LOSER

15⁰⁰
b

LOSER

The Real
Seattle Music Story

by Clark Humphrey

Feral House • Portland

SONG COPYRIGHTS

Chapter 1 "The Wilting Willie Song" by Ruth Prins, © 1962 King Broadcasting Co. **Chapter 2** "Granny's Pad" by Al Berry, © 1962 Bolmin Publishing (BMI). **Chapter 5** "Better World" © 1977 the Screamers. Used by permission of Tomata du Plenty. "For the Rich" by Cynthia Genser and Rich Riggins, © 1979 Living Page Music (BMI). Used by permission. "I'm Not An Astronaut, I'm A Nut" by Gary Minkler, © 1978 Listen You! Music (BMI). Used by permission. **Chapter 6** "Golden Showers" © 1980 the Mentors, administered by D.U.P. Publishing (ASCAP). Used by permission.**Chapter 8** "Searchin' USA" by Scott McCaughey, © 1985 Mac/Nor Music (BMI), administered by Bug Music Group. Used by permission.**Chapter 9** "I'm a Refuzor" © 1981 Mike Refuzor. Used by permission. "P.C.C." lyric by Mark Arm, © 1987 Bad Moon Music. "Kill Lou Guzzo" by the Dehumanizers, © 1986 D.U.P. Publishing (ASCAP). Used by permission.**Chapter 10** "Kill the President" lyric by Peter Litwin, © 1991 Coffin Break. Used by permission. "Feast or Famine" by Chris Eckman and Carla Torgerson, © 1988 Fire and Skill Publishing (BMI). "Sandfleas" by Gas Huffer, © 1992 Lead Head Music. Used by permission. "Down By the Pool" by Richie Ray and Terry Hanisch, © 1990 Half the World Publishing (BMI). Used by permission. **Chapter 11** "Captain Hi-Top" by Mother Love Bone, © 1990 PolyGram International Publishing/Stardog Music (ASCAP). "Dive" by Kurt Cobain, © 1989 EMI Virgin Music/The End of Music (BMI), rights controlled by EMI Virgin Songs Inc. "Golden Blunders" and "Definite Door" by Jon Auer and Ken Stringfellow, © 1990, 1993 Number 23 Music (ASCAP)/Twenty-Three Songs Music (BMI). Used by permission. "Crucifuckin" by Ben McMillan, © 1991 Roadblock Music Inc./Four Wheel Groove Publishing (ASCAP). Used by permission. "Slaughter of Bruce" lyric by Mia Zapata, © 1990 the Gits. Used by permission. "Regrets" by Rusty Willoughby, © 1993 Fatbald Music (BMI). "Under 10 Handicap" © 1993 Edwin Judah Fotheringham and Nate Johnson. Used by permission of Super Electro Sound Recordings. "More Noise Please" © 1989 Steven Jesse Bernstein. Used by permission of the S.J. Bernstein Archives. For information on Jesse Bernstein's writings and recordings contact 1202 E. Pike St., #922, Seattle, WA 98122-3934. "White Boy" © 1991 Bikini Kill, used by permission of Kill Rock Stars. **Chapter 12** "In Bloom" by Kurt Cobain, Krist Novoselic and Dave Grohl, © 1991 EMI Virgin Music/The End of Music (BMI), rights controlled by EMI Virgin Songs Inc. "Junkhead" by Jerry Cantrell and Layne Staley, © 1992 Buttnuggett Publishing/Jack Lord Music (ASCAP). "Second Skin" lyric by Mia Zapata, © 1992 the Gits. Used by permission.

For a free catalog of publications, send SASE to: Feral House, PO Box 3466, Portland, OR 97208-3466.

9 8 7 6 5 4 3 2 1

Feral House publications are distributed to the book trade by Publishers Group West.

Designed by Art Chantry. *Typography by* Hank Trotter.
Darkroom tech by Jeri Francis. *Proofreading by* Sara DeBell.

CONTENTS

ACKNOWLEDGEMENTS

Initial research on this book began in April 1993. This was a time when the New York media industry had declared Seattle "over," that we had merely been a source for a few bands and styles to be incorporated into the business-as-usual star machines of the entertainment industry. The New York music world, and the New York book world, didn't (and still doesn't) understand that Seattle represented a threat to those star machines. New York publishers, therefore, rejected the book; no established Seattle publishers were willing to take on a project not aimed at yuppies or academics.

I'd completed a rough draft in February 1994, and circulated photocopies to some of my sources for fact-checking. I was negotiating with Feral House in Oregon at the time of Kurt Cobain's death; after which some New York agents suddenly took an interest in my work. But I'd never wanted to write a Cobain gossip book while he was alive, and didn't want to turn this book into that. Feral House assured me that I wouldn't have to.

Thanks to the more than 200 people who let me interview them, especially to the ones I didn't quote or whose stories I didn't use (for space, I had to cut bands that neither recorded nor performed in public, even if "we had really hot practices").

Aside from the Cobain/Love camp, the only people I wanted to talk to but couldn't either were on perpetual tour or otherwise busy, or left town long ago and couldn't be reached. Only one person completely refused to cooperate with the project; I'm honoring his request by not naming him.

Most research projects are built on earlier work. So is this. I'm particularly indebted to published pieces by Dawn Anderson, J.A. Anderson, George Arthur, Michael Azerrad, Patrick Barber, Peter Blecha, John Book, Art Chantry, Paul Dorpat, Gillian G. Gaar, Jeff Gilbert, Jo-Ann Greene, Dan Halligan, Danny Housman, Milo Johnstone, Tom Phalen, Gene Stout, and Dave Thompson; and to the collective minds of the *Rocket, Backlash, Hype* and the *Stranger*.

Visual material was donated by many many people. Particular thanks go to Grant Alden/Vox Populi Gallery, Dawn Anderson, J.A. Anderson, Jim Anderson, Jim Basnight, Leighton Beezer, Mark Bendix, Jim Blanchard, Gary Browne, Art Chantry, Owel Connell, David Crider, Tammy DeCroff, Jerry Dennon, Curt Doughty, Frank Edie, Ed Fotheringham, Leslie Fried, Cam Garrett, Jeff Gilbert, Graham, the Greater Zenith/Des Moines Historical Society, Frank Harlan/No Budget Production, Chris Hartshaw, Ben Ireland, Milo Johnstone, Jeff Kleinsmith, Joey Kline, Jeff Long, Lee Lumsden, Maire Masco, Scott McDougall, Lance Mercer, Courtney Miller, Gary Minkler, Billski Moore, Rob Morgan, Tim Muck, Buck Ormsby, Lisa Orth, Charles Peterson, Wilum Pugmire, Stephen Rabow, Mike Refuzor, Jesse Reyes, Roderick and Anisa Romero, Cha Cha Samoa, Christine Sievanen, Mike Stein, Sub Pop Ltd., Hank Trotter, Bon Von Wheelie, Kim Warnick, Dennis White, and △.

Contributing photographers include Mike Andeel, J.A. Anderson, Arthur S. Aubry, Skip Beattie, Gary Browne, Marsha Burns, Tom Collicott, Jini Dellaccio, Cam Garrett, Gary Hall, David Hawkes, Bob Kondrack, Kristine Larsen, Lance Mercer, Kelly Mercier, Karen Moskowitz, Charles Peterson, Deena Rosenberg, Rex Rystedt, Elisa Shebaro, Mark Van S., Kevin Westenberg, Alice Wheeler, and others lost to time.

Thanks also to all the employers who declined to hire me, leaving me with the time to do this; to the out-of-towners who wrote all those inaccurate or incomplete Seattle scene books, leaving me to set the story straight; to all the local writers who thought about writing a Seattle scene book but backed out of the task; to all the people who risked their friendships by giving me other people's phone numbers; to the record collectors, zine writers, DJs, poster artists and photographers who let me borrow from their collections; and to 911 Media Arts for setting up a five-hour private screening of local music videos (nobody said it'd be easy...).

Mr. Humphrey uses Apple computers 'cuz he demands the best.

INTRODUCTION

Natalie Wood, 1962: "Look! It's me! Gypsy Rose Lee! From Seattle!"
Bill Wendall, 1992: "And now, the latest hot new band from Seattle, David Letterman!"

In the winter of 1991-92, the Seattle music scene became the darling of the world. Media outlets around the world issued lengthy stories about the angry, disheveled "grunge" rock emanating from our city's bands—stories complete with misconceptions and more than a few downright lies. New York and London rock scribes delivered a stream of Nirvana/Pearl Jam gossip books, full of mis- and dis-information. Most neglected every local band that didn't record for Sub Pop or didn't include one of the latter-day superstars. One book dismissed the U-Men, arguably the first true grunge band, as "art rock." None gave the Young Fresh Fellows, Seattle's first indie-record stars, more than half a sentence. We're here to correct some of that, and to tell a story.

One of the biggest aspects about the Seattle Scene mania was its supposed authenticity. As the myth goes, this isn't something a couple of packagers in a penthouse office dreamed up. It's supposed to be a folk phenomenon, a community of ideas and styles that came up from the street.

In fact, a lot of it *was* dreamed up by a couple of packagers in a penthouse office, but they exploited something that had been developing haphazardly for over a decade, digesting and rejecting assorted influences along the way. As with anything real, its creators didn't give a damn about authenticity (much of the apparel and terminology was lifted from 1981 hardcore bands; a lot of the ideology was lifted from old Morrissey interviews).

There *is* a real Seattle scene, and this is its story. It's a long story, with a lot of people who built the foundations for other people's success. As fate usually has it, a lot of influential people never got their due; we hope to correct some of that. We'll get to the latter-day celebrities around Chapter 9 or so—be patient.

We won't talk much about local concerts by out-of-town bands; a Black Flag gig in Seattle assuredly rocked just as hard as a Black Flag gig in Cleveland. We're glancing lightly over the achievements of ex-local people after they left town, with a few exceptions; this is primarily a book about stuff created here. And we won't talk too much about the Sixties Generation; there were a lot of hippie musicians here, but their culture veered away from energetic original rock and toward imitating established trends. Those hippies who did influence the punks are noted in Chapter 5.

Throughout the text, the term "album" refers to any recording with at least 10 selections and/or over 30 minutes of playing time, whether its primary medium of release was on vinyl or compact disc. After all, the term "album" dates back sets of 78s in sleeves that were bound in a photo album-like book.

I've made every attempt to verify all the information in this account. Some people, however, have vastly different recollections of the same events (times, places, details, et al.) But as they used to say about the hippie days, "If you remember everything about it, you weren't there." Any proven discrepencies will be corrected in future editions.

Despite the mighty length of this tome, it still gives short shrift to many popular local performers of the past and present. My apologies to all the bands I said little or nothing about, and to their fans.

I've been watching and documenting this scene all this time. I was one of the original new-music DJs on KCMU, the college station that nurtured the scene for a decade. I've written for local and national zines and newspapers. For the past three and a half years I've been the pop-culture columnist for the *Stranger*, Seattle's top alternative weekly. I've also dabbled in experimental fiction and published a hypertext novel on computer disc, but that's a story for another time.

Some things to remember

But before all that, we need a brief overview of the city's past so we can trace some of the roots of what came later. And before we get to *that*, we need to correct a few misconceptions:

■ Seattle is *not* some tiny podunk village in the wilderness, OK? We're a major world seaport and a high-tech mecca. We gave you a lot of neat inventions: jet planes, microcomputer software, kidney dialysis machines, condensed milk, Erector sets, and even the Slinky.

We're not (or weren't) a wealthy town, though. Our few rich families keep low profiles on suburban estates. It took decades for high-culture interests to set up a viable patronage network. The trust-fund wealth that supported cultural ventures in big media cities hardly existed here. Ours was not a scene of *Vogue* dillentantes partying 'til dawn in Chanel dresses. When Billy Joel sneered in "Still Rock n' Roll to Me" that you needed lots of money to go new wave, we who scoured thrift stores for $25 outfits laughed out loud.

We're also a pretty private place, influenced by Nordic Lutheran and Calvinist pioneers who spoke little and socialized less. Seattle has a social air of sullen timidity which some outsiders mistake for haughtiness. We *don't* think we're too cool to talk to you; we're afraid you're too cool to want to talk to us. When a new-music community developed here, local "arts supporters" reacted with open hostility or (worse) smug condescension. Our so-called "tolerant," "diverse" city tried to crush anything that contradicted the mandatory mellowness. That, of course, just made our angry young men and women even angrier.

■ The media claimed Seattle music's success had to do with the city's "isolation." It's true that we're a day's drive from US cities bigger than us, surrounded (except for Portland and Vancouver) by vast rural areas and a few college, industrial and shipping towns. That kept some bus-and-truck level bands from touring here. But many of those bands did come here. And a lot of the people we'll talk about became interconnected with what Calvin Johnson labeled the "International Pop Underground," communicating by zines, computers, phones and self-recorded cassettes with labels, clubs, radio stations and bands from Washington, DC to Japan.

Seattle *was* isolated from the record industry. The Big Six labels and their subsidiaries had no A&R people in the Northwest states. In the early '80s Seattle had one superstar rock act, a couple of national jazz acts, a symphony that made CDs for a classical indie label, a couple of studios that recorded big-name acts, and a few established stars who bought suburban homes near here. But there was no established path for a local band to rise out of the local clubs, and those clubs were few and sparsely attended. We'd always had talented people but didn't have the infrastructure to support them—until somebody got the idea to promote local records directly to the underground across North America and Europe.

■ Nobody intended for the mania to happen the way it did, and just about everybody was glad to see it subside. We're grateful for the attention, sort of, and it's great to see good bands get the breaks they deserve. But nobody wanted the world to think we adhered slavishly to one kind of music and one kind of clothes. Indeed, the little segment of the scene the world first heard about was pretty much over by the time the world heard about it. And *please* don't blame anybody here for "designer grunge" fashion. That was all invented in New York.

■ There is no singular "Seattle Sound," but there is a common Seattle attitude. We believe in making great music and art, not in the trappings of celebrity. Remember the L.A. rock movie *The Decline of Western Civilization Part II: The Metal Years*? Remember the part where everybody insists, "I *will* be a Rock Star?" If you said that in Seattle, you'd get laughed out of town. (Unless you were Andrew Wood and said it half in jest.)

Of the people here who've made it big, only Sir Mix-A-Lot drives a limo, and *he* does it out of black-middle-class materialism, not showbiz affectations. Hollywood stars move here to build expensive homes on Puget Sound islands; our homegrown stars buy old bungalows in town, and many still share their digs with housemates. Many people left Seattle for California to try to become big, but nobody since Robert Cray in 1987 moved south *after* making it big.

If there's a common message among these bands, it's that *your life and your culture count*. You'll find this message in most everything done here, from Sir Mix-A-Lot's tales of young black Americans who don't sell drugs or shoot each other, to Bikini Kill's anthems about surviving abusive relationships with pride intact, to Nirvana's elliptical pop songs about emotional confusion. You don't have to be from a media capital, you don't have to have the proper demographics, to have something worth saying. Make your own scene, don't conform to anybody—not even us.

■ Aside from an ocean and a time zone, Seattle has little in common with what the world thinks of as "The West Coast." We didn't have anything like the corporate entertainment machine of Los Angeles or the bohemian entertainment machine of San Francisco. You will read the terms "Los Angeles," "Hollywood," and just "L.A." throughout this book, usually in negative contexts. The Hollywood starmaking machinery is what most Seattle bands treated as the bad guys: pay-to-play "showcase" clubs (where bands fork over up to $1000 to be seen), bimbos, big hair, wasteful company spending charged against the band's royalties, gold-chain-clad agents, drugs-and-hookers payola to radio stations, target marketing, the grooming and dumbing-down of bands for mass acceptance, and producer-driven concept bands.

These feelings were augmented by the degree to which the Seattle punks were influenced by the L.A. hardcore scene, which attempted to create authentic music in the shadow of the conglomerates, but wound up making virtually unlistenable sounds in order to avoid the rock-star machine, and eventually became just another consumer lifestyle option. When Seattle bands finally attracted the majors' attention, they tried to negotiate everything from a position of strength. Even then, they often found problems, as we shall see.

■ The Pacific Northwest is *not* some mellow wonderland where all is prosperous and serene. Everybody believed that Washington's (and America's) first pop superstar, Bing Crosby, was an easygoing gent and fine family man. His sons since revealed that he beat and tormented them. The Northwest School painters led the world to believe the Skagit Valley was heaven on earth. In his memoir *This Boy's Life*, Tobias Wolff begged to differ: the valley town of Concrete was a living hell for him.

David Lynch was right: There *is* an evil in these woods. This may be a land of perky backpackers and nerdy engineers, but it's also a land of environmental destruction, deliberately-released radiation clouds, racist fraternal lodges, brutal gangs of every race, serial killers, child-abuse cults, Satanic and occult groups, white-supremacist bombings, neo-Nazi safe houses, UFO sightings, mysterious cattle mutilations, ice skaters with thug boyfriends, and other phenomena you'll never find in a tourist guide. Even our early heritage is one of brutality, exploitation and genocide.

Wherever you see an obsessive fetish with niceness, you've got to look past that false front to find the face of sheer terror beneath, whether you're in Concrete, Twin Peaks, Bainbridge Island, Bellevue, Aberdeen, or Seattle (mistakenly proclaimed by tourist promoters as "The Emerald City").

Or, for that matter, in the oft-romanticized native nations that came before all this.

PART ONE

CHAPTER ONE:

PREHISTORY (1850-1958)

"Northwest Lifestyle" advocates like to pretend that this is a corner of God's Country unspoiled by mankind. In fact, this is an inhabited area and has been for 5,000 years. Local tribes fished in the summer, sat inside and made art in the winter. The various (often hostile, sometimes cannibalistic) tribes of the region developed customs and legends that inspired others since, including potlatches (ritual dinner parties with gift exchanges), totems, long-houses, sweat lodges, and stories. In some stories, Snoqualmie Falls is the source of life. To these people, art, music and stories weren't consumer products but expressions of the soul. The tribal culture was known as "Northwest Coast" by later historians—most of the local nations settled along the coastline and rivers; many avoided the deep woods, said to be the home of evil spirits.

Taking over

White explorers first came to present-day Washington state in the late 1700s. Settlers started trickling in the 1820s. By the 1850s, the indigenous nations were targeted for conquest and/or removal. Some tribes were forced to march hundreds of miles, with most members dying along the way. Some were attacked by armies. Others were decimated by "gifts" of liquor and of blankets laced with smallpox.

"New York-Alki" ("...by and by") was founded in 1851 at an unprotected harbor in present-day West Seattle, followed the next spring by a settlement at the protected inland shores of Elliot Bay, surrounded by tall wooded hills and muddy tide flats. This became Pioneer Square, the foot of the present-day downtown.

The early pioneer boomtown culture quickly developed into a dichotomy between the wide-open and the uptight, between the high-livers (symbolized by Dr. David Maynard, the hard-drinking secular-humanist founder of the settlement at Pioneer Square) and the puritans and entrepreneurs (symbolized by David Denny, a member of the original Alki party and a teetotaling Republican). The two platted the street grids on their adjacent claims so that the streets didn't run parallel.

Maynard persuaded pioneer Henry Yesler to build a sawmill on his claim. The trees for the mill came from the hills outside the settlement, and were skidded down the hill on Yesler Way, the street between the Maynard and Denny tracts. This

became the original Skid Road (*not* "row").

A big fire destroyed a lot of the original settlements in 1889, the same year Washington became a state. The new buildings were built of brick and steel; many came to house saloons, cheap hotels and brothels for timber workers (the only solaces in a truly miserable way of life).

Early booster Asa Mercer brought in a shipload of young widows from Massachusetts, the Mercer Girls, to save frontier men from the sin of mating with native women (their story was later sanitized into TV's *Here Come the Brides*). Immigration to the region took on a standard pattern when James J. Hill's Great Northern and Henry Villard's Northern Pacific railroads reached Puget Sound from the upper Midwest. The Northwest was settled as more "north" than "west," by third- and fourth-generation American families of repressed Calvinistic farmers lured by cheap real estate offers along railroad-owned grant lands. The tracks were built by large crews of Chinese immigrants; many settled in Seattle despite a harsh racial climate including anti-Chinese riots (to this day, King County has more Asian than African Americans). Hill's Great Northern took over the Northern Pacific, and (with Hill's friend, timber boss Frederick Weyerhaeuser) dictated Washington's economic life for a generation.

Opposition to the railroads' monopolistic practices spawned labor organizing and the progressive political movement, the latter reaching here from Minnesota and Wisconsin—another way our regional culture grew more from the Midwest than the Southwest.

The railroads also brought Seattle into the mainstream American economy, just in time for the town to be devastated in the economic Panic of 1893. Do-gooder drives to help Panic victims fueled Seattle's progressive movement, which by the 1960s took over City Hall (though the business community still weilded the real power). Reform politicians tried to crush the bordellos with an 1894 law prohibiting women from working where liquor was served. My great-grandfather came here from Wales as a circuit-riding Methodist preacher, out to convert the whoremongering lumberjacks.

The 1907 gold rush sent hundreds of prospectors through here to the Yukon, but the real money was made here by merchants, outfitters and madams. Condensed milk, a stay-fresh frontier provision, was one of the many inventions from here.

Doc Maynard

David Denny

James J. Hill

Bertha Landes

Nellie Cornish

John Cage

Elks

Dave Beck

Other local tinkerers over the years came up with the "Dick and Jane" books, the kidney dialysis machine, and one of the first electric guitars (by Bud Tutmarc, who added an electrical pickup to a modified Hawaiian pedal-steel guitar).

Seattle's economic agenda was controlled by 1910 by a tight elite of timber and rail bosses, newspaper publishers and bankers. These men (and their ladies' auxiliary) established a dull, puritanical urban culture (with appropriate outlets of escape for rich white men, including a revived tolerance policy on brothels and saloons).

City engineer R.H. Thompson decreed that some of the steep hills surrounding downtown impeded the city's expansion. He started a regrading project that lowered the grades of several downtown avenues and (by 1931) obliterated steep Denny Hill, replacing it with a flat expanse (the Denny Regrade, also known as Belltown after pioneer Austin Bell) that became a forlorn site of car dealerships and residence hotels. The dirt was used to make a big industrial district out of tide flats south of downtown, including the site of the Kingdome stadium.

Seattle grew to be the preeminent economic force of the region, outdistancing the older Portland, 150 miles to the south, and Tacoma, 40 miles to the south. As Seattle became the hub of the region's banking, education, and commercial administration, Tacoma grew into a rough-hewn town of factories, lumber mills and military bases, a place with fewer pretensions and more vices.

In 1916 William Boeing started building mail planes in an old boathouse on the waterfront; his company soon led the post-WWI passenger aircraft business and was the first owner of United Airlines (United's first coast-to-coast route, Seattle-Chicago-New York, was called the "Main Line;" through the '60s its in-flight magazine was called the *Mainliner!*)

The ratio of women to men in Seattle wasn't equalized until the '20s. With no room for daintiness, the pioneer life bred tough and stoic women. The Pike Place Market started in 1907 to bring local produce to local housewives without costly middlemen. These women launched an early feminism, making this one of the first places to let women vote (in 1884, rescinded with Washington's statehood in 1889 and reinstated in 1920 with national women's suffrage) and to enact prohibition (in 1916). In 1910, Imogen Cunningham became one of the first women in the world to open her own photo studio, pioneering the use of nude figures (female *and* male) in highbrow photography. In 1926, Bertha Landes was elected as the first female mayor of a big city. Another pioneer in nontraditional careers for women was tugboat owner Thea Foss, fictionalized by writer Norman Reilly Raine into the hard-working and tough-talking Tugboat Annie.

Other "women's work" was undertaken by more conservative (but still strong-willed) women, including wives of the rich: campaigning against brothels (not fully shut down until the last months of World War II), the "carriage trade" society serviced at the Frederick & Nelson department store and tearoom (closed in 1992), and the roots of a high-culture community centered around Nellie Cornish's art school, where composer John Cage and choreographer Martha Graham served residencies. There was a small scandal when British conductor Thomas Beecham, brought in to lead the Seattle Symphony in the early 1940s, resigned and either called Seattle a "cultural dustbin" or warned that it could become one, depending on whose account you read.

The society ladies tried to establish the city as an outpost of high culture, but it remained in the cultural shadow of San Francisco. The first clothing stores in a lot of Midwest towns were called "The Boston Store;" Seattle's first was "The San Francisco Store." Cunningham moved south in 1917, in search of an established art community; many artists and musicians would follow her over the following decades.

Let me entertain you

As a remote place that had to import commercial entertainment by steamer and later by rail, Seattle became a major business center for the great vaudeville touring circuits, including the powerful Consodine and Pantages theater chains. One of our great traveling-show houses, the 1,300-seat Moore, plays a part in our later story. One local girl who grew up on the stage became the premier exotic dancer Gypsy Rose Lee (later an author and racounteur). Jazz great Jelly Roll Morton lived here for a while and wrote a tribute to the town, "Seattle Hunch."

Prohibition brought a wild subculture of speakeasies, roadhouses, and rum-running from Canada by boats and back roads. I grew up near a Snohomish County hill still known as Whiskey Ridge. With repeal, the state allowed only 3.2 percent beer in taverns (and nothing closer than a half mile from the UW campus). The state established a liquor-store monopoly; liquor by the drink was only allowed in private clubs, the elite's favorite hangouts. The state was officially dry on Sundays.

The national fraternal-lodge movement (Elks, Moose, Eagles) largely began in Seattle. With only whites allowed to join, and women relegated to wives' auxiliaries, the lodges professed to provide "community leadership" while providing a site for "men of prominence" to guzzle bourbon (even during the dry years) and watch blue movies. The lodges thrived for half a century, but plummeted as their racial, cultural and political philosophies became passé in the '60s. Elks Lodge #1 in downtown Seattle was torn down in 1968 for a bank tower. The auditorium at Eagles Aerie #1 featured hot jazz bands in the 1940s, hippie bands in the '60s, and punks in the early '80s.

One big union

Authorities in Seattle, Everett and Centralia resorted to gangs of thugs to suppress the Industrial Workers of the World, the most radical labor union in U.S. history (vowing to create "One big union of all the workers, the greatest thing in the world"), and to stop a February 1919 general strike (America's first citywide labor unrest). Eventually they had to settle with more moderate labor interests, leading FDR's Postmaster General to make a snide remark about "the 47 states and the Soviet of Washington." Washington became one of the most unionized jurisdictions in North America. But by then radicalism was being excised from the labor movement by local Teamsters organizer Dave Beck, who in the late '30s promised peace to employers in return for wage and benefit hikes. Beck became the national leader of the Teamsters, proving his loyalty to employers by helping break other unions' strikes (starting the long rift between the Teamsters and the AFL-CIO).

Roll on, Columbia

We were still one of the world's youngest major cities when the national media business cranked up in the 1920s. We'd developed precious little regional culture by the time magazines, movies and radio began to impose one mass culture on the whole nation.

The radical element supported an early folk music circuit, including several long stays by Woody Guthrie. In the mid-1930s, the federal government commissioned him to write "Roll On Columbia," an ode to the series of dams being built along the Columbia River that provided irrigation and electricity to eastern Washington (decimating fish runs in the process). The feds had another purpose for the dams besides stimulating the economy: they supplied cheap electricity to the new aluminum factories that supplied Boeing's aircraft plants, already preparing for future war production.

One of Guthrie's local friends was Ivar Haglund, a folk singer and onetime socialist sympathizer who parlayed a waterfront amusement arcade and curio shop into a successful chain of seafood restaurants.

Frances Farmer

Jazz musician and nightclub owner Vic Meyers ran for lieutenant governor in 1932 as a publicity stunt, won as part of the FDR landslide, and stayed in office 20 years. Meyers's stunt was repeated in the early 1970s by Red Kelly, who ran a jazz bar in Olympia; he and some friends ran losing campaigns for state offices as the OWL Party ("Out With Logic, On With Lunacy").

A close-knit bohemian community lived in houseboats along Lake Union, a mostly industrial waterway in the center of town tainted with industrial and human wastes, and dominated on its north side by a smoke-belching coal gasification plant. The houseboats were notorious for all-night parties, drunken revelry, and the discussion (and alleged practice) of free love. Like many artistic neighborhoods across the country, it was overrun by the well-to-do.

Less glamorous depression victims lived in squatter shacks along the Duwamish river and at a 1,000-resident Hooverville near the present Kingdome site, ordered demolished by City Hall. An Unemployed Citizens' League established an underground barter economy, which they called "the Republic of the Penniless;" at its peak it involved 50,000 residents.

The University of Washington employed noted poet Theodore Roethke and other progressive thinkers, some of whom clashed with conservative state bigwigs. The state fired '30s UW president Henry Suzzalo, officially over his costly new library

Ivar Haglund & the Smith Tower

Wobblies

**Opposite:
Woody Guthrie**

"Noodles " Smith

Richland H.S. "Bombers"

R.C. Robinson
(Ray Charles)

Early Quincy Jones

A Hot Jazz Scene

but really over his tolerance toward free thinkers.

The '30s also brought America's first pop super-star, Tacoma-born Bing Crosby, and the Golden Age of Radio, with local son Edward R. Murrow as its conscience. It also had a fairly radical local the-ater scene, with Burton and Florence James's Seat-tle Repertory Playhouse in the "U District" next to the UW campus (driven out of business in the late '40s by a conservative smear campaign) and an ill-fated UW student actress, Frances Farmer.

Farmer first gained attention starring in a 1935 student production of *Alien Corn* that got extend-ed from two weeks to six months. She'd also acted in other productions with fellow drama student Chet Huntley, a future TV news anchorman. She entered a radical magazine's essay contest and won a trip to Moscow; she insisted to a Red-baiting lo-cal press that she only wanted the trip because it would drop her off in New York. She got to the New York stage, and to 14 Hollywood roles from 1936 until 1942, when she was arrested for drunk driving. She burned out on the stress and corrup-tion of Hollywood, retreating into the bottle. After several drunk-and-disorderly arrests, her mother put her in a series of mental institutions. Unsub-stantiated reports had her gang-raped there by sol-diers and receiving a lobotomy; there are no official records of the latter. She *was* hooked onto mood-numbing drugs. She lay low for several years after her release, agreeing only in 1958 to tell her story on a TV show; that led to one movie, a touring play, and a long stint on an Indianapolis TV station. Her film career would have ended in the late '40s any-way, when anybody with a hint of past sympathy to leftist causes was blackballed from the industry.

Wings to victory

WWII brought Japanese-American internment camps, unprecedented industrial growth at Boeing (and the camouflage "city" on the roof of its bomber assembly plant), many women entering in-dustrial jobs, African-Americans moving here, and an open vice scene downtown. Booze, gambling and prostitution flourished under the winking eyes of paid-off cops.

The 1939-built Showbox Ballroom and its ground-floor Amusement Center (a bowling alley and penny arcade, converted years later into a peep show), were open to service servicemen 24 hours a day with bands, burlesque dancers and food. Local hero Gypsy Rose Lee held a three-month starring engagement there, stripping (incompletely) and singing her hit "Shoo Fly Pie and Apple Pan Dowdy." Young women were bused in to dance with the sailors; some of them turned tricks in the basement. Army MPs came in at one point to shut down some of the more active down-town brothels. The Showbox struggled after the war and closed in 1948; it briefly reopened in 1954-55 and again as a hippie club in 1967. Over the years it also served as a furniture store, a day-rental meeting hall, and a bingo parlor.

Other local big-band ballrooms included sever-al future rock venues: Parker's on Aurora Avenue (U.S. Highway 99), the Trianon in Belltown, the Odd Fellows Temple on Capitol Hill, and Washing-ton Hall in the Central District.

Jazz also lived at after-hours bottle clubs in and around the city's Chinatown, south of Yesler Way, allowed to stay open by bribed cops under an un-written "tolerance policy." The best known was Russell "Noodles" Smith's Black and Tan Club, which operated on a noon-to-dawn basis from 1922 to 1965 (its space was most recently a Vietnamese disco).

One of the top local bandleaders was Bumps Blackwell, whose bands included singer Ernestine Anderson and multi-instrumentalist Quincy Jones, a graduate of Garfield High School. Jones and Blackwell went to Hollywood in the '50s. Blackwell became an executive with Specialty Records, where he launched the careers of Little Richard and other early rockers. Jones became a record mogul, composer, arranger, producer, and film pro-ducer of world renown; in 1995 he received a spe-cial Academy Award for his humanitarian contribu-tions. Ray Charles spent a couple of years here in the late '40s, making his first radio and TV appear-ances and cutting his first single.

UW student Harry Smith happened upon some old hillbilly, cajun and "race music" 78s at a Salva-tion Army depot, where they'd been gathered for a war-recycling drive. Smith rescued as many of the discs as he could; they became the basis of a small coterie of students and academicians who col-lected and traded these '20s and '30s rarities. In 1952 Smith persuaded Folkways Records to release highlights of his collection on a six-record *Antholo-gy of American Folk Music*. Some historians count this as the start of the '50s folk movement.

The war ended with atomic weapons produced in part at the Hanford Nuclear Reservation, a huge top-secret factory complex situated in a Rhode Is-land-sized section of Eastern Washington. The U.S. Navy ship where the Japanese army signed the sur-render papers later became a tourist attraction at the Naval Shipyard in Bremerton, on the Olympic Peninsula across Puget Sound from Seattle.

Down in Hollywood, native son Bing Crosby was frustrated by live radio. He wanted to record and edit his shows; the only sound recording media at the time were shellac discs and film sound-tracks, both of which were cumbersome and had lower sound quality than live radio. He was intro-duced to a captured German tape recorder and co-founded Ampex, the company that developed that technology into professional audio tape (and even-tually into videotape). Tape recording arrived just in time to save the sanity of Seattle-born Mary Liv-ingstone (Sadie Marks); the extremely shy actress could now record her lines for husband Jack Ben-ny's show in a private studio, away from the stress of a live audience.

Shortly after the war's end, Betty McDonald published a nonfiction memoir about her move from Seattle to a small farm on the Olympic Penin-

Kenneth Arnold

J.P. & Gertrude

Scoop & Maggie

sula. *The Egg and I* was a surprise national best-seller and launched the "Ma and Pa Kettle" movie comedies, based on McDonald's real-life neighbors.

Jet city

On June 24, 1947, Idaho businessman Kenneth Arnold was flying his Cessna near Mt. Rainier when he saw what he called nine "disc-shaped" craft the size of airplanes, flying "like saucers being skipped over the water" at up to 1,000 miles an hour. The phrase "flying saucers" quickly appeared in pulp fiction magazines and B-movies. Thousands reported to have seen or entered alien spacecraft in subsequent decades, including dozens of sightings in the Washington Cascades and on the Yakima Indian Reservation. Some local UFO faithful formed a religion based on their belief in otherworldly beings, the New Age Church (probably the first use of that phrase).

Liquor by the drink expanded from private clubs into restaurant-lounge combinations in 1949, under regulations that favored the big stuffy operations that businessmen and their political cronies personally preferred. This steak-and-scotch industry didn't support much in the line of creative nightlife; indeed, the legal competition helped to drive the underground jazz clubs out of business. Around 1955, editors at Hearst's morning *Post-Intelligencer* asked reporter Emmett Watson to begin a Walter Winchell-like column on everything going on in Seattle; his first response was that there was nothing going on worth writing about. If his editors had cared, Watson could have written about the rhythm and blues being cooked up in scattered race-music clubs around the city, or the hot country swing being played in Washington's small-town dance halls, where Loretta Lynn and Buck Owens gave some of their first performances.

Seven miles north of downtown, Northgate opened in 1950 as the world's first modern shopping mall.

Conservative thinking so pervasively took over in the '50s, people growing up in it thought it had always been that way. Local politics were run by bourbon-swilling WWII vets with ties to fraternal lodges, private clubs and the business community. Even with a solid Democratic machine in place, McCarthyism drove many good people from the UW and from state government. Our powerful U.S. Senators Warren Magnuson (an "industrial policy" New Dealer) and Henry Jackson (a Cold War hawk) adhered to the WWII formula for domestic prosperity through big government contracts in industry and technology. They tirelessly promoted the coalition of money and power that President Eisenhower derisively called "the military-industrial complex." They saw no contradiction between this and their liberal votes on domestic social issues; they viewed the battle against racism in the South and the battle against Communism abroad as equally righteous. To Magnuson and Jackson, the Cold War was great for business, especially when it started heating up in Indochina, providing an excuse to order more B-52 bombers from Boeing.

Boeing made the "international jet sèt" possible with its passenger jetliners, but its own corporate culture was decidedly un-swinging. Under the influence of Boeing, Seattle developed the mentality of engineers: quiet, orderly, dull. When author J.D. Sallinger created the squarest possible New York tourists to be ridiculed in *The Catcher in the Rye*, he symbolized their utter unhipness by making them from Seattle.

While other industrial giants built expendable factories in the city and moved office jobs out to the suburbs, Boeing was forced by Seattle's hemmed-in geography to build assembly plants in the sticks, but kept most of its engineering and executive jobs at its complex in south Seattle. This made Seattle a relentlessly middlebrow, middle-class town in sharp contrast to the blue-collar nature of the surrounding region (or to the affluent suburbs of Bellevue and Bainbridge Island).

The same button-down mentality took over Seattle's other top employer, the University of Washington. Under a flood of federal grant money shipped our way by Magnuson and Jackson, the UW became a giant engineering and medical research lab with a vestigial appendage of a liberal arts college.

Patches pals

The new medium of television provided early quaint experiments in local entertainment shows. But by the end of the '50s, the only local entertainers were on kiddie shows, most notably KIRO's roughhousing J.P. Patches (Chris Wedes), sometimes cited as Matt Groening's inspiration for the *Simpsons* character Krusty the Klown. Between cartoons and live commercials, J.P. subverted most every rule of wholesome family entertainment via his raucous improvised skits with sidekick Bob Newman, whose dozen stock characters included the Queen of the City Dump, Gertrude Bleech. J.P. entertained and subverted young minds from 1958 to 1981.

When J.P. started, KING already had its own cartoon package show starring Scandinavian-dialect vaudevillian Stan Boreson and his ill-fated sidekick Doug Setterberg, that ran until 1967. They performed local humor and sang Swedish-accent songs by '40s radio comic Yogi Yorgesson; they recorded several LPs of this material for New York's Golden Crest Records. Setterberg got throat cancer in the early '60s and had to speak to the kiddies through an electronic voice box (the man who played the computer voice in the Godard film *Alphaville* had a similar implant).

Another KING kids' host, the harlequin-suited Wunda Wunda (Ruth Prins), had a puppet potted plant for a co-star, Wilting Willie. Every day she watered his pot and sang the Wilting Willie song: "Willie, won't he/Willie, won't he/Stand up today?/Willie, won't he/Willie, won't he/What do you say?" You never knew if he'd stay Wilting Willie, drooped over the edge of the pot, or become Stand Up Willie, rising straight and narrow to a fanfare by the show's organist.

KING compensated for the lack of visual content in its early newscasts by hiring a succession of three "cartooning weathermen." Bob Hale, Bob Cram and Tom Davie drew engagingly cute characters to accompany the regular map and forecast graphics. They also communicated the joys of cartooning to a generation of local kids. Washington had already given the world the far-out and gross-out visions of cartoonist Basil Wolverton, who drew surrealistic farces for the early comic book

version of *Mad* and designed the *Li'l Abner* character Lena the Hyena, the Ugliest Woman on Earth.

The Northwest school

Aesthetic opposition to the stuffed-shirt era began to emerge. Seattle (particularly the Blue Moon Tavern, a hangout for UW literary types including Roethke) was a frequent traveling stop for the early Beats. A Cornell grad and Boeing technical writer, Thomas Pynchon, wrote much of his first novel *V.* in his U District basement apartment, using Boeing as the model for his fictional Yoyodyne Corp. Richard Brautigan fled his native Tacoma for San Francisco to write *The Abortion, In Watermelon Sugar* and other gentle fables that belied the storms in his life (he died at his own hand in 1986).

The national art world recognized a set of Asian-influenced landscape painters in Seattle and the Skagit Valley (including Mark Tobey, Morris Graves and Kenneth Callahan) as a "Northwest School" (as named in a 1953 *Life* article). Their visions of muted serenity complemented the Beats' interest in Asian spiritual philosophies, and were also influenced by the massive Asian art collection at the Seattle Art Museum (founded during the Depression and lacking the funds for European masterworks). La Conner, a remote fishing village in the Skagit Valley halfway between Seattle and the Canadian border, became a mecca for these painters and their wannabes.

Rocking 'round the clock

By the mid-'50s, hip white kids here and across the country were catching on to black R&B 45s. Robert E. Lee Hardwick, a DJ on middle-of-the-road station KVI, publicized this music as much as his station allowed; but when white musicians turned R&B into rock 'n roll, Hardwick was one of the many adult music lovers who (like Steve Allen and Jack Kerouac) pooh-poohed the bastardization of authentic black music into commercial teenybopper fodder. That didn't stop other enterprising guys from marketing R&B to white kids.

In 1955 mercurial Seattle businessman John Elroy McCaw bought New York radio station WINS. McCaw fired the news department, the studio orchestra, and the other trappings of the Golden Age of Radio. He was content to just use records for his programming, including the rhythm and blues 45s spun by a disc jockey McCaw's staff discovered in Cleveland, Alan Freed (who popularized the term "rock n' roll," taken from an old blues sex metaphor). McCaw's station helped turn the white rock scene from a few knowledgeable teens collecting "race records" into the beat that took over the world. (McCaw got overextended, sold the station, and died owning little more than a small-town cable TV system. His sons parlayed that into a national cellular-phone empire, which they sold to AT&T for $13 billion.)

The story of rock in Seattle, however, begins a couple of years later, and it largely begins in Tacoma.

Stan Boreson

A Bob Hale Cartoon

Basil Wolverton
(self portrait)

Mark Tobey

CHAPTER TWO:
AT THE CASTLE (1959-1966)

Bonnie Guitar

The Fleetwoods

As the Space Needle's foundations were poured, a lively little dance-club circuit was underway. It was housed in clubs like Parker's on Aurora, the Trianon downtown, and the Spanish Castle in Federal Way, and in high school gyms from Bellingham to Olympia. It starred a tight community of a few dozen players. Some were just out of (or still in) high school; some were slightly older but had already gigged heavily in pop and country dance bands, playing off-the-shelf arrangements of current hits.

Come softly

The Fleetwoods (named not for the Cadillac but their Olympia telephone exchange) scored the first national pop hit from the Northwest, "Come Softly to Me," in early 1959. Gretchen Christopher, Barbara Ellis and Gary Troxel wrote the sweet ballad for an Olympia High School talent show. They were discovered by Seattle producer Bob Reisdorff; they recorded the song at Joe Boles's West Seattle home studio, as arranged by country singer Bonnie Guitar. The group projected a mature innocence on this and subsequent records on Reisdorff's Dolton Records (distributed by Liberty). Like the later local vocal team the Brothers Four (four UW frat boys, led by future local TV personality Dick Foley), their acoustic harmonies appealed to radio stations that wanted to exploit the folk craze without airing anything political. "Come Softly" spent 16 weeks on the *Billboard* singles chart, four of them at #1. The Fleetwoods continued to make records, live performances and TV appearances until 1966. All three still live in the area; Troxel now sings with a new Fleetwoods group, while Christopher is a music therapist.

O'Day days

Paul W. Berg, the 22-year-old son of a Tacoma radio preacher, got a radio job in 1956 in Astoria, Ore. While there, he held live "platter parties" broadcast from teenage sockhops. He came to Seattle in 1958 to work at country station KAYO. He took the name Pat O'Day; it came from Seattle's Catholic O'Dea High School, and also from the radio-industry term "daypart."

In the fall of 1959 O'Day became the afternoon DJ on KJR, the former NBC Blue Network affiliate that went to a top 40 format in 1955 under owner Lester Smith, who later sold half his company to actor Danny Kaye. (Smith's daughter Laura Lee now hosts a new age talk show on KVI.) O'Day commanded the airwaves with his fast, driving, monotonic voice, perfect for tinny AM car radios.

Peter Blecha: "Almost singlehandedly, O'Day transformed what radio was and helped mold the perceptions of thousands of teenagers into what it could be."

Rock was in a steep decline. Elvis was in the Army (having played Sick's Seattle Stadium on his last pre-draft tour), Buddy Holly was dead, Jerry Lee Lewis was disgraced, Carl Perkins was laid up after a car wreck. The national labels were promoting fashion plates like Fabian. There was virtually no live rock in the region when O'Day mounted his first teen dances in November 1959. He hired the Fabulous Wailers, formed at Tacoma's Stadium High School (several years before Bob Marley formed his first Wailin' Wailers in Jamaica), to play a series of dances at the Spanish Castle, a crumbling dance hall with a kitschy castle storefront on Highway 99 between Seattle and Tacoma. The Wailers (who included Buck Ormsby, Kent Morrill, Ron Gardner, Rich Dangel, John Greck, Mark Marus, Mike Burk and a half dozen other members during their 11-year tenure) already had a regional hit with the cool-piano instrumental "Tall Cool One," which spent 13 weeks on the *Billboard* Hot 100. They made a two-month East Coast tour supporting the hit (with Morrill's mom serving as chaperone), including appearances on *American Bandstand* and Alan Freed's radio show.

Kent Morrill to the Seattle Times, *8/79: "We recorded that song ("Tall Cool One") in one take at the K of C Hall in Tacoma one night after a dance. Three weeks later it was a hit.... We had an offer to sign with GAC, the biggest booking agency at the time. They wanted us to move to New York, sign a record contract and everything, but we were too young and stupid to do it. We missed our girlfriends and cars and wanted to go home to Tacoma. We passed it up and that was it. I honestly feel that if we would have signed we would have become one of the great groups."*

The Wailers released the first of their seven albums on Golden Crest Records (the same New York label that released Stan Boreson's novelty records). After that, they became one of the first

Rockin' Robin Roberts

The Viceroys

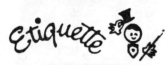

of the scene's top vocalists) and bass player Pete Leinonen. Leinonen, son of a onetime Wobbly newspaper editor, was one of the few original Northwest Rock musicians to later play the punk circuit (with the Magnetics, Pagan Agents, Nordstroms, Born Again Aliens, Anti-Fascist Marching Band and Jesse Bernstein Band). His sons Walter and Henry played in several punk bands: the former in Hobo Skank and SWAK (Sealed With A Kiss), the latter in FAST (Fuck Authority Skate Team), Necroticism and Boraxx.

Pete Leinonen: "The Swaggerz alternated with the Wailers, Friday and Saturday nights at the Lakewood Community Center in south Tacoma. The tunes were all really simple.… When rock n' roll started, the rhythm section came out front for the first time, instead of being in back of all the horns. People hadn't really heard amplified music before, either, so that added to the newness of it all. Teenage girls would go crazy about it. That gave rock n' roll musicians a terrible social stigma. Nobody wanted their daughters seen in your company. We became erratic, we all had cars, we played over big territories from Bellingham to Olympia. We wore suits but they were more like beatnik suits, not the white jackets and bowties of the dance bands. The look was black slacks and white shirts; we were all trying to afford black shirts. You couldn't buy black shirts at Penney's."

Buck Ormsby: "We played mostly teen dances, but not actually in the high schools. The powers that be in the schools still thought this was the devil's music. We played ballrooms, dance halls, parties, drive-in restaurants, whatever place was available to us on a Friday night."

These bands learned their chops the way all early white rockers did, by copying black musicians who couldn't get the opportunities white kids could get. The Wailers went straight to local black clubs like the Black and Tan, Birdland, the Esquire, the Washington Social Club, the Empire Bar Room, the Galaxy (the future Off Ramp), and Gabe's jukebox bar.

Buck Ormsby to the Rocket, 9/83: "A lot of the groups around here learned a lot from black music…people like Bobby Blue Bland, Little Willie John and Little Richard and the Upsetters, they would play at a dance hall in Seattle called the Empire Bar Room and in a place in Olympia called the Evergreen Ballroom. It was all black people, and we'd be standing out in the middle listening to this great, high energy music. We'd just go out there and stand and not move—just watch.… We'd see black groups and cover the songs the next week, and a lot of people would think they were our tunes."

bands to form its own record label, Etiquette (distributed by United Artists). They cranked out one more national hit, "Mau Mau," and a string of regional hits: "Mashi," "Seattle," "Dirty Robber," "Since You've Been Gone," and "Wailers House Party."

Over the next eight years, O'Day put lots of local records on KJR's "Fab 50" playlist and booked the same bands into his O'Day and Associates dance circuit, centered at the Spanish Castle. At its peak, O'Day's firm held 58 dances a week in western Washington, and KJR had up to 37 percent of the local radio audience (despite fierce competition from KOL).

Tacoma rocks

Like the Wailers, many of O'Day's top bands (the Ventures, Little Bill and the Bluenotes, the Sonics) came from Tacoma, where the button-down Boeing corporate culture hadn't stifled the creative spirit. Another band from Tacoma, the Swaggerz, included guitarists Jim Clockner and Neil Rush (whose then-wife Merrilee became one

In 1961 the Wailers added a singer, Buddy Holly lookalike Rockin' Robin Roberts. The instrumental-combo basis of Northwest bands, in which the vocalist was treated as just another sideman, is why the Boise-founded band with singer Mark Lindsey was always billed under its lead guitarist's name, as Paul Revere and the Raiders.

Roberts and the Wailers recorded a guitar-combo version of a proto-reggae song written in 1958 by L.A. R&B singer Richard Berry. Berry had sold his publishing rights for a trifle, and never prospered from the dozens of versions of "Louie Louie" recorded by local bands from 1961 to 1965. Ormsby's Stadium High classmate Bill Englehart was the first local artist to perform and record the song, with his band Little Bill and the Bluenotes, but the Wailers' version was the first to get local airplay. (Englehart later had the local hit "I Love an Angel," and still performs in the area.)

More hitmakers

The Frantics (Ron Peterson, Jimmy Manolides, Bob Hosko, Dick Goodman, Chuck Schoning) also performed, but didn't record, "Louie Louie." They still became the second big act on Dolton Records. O'Day made regional hits out of their instrumental singles "Straight Flush" and "Werewolf" (which included a chilling introductory poem spoken by Reisdorff, snarls by engineer Kearney Barton, and wolf howls by Bonnie Guitar), but their only national hit came as the anonymous backing band on "Dream Lover," Bobby Darin's last rock record. After several years of steady local gigs and personnel changes, the remaining Frantics (Schoning, Hosko, Don Stevenson, Jerry Miller) moved to San Francisco in hopes of greater industry attention, changing their name to Luminous Marsh Gas. Manolides ran a Seattle art gallery in the 1980s and now has a cigar store in Pioneer Square.

Rockin' Robin Roberts also headed to California, where he died in a 1967 auto accident; the Wailers replaced him with 15-year-old Gail Harris, Seattle's first real female rock singer.

The Ventures scored a #2 national hit in 1960 with "Walk Don't Run," a rocked-up version of Chet Atkins's arrangement of a Johnny Smith jazz-guitar staple. Their twangy guitar/driving beat style kept Bob Noble, Don Wilson, Nokie Edwards and Howie Johnston on the charts for nearly a decade (recording over 80 albums then and since). Though often lumped in with "surf music," *Rocket* critic Jim Emerson wrote that their intricate guitar interplay sounded more like "the resonant echo of a slightly rusty gasoline can on a rainy day." They also served the house band for many months at the Java Jive, a South Tacoma dive in a building shaped like a teapot (still a regional landmark). While known as an instrumental outfit, they did have a singer for a time, Nancy Claire, who also sang for the Frantics, Exotics, Dynamics and Viceroys.

The biggest hit of the Viceroys (led by guitarist Jim Valley and drummer Fred Zuefeldt) was 1962's "Granny's Pad," named for O'Day's radio alter ego Granny Peters. It was one of those instrumentals that snuck in a vocal exclamation of the title, with some mumbling at the fadeout: "Going down to Granny's pad/She really swings/Granny do the wa-

tusi…" Valley went on to Don and the Goodtimes and wrote their local hit "Little Sally Tease," covered by the Standells. Some Viceroys gigs included Clif Lenz, who grew up to be a local radio DJ and TV talk show host. The Viceroys went to L.A., where major-label groomers turned them into the short-lived Surprise Package; Zeufeldt came home to be a producer and engineer. The leader of the Goodtimes, ex-Kingsman Don Galluci, wound up in L.A.; in the spring of 1970 he produced Iggy and the Stooges' seminal album *Funhouse*.

Jimmy Hanna and the Dynamics were noted for their lead guitarist, UW journalism student Larry Coryell. Their main regional hit was Dave Lewis's composition "J.A.J." (for Jive Ass Jerry—an alleged reference to Lewis's record producer, former Dolton promo man Jerry Dennon). Coryell moved to New York in 1965 to make it big in jazz, though several of his projects (including the pre-fusion Free Spirits) reflected his rock interests.

Larry Coryell *on his Seattle years in* The Journal of NW Music, *1992: "I think the kids in Seattle and the Northwest were into a much stronger*

Don & The Goodtimes

The Frantics

Pat O'Day

Kearney Barton

Jimi Hendrix in
The Rocking Kings

Elvis at the Fair

form of R&B than in other parts of the country."

Coryell *on his early New York years in* Tower Records Pulse!, *1993: "We were in the middle of a world cultural revolution. Everybody was dropping acid and the prevailing attitude was, 'Let's do something different.' We loved Wes [Montgomery] but we also loved Bob Dylan. We loved Coltrane but we also dug the Beatles. We loved Miles but we also loved the Rolling Stones."*

Bringing up the female contingent of the scene were early country-rockers Bonnie Guitar and Merrilee Rush (who scored a national hit in 1968 with "Angel of the Morning"). The relative lack of female vocalists was related to the lack of prominence for local rock vocalists in general. The scene was fueled by dance guitarists who rose to prominence through O'Day's shows, including hyped-up "battles of the bands" where the beat and the energy were what mattered.

A few black musicians managed to break through the city's semi-official color line on Yesler Way. Ron Holden's soul ballad "Love You So" reached *Billboard*'s #7 under the tutelage of ex-Ritchie Valens producer Bob Keene. Tiny Tony (who, naturally, was quite un-tiny) had a regional hit with the dirty-blues ditty "Hey Mrs. Jones" (with a backing vocal of Tony's illicit lover by the white Merrilee Rush). Tony also worked with a vocal combo, the Gallahads, who reached #111 on the *Billboard* charts with "Lonely Guy." Dave Lewis scored with the R&B instrumentals "Dave's Mood" and "Little Green Thing" (named after a catch phrase of KOL DJ Lan Roberts). He ran the house band at Birdland, an after-hours R&B club in the Central District; he later had his own downtown club, Dave's Fifth Avenue. "Little Green Thing" was picked up in 1964 as the title cut on the fifth LP ever released on Herb Alpert's new A&M Records. Lewis made eight other albums but his career declined later on. He was hooked on cocaine and/or heroin at several times, and spent some time in prison after robbing a pharmacy in 1985. In 1994 he resurfaced with a jazz band, Carousel.

Lewis's records were among the first produced by Jerry Dennon, who always admitted his business talents were superior to his recording talents (though his raw sound influenced many). Dennon ran a string of record labels from 1962 to 1983, including Jerden, Burdette, Panorama, Picadilly, Great Northwest, First American, and Music Is Medicine.

A lot of the local rock records were cut at Audio Recording, a small downtown studio run by engineer Kearney Barton. He's still recording today, on much of the same equipment the '60s bands had used.

Teenage guitarist James Marshall Hendrix spent many an evening from 1959 to 1961 playing blues on the streets with his friend Junior Heath, or hanging around outside the Spanish Castle or the Empire, guitar and amp at his side, hoping for a

chance to sit in. If a band turned out to be short an amp or blew out one of the amps they'd brought, he'd let them use his, but only if he got to play. He joined a pick-up band for Little Richard at the Spanish Castle, only to get dismissed midway through for upstaging the star. He played in some local teen bands (the Velvetones, the Tomcats, the Rocking Kings) before he dropped out of Garfield High School and joined the Army in May 1961, shortly after his 18th birthday. Upon his discharge he traveled between Nashville, Vancouver (where he played with future comedian Tommy Chong) and New York, as well as traveling in Richard's and other touring bands, before getting discovered in England. He wrote a song in tribute to his teen experiences, "Spanish Castle Magic," but never resided in Seattle as a professional musician. His achievements were made far from here, and hence are beyond the scope of this book. Calling Hendrix a Seattle artist is as misleading as calling Madonna a Detroit artist.

The world of tomorrow

The "Jet City" era of industrial utopianism peaked in 1962 with the Seattle World's Fair (a.k.a. the Century 21 Exposition), which brought a lot of wondrous things to our stuffy little town: kitsch-futuristic architecture, a Space Needle, strip shows, an Elvis movie (*It Happened at the World's Fair*), two professional theater companies, an opera company, a 14,000-seat coliseum, and brief worldwide recognition. Local TV stations hyped the fair on weekly prime-time shows, and found time for live music shows with fair tie-in themes (*Deck Dance, Hootenanny*).

The fair was built at the foot of Queen Anne Hill, on a traditional site for old native gatherings. Some sources claim it had been a site for potlatches, intertribal parties where chiefs tried to outgive one another. The fair's "futuristic" buildings were cheap modern constructions designed for multipurpose use in the post-fair complex, Seattle Center, and fell into disrepair well in advance of the 21st century. The fair's "World of Tomorrow" exhibits promised that by now we'd be living in a wonderland of domed cities, speedy peoplemovers, and spacious plastic homes, powered by cheap, clean atomic energy. What we got was suburban sprawl, freeways, bland office towers, and tacky subdivisions and condos, powered by imported oil, fish-killing dams, and expensive, dangerous atomic energy.

Cultural organizer Lorenzo Milam started a volunteer radio station in 1963 on the then-little-used FM band, KRAB. It was a revolutionary concept: run on volunteer labor and listener donations, it played blocks of everything from Early Music to bebop to Appalachian folk to children's stories to big band classics to audio documentaries about professional wrestling and greasy-spoon diners. Milam, a self-described "closet cripple" who suffered from polio and believed in the power of the imagination, went off to organize similar stations across the country. In his absence, KRAB's parent Jack Straw Memorial Foundation became more careerist and the station became more tame.

In 1964, KING-TV started *Seattle* magazine, the city's first major commercial publication not bound to a Chamber of Commerce ideology. The slick monthly's writers (including southern transplant Tom Robbins and former Princeton poli-sci prof David Brewster) made what now seem tame stabs at the short-sighted local cultural and political machines. It was shocking for a town used to hearing only what the business community wanted it to hear; businesses pulled their ads from the magazine, and threatened to pull their ads from KING. *Seattle*'s lack of fiscal success may have influenced the more conservative tone Brewster later took in his own *Seattle Weekly*.

Where the action was

The biggest version of "Louie Louie" was produced in 1963 by Dennon as a cheap demo for a Portland band, the Kingsmen. The tape was picked up by Scepter/Wand, a New York R&B label. A Boston soul station, presuming the band to be black, put it on its playlist.

The resulting worldwide hit propelled the local circuit to continued prosperity in the face of encroaching Beatlemania in 1964. Paul Revere and the Raiders (who'd recorded their own "Louie Louie" the same week as the Kingsmen's version) took advantage of their existing name by adopting an anti-British image with Minuteman costumes. The Raiders moved to L.A. and became the house band on Dick Clark's TV show *Where The Action Is*.

The Kingsmen toured and recorded for the rest of the decade, scoring a few national hits (including the novelty "Jolly Green Giant") and appearing with Annette Funicello in *How to Stuff A Wild Bikini*, but without the original impact. The drummer's mother may have been the reason. Jack Ely was the lead singer on "Louie Louie," but (according to the most commonly retold version of the story) drummer/saxophonist Lynn Easton's mom took care of trademarking the name. When the record was picked up by Specter/Wand, Mrs. Easton said the band could keep using the Kingsmen name, as long as her son became the singer. For the band's first LP (with no pictures of band members), every track was recorded live with Easton except "Louie Louie," for which the original single with Ely was overdubbed with concert noise.

British musicologist Ian Whitcomb lived in Seattle for a spell, and played R&B covers and English music hall ditties in a coffeehouse in the basement of the Mutual Life Building at 92 Yesler in Pioneer Square. Dennon recorded Whitcomb's blues-rock arrangement of an English drinking song, "This Sporting Life," with Gerry Rosalie of the Sonics (see below) on backup vocals. It was a success, but the real hit came with the follow-up. During the instrumental intro to the gritty blues song "You Really Turn Me On," Whitcomb accidentally knocked

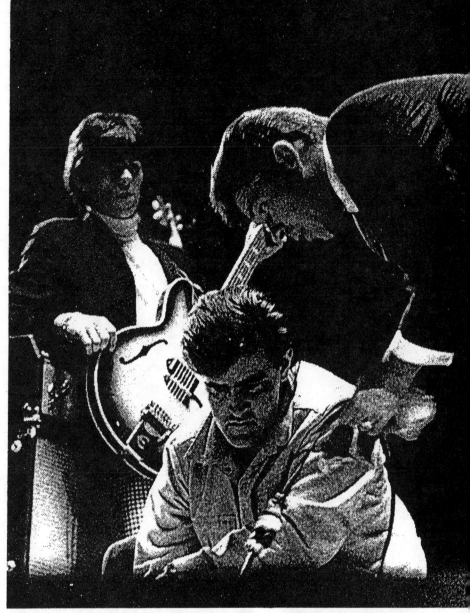

an ashtray onto the studio floor. Believing the take to be ruined, Whitcomb started singing in a campy falsetto, while the session band churned behind him as usual. That take, ashtray and all, became a #1 hit in 1965 and an anthem for the still-underground gay scene. Whitcomb returned to England, where he remains a leading historian on early American music.

The Beatles came to Seattle on Aug. 31, 1964. They were promoted by Pat O'Day and partner Tom Hewlett under the name Concerts West. The Beatles played at the Seattle Center Coliseum and stayed at the Edgewater Inn. Entrepreneurs bought up the hotel carpet the Fab Four had walked on and sold it in little pieces to devoted fans. The Edgewater, built on a waterfront pier where you could (at the time) "Fish From Your Window," became *the* local hostelry for touring rockers, as later honored in Frank Zappa's song "Mudshark" (which described an allegedly-true incident involving a Led Zeppelin groupie persuaded to commit an unnatural act with a fish). O'Day also produced shows by the Rolling Stones in 1965 and 1966 (the latter with the Raiders and Whitcomb opening), and the Kinks

Keith Richards, Ian Stewart and Pat O'Day at the 1966 "Teen Spectacular"

Paul Revere & The Raiders

The Sonics   in 1965 (opened by Tacoma's Sonics).

Sonics boom

The Sonics, formed in 1963 and named after the sonic booms heard in their neighborhood near McChord Air Force Base, recorded originally for the Wailers' Etiquette label and later for Dennon's Jerden Records. They took the Wailers' guitar-bass-drums-sax formula further away from slick teeny-bopper innocence and into a rough-hewn assault. They played Wailers songs and some of the R&B tunes the Wailers also covered, but with a harsher edge. Their horror-movie-inspired originals ("Psycho," "The Witch," "Strychnine") were delivered in a madman manner by singer Gerry Rosalie, whose on-stage aggression and off-stage high living inspired comparisons to Jerry Lee Lewis. Andy and Larry Parypa churned out guitar and bass chords with abandon; drummer Bob Bennett's beats affirmed everything parents believed about the evils of rock n' roll; even obligatory sax player Rob Lind sounded like a clarion call to debauchery. In three years the band went from the Parypas' basement to high school dances to opening in arenas to headlining in large auditoriums to oblivion.

Rob Lind *to the* Rocket *on the Sonics' sound: "Everything that was technically right was technically wrong for us."*

Paul de Barros: *"I had the privilege of being in Seattle in 1965 on a vacation. I was taken on a blind date to the Evergreen Ballroom outside Olympia to see the Sonics. The place was packed and with good reason. This was one kick-ass rock n' roll band."*

Art Chantry: *"The Sonics were one of those bands that, even if not very many people heard them, those that did hear them were tremendously affected by them."*

Their mystery image was enhanced by the cover for their first LP, by Etiquette's resident photographer Jini Dellaccio. Beneath the bold-type heading HERE ARE THE SONICS!!!, you could only barely see a faint sepiatone image of the five band members' faces. A Sonics gig at Parker's was seen by members of the Who, in town on their first American tour; in London weeks later, Pete Townshend told Barbara Walters and a live *Today* show audience that seeing the Sonics was one of his few good memories of America. The band was courted by London Records and got as far as a test-pressing 45 before contract negotiations fell through. Despite releasing only three crudely-recorded LPs, a few extra singles, and a split Christmas album (with the Wailers and the Galaxies), the Sonics are cited as an influence by countless bands who never saw them.

In 1966, Hollywood movie-theatre executive Sam Schulman brought professional basketball to Seattle. He paid Rosalie and company $10,000 for the right to use "Sonics" as the short name of his team, fully known as the SuperSonics (after the Super Sonic Transport, a plane being developed at Boeing with federal money). The members took advantage of the opportunity to take time off from the business; the rigors of touring, combined with growing personality conflicts and their own raucous lifestyles, had done them in. One member was even arraigned in a trumped-up statutory rape charge, filed by a Yakima groupie's dad. Andy Parypa sold the band's equipment and name to a lounge act, which performed into the mid-'70s.

The Sonics' era was ending anyway. The first LSD showed up in the U District sometime in 1966. The Beatles' *Sgt. Pepper* album would come out the next year, popularizing a new brand of pop. The local big-beat bands would soon leave town, break up, or change their sound to meet the changing tastes. In later years, the Sonics' music would be regularly rediscovered and reinterpreted. Promoters of their reissue records called them the fathers of punk (a label more aptly applied to Detroit's Stooges and MC5). Foreign writers later mistakenly credited them with directly starting grunge. There was little or no direct lineage of hard garage bands from the Sonics to the local '80s punks; Seattle had to relearn it all a decade later from New York. During their day the Sonics were popular with local audiences (if not among other musicians, who often thought they were sloppy and unprofessional), but were unknown anywhere else—except in Cleveland, where they appeared on a local TV show. After all the hype, what remains of the Sonics is a handful of the rawest 2:30 songs ever made—songs that became even rougher-sounding in later reissues, many of which were produced without access to the original masters.

Suffering a similar tragic fate was an Olympia band, the Bootmen (also known as Cottonmouth). They released the regional hits "1, 2, 3, 4," "Black Widow," and "Ain't It the Truth." Then guitarist Fred Dickerson was drafted. In what may have been attempt to get a dishonorable discharge, Dickerson got into a drunken fist fight with his sergeant, punching him in the face and breaking his own hand in several places. He got the discharge but couldn't play guitar again. Dickerson's younger brother Mike played in several early-'80s Olympia punk bands.

The wethead is dead

One of the last local bands with a chance for success was the Daily Flash, the first band to promote its own shows at rental halls and to create its own advertising (including "I Flash Daily" bumper stickers). The band, which included Don MacAllister, Doug Hastings and Jon Keliehor (replaced by ex-Dynamics drummer Ron Woods), incorporated folk and jazz elements within its pop sound. After playing in Seattle for a year the band moved to L.A. in 1966, where It recorded for Parrot and Uni. It performed with the Raiders on *Where the Action Is* (playing the hit "French Girl") and appeared on *The Girl From U.N.C.L.E.* (playing "Oi Oi Oi Oi, My Bulgarian Baby"). Guitarist Hastings replaced Neil Young in the Buffalo Springfield. The group continued without him, performing here and in California until early 1969; in an attempt to conform to the flower-power fad, it briefly changed its name to Nirvana (there was also a minor British band with that

name around that time). Keliehor resurfaced locally in the 1980s with the world-beat ensembles Gamelan Pacifica and Je Ka Jo.

When the *Cruisin'* series of oldies LPs (re-created AM radio hours complete with DJs and ads) came out in the '70s, Pat O'Day was chosen to host the 1966 volume; an appropriate choice, since that was the last year the Spanish Castle operated (it was demolished a decade later) and the last year O'Day's dance circuit ruled unopposed in the Seattle music market. That December, O'Day's company produced a teen dance in Burien starring Merrilee Rush. As an extra attraction, he added one of the area's first touring psychedelic light shows: slides of abstract and nature scenes, synchronized to records, plus 2,000 watts of aviation strobe lights. Rush's band refused to be upstaged by the lights and wouldn't play until they stopped; the audience nearly rioted.

The following year, O'Day was sued for $3 million for allegedly monopolizing the local concert biz; the three businessmen who sued him implied that he'd been involved in payola and kickbacks from the bands he supported. O'Day promoted fewer, bigger shows during the three years of litigation (he was eventually exonerated), but sold his teen-dance company. That business was fading anyway. The music industry was changing, and Seattle's foothold in it would be lost in the transition.

The Daily Flash

The Edgewater Inn
"Fish From Your Window"

The Java Jive —
where The Ventures
were the house band

At The Castle (1959-1966)   **15**   Left: Ian Whitecomb

CHAPTER THREE:
PURPLE HAZE DAYS (1967-70)

As major college towns, Seattle and the Canadian-border town of Bellingham (home of Western Washington University) had their share of hippie-era activity. There were underground papers (the *Helix*, *Seattle Flag* and the 13-year-lasting *Northwest Passage*), longhair lifestyles, panhandlers, pot, junkies, campus marches and sit-ins, ROTC and supermarket bombings, black light posters, gelatin/color wheel light shows, very raucous bars, and bullying cops. On other fronts, we had a thriving Black Panthers branch and a black theater movement.

As the media turned beat generation ideas into an increasingly superficial mass movement, the music industry commodified Beatlemania into a big business ruled by a few supergroups.

I'll leave the main chronicling of that era to the thousands of '60s-nostalgia writers. But I will highlight a few points.

Jimi Hendrix experiences

Pat O'Day ran the first national headlining tour (after a few disastrous dates opening for the Monkees) of Jimi Hendrix, the Seattle-born guitarist who became young white America's ultimate fantasy of the dangerous black rebel child. Hendrix performed four headlining gigs in Seattle: in February and August 1968, May 1969, and July 1970. (Before that, he'd appeared here in 1964 as part of the Isley Brothers' touring band.)

Before his first local starring show he made a trip to his alma mater, Garfield High. A student asked how long it had been since he'd been to Seattle. Accounts of his response vary but generally run along the lines of "About a thousand years ago."

Seasons in the sun

"Pat O'Day Is A Shmuck" bumper stickers were sold on the Ave in 1967, spread by advocates of a different music scene. The epithet was derived from a KRAB DJ who'd actually called O'Day a "shuck," an old jazz term for a shady hustler, over his monopolization of the local rock business. Some of their first sightings were at the UW HUB Auditorium, where a March 1967 Country Joe and the Fish gig provided the first big local showcase for the new political folk music. Joe McDonald later lived in Bellingham for a spell, always ready to donate his services to a benefit concert. By the time of his first local show, Seattle already had the

Helix, a network of folk coffeehouses, active chapters of Students for a Democratic Society and the Committee to End the War in Vietnam, a thriving Free University, and local action groups such as the Brothers and the U District Movement.

That summer's Sky River Rock Festival and Lighter Than Air Fair is reputed to have been America's first outdoor, multi-band rock festival. It featured the Allman Brothers, Pink Floyd, It's A Beautiful Day, the Youngbloods, Santana and the Grateful Dead, before 20,000 people over two days. It was held on a raspberry farm on the banks of the Skykomish River owned by Betty Nelson, known among the freaks as Universal Mother. Her son Ward, nine at the time, grew up to play hardcore punk guitar, first for Joe Despair and the Future and later for the Refuzors.

Sky River was followed by the Sunshine Freedom Festival, the Underground Rock Festival, the Bullfrog Festival, the indoor Trips Festival at the Seattle Center Exhibition Hall (the city originally refused to rent the hall to the promoters, until Tom Robbins wrote a *P-I* commentary pleading for open minds) and two more Sky River festivals. At the third Sky River, an 11-day affair held in southwest Washington, West Seattle art-school student Shary Flenniken met up with some San Francisco underground cartoonists and joined the Air Pirates collective, which got sued for its X-rated Mickey Mouse parodies; she later drew the *Trots and Bonnie* series for *National Lampoon*.

The biggest of all was the 1969 Seattle Pop Festival, bringing over 50,000 to a private campground to see Led Zeppelin, the Doors (with the fat burnout version of Jim Morrison), the Byrds, the Guess Who, Ike and Tina Turner, Chicago, the Youngbloods, Vanilla Fudge, Ten Years After, Chuck Berry, Bo Diddley, and a non-singing performance act billed as "Frank Zappa Presents Alice Cooper." Some people said it was a better show than Woodstock, held the previous weekend.

Smaller outdoor shows took place all the time, at least during spring and summer seasons. There were be-ins and love-ins in Volunteer Park and the Seattle Center lawns, and an ongoing "hippie hill" on the UW campus. All featured girls in long dresses, boys in brown leather, and the narc squad on the watch for pot. But any longhairs who tried to relax by the reflecting pools at Pacific Science Center (the old World's Fair science exhibit) were

First light show

Helix benefit concert

A "Be-in"

Early OCA show

rented for rock shows in early 1967 by the Overall Cooperative Structure, a booking collective that folded after five months. OCS was succeeded by UW drama major Boyd Grafmyre (who also promoted the Seattle Pop Festival). Over the next four years, the Eagles hosted gigs by almost all the national hippie bands, busing up from San Francisco on the new Interstate 5 freeway: the Grateful Dead, Janis Joplin, Joe Cocker, Steve Miller (who later settled in a Seattle suburb), the Doors, Paul Butterfield, and the Youngbloods—but not Hendrix, who was scheduled there in February 1968 but got moved by Pat O'Day into the bigger Seattle Center Arena.

L.E. Bonow, *ex-wife of hippie musician Dan Bonow: "The Eagles was big, but it was intimate. It was dark. The light shows really made it come alive: Lux Sit and Dance, the Union Light Company, the Electric Light Company. It was really informal: bands talked to you. Groupies could get full access and fuck anybody in the bands. None of the guys in the bands had wives, or at least they didn't bring them up."*

At first, the air in the big ballroom could be so laced with pot smoke that it bordered on unbreathable. The hippie insiders soon got perturbed as Grafmyre turned the Eagles scene into a well-oiled business venture where on-premises pot smoking and making out got banned. The purists were more enraged when O'Day, the local symbol of corporate rock, turned out to be a silent partner in Grafmyre's company. Grafmyre controlled local gigs by the top California bands until 1970; other promoters kept the Eagles open until 1972.

Other spacey venues included the Happening (the temporarily renamed Showbox), Freeway Hall (a socialist meeting hall on land owned by ex-sympathizer Ivar Haglund, where punk shows would later be held), the Walrus in the U District (a former hayloft, later a cover-band bar called the Rathskeller and now a hot-tub salon), the Fresh Air Tavern on Broadway (later a gay disco), the Warehouse, the Travel Agency, the Medicine Show, the Chalet, and even a *franchise* club at 13th and Pike on Capitol Hill called The San Francisco Sound. O'Day got in further on the new action with the BFD (an old church) and a space on Aurora called O'Day's Bummer, but he found more money in arena rock with his promotion company Concerts West (later sold to KJR owners Kaye-Smith). The city tried to ban psychedelic light shows, citing an obscure old law against "shadow dancing" by strippers; the case was thrown out of court.

With the music business getting bigger and more consolidated (despite anti-establishment messages in the lyrics) and Seattle a lucrative tour stop for California acts, there was no room for local bands to forge their own identities. Local bands that played the hippie bars kept to covers for their first few sets, only bringing out original tunes at the end of the night.

A few of the pre-1967 bands stayed on. The

sternly shooed away by the humorless schoolmarm presence of director Dr. Dixy Lee Ray (an adamant promoter of the nuclear industry, and later a one-term governor with a strident anti-environmentalist agenda).

Drugs were used and sold freely along University Way, on Hippie Hill, and at the out-of-town rock festivals. The second Sky River festival had dealers hawking their wares out loud, plus hippie hookers offering blow jobs in tents. Authorities passed laws to crack down on the festivals, forbidding drugs and alcohol and mandating heavy security and plenty of sanitation facilities. The owner of Ballard's Buffalo Tavern tried to avoid the restrictions by billing his festival as a political gathering, the Buffalo Party Convention; the state didn't buy his claims and imposed roadblocks around the festival site.

The Eagles flies

The primary psychedelic temple became the Eagles Auditorium. The world headquarters building of the fraternal lodge organization was first

Ventures proved resilient to changing fads (their 1968 cover of the *Hawaii Five-O* theme became their second biggest hit). Paul Revere and the Raiders (or their name) appeared on a string of hits conceived by singer Mark Lindsey and producer Terry Melcher, and executed by studio musicians. They peaked with the 1971 hit "Indian Reservation." Lindsey disappeared into the netherworld of Hollywood production work, surfacing in 1980 with a score for the re-edited samurai movie *Shogun Assassin*; he later appeared with other former rock stars on a *Married...With Children* episode. Revere formed a Raiders nostalgia band that still plays auto shows and county fairs.

Other wetheads tried to cash in on flower power. Members of the Frantics wound up in the California bands Moby Grape and Quicksilver Messenger Service. When singer Jimmy Hanna left the Dynamics (Larry Coryell's old band), saxophonist Jeff Afdem took the reins and turned the band into the Springfield Rifle, later renamed the Springfield Flute. R&B singer Tiny Tony turned his band, the Statics, into the acid-blues International Brick. The Wailers tried to stay hip by adding a quote from Buddha's *Dhammapada* to an LP cover.

Outside the bars, local bands settled to serve as opening acts for San Francisco stars or political rallies, or as part of multi-act bills at free outdoor shows. Dozens of bands appeared, including many who only got together once for improvised doodling.

Calliope, one of the Eagles' opening bands, released the LP *Steamed* on the Buddha label, briefly cracking the bottom of the Top 40. Its singer, Danny O'Keefe, scored a solo hit with the '70s ballad "Goodtime Charlie's Got the Blues," covered by Elvis.

Other local bands of the time included Dan Bonow's mixed-race Juggernaut, the PH Phactor Jug Band, Crome Sycrus, Mirage, Magic Fern, Floating Bridge, Easy Chair, Blues Interchange, Indian Puddin and Pipe, Ethiopia, and West Coast Natural Gas. A few of these got signed to national labels but were dropped after one or two failed releases. None lasted beyond their era.

In visual art, the Northwest School boys attracted a scad of imitators and followers, hanging out in dangerous Seattle dives like the Blue Moon and Century in the U District, the Pigalle in the Pike Place Market, the J&M in Pioneer Square, and the Elite, Deluxe and Comet on Capitol Hill and taking over the Skagit Valley fishing town of La Conner. As art critic Charles Krafft noted, "there was a lot of drinking and drugging and driving going on."

Seattle had its own resident "tribe" of the hippie-exploitation musical *Hair*, at the Moore Theatre. Eyeing the success of *Hair*, the Seattle Opera produced the world's first stage production of the Who's rock opera *Tommy* in 1971, premiering at the Moore soon after *Hair* closed. Appearing topless as Tommy's mother and the Acid Queen was an aspiring singer-actress from Hawaii, Bette Midler.

Legends past and future

The Sonics returned in 1968-69, sort of: producer Jerry Dennon issued some tracks made before the band's breakup, and later sent vocalist Gerry Rosalie to California to record pseudo-hippie sides under the Sonics name with studio musicians; these included a blasé cover of Frank Zappa's "Any Way the Wind Blows." Rosalie left the business and became a carpenter. The original Sonics performed a three-song reunion gig in 1972 at the 1928-built Paramount Theatre, newly rechristened as a rock palace (it was managed for several years by Dave Lewis's brother Ulysses). Dennon's other late-'60s releases (including the New Yorkers, three Portland brothers named Hudson who became minor TV comics) went nowhere fast. Rosalie resurfaced in 1980 with a "new" Sonics LP, produced by Dennon with a cover band called the Invaders.

Bruce Lee, a San Francisco-born martial arts enthusiast, came to Seattle and worked in the restaurant of King County Councilwoman Ruby Chow, while studying philosophy at the UW and teaching kung fu to local young adults. He went to Hollywood and got his break as Kato on *The Green Hornet*. When the show was cancelled in 1968 he went to Hong Kong and spent five years introducing martial-arts action to film audiences around the world, until his mysterious death at age 32.

Bruce Lee's gravesite

**the Moby Grape
(with former Frantics)
in collaboration with
Seattle's Joffrey Ballet (!)**

Seattle

75 CENTS
FEBRUARY 1970

Boyd Grafmyre,
Seattle's Mahatma of Rock

Boyd Grafmyre

Seattle Black Panther leader Curtis Harris with his bodygaurds

The Pilots beat the Mariners to the idea of hapless

Tikkun; his writings about "the politics of meaning" and "the sleeping sickness of the soul" were paraphrased in speeches by first lady Hillary Rodham Clinton. (Boldt proved pretty radical himself in 1974 when he ruled that local native Americans deserved half the salmon in their historic fishing grounds, based on treaties that allowed them access "in common" with their white conquerers.)

Between the courthouse riot and the subsequent trial came the town's biggest protest rally on May 8, 1970. After the Kent State killings, about 50,000 people took to the streets, blocking all traffic on the Express Lanes of the Interstate 5 bridge over the Montlake Cut. It was one of the last big radical events covered in the *Helix*; its fortnightly circulation had dropped from 17,000 to below 10,000. One of its editors, Walt Crowley, became a TV news commentator and a publicist for local Democrats.

Wilting flowers, growing seeds

The last *Helix* in June 1970 reviewed a gig by the Lamar Harrington Band, a hippie-rock group (named after a UW gallery director) co-founded by Danny Eskenazi (owner of Dreamland, Seattle's first vintage clothing store). Eskenazi recalls that the group played "noncommercial gigs" at art galleries and rental halls; "the bars wouldn't take us because of our infamous wall of sound." Some 50 people played in it over the next four years; its core line-up included guitarist Eskenazi, singer Phil Miller, and on bass a UW economics professor, ham radio buff, baseball fan and amateur astronomer who'd gone longhair. That soon-to-be ex-professor, Homer Spence, would become one of the few links between the '60s and '80s alternative scenes.

Another such link was Steven J. Bernstein (known to friends by his middle name, Jesse), who came up from California in 1966 at age 16 and immediately started playing bass and trumpet in post-beatnik jazz bands with Pete Leinonen at the Llahngaelhyn, a restaurant south of the U District that reappears later in our story as Scoundrel's Lair. It was across from the Red Robin tavern, a popular freaks' watering hole and site of countless pot and acid deals. After that scene faded, Bernstein and Leinonen played in assorted jazz and rock bands.

Wilting flowers

The war-bloated prosperity that made "dropping out" feasible collapsed. Boeing laid off a third of its 100,000 area employees, after setbacks including the cancellation of the SST project (the unbuilt plane the SuperSonics were named after). *Seattle* magazine folded; KING couldn't subsidize its losses. An anonymous billboard near Boeing Field showed a lightbulb with the headline, "Will the last person leaving Seattle please turn out the lights?"

The Seattle Pilots, our second major league sports team (memorialized in pitcher Jim Bouton's memoir *Ball Four*), left town in early 1970 after

Politics and retribution

Terrorist acts on both sides of the antiwar movement set people wondering where we were headed. The Black Panthers office was the target of a police sting operation — an undercover cop showed up to "donate" some used typewriters to the office; once he left, cops showed up to bust the Panthers for possession of stolen property.

Two thousand protesters attended a February 1970 sit-in at the Federal Courthouse protesting the Chicago Seven verdicts. The protest was met by a mass billy-club and tear gas attack by police, which led some protesters on melee of downtown vandalism (broken windows, an overturned cop car or two), hundreds of injuries and 89 arrests. Protest organizers were charged with conspiracy to provoke violence. The resulting "Seattle Seven" trial turned into a road-show re-enactment of the Chicago trial. The defendants harassed old Judge George Boldt until he cited them for contempt of court and issued six-month sentences, dropping their original charges. One of the Seven, psychology teacher Michael Lerner, moved to San Francisco and co-founded the political magazines *Ramparts* and

one pathetic season at Sick's Stadium; the city sued the American League over the move and eventually won a new franchise, the hapless Mariners. In the summer of 1970, Sick's Stadium hosted Jimi Hendrix's final Seattle show. During the gig he bad-mouthed Seattle, Garfield High and the audience, who started to leave during a sudden downpour. He said nobody here had ever appreciated his music and he was glad he'd left. Hendrix died in England that September. The official cause of death was choking on his own vomit; his family continues to insist it wasn't drug-related.

The freewheeling '60s music scene collapsed as thoroughly as the economy.

Pete Leinonen: "All the bands had booked their own gigs up to this time, and they were getting as much as $250 a night; one band playing the whole five hours. The clubs were packed; the prices were cheap; we were all making a modest living. But in San Francisco and Los Angeles, so many people had moved there hoping to be musicians that bars could get bands to play for free, and then they got bands to pay to play. So a bunch of musicians came up here and told bars they'd work for $100 a night. Then they saw they could make more money on the other side of the till. They came up to the bar owners and offered to take care of all the music; they'd take all the door fees and book all the bands, and the owners wouldn't have to worry about a thing. All the bar owners had a meeting at a hotel and all lowered their fees from

Jimi Hendrix's gravesite

$250 a night to $250 a weekend.

"These new booking people held open auditions for all the bands that had been playing these places. They picked a few bands and told them, 'Here are the songs you have to play, and you have to get a girl singer with a short skirt.' And that was the end of original music in Seattle."

By the end of 1970, the best-known longhair in town was Dick Balch, a Chevrolet dealer who smashed cars with a sledgehammer in TV ads and proclaimed, "If you can't trust your car dealer, who can you trust? Peace!"

Dick Balch

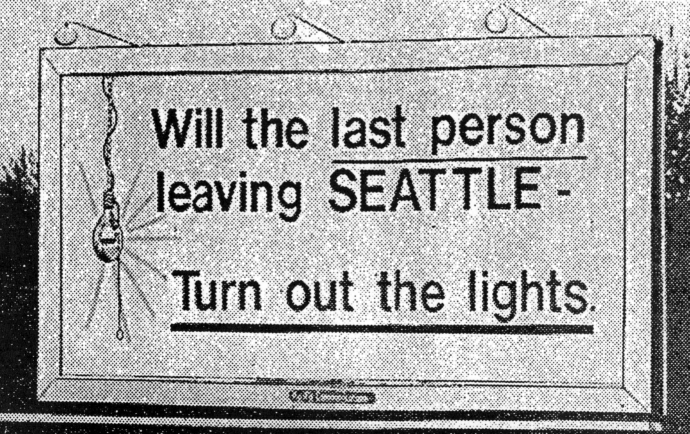

CHAPTER FOUR:
HAPPY FACE (1970-1976)

1973

1974

1975

One of the original foundations of punk rock was a reaction against the passionless, smug materialism of the mid-1970s. As such, Seattle was a perfect place for punk to fester. Perhaps no other city so embraced the gourmet-ized mediocrity that was '70s culture. I don't mean the goofy, outrageously-dressed, fun '70s. I mean the self-centered, lifestyle-obsessed boring '70s. Seattle changed from a town of uptight, quietly dull, self-deprecating squares to a town of uptight, righteously dull, self-aggrandizing boomers. In many ways, the squares had been more open-minded.

To those of us who came of age then, the '70s music scene was the most boring thing imaginable. But beneath the bland content of the post-hippie bands, this crowd developed a network of hangouts, studios, health food co-ops, record stores, arts agencies, media (the *Seattle Sun*, a weekly tabloid of politics and arts reviews where Franklin High/Evergreen State grad Lynda Barry published her first professional cartoons), and other institutions.

Two dots and a curve

The Happy Face button, fetishistically perky and soulless, was the perfect icon of '70s Seattle. The symbol was allegedly designed by Seattle ad man David Stern in 1967 for a local savings and loan. He claimed to have based it on the animated happy face that danced with Dick Van Dyke in the movie *Bye Bye Birdie*. Two groups on the east coast claimed to have used the image before Stern did. The image of two oval eyes and a curved-line smile in a yellow circle, never copyrighted, was picked up by clever entrepreneurs starting in 1970. In the late '80s, it was revived by British rave promoters to symbolize neo-psychedelia.

Cracking down

New "progressive" Mayor Wes Uhlman entered office in 1969 and ordered an immediate end to the city's "tolerance policy," an unwritten premise that basically said cops had better things to do than enforce archaic liquor and vice laws. Until then, local taverns could be intense places. Hardly a week went by that somebody didn't drive a motorcycle into one of the dozen hippies' and painters' hangouts. Underage drinkers, nude barmaids, and after-hours service were not uncommon. The policy also meant cops looked the other way at (or were paid

off by) hookers and drug dealers.

That ended, in the name of Clean Government. The U District's open-air drug bazaar got driven underground. Under Uhlman, and his successors Charles Royer and Norm Rice, the city strictly enforced an official culture of passivity. By 1976, all the raucous hippie taverns got toned down, cleaned up, or closed. In their place came fern bars, singles bars, sports bars, and mellow-music bars. Suffering perhaps the worst fate was the Red Robin tavern—it became the flagship outlet of an upscale burger chain.

The wide-open frontier city was dead. You had to conform to the new complacency (euphemistically labeled "Seattle Style" or "the Northwest Lifestyle") or else. Two decades later, our "liberal" leaders (including many ex-hippies) still mistake blandness for a virtue.

The Green-ing of Washington

In the mid-'60s, the fiscally conservative state legislature approved a new four-year college. Golf-course gladhanding between politicians and local officials sited the college near the state capital of Olympia, far from the state's population-growth pattern. The Evergreen State College, opened in October 1971, was devised as a liberal arts college without rigid testing or formal class structures. This policy appeased legislators who didn't want to duplicate existing colleges. It proved a boon to the state coffers, attracting thousands of students over the years at full out-of-state tuition.

Slowing down

In 1970-71, the whole Youth Movement emerged from its countercultural Shangri-La and instantly turned ancient like Margo in *Lost Horizon*. As the student draft was phased out, college politics became less activist, more ivory-tower ideological. As the Bay Area scene collapsed from its own weight, many of the original hippies fanned out across the west. Many settled in Seattle and northwest Washington inspired by the local scenery, the local mushrooms and the local weed, they retreated from the outside world.

Not everyone gave up on radical politics. There were leftist splinter groups (the Freedom Socialists, the Revolutionary Communist Youth Brigade) and single-issue groups (environmental, anti-nuke, feminist, gay, pro-pot, neighborhood-preservation).

1976

1977

1978

1979

Below:
As he appears today

The Seattle Sun
celebrates at the
new Gasworks Park

The little button
that started it all

Lynda Barry ad
for The Sun

grocery stores in the country.

Thousands of low-income housing units fell, their sites becoming office towers and luxury condos scores of old-man taverns and diners got hopelessly gentrified. As nondescript towers dominated the skyline, Seattle became a city of bureaucrats with little connection to the city's past or to the rural/industrial economy of the rest of the state. To the new office hordes, "The Country" was not the source of life or wealth but one big "romantic getaway," highlighted by tourist streets in Port Townsend and La Conner full of trinket shops and ice cream parlors.

The "young professionals" who filled the towers (the term *yuppie* didn't emerge until 1984) seemed to have incomes exceeded only by their egos there may not have been many of them, but the media and consumer industries bowed to their every whim. Nordstrom, a local shoe chain that expanded into apparel in 1968, thrived by outfitting these office jockeys in "power" clothes.

Some of these people went to work in politics under Uhlman and Royer (an ex-TV reporter and brother-in-law of local advice columnist Jennifer James). The city and county had already pushed through a cheap and homely domed stadium that opened in April 1976, the same week ex-*Seattle* magazine writer David Brewster's *Seattle Weekly* began. Unlike "alternative" papers in other towns, the *Weekly* never cared for left-of-center politics or youth culture. Rather, it ran breathless accounts of insider politics and reviews of upscale entertainments, especially trendy restaurants.

Art as lifestyle

Officials promoted Seattle as an arts mecca, a reputation based more on consumption than production.

Galleries popped up in Pioneer Square to supply costly decor for the office towers and for executives' homes but artists, particularly those who didn't make decorative crafts, struggled to hold onto a diminishing stock of studio space in gentrifying neighborhoods. Uhlmann instigated a "1 Percent for Art" program, allocating a piece of municipal building budgets to art installations. That and other programs built a public-art bureaucracy which encouraged artists to abandon personal expression in favor of grant writing, nepotism and big bland sculpture—though the bigger public art contracts usually went to out-of-town artists. California artist Douglas Hollis built a piece on the shore of Lake Washington in 1983 involving organ pipes strung up so they whistled in the winds blowing in from Lake Washington. Hollis titled it "A Sound Garden."

Film was the perfect artform for the ex-hippie mindset, offering passive consumption with upper-middlebrow good taste. Art Bernstein and Jim O'Steen started the Harvard Exit in an old women's club on Capitol Hill, the first of a new generation of art-house cinemas. Randy Finley, brother of *Bob Newhart Show* co-star Pat Finley, started Seven

But many adult hippies preferred "personal politics," cleansing their consciences through lifestyle choices.

To older Seattleites, a weekend in the country had meant driving to a campsite or a vacation home for downhill skiing, motorboating, fishing and hunting. To a smaller bohemian cult, started in the '30s and centered in the Mountaineers Club (whose meeting hall would later be rented by punk shows), "roughing it" was a spiritual, quasi-socialistic way of life, a means of connecting with a world that industry didn't control. "Pure foods" like yogurt and bulk grains mattered to this clique. The later adult hippies found more apolitical, self-centered joys in backpacking, cross-country skiing, white-water rafting and bicycling. Recreational Equipment Inc., a retail co-op that originally supplied hardcore outdoorspeople, thrived as the sporting goods mecca for the new office set. REI was headed during its growth phase by mountain climber Jim Whittaker, the first American to reach the top of Mt. Everest his son Bob is now Mudhoney's manager. Puget Consumers Co-op, a bulk buying club for the original pure-foods sect, grew into a chain of health-food supermarkets with some of the highest sales per square foot of any

Gables Theatres, which owned 28 screens in nine buildings by the time it was sold to the Samuel Goldwyn Co. Vancouver entrepreneurs Darryl McDonald and Dan Ireland leased the Moore Theatre as a foreign-film house, starting with a two-week promotional event pompously called The First Seattle International Film Festival; it later became a true festival, with over 150 films in three weeks each May.

Seattle supported over a dozen nonprofit live theatres, performing most of the scripts you could see at other "regional" (non-New York) theatres. Most of the popular locally-created plays involved light whimsical farce, influenced in part by a cabaret troupe called Ze Whiz Kidz (more about them in a few pages). The more adventuresome companies included A Contemporary Theatre, the Empty Space, the Evergreen Theatre Conservatory (which became the New City), and the multicultural Group Theatre (based at the UW Ethnic Cultural Theatre, where some punk shows were also held, and named after a New York company where Frances Farmer once acted). Seattle's theatres attracted a community of actors, designers and costumers who came here specifically for low-wage artsy work. They godfathered local scenes in performance art and modern dance. Today, boosters claim if all the "professional arts organizations" in town were counted together, they'd be the city's 10th largest employer (that figure doesn't include rock bands or those who make money off them).

We patronized big new bookstores; but with a few big exceptions, the only popular local books were travelogues or mysteries with by-the-numbers local scenery, or Southern writers who moved here while still writing only about the South. Tom Robbins wrote a novel about "the search for the cosmic goof" in 1971. *Another Roadside Attraction* sold 250,000 paperbacks and led to a series of comic odysseys, starring fictional versions of local hippie celebrities. Frank Herbert, who'd moved to the gentrified timber town of Port Townsend, became a worldwide success with his *Dune* novels, injecting science fiction with environmental and spiritual themes. Raymond Carver, a poet and short story writer from Yakima, published spare, stripped-down stories of people who spoke plainly and kept

their emotions tightly to themselves—a highly accurate portrayal of pre-yuppie Washington.

One of the few art forms where creativity was encouraged was in advertising, particularly in ex-hippie Terry Heckler's remarkable ads for Rainier Beer: woodland herds of six-foot, legged "Wild Rainiers" Mickey Rooney and Buster Crabbe reworking their old film images; "Northwest Beer-graphic" magazine-parody posters. Heckler's ads made Rainier #1 in the region, until new out-of-state owners dumped them for a California agency's notion of "Northwest style": Quick-cut images of cheekboned airheads engaged in outdoor sports.

Jesus people

Hippie stylings (without the sex or drugs) were preserved for a couple of years by the Jesus People (called "Jesus Freaks" by outsiders), an underground of longhaired proselytizers who began in Seattle around 1969. Linda Meissner, their chief local organizer, started a co-op coffeehouse near the Space Needle with its own monthly paper (*The Truth*) and its own Christian rock band (The Wilson-McKinley). The movement split apart when Meissner joined European street evangelist Moses David's Children of God.

Another famous cult around here was the Love Family, led by a bearded guru known as Love Israel with communal households in Seattle and a farm out north; its devotees included the grandson of TV personality Steve Allen. When the Bhagwan Shree Rajneesh had to close down his big Oregon commune, many of his devotees settled here.

Rock goes safe

Baby-boomer writers often blame disco for the dearth of vital music in the period. In fact, disco was a liberating landmark for black and gay cultures, and a revitalizing force for urban nightlife. Seattle's hippest disco at the time was Shelley's Leg, a waterfront gay dive with a hip-straight crossover clientele. The owner opened it with settlement money after she lost a leg in a car crash.

The real musical dead end in the era wasn't disco, it was soft rock (also known as mellow rock, country-rock, blues-rock, folk-rock, or singer-song-

D.B. Cooper happens!

The Red Robin goes mainstream

Spot the difference:

Janis in 1960

Duffy in 1971

Below: Shelley's Leg Disco

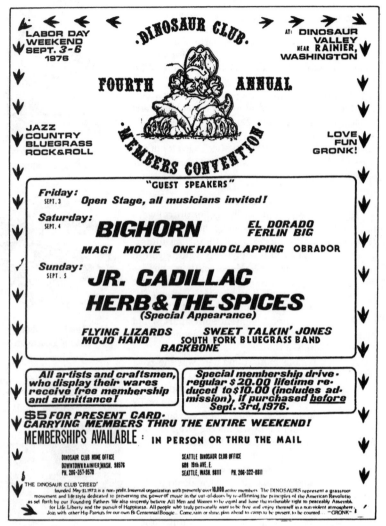

Gronk! if you're a dinosaur

The new Kingdome

writer music).

The Wailers and their friends founded the first local music scene their reincarnation as Jr. Cadillac founded the second. The new group (founded by original Northwest Rock musicians Ned Neltner, Les Clinkingbeard, Andy Parypa, Jim Manolides, and Bob Hosko) took a different variation on the same '50s R&B the Wailers were built on. The old white R&B was lean and crisp; the new white R&B was fat and soft. Old Wailers records still sound great today because their sound is forever young; Jr. Cadillac's sound was old when it began and grew older over the next 24 years. It was the sound of a self-satisfied generation that had finished sowing its wild oats. Ex-Wailer Buck Ormsby joined the band soon after its inception, then left in 1983 to concentrate on studio work. He's reissued the cream of the Etiquette Records catalog on CD, and in 1994 started a local country label, Black Boot.

Several female acts emerged at this time (Linda Waterfall, Kathy Hart, Annie Rose and the Thrillers, Sandy Bradley), soft rock being more amenable to traditional feminine roles. These women ranged from bland folk to bland blues to bland Motown covers to Janis Joplin impersonations. An '80s addition to the hippie-blues circuit, Duffy Bishop, imitated the Joplin sound so perfectly that local promoters crafted a Joplin bio-musical starring her.

The granola-blues bands played at the Rainbow tavern (next to the Blue Moon in the U District), the Buffalo and New Melody in Ballard, and assorted spaces in Pioneer Square: the Central Tavern, the Bombay Bicycle Shop, the Merchant's Cafe, Doc Maynard's, and Hibble & Hyde's. In the '60s, developers had tried to raze the historic district for a big parking lot. Citizen outcries saved the buildings, but not their old uses. Old flophouse hotels and greasy spoons became sports bars and tourist shops. Many of the former black R&B clubs became dedicated to white macho blues, one-dimensional reinterpretations of the Chicago blues sound. Bill Englehart, one of the original Spanish Castle musicians, became a favorite on the white-blues circuit with his new Little Bill and the Bluenotes. Ex-Sonics Andy and Larry Parypa appeared in Charlie Kester's blues band Charlie and the Tunas.

In the new Pioneer Square bars, black musicians were actively discouraged. It was common knowledge that a five-piece band could have no more than two black members and hope to get booked. Tacoma-raised black guitarist Robert Cray could only get playdates in Pioneer Square by heading an otherwise all-white band, which originally included white singer Curtis Salgado. In 1977, Cray and Salgado played a Eugene, Oregon bar to a small crowd that included John Belushi, in town filming *Animal House*. Belushi later acknowledged Salgado as his chief inspiration for the Blues Brothers.

The black musicians who managed to achieve gigs in white bars were either touring blues-nostalgia acts or first-generation African and Caribbean artists, playing the watered-down ethnic sounds later known as "world beat." The only exceptions were at the Rainbow, Buffalo and New Melody taverns, where Cray was booked alongside white Motown cover bands.

The local soft-rock bands were even more predictable than the blues revivalists. The mixed duo Reilly and Maloney recorded LPs of dispassionate love songs and the world's tamest cover of Buddy Holly's "Everyday" on a label run by Reilly's husband, with the decidedly un-rocking name of Freckle Records.

The hard rock scene was even more pathetic still. The Aquarius tavern (the once and future Parker's Ballroom on Aurora), the Rathskeller, the Top of the Hilton, the Medieval Cellar and Pier 70 were all booked by cover-band circuits. To play there, you had to play the hits and you had to play them like the hitmakers. You graduated to the downtown lounges after proving your chops at proms and suburban bars. The more accurate your "Stairway to Heaven," the faster you rose.

Rock radio sucked in most of the country, as executives and consultants imposed tight playlists onto former freeform FM stations. It was worse here than in some towns. The top-rated KISW and KZOK played lowest-common-denominator lists of predictable hard-rock cuts. "Stairway" was Seattle's most-played rock song for more than 10 years. Seattle radio broke AC/DC in the U.S. If it now seems like today's hit Seattle bands (even Sir Mix-A-Lot) cite Black Sabbath and Van Halen as major influences, it's partly because there was little else a local teenager from 1970 to 1980 got to hear—unless you lived in the multiethnic South Seattle and got turned onto James Brown at an early age, like the young Filipino-American Lynda Barry (who wrote about the experience in her novella *The Good Times Are Killing Me*).

KISW was owned by Kaye-Smith Enterprises, which also owned KJR-AM; but while KJR at its peak was extremely locally-oriented, KISW was essentially managed by the national Burkhart-Abrams consulting firm. Kaye-Smith opened a recording studio in Belltown, where former Philly soul producer Thom Bell cut national hits for Elton John, Tower of Power, the Spinners, and other top acts of the time.

Dreamboat Annie and Nancy

The Bellevue-founded band Heart (originally White Heart), rose to the top of the cover circuit playing an all-Led Zeppelin set at the Aquarius. Ann and Nancy Wilson were brought into the band as singers in 1973; Nancy was guitarist Roger Fisher's brother's girlfriend at the time. The sisters had sung together since kids, in church and at weddings and officers' clubs. They progressively took control of the group, added original tunes, then relocated to Vancouver, where some of the guys in the band and its entourage had moved to avoid the draft. They found more of a music industry to plug into up north, thanks to radio stations' mandated Canadian quotas. They became world-famous starting in 1976 with the *Dreamboat Annie* album on the independent Mushroom label. Its slickly produced blend of radio-friendly rockers ("Crazy On You") and ballads ("Dog and Butterfly") led to two decades' worth of hits.

Nancy Wilson: "We promoted the record ourselves, driving to radio stations through the midwest. We said we were a band from Vancouver, B.C., because it sounded more exotic and more interesting than to say we were from Seattle."

The Wilsons now own the former Kaye-Smith recording studio; through their acoustic side project, the Lovemongers, they perform a lot more local gigs these days than any of the grunge superstars. The Wilsons and guitarist Howard Leese are the only remaining members from Heart's early days; ex-members Fisher, Steve Fossen (who both also served in the spandex-pop Strypes) and Michael Derosier regrouped in the late 1980s as Alias, with the minor hits "Haunted Heart" and

"More Than Words Can Say." One of Heart's early tour truck drivers, Kelly Curtis, moved up to become the band's tour manager, then left to co-own a management company (where we'll meet him again in chapter 10).

Ex-Guess Who member Randy Bachman roamed from Canada to Tacoma for a while with his new band, Bachman-Turner Overdrive; after they returned to Canada to start recording, they cut a tribute song to Tacoma called "Blue Collar."

Ze Whiz Kidz

One big exception to the cover-band tedium was Ze Fabulous Whiz Kidz, a mostly gay lip-sync cabaret troupe originally formed by Tomata du Plenty (David Harrigan) and Gorilla Rose (Michael Farris) in 1969, the year the gay liberation movement began in New York. The troupe was ensconced by 1970 at the Exotic Paradise Room in the basement of the historic Smith Tower (now a health club). They were the first guys in Seattle to wear dresses in public (with beards). The casts of their nearly 100 mini-musical shows included the stage names Satin Sheets, Co Co Ritz, Daily Flo, Benny Whiplash, Michael Hautepants (costume designer Michael Murphy), Leah Vigeah, and genuine females Louise Lovely (DiLinge) and Cha Cha Samoa (Cha Davis; now a painter). They opened for Alice Cooper at the Paramount in 1972 with a '50s-theme musical, "Puttin' Out Is Dreamsville;" Samoa appeared with a giant papier-mache phallus as she belted a song called "Rock Around the Cock." They made a special for PBS affiliate KCTS, and shot a few mini-movies with black and white school-model videotape recorders.

Cha Cha Samoa: "There was a saying among Ze Whiz Kidz that someday Seattle was going to happen. It's finally happened, though a lot of Ze Whiz Kidz didn't live to see it."

By the time they opened for the glamrock-pioneer New York Dolls at the Moore Theatre in 1974, the Kidz had changed their act (along with several of their core members). Under the direction of Satin Sheets (Dennis Weikel, who later changed his stage name to J. Satz Beret) they threw out the lounge act and became a rock band with the addition of the Fabulous Pickle Sisters, including Brad Sinsel and Rick Pierce. Sinsel had been in a number of cover bands, and once billed himself as "British rock god Bradford Tolnby" to get gigs.

Brad Sinsel to the Rocket on Ze Whiz Kidz, 1986: "They were gay; this was the first touch of glam in the Northwest before they called it punk. We looked like Motley Crue does now. But at the time, it wasn't accessible.... We tried playing clubs, but were met with the 'what the hell's that' attitude so common in Washington. Still, we never really had any competition, because back then, no one wanted to do that kinda thing.... At least we had the balls to dress real funny and take whatever people had to say with it."

Mountain Fresh to You Each Evening

Some Whiz Kidz:
Satin Sheets (Satz), Rio
de Janiero, Coco Ritz

A Whiz Kid

The first import record store

Rob Morgan on Ze Whiz Kidz in his Pop Lust/Super Boss Rock zine, 1982: "At the time people may have thought they were weird, but they were an idea whose time had come. This strange collection of writers, would-be actors and basic stage hams put on shows the likes of which Seattle (or anywhere else) would never see again. These pre-Tube-escents, if you will, collaborated on these shows in their humble homes, which also all had names—Heartbreak Hotel, Bella Donna House, Lavender Shadows, Harlow House, Casablanca—each house decorated to outdo the next with stuff from St. Vincent de Paul (a now-defunct thrift store) and props from Costume & Display Supply.... .Amongst the bigger hits, "Lay Me Down & Knock Me Up," "Fist Full of Douche Bags," "Swastika Sweethearts," "Every Bracelet Has A Price Tag," "Boardwalk of Broken Dreams," "I Love Your Face, I Want to Stab It"—all predecessors of their videos, The Great Pussy Snatch, Sex Me, and Tinsel Town Review (KCTS's finest hour)."

The Dolls' other opening act at the Moore was the Lamar Harrington Band (Homer Spence, Danny Eskenazi, Phil Miller, and a host of others). Eskenazi recalls having invited "everyone we knew and everyone that everyone we knew knew to bring an instrument and join us. There were almost as many people on stage as there were in the audience." The Harrington Band and its side project, Ace Oom and the Eons, had appeared in May 1973 on opposite sides of a self-released single, with the neo-surf "Oom Cocka Mau-Mau" on the A side (playing at 45 rpm) and the pseudo-lounge-jazz "Paralyzed" (playing at 33, clocking in at 7:01). This kind of DIY production and marketing would prove important in the scene to follow. That year Spence and Eskenazi entered their living room, designed with Eskenazi's exquisite taste in camp furnishings, into the Northwest Annual art competition and *won*.

The later glam version of Ze Whiz Kidz was briefly joined by Charles Gerra. In a 1988 bio he claimed to have been an underage street survivor whose family had committed him to a mental institution to "cure" his homosexuality. He wrote that he escaped from that, joined a foster home, escaped from *that*, and wound up selling himself at Second and Pike, then as now one of downtown's rowdiest corners. He got into performing partly as a non-street way to attract johns. But he found himself shaping his persona in Ze Whiz Kidz toward glitter and glamour, away from drag. Gerra took the stage name Charles Garrish, later changed to Upchuck.

Years ahead of their time in their style, spelling and attitude (and their use of street posters and on-stage video projection), the last Whiz Kidz dispersed in 1975 to punk bands The Lewd and Tupperwares, the pop-metal band TKO, costume design, and L.A. video/film production. Michael Murphy costumed Led Zeppelin for a couple of tours. Tomata Du Plenty and Gorilla Rose, who both left the group before its final breakup, spent some time in New York in 1974-75; they hung out in the Andy Warhol entourage, and designed concepts and costumes for Bette Midler, the Manhattan Transfer, and some of the early CBGB bands. Louise Lovely and fellow Whiz Kid Michael Campbell joined with theatrical director Norm Langill to form the One Reel Vaudeville Show, which put on farcical plays at street fairs One Reel turned into a production company that ran the giant Bumbershoot Arts Festival in Seattle Center every Labor Day weekend.

Teens strike back

Despite all this, youth culture was at a low point. The media no longer cared about teens (or even college kids). Rock radio stations went to oldies, soft rock, or bombastic metal by industry-generated superstars. The tail end of the baby boom was subjected to ugly jeans with wider cuffs than waists (some designed locally by Britannia, Generra and Unionbay, firms that supplied local stores with styles that the rest of the country had abandoned). To many members of a generation weaned on the Beatles and bubblegum, both Ozzy Osbourne and Linda Ronstadt left a lot to be desired.

Some people refused this status quo. They sought inspiration from London (where the music business still cared about youth appeal and street credibility), New York (where the disco scene revitalized nightlife, indirectly sparking a renewal of live rock clubs), and Detroit (where the MC5 and Iggy Pop's Stooges had kept the brash garage sound alive). Taking their lead from the New York Dolls, the Pretty Things, Gary Glitter, T. Rex, and especially David Bowie (and later by the CBGB bands), kids in towns across North America built their own scenes. In Seattle, a nascent scene of a few dozen teens hung out in the U District, at Kim Harris's Campus Music (the first store in town with import records), the Dreamland clothing store and the 456 Cafe and downtown, at the Time Travelers record/comics store and Scotty's Juice Bar. These kids formed bands in basements and garages.

Their first major public show took place on May 1, 1976—May Day of the Bicentennial year.

Opposite:
First punk show
poster (by Tomata)

CHAPTER FIVE:
THE TELEPATHIC FOUNDATION (1976-1977)

On May 1, 1976 in the big musty second-floor ballroom of the Odd Fellows Temple on Capitol Hill came the TMT Show, a self-promoted show with the Telepaths, Meyce and Tupperwares. The Seattle Scene was born, two months before England's first punk show.

Mind you, the scene had a low birth weight.

Neil Hubbard in Rescue, 5/81: *"Admission to the TMT Show was one dollar (yes, $1), about a hundred people showed up, the groups paid for the room and made their nut. This show (please correct me if I'm wrong) was the first self-promoted show in town. The bands rented the hall, got a P.A. and DID IT. It was as much fun or more than many of the shows now."*

Larry Rosen in Pandemonium, 6/93: *"To begin with, all music scenes share a few common elements. Scenes need young, disenfranchised, poverty-bound people. Most scenes happen in college towns. All scenes happen in places full of kids with lots of time, not much money, and too much hair. Since most young people want to be writers or rock stars, eventually some of them form bands, admiration societies, and there they are: the seeds of a scene. Spare time, youthful angst, over-simplified world views, and guitars."*

The Telepaths

The Telepaths (originally Godzilla and the Flaming Telepaths, after a Blue Oyster Cult song) originally were singer Dan Rabinowitz, guitarists Erich Werner and Reid Vance, bassist Geoff Cade, and drummer Dean Helgeson. By the TMT show they included Erich's brother Curt on vocals, Bill Rieflin on drums, and in Vance's guitar spot the 35-year-old ex-professor Homer Spence.

At the time, 35 seemed ancient for someone who still cared about original music (Reiflin and the Barkers are approaching that age now and it doesn't seem weird that they're still going strong). Spence had known the early Seattle rock scene, came of age in the hippie scene, but (unlike many people his age) hadn't become a mellow burnout. He possessed a sharp wit, an unlimited imagination, and a caring heart. He never treated his younger bandmates as kids; they were full partners in everything. During and after his Telepaths stint, Spence produced several bands' 45s and became a

spiritual mentor to the scene.

Bill Rieflin: *"Dan Rabinowitz asked me to join this band he was getting together. I told him I hadn't played drums in three years, but that I'd go over and try out with his band. There was talk about this old guy who was going to be in the band, but he was in the Bahamas or Jamaica. I said OK.... My first experience of Homer was when Dan decided to replace me with another drummer, which made Homer really angry. He thought it was an incredibly audacious move, and had me stay. Shortly after that, Dan left the group."*

After Rabinowitz left (he briefly led another band, Daniel and the Lions, before pursuing a Ph.D. in philosophy at the UW), the leading stage presence in the Telepaths was Curt Werner (also known as Eliot Crimson and Druid S. Patrick). A self-taught student of decadent poets and obscure philosophers, Curt also claimed to be a real telepath, someone who can read people's minds. At one gig he decapitated a mannequin head on stage. Gregor Gayden took turns with Curt fronting the group before its 1978 demise, with Roosevelt High grad Mike Davidson replacing Cade on bass.

Curt Werner: *"I was schizo. Dan got me into Nietzsche and got me out of my paranoia by bringing me into the band. It was an island of sanity, not for anybody else, just for us. When the band got other people, it got stupid.... Gregor and I had robbed a beer truck. We were carrying off a few cases of beer up 42nd Street. There was this guy from Borneo at Dreamland who was holding a copy of (the Stooges LP) Funhouse. We knew we had to know this guy. He had hair out to here. Homer got in the band, then Gregor was in the band. Then Reid quit, and Dan just became our guru; he stopped playing.... Erich said three things that made me quit. He said I was too operatic, that Pam Lillig (Girls guitarist) told me to get me out of the band, and that I was too old to be in a rock n' roll band. I was 20."*

With a grab-bag of influences ranging from Iggy to Roxy Music to Jean Cocteau, the Telepaths created an ever-changing set that rocked without losing its smarts.

Bill Rieflin: *"We were turned on by the New York*

Erich Werner

Stub from cancelled T.T. Oh! Show

Bill Rieflin

right:
**Early Telepaths
(Homer Spence on left)**

Penelope Houston

**Tomata du Plenty
and Joey Ramone
record shopping**

Dolls and the Stooges. We were playing Stooges songs, writing our own tunes, real intensity and power. They were outrageous, multi-chord songs; every 30 seconds or so a new thing would happen. It was like Bartok on acid. Whenever Erich did a guitar solo he hit an E chord as hard and long as he could, no matter what key the song was in; to him that was the heaviest thing possible. The Telepaths defied logic, defied description."

The Telepaths played back yards and basements in the summer and fall of 1975. They achieved a public gig on New Year's Day 1976 at the local midnight premiere of John Waters's *Pink Flamingos*, held at the Moore Theatre. At that gig, the Telepaths also served as the backup band to an all-drag vocal trio, the Tupperwares.

Weeks before the TMT Show, the Telepaths played an after-school talent show at Nova Alternative High School (a small program with nontraditional learning structures), where some members attended; authorities pulled the plug on the glitter-inspired set. When the band agreed to do just one more song, power was restored; Curt screamed a high-defiance rendition of Iggy Pop's "L.A. Blues," while the boys in the band belted out what Hubbard later called "a thick, jarring, toneless blast" and destroyed their instruments plus parts of the school-owned PA. Random fights broke out in the halls.

Erich Werner: *"The Moore show was our first chance to get out there and really make some impact. There were no resources in that town for playing; that just made us more pissed off. There were no clubs, just bars with boogie rock and cover bands.... Our whole attitude as a gang was a perpetual state of anger about our environment. We opposed just about everything we felt Seattle stood for. We hated suburbia; we were completely opposed to complacent happiness, and we felt the world at large wouldn't tolerate us. People constantly called us names because of how we looked, so we had a strong identity, a them-and-us polarity."*

Under the Telepathic Foundation label, the Telepaths released a 7-inch record in 1978 that expressed the range of influences the band had absorbed in two years. The bass-laden A-side,

"Frozen Darling," was a driving, hypnotic ballad heavily flavored by the poetic side of the early CBGB scene. The 5:30 B-side, "Must I Perform," started out with slow, loud guitar fuzz and feedback. It picked up the pace into a vocal bridge energetic angst. It slowed down again, collapsing upon itself at the close into a sludgy, chaotic wail of noise. They were one of the first punk bands anywhere to be loud, messy and slow all at once (California's Cramps and Flipper would experiment in similar ideas). The concept didn't catch on at first; to local bands like Chinas Comidas and the Enemy, "Loud Fast Rules" still applied.

A floor of an old sailors' hotel in the working-class Ballard neighborhood was christened the Telepathic Apartments. Iggy Pop and members of Blondie played an impromptu set to a packed party there after a Paramount show, on a "stage" made of plywood boards atop an old mattress in Greg Ragan's bedroom. David Bowie, in Iggy's band on that tour, reportedly rode up and down the cobblestoned Ballard Avenue in a limo looking for the place but never showed up.

In 1978, several Telepaths (including Spence) moved into a house near Northgate. Curt Werner gave it the name Chez Macabre. It was among the first of a network of band-party houses where musicians and their pals hung out, practiced, and held wild private performance parties.

Some of the band houses and party houses became infamous dens of debauchery: the House of Ken, the Madhouse, the Gas Chamber, Cleave Land, the House of Five, the Academy (still in operation), Shelby House, the Lagoon, the White House, Dogma House, Holy War Cadets House, Death House, and the Eastlake House. The latter is still occupied by early scene members James Babyteeth (Carbo) and Pony Maurice, who have made it a silver-painted shrine to their pre-punk idols: the New York Dolls, Bowie, Twiggy, Patti Smith.

The Tupperwares and Screamers

The Tupperwares (soon renamed the Screamers to avoid trademark trouble) were fronted by ex-Whiz Kid Tomata du Plenty, with Melba Toast (Tommy Gear) and Rio de Janeiro (David Gulbransen, whose family owned Belltown's legendary Dog House diner-piano bar). By the TMT show they'd added a backing band, including Pam Lillig

the Tupperwares

Tomata

RIO

MELBA

(later in the Girls), Eldon Hoke (later in the Mentors) and Dan Rabinowitz's brother Ben (later in the L.A. band Lone Justice). Their set included a dirgelike ode to Eva Braun, a peppy ditty called "Instamatic Fanatic," and a faux-bubblegum love song called "Goin' Steady With Twiggy;" co-written by Rieflin and Erich Werner.

Du Plenty organized an underground film screening later that year, with footage of New York rock poet Patti Smith. The sight of Smith on screen that night, combined with the later sight of the Sex Pistols on the NBC News show *Weekend*, convinced the Tupperwares' 18-year-old "bodyguard" Penelope Houston to split for San Francisco and form the cult-hit Avengers.

The Screamers split for L.A. in early 1977, after they'd become a self-contained band and traded in the glitter look for bare chests in open leather jackets. They found themselves making more videos and fanzine interviews than actual live shows, and never officially released a record. By the band's end two years and a few personnel changes later, their intelligence and offstage gentility had become out of place as L.A. punk grew louder, faster and dumber. Du Plenty starred as the last survivor of a post-nuclear Earth in Dutch director Rene Raalder's 1986 film *Population One*, and later ran art galleries in L.A. and Miami Beach. Gear became a musical-instrument salesperson. Gulbransen (the first to leave the group) became the Dog House's manager, closing the beloved greasy spoon in January 1994 amidst competition from newer, trendier eateries. Later that year he opened a successor restaurant, the Puppy Club, on the ground floor of the Belltown building that housed Pearl Jam's management offices.

From the Screamers song "Better World": "Why are we consumers? There's our product that you're buying/Your love affair with the government is over/But you're still getting butt-fucked!"

Jello Biafra on the Screamers in the book Incredibly Strange Music Volume II*: "They were my favorite of all the early West Coast punk bands. No guitar—just an Arp Odyssey synthesizer on milk crates, fuzzed electric piano, drums, and a trained mime for a singer who could startle a whole audience just by lifting an eyebrow. Their* live shows were dynamite—not just the powerful visuals, but their music took more twists and turns than anyone I knew then. It's the ultimate musical tragedy that they held out for the big record deal that never came, and wound up not being properly recorded at all. Only a bootleg single and the Target video survive. No one has sounded anything like them since. If they'd cracked Europe, 15 years of synth-pop and techno-dance dreck might never have happened!"*

The Meyce and Moberlys

The Meyce included singer-guitarist Jim Basnight, bassist Paul Hood, singer Jennie Skirvin and drummer Lee Lumsden (editor of two of the first local proto-punk zines, the mimeographed *District Diary* in 1974 and the offset-printed *Chatterbox* in 1975-77). Lumsden's *Chatterbox* partner, Neil Hubbard, later described the Meyce as "a young, fresh pop band...soft vocals, melodic bass lines, quirky drumming and an intelligent sensibility." In one of the *Seattle Times*'s first punk reviews in January 1977, critic Patrick MacDonald wrote that "they could be the forerunners of an important new trend in local rock music."

Basnight (whose father was an old Theodore Roethke cohort and KRAB DJ) and Hood had debuted at a 1975 Roosevelt High student talent show. Their band, the Lover Boys (named for a Shangri-Las song the New York Dolls had covered; no relation to the later Vancouver band Loverboy), got the plug pulled on them after three songs during the talent show, at which Basnight wore a silver "X" painted on his bare chest. The show's audience included Roosevelt student Frank Ferana, who soon went to L.A. and became Motley Crüe bassist Nikki Sixx. Basnight got beat up after the show by some of the school jocks.

The Meyce opened in March 1977 for the Ramones (whose first LP had come out the previous summer), in the only punk show ever held in the stately Olympic Hotel. If the TMT Show was the scene's birth, the Ramones show was its first walking step. About 500 people paid $5 to Blitzkrieg Bop with the four faux-bros from Queens, who played a 20-minute set of the only songs they knew at the time, took a short break, then played the same set all over again. The group only charged

The Meyce

Ian Fisher

Geoff Cade

$500, providing a tidy profit to promoter Robert Bennett, editor of the early local punkzine *Twisted*. Bennett went on to a string of ventures including catering and limousine rentals. He was about to re-enter the concert business in 1992 when a federal grand jury indicted him for running a prostitution ring under the front of an escort service, laundering the profits through his other companies. Those charges were dropped, but he was jailed under a related charge of income-tax evasion.

The night before the Olympic show, the Ramones played the Rocker Tavern in Aberdeen, a tough logging town on the Washington coast 100 miles southwest of Seattle. By all accounts it was a horrid experience for the band members, who were repeatedly confronted by shit-faced metal-heads. From the moment their PA came on, before they'd played a note, the locals were yelling at them to turn themselves down. The local guys were used to cover bands and to long breaks between songs for asking women to dance; they were uncomfortably stuck on the dance floor through the band's entire nonstop set. Before the second set, the band was given an ultimatum to turn down the volume for the second set or leave now, unpaid; they reluctantly agreed to crank down the amps just this once. The only Aberdeen residents who'd heard of the band were a couple of high school kids who couldn't get in, so they just hung around outside during the show. One of them was a heavy-set 16-year-old named Kurdt Vanderhoof, who'd seen a brief item about the Ramones in *Rock Scene* magazine and promptly bought the local record store's only copy of their first album. He soon started driving up to Seattle every weekend to see punk shows and got into a band called the Lewd, using the stage name Blobbo.

Meyce singer Jim Basnight moved to New York soon after the Seattle Ramones show, learning the tricks of music promotion but burning out on the cost of living. He came back three months later and recorded a solo 45, pairing the breezy ditty "Live In The Sun" with the more downbeat "She Got Fucked." He then founded the Moberlys (named after a sign Basnight saw in front of a north end house; not, as rumored, after Seattle School Superintendent David Moberly). That band took teen love songs *very* seriously, in the manner of Jonathan Richman's early work. Early members included Steve Pearson and Jeff Cerar, who took the danceable-pop concept further in their respective next bands, the Heats and the Cowboys.

The Moberlys broke up in early 1980, just after they recorded a self-titled album, produced in part by Jr. Cadillac's Ned Neltner. The first full-length LP by a band on the Seattle underground circuit, it made *Trouser Press*'s "Underground Top 10" list for 1980.

Basnight sang in a '60s-cover band called the Pins (after he left, it evolved into the still-gigging Rangehoods), then left for New York, formed a new Moberlys there that failed to break into the business, came home in the mid-'80s and started

another Moberlys, moved with that band to L.A., recorded tracks with R.E.M.'s Peter Buck and almost got signed by EMI before a label "restructuring" passed him by. After that fiasco Basnight came home and formed a pair of new bands, Sway and the Rockinghams. (Buck also moved to Seattle recently.)

Lumsden next played in Alan Michaels and Dave Fisher's Radios (who played what Lumsden called "silly pop songs" on guitar, drums and Farfisa organ). He played a few gigs with Up-chuck's Fags, then went to the east coast to study the philosophies of G.I. Gurdjieff (following in the footsteps of his musical idol, Robert Fripp). After he came back he led his own mid-'80s band, the Celestial Pygmies.

Rental hall shows

The infant scene grew as young Anglophiles and Manhattanphiles took inspiration from the punk explosion. Record stores in the U District (Campus Music, Cellophane Square) and downtown (Time Travelers) started carrying punk zines, UK music papers, and import releases (some by US bands who couldn't get a domestic deal).

Over the next two years, a score of punk and new wave bands formed in party houses, but had no regular place to play, just rental-hall shows at places like the Norway Center, the Freedom Socialist Party's Freeway Hall, and the performance-art space Washington Hall. They also got the occasional opening gig at the Paramount for appropriate national acts like Iggy Pop, Blondie, David Bowie and Talking Heads.

Shelli Story: *"The '70s scene was about 50 people at its core. There were no clubs, but there were shows all the time. We always had theme invitational parties, with Xerox flyers. You'd go there and everyone in Seattle who counted was at that party. There was one party in 1977 called Rock Au Go Go. It was in the basement of an apartment house in the U District. We put on wigs and glam clothes, there was '60s go-go dancing."*

One of the first Freeway Hall shows, in February 1977, starred ex-Telepath Geoff Cade's next band, the Feelies, who soon learned of another Feelies (both were named after the virtual-sex movie in the novel *Brave New World*) and became the Feelings. That group (with Rob Vasquez, later of the Look, a neo-garage-rock band) was one of the first here to get into the snarly, surly attitude rock being spread in England by the Sex Pistols and the Damned. Its songs included "Turds of Love." Guitarist-singer Greg Ragan used to hang from curtains and rafters and scream his lyrics while writhing about. At one Odd Fellows show, Ragan went into convulsions during the set and crawled to a restroom to vomit while drummer Dean Helgeson tore up his rented kit. Ragan was replaced in September 1977 with Ian Fisher, later of the power-pop Cowboys. Helgeson also joined the Cowboys' first line-up, but had to leave after he

was diagnosed with leukemia, which took his life in 1986.

Ex-Whiz Kid J. Satz Beret formed the Sixteen Year Old Virgins (soon revamped as the Knobs) with Drake Eubank (who later played in several suburban metal bands), Mark Cain, Sheldon Gomberg, Mark Bowen (later in San Francisco's Pop-O-Pies) and Jeff Gossard (later in Upchuck's band Clone; Jeff's younger cousin Stone would join the music scene several years later). The Knobs were best known for the song "Chain Saw Sex" (Satz ended their first show by taking a chain saw to a monitor amp). After that Satz formed his best-known band, the Lewd, with Eubank, drummers John Nay and Dave Drewery, and bassists Buttboy and Mike Davidson, and guitarist Brad Rammels (replaced by Blobbo). Eubank, Rieflin, Gomberg and Mark Cain also briefly formed the S'Nots, who released perhaps the first local punk 45, *No Picture Necessary*, several months before the Telepaths single.

Jack Endino: *"Drake Eubank booked some time at Reciprocal Recording one day in 1986 or '87. He came in to overdub hours of indistinguishable guitar noise tapes. John Goodmanson at the Music Source later told me Eubank went in there to erase a bunch of the tapes, at $80 an hour."*

Another ex-Whiz Kid, chanteuse Cha Cha Samoa (one of the few local women into the sequined showbiz glamour now associated mostly with drag queens), formed the dress-up band Sex Therapy with hippie bluesmen Robert DyLong and Pontiac Jones. She went to England from 1981 to 1984, then came back and joined the Treeclimbers, led by guitarist and booking agent Jonathan Poneman, a native of Toledo, Ohio who'd hitchhiked here in 1980 from a West Virginia military school carrying only a briefcase of coveralls and a bible. Poneman's first local band was the 1980-81-era Rockefellers; contemporaries recall the band with terms like "generic new wave."

Helena and Johnny

It's important to note that women were in-volved in punk rock up front and from the start; unlike other art movements where women were ghettoized into an auxiliary or a subsequent second wave. Punk was originally about self-empowerment and self-expression, not macho licentiousness. It was boys and girls creating their own world, not boys blazing a trail and girls following along.

Female musicians in the early scene included Helena Rogers, daughter of a Dutch WWII refugee and co-leader of the band Student Nurse (with her drumming-songwritng husband, record store owner Johnny "Rubato" Rogers); Cynthia Genser of Chinas Comidas; Suzanne Grant, singer for the Enemy; Pam Lillig, guitarist and back-up singer for the Girls; and Shelli Story, guitarist for Mondo Bando, whose singer Electra claimed to be a hermaphrodite. Electra, whom Story called "a long haired, skinny, freaky guy who was also a chick," also served as the Lewd's sound operator, and later ran sound boards in several San Francisco clubs.

The Beakers (see next chapter) may have been the first area band with a non-singing female musician, art student/bassist Frankie Sundsten. There would eventually be all-female bands, including Sundsten's Children of Kellogg. The 1979-82 band Rally Go initially had all-female instrumentalists (Danielle Elliot, Kim Jennings, Heidi Sutter and Tamara Jones, the latter two later in the Pre-Fabs and Mad Dash) backing male singer Bill Borden (replaced by Jim Basnight's sister Beatrice).

Jim Anderson, *Beakers/Little Bears from Bangkok/Gardenias: "I always went out of my way to find women to play in all the bands I played in. I've always hated what happens when four men get together making stupid fuckin' music."*

Student Nurse began as a two-concept band: improvisational avant/jazz/pop (with freeform dancer Sharon Gannon) in the first set, hard-drivin' tunes in the second. John and Helena had a succession of bassists and rhythm guitarists, and evolved into a not-quite-straightforward art-rock outfit with Eric Muhs and Tom Boettcher. Johnny's drumming would unexpectedly slow down mid-song, forcing the audience to stop dancing and listen to Helena's words. Muhs sometimes appeared covered in red tape and leaped about on stage; he also invented his own instruments, including the Particle Board (a slab of wood with one piano string). The group put out a couple of singles and a 12-inch EP (*As Seen on Television*), with the Rogerses playing out the postmodern bold woman/ meek man relationship. By their final gigs in 1984-85 they'd "graduated" to just the Nurse. Johnny also dabbled in other outfits, including the dance-funk No News.

The Enemy was born when the Fruitland Famine Band, a hippie soft-rock outfit formed in 1975 in Olympia, was booked into an Odd Fellows Hall show by its manager, insurance adjustor Roger Husbands. Singer Suzanne Grant, guitarist Damon Titus, bassist George Gleason and drummer Peter

S'nots

The Lewd

P.K. Dwyer

Barnes christened their new-wave rebirth by changing their clothes onstage while bathed in strobe lights. (Paul Hood joined the band on bass later, with Gleason moving to rhythm guitar.)

Suzanne Grant: *"The Fruitland Famine Band was formed by George and Damon. They played four different sets every night. One was a punk set, one was a "crazy" set, one was country-rock, one was lounge music. They brought me in at first as a back-up singer; I was in a swing jazz band in Olympia with an even longer name. We toured with Far West Entertainment (a cover-band circuit) up to Canada. It had beginnings as a much more organic band. We played the hippie dances on farms and in Mt. Vernon and Bellingham. But even before we turned punk we had songs with political messages like 'Eat the Rich.' "*

Chinas and Gary

Chinas Comidas was started in 1977 by Genser, a New York-bred poet who often chided Seattleites for being insufficiently New Yorkish. She took her band name (also her stage name) from Manhattan's Spanish-language signs for Chinese food. While in New York she'd published a book of Patti Smith-inspired poetry, *Taking On the Local Color.* While in Seattle she made two 45s, "Peasant Slave"/"Lover Lover" and "Snaps"/ "For the Rich" ("They're the rich/and they eat the world!"). Her core backing musicians were Rich Riggins, Mark and Brock Wheaton, and Dog Midtskog (whose brother Tor shows up in chapter 7).

Chinas Comidas was one of the first bands to get caught up in offstage brawls, a sign that stupidity was already infiltrating the scene. In some of these brawls, band members sometimes got their instruments trashed by members of rival bands. Genser once had a plate of shrimp thrown at her by an audience member when she stopped the music to read her poems.

Cynthia Genser *on punk violence to the San Francisco zine* Search and Destroy, *1978: "There are some impromptu responses brought about by the show or by me—'cause I look somebody in the eye—'cause sometimes I'm up there and I wanna wipe the smile off everybody's face and sure enough I'm gonna catch somebody's eye and they're gonna be pissed off and feel attacked and throw stuff...but there's staged violence, mostly by people who are reading too much* Rolling Stone, *and that's what I can't stand.... All these bands in Seattle are piss poor. They can't afford to have their equipment trashed.... They should go trash equipment of some band they really can't stand that's making it big!"*

The group decided it had to go to L.A. to make it; it got swallowed into the starving-entertainer culture there, and broke up. Genser now teaches literature back in New York, where she's published two more poetry books. Mark Wheaton stayed in L.A. to compose and arrange for fellow ex-Seattlite

Johanna Went (see below); he now works at the *LA Weekly.* Riggins came back and now runs a practice studio. Brock Wheaton now works at a motorcycle dealership.

Rich Riggins: *"There was no local music business then. You had to put on your own shows, convince a bar to have you or rent a hall yourself, get enough other bands onto the bill to make it worthwhile for the bar owner to have you, then try to convince your friends to show up. Even when there were 'professional' promoters, they'd turn out to be scam artists who'd find any way to cheat you out of your money. To make a record you had to pay for it all yourself, handle your own distribution, then follow-up by going to all the local stores. The few studios in town didn't know what to do with you. You'd say you wanted it to sound like the Sex Pistols and they'd insist it had to sound like the Eagles."*

Before Genser formed her own band, she performed her first gigs under the Chinas name with four guys who also played with 1968 Roosevelt High graduate Gary Minkler, under the name Red Dress. These musicians did several rental-hall shows with each singer fronting a different set (starting in January 1977 with the "Alive in Underground Seattle" show at the UW HUB Ballroom).

Minkler was the first performer to straddle the emerging rock underground and the established hippie-rock circuit centered at the Rainbow Tavern. The band was founded by Minkler, guitarist John Olufs and bassist Riggins, who left with Genser. Olufs, guitarist Pete Pendras, bassist Jerry Anderson, keyboardist Bill Bagley and drummer Billy Shaw were among Red Dress's core members over the subsequent 14 years. The rental-hall showcases gave Minkler the chance to break away from white-R&B cliches, exploring the possibilities of rhythm guitars and screeching-crooning vocals. Minkler, short, bald and scrawny, pranced and lurched about like a bird of prey, whether belting out the Captain Beefheart-esque ballad "Bob Was a Robot" or an ode to love among the extinct, "Teenage Pterodactyls." The original Red Dress hung in until 1985. Minkler formed new lineups in late 1986 and again in 1988-90; the later versions were less experimental, more dance-predictable.

From **Red Dress's** *"I'm Not An Astronaut, I'm A Nut": "I'm gonna blow a hole/In a famous face/I'm gonna put my face/In that famous place/Then even an astronaut/Up in outer space/He will see me/And sitting in their little rooms/Others will know who I am/On their TVs."*

The Jitters, who also premiered at the Alive in Underground Seattle show, also straddled the soft-rock circuit and the new underground. P.K. Dwyer ran the novelty-rock outfit with co-singer Donna Beck (her real name, not taken from the *All My Children* floosie), performing odes to soup kitchens and other good-life amenities. Dwyer split for L.A. in 1980, then came back with the Holly-

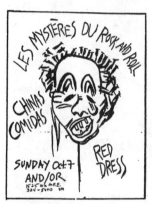

wood Dick Doll Revue, and recently made two solo records (one under the name George Michael Jackson).

More oldster-dominated was Roland Rock, a dance-oldies band that claimed to qualify as new wave because it redid bubblegum pop tunes that had been forgotten in the hard-rock '70s (later switching to a gothic-metal concept). It was run by Ron Woods (formerly of Jimmy Hanna and the Dynamics), Tim Bonow (who'd played with his brother Dan in several hippie R&B outfits) and Marty Frasu (who later started the pop-nostalgia Frazz).

Early emigrants, Monster Wax, party people

Johanna Went, daughter of a struggling working-class family in south Seattle (her mother died of TB, she and her siblings worked with her father's demolition business), was recruited at a party one night to join Tom Murrin's Balloon Theatre. As she told the 1981 zine *Desperate Times*, "He said, 'Well, it's just going around with balloons acting silly.' It sounded real interesting so I signed up." Went and Murrin debuted in a Mother's Day show at painter Billy King's studio. ("I'd never done anything free-form before, so it was really amazing.") They continued to create free-form performances here and on self-funded tours in Europe, where she got caught up in the 1977 London punk revolt. She brought her invigorated sense of the possible to Seattle, where she staged sidewalk performances outside the Bon Marché department store involving creamed corn squirted out of rubber fish. In 1979 she moved to L.A., where she embarked on a series of performance pieces involving found props, dildos, animal parts and surgical tools; some of her pieces featured music by Mark and Brock Wheaton, previously of Chinas Comidas.

Johanna Went to Desperate Times, *1981:* "I observed the beginning of the punk thing in London. I thought it was great, but I wondered if it would ever move across the ocean to America. In London it was evolving from economic need, and middle class America was just too damn comfortable.... It came to America as a fashion. In Britain, it came out of the soul, and here it was calculated, thought-out."

The Chinas Comidas 45s were produced under the band's Exquisite Corpse imprint and released by Wes Geesman's Monster Wax Records. Geesman, who owned three used-record stores in the U District, once ran an in-store contest for local tapes. Winners would get $100 and a single on his label. One of the three winners was submitted by Mark Wheaton under the name Pink Chunk. Geesman had the 45 pressed on clear vinyl with pink streaks. Predating industrial music, the "Kitchen Cantata" featured Wheaton and members of the hippie band Uncle Cookie using kitchen utensils as percussion instruments; painter-textile artist Carl Smool, a housemate of the Cookie members, was one of the egg-beater beaters. That was the B side. For the A side, Wheaton submitted a dirge-paced "Louie Louie" with plenty of overdubs and guitar distortions. The track had been laid down in 1973 by Uncle Cookie's bass player on a simple sound-on-sound tape recorder, starting with a practice session he taped while learning to sing and play at the same time. It was the first recording "produced" by that aspiring bassist, Conrad Uno.

The Monster Wax records were made in small quantities and took forever to sell out. Seattle punk lived in party houses and record stores, with occasional forays in public settings. The initial wave of New York and London bands formed (and, in cases like the Sex Pistols and Television, broke up), while punks here still struggled to mount self-promoted gigs, waiting impatiently to be unleashed onto the world.

In the spring of 1978, Roger Husbands became that unleasher.

CHAPTER SIX:
I NEED AN ENEMY (1978-1979)

Roger Husbands rented the old John L. Bird office-supply store on Spring Street, across the alley from the local Federal Reserve Bank office, as the Enemy's rehearsal space and the northwest's first punk club.

The Bird opened on March 4, 1978. Admission was $3. It was a dark, narrow, warehouse-like space with a makeshift stage and a second-hand PA. As many as 200 crowded into the room, whose official capacity was 99. Graphic designer Art Chantry later speculated that "the entire audience on opening night eventually formed their own bands."

Stella Kramer: "The first Bird show was treated by Roger as a big media event. He got a performance-art group he knew (Friends of the Rag) to show up. He set up a little photo area outside. The only people who used it were the snobby, not-in-the-scene publicity hounds who never showed up again.... All you did was wait for the weekend to go there. There was maybe one party house in the U District at the time, so the Bird was the place to go.

"...As soon as it was obvious what was happening at the Bird, there was no way it was going to survive. It had no sign on the door, the windows were curtained off. Roger had these big bags of pre-popped popcorn so people would have something to throw at bands they hated. It was a very controlled situation. There was no differentiation between the bands and the audience."

Shelli Story: "I ran the door at the Bird. You had to convince me to let you in, then you had to get past Neil Hubbard and Gregor Gayden in the hallway with baseball bats. Then you walked up a hallway to this huge room. The walls were all painted with profanities; after the Fire Department started showing up Roger (Husbands) asked us to repaint the walls. We painted them all black."

The Mentors

The first show featured the Enemy, the Telepaths (in blue blazers borrowed from Danny Eskenazi's vintage-clothing store) and the debut of the Mentors, a group devoted to what would later be called "political incorrectness." Vocalist/drummer El Duce (Eldon Hoke, who sometimes used dildos as drumsticks), guitarist Sicky Wifebeater (Eric Carlson), and bassist Dr. Heathen Scum (Steve Broy) wore hooded masks onstage even though everyone knew who they were, and described themselves as "the masked villains of Rape Rock." Song titles included "Secretary Hump," "Macho Package," "Butt Odor #5," "Can't Get It Up," "Golden Showers," and "Total Crap." They had a dominatrix (played by Linda Van Etta) whip them on stage as punishment for their bad attitudes.

The Mentors moved to L.A. the following year, and recorded a number of indie releases for the Mystic, Death, Ever Rat, Metal Blade and Red Light labels, with such titles as *Up the Dose* and *You Axed For It.*

Their biggest fame came during future Second Lady Tipper Gore's 1985 crusade to censor rock lyrics, when fundamentalist minister Jeff Ling read their song "Golden Showers" aloud at a Congressional hearing: "Bend and smell my anal vapor/Your face is my toilet paper." They're the only Bird-era band still performing under their original name, but few people here take much pride in them. But it's important to note that in their Seattle days, they shared a stage with an intellectual-rock band and a new wave band with a female singer.

El Duce of
The Mentors

Enter Upchuck, pretentiously

Another Bird highlight was the March 31 debut show of Upchuck's first band, Clone. The teen glam monarch had attracted a "sugar daddy" who had installed him in a house with several gay-hooker housemates and a full PA setup in the basement. With this new-found wealth, Upchuck rented a limo to make his entrance into the small space, where he and his band performed David Bowie's entire *Station to Station* LP. The band included Jeff Gossard, Dave Drewery (later in Rob Morgan's Pudz), and Mike Davidson (also in the Lewd). After that first gig and the self-released 45 "Jacuzzi Floozie Suzie" (Upchuck's only released vinyl), the group added Sammamish High School graduate Gordon Halpern, previously a keyboardist in the cover band Sorcerer's Apprentice; he soon adopted the stage name Gordon Raphael. (He also played on the first Chinas Comidas 45.)

Clone played about a year and a half. As Upchuck gathered more original material, he reshuffled his players into Mental Mannequin. The new

group included Raphael, Davidson, Tor Midtskog, Pony Maurice, and siblings Ben and Barbie Ireland. Mental Mannequin played what Raphael called "a fusion of punk, new wave, and keyboard progressive rock" in odd time signatures to audiences that wanted to hear only loud guitars.

Members of Upchuck's bands and their small gothic entourage found side work as nude and/or black-clad models for Marsha Burns, a gallery photographer who specialized in portraits of "offbeat" subjects.

The Bird riot

To avoid Liquor Board harassment, Bird owner Roger Husbands neither sold nor allowed alcohol. Other than that, its atmosphere was like a punk party house cubed, crammed with up to 300 revelers (many underage, some pushing 40, some on pot or acid). Like London's seminal Roxy, it showcased a score of bands and forged a new community of musicians and fans in just three months.

The Bird's first taste of trouble came on April 14, the club's sixth weekend. In the midst of a show by the Mentors, the Dimes and San Francisco's Dils, fire marshals showed up with papers asserting "Violations too numerous to list. You must cease operation immediately." Husbands refunded everyone's admission, turning the "business" into a "private party," and the show continued, closing with an improvised song called "Fuck the Fire Marshal" performed by various band and audience members. Husbands tried to keep the space open on a volunteer basis, but was given notice to vacate by his landlord effective June 1.

The closing night party went smoothly, until one passerby called the police around 2 a.m. to complain about the remaining partiers throwing things off the roof. Minutes later, the club was invaded by three rampaging plainclothes cops, who initially refused to identify themselves. They ordered everyone to stay inside, enforcing their orders with billy clubs and plenty of head-bustin'. Homer Spence asked one of the still-anonymous thugs to identify himself; as Spence told the *Seattle Times*, the attacker opened his wallet in the dark lobby to briefly flash "something that could have been a badge." Spence added that most of the people in the club were "just trying to find out what was going on. There was no physical resistance that I'm aware of."

Enemy guitarist Damon Titus got kicked in the balls; Bob Kondrak was hit twice in the mouth. Enemy singer Suzanne Grant escaped out the front door during the melee, but was caught outside by a uniformed cop who hit her across the chest with a billy club and twisted her arm behind her back until he fractured her wrist. She went limp; the cops picked her up, pushed her face into a window, and warned her not to complain about police brutality. Grant called out to a passerby outside, who himself got shoved around by cops, beating his face in. Fifteen people were arrested, eight of whom were charged with reckless endangerment, obstructing or menacing.

Bob Kondrak recorded the police brutality on audio tape. The Enemy used the tape in the band's subsequent 45 "Trendy Violence" (they'd written the song before the bashing, originally to comment on punk-on-punk fights). The tape was also used in a class-action suit brought by victims of the police; at the trial, officers tried to say the brutality was fabricated and the tape faked, but the judge ruled with the punks and ordered a small cash settlement. The police would continue to harass punks and punk shows over the next 15 years—closing shows and clubs on the flimsiest excuses, verbally harassing punks on the streets, strictly subjecting punk clubs to fire, liquor and noise ordinances that yuppie blues bars seemed able to violate freely. The original Bird space is now divided into architects' offices.

Under the Bird name, Husbands booked shows in the Carpenters Union hall and other sites, eventually booking weekly shows at the Odd Fellows Hall through that November. The Halloween show had the Lewd, Roland Rock, and the debut of the Frazz. The latter was a '60s pop-revival band fronted by Marty Frasu, an ex-San Franciscan who'd played with white Hendrix impersonator Randy Hansen. The Frazz played with assorted members for five years, including two go-go dancers; they released a 45 on their own Du-Tel Records with a cover of the Shocking Blue's "Venus" (another of that band's songs would be covered on the first Nirvana 45). Husbands was kicked out by the Odd Fellows for attracting unruly-looking patrons (another syndrome which would be repeated over the years).

During and just after the Bird era, the chief punk print medium was the tabloid *Stelazine*. Stella Kramer, using a variety of names including "Stella Street," published six issues of the taboid, *Stelazine*, sold for 50 cents at the punk-friendly record stores. In unscreened photos and handwritten text, it depicted the local punks as angry, cute, wild fun seekers anxious to break free from the suffocating constraints of the cultures around them.

Stella Kramer: *"I knew the Enemy people from college days. I moved back to Seattle from Washington, D.C. in 1976. I lived at the Enemy's house on Minor Avenue, 'Minor Manor.' I did some publicity for them, until Roger fired me. Then the Bird opened. I was at all the shows. I wrote the whole time I was there; I realized I should do something with it. I started* Stelazine *with Frank Edy, who designed all the Bird's posters. He did all the art, I did all the writing. I tried to get other people to contribute and to advertise; everybody said they loved what I was doing but they didn't want to be a part of it. The second issue was all about the harassment people were getting from the cops, closing parties and harassing people on the street. I called it 'Punk, the National Crime.'* Stelazine *was the only thing coming out at the time. Cops were closing everything down, so there was almost no scene going on. After the first Bird closed, nobody knew if there would ever be anything else except one-off shows.* Stelazine *was the only thing that kept things going when nothing was going. Seattle had a 'real scene' that was*

maybe 35 people, and an outer ring of part-timers around that. I was getting harassed on the streets. People would throw rocks. I was with two other women crossing First Avenue in our punk outfits one day when I noticed a cameraman (for KSTW-TV) filming us. We were shown the next night, for a report about child prostitutes. We sued the station and won. I left Seattle right after that, because I just felt very unsafe, overexposed."*

It wasn't until February 1979 before the next dedicated new-music space opened: the Golden Crown, a Chinese restaurant that had a drag-queen bar on its lower level. For seven years, audiences climbed a flight of steep stairs to the restaurant's old upstairs banquet room, to see a succession of bands from the Beakers to Soundgarden. The room was all-ages for its first few shows, until economics led owner John Louie to install a bar.

The Funhole and the Edmonds
Bands continued to play at party houses and practice spaces. Some notably crowded and loud shows were promoted by Ed Shepherd and Bob Kondrak at the Funhole, a small garage-like studio and band practice space in the aging-hippie neighborhood of Fremont, run by painter Jacques Moitoret (it's now a hair salon).

Jacques Moiteret: *"The Funhole space was 10 by 60 feet. We divided that up into an audience area and gallery at one end, the stage in the middle, and a backstage behind that. We had no licenses or permits. We postered all over town and got 250 people crammed into 150 square feet. You could walk on the heads of the people there. They paid $1, except for 50 of our friends who got in free.*

"The first two shows went well; the third show was shut down halfway through; so there were officially two and a half shows there before the city

**Below: Rob Morgan
in office of the Bird**

**The Heaters
(aka The Heats)**

The Cowboys

**The Radios
at IOGT Hall**

stopped us."

Rental-hall shows were held at the UW Ethnic Cultural Theatre, Washington Hall, the Polish Hall, and the 300-capacity IOGT Hall (home of the International Order of Good Templars, a minor Elks spin-off group; since demolished). One of the IOGT shows featured the debut of the Fishsticks, with Rob Morgan (the only member of the suburban Edmonds Woodway High School class of 1976 to own a Monkees T-shirt), Eric Erickson and Peter Barnes. Morgan went on to form the Pudz, who played blistering serious-fun covers of the cheesiest pop songs ever made.

More all-ages shows were held for a few weekends at the Puppet Theater, run by a marionette troupe that only used the place in the daytime. The puppeteers had built a catwalk above the stage. Someone got up there during a gig by Greg Ragan's band Janitors of Love. The guy poured beer all over Ragan during his second song. He ran out and never came back. Ragan soon left the music scene and struggled with a drug habit for many years; he'd overcome it and had developed a career in retailing when he died in May 1993.

Bob Kondrak on the rental-hall circuit: "I was a philosophy major at the UW when I first got into these shows and these parties. It was like all these little dadas springing up."

Modern rock came to the suburbs when ex-*Helix* writer Norm Caldwell got a job managing the Edmonds Theater, a minor art house north of the Snohomish County line. In the spring of 1979 Caldwell and his partner, Harvard Exit co-owner Art Bernstein, rechristened it the Edmonds Rock n' Roll Theater. Each Friday and Saturday Caldwell offered a rock movie (*The Girl Can't Help It* or *Go Johnny Go*) and a band. (The concept was first tried out at the Harvard Exit, with the Moberlys and *A Clockwork Orange*.) According to former *Post-Intelligencer* rock critic George Arthur, "the Edmonds Theater's existence was predicated on the summer release of the Ramones' *Rock n' Roll High School* with Caldwell figuring, correctly, that he'd be the only non-drive-in in Washington to book it." The concept didn't last: Caldwell realized that most punks didn't have cars and hence couldn't go to drive-ins, but forgot that you needed a car to get from Seattle to Edmonds. He later booked some of the same bands at the video-game tavern Goldie's On Broadway, including some of the first paid gigs by the Girls and a couple of Knack-esque power pop bands, the Heats (original-

ly the Heaters) and the Cowboys. He later moved to Mexico, where he now works in real estate.

Power pop

The Cowboys and Heats would become the local kings of commercial "new wave," the bands critics and radio stations deemed the most likely to succeed.

Ian Fisher and Jeff Cerar's Cowboys were a pop-reggae-funk-dance party band, a concept that proved more commercially durable in Portland with the Crazy 8's and Sweaty Nipples. Typical Fisher lyrics included "Lovesick girls! Touch me!" and "Standing in the Rain, Waiting on a Bus." They released a couple of singles, an EP in late 1982, and an LP in 1986, by which time they had already passed their peak as dance-floor headliners. But during their heyday they were one of the first to "graduate" from the new wave circuit into some of the suburban dance bars that normally only booked cover bands. They appeared on the cover of the *Times* Sunday magazine section and were honored by AOR station KZOK as "Best Local Band," daring to accept the award before a very hostile audience at a Sammy Hagar/Loverboy concert.

Ian Fisher to the Rocket *on the trials of small-time fame, 10/84: "I lost a lot of friends when the Cowboys started getting press. It was like 'Ian and these guys are on a massive ego trip, these guys think they're the hottest thing.' OK, when you're 22, 23 years old, and all of a sudden people are writing about you and you have all these people in bars coming up to you and giving you phone numbers, girls, and all of a sudden you have these drug people putting cocaine in your face. Yeah, you trip out on it for a while."*

The Heats (Steve Pearson, Don Short, Ken Deans, Keith Lilly) played what John Keister called "cute, high-pitched, two-part harmony." They appeared in a TV commercial for the local horse track, labeled as a "Soon To Be Famous Rock Band." They were signed by Heart's then-manager Ken Kinnear, who lavished them with costly (for Seattle) promotion. Kinnear splurged for an LP with a major-label budget; it featured the snide-rock anthems "Ordinary Girls" and "I Don't Like Your Face" (allegedly written in response to a negative *Rocket* story). *Times* columnist Eric Lacitis hyped them as the one local band with a real chance for national success. It didn't work out that way: the punks despised their snot-rock attitude and Pearson's whiny vocals; the general public didn't pay attention to them—outside of a core of pubgoers who normally only went to cover bands.

John Keister: "People like the Heats were vilified by the true punk rock hipsters, but they did more for the new wave-original rock scene than the hardcore bands ever did. They proved to club owners that bands that played their own music could draw crowds. They were poppy; they didn't have those credentials of being hardcore socialist left-wing insane punks; but they really were crucial at a certain time toward opening the scene up."

The Heats and Cowboys invaded punk spaces often enough, to the punks' chagrin, but their home base was Astor Park, an old jazz lounge on Fifth Avenue with a red-velour, businessmen's-smoker variety of sleaze about it. Astor Park dance-floor faves from 1979 to 1984 included Steve Aliment's No Cheese Please, Jim and John Irwin's Moving Parts, Christian Fulghum's Attachments, Uncle Cookie vet Mark Sargent's Mondo Vita, Jim and David Keller's New Flamingos, and David Surkamp's Hi-Fi (with Fairport Convention vet Ian Matthews). The place was eventually closed by the Liquor Board for not meeting its food-sales quota.

Daina Darzin in Rescue, 1981: "Astor Park reminds me, in decor, of a lounge I was once at in Miami which featured a Cuban-flavored disco band, little quiche hors d'oeuvres, and a guy who was trying to sell me very stepped-on coke. That, with a little Elks' Lodge thrown in. (That fake-fireplace boulder stuff behind the stage has GOT TO GO.) Astor Park also charges two bucks for a beer. Much of the audience looked like they were secretly afraid they were too old to rock n' roll and too young to die."

Christian Fulghum, Attachments/Sister Psychic: "The Attachments were a classic example of a band that was less than the sum of its parts. They were all good musicians, but half wanted to be metal and half wanted to be the Eurythmics. We had some financial backing for a while. It's better to be broke like Sister Psychic than to have the distractions of backing."

Astor Park was booked by Jean Baptise, an ambitious entrepreneur who had a reputation for picking popular (if not always good) bands—and for striking hard deals. He sometimes tried to reduce or eliminate his promised fees to bands if he decided the audience was too small or his costs were too high. He also booked several other spaces including the Bahamas Underground, the former 92 Yesler coffeehouse in Pioneer Square (now a toy store). Many of the former Bird bands and their friends got their first 21-and-over gigs at the Bahamas, before it was closed over liquor-law violations. Baptise now books nostalgia and world-beat bands at the Ballard Firehouse and Under the Rail.

Karen Hansen, concert promoter, on the Bahamas Underground: "It was large, it was dark, the drinks were strong. The place rocked."

Other venues

A few modern bands, particularly those that avoided the more dissonant sounds, got occasional gigs at the old-hippie Buffalo and New Melody taverns in Ballard. One band that often played the Ballard bars was Fred, a punk-jazz-noise conglomera-tion formed by trumpet-guitar player Jeff McGrath and trombone player/UW musicology student Greg Powers. McGrath and Powers gigged with assorted additional players under the Fred name (it didn't mean anything) until 1991; by the end they played mostly at private parties. They also organized sporadic midnight acoustic jams of four to 100 people on the UW campus's "Red Square" (officially the Central Plaza) from 1980 to 1985; posters for the jams invited people to bring their own instruments, store-bought or homemade.

Jeff McGrath: "I was playing in musicals with Greg. I met some of his friends at a party on Queen Anne Hill. None of us played guitars or drums. We started asking, 'If we had a band, what would we call it?' The consensus was that we'd call it Fred.... We had to pester Modern Productions to let us play in the Showbox. They thought we were a joke. They finally booked us on a bill with a band called Bob and a band called the Debbies."

The Monestary, an all-ages gay disco, opened in an old church building operated by a Universal Life Church mail-order "ministry." A few punk shows were held there in the early days, but it soon went all-DJ. It attracted police attention over underage gay prostitution and drug dealing on the premises; it was eventually shut down as part of a series of crackdowns against independent youth culture.

The city had long treated all public gatherings of teenagers, for legal or illegal purposes, as menaces to be crushed, from car cruising near Alki Beach to parking-lot scenes at Dick's Drive-Ins. Officials never understood that shutting teen hangouts never stopped illicit activity, it just dispersed it. Art Bernstein's son Nils was one of the underage kids who went to the all-ages clubs. He later ran a record store on Capitol Hill, the Rebellious Jukebox (named after a Fall song) and now does PR for Sub Pop.

Nils Bernstein: "I started going to shows when I was 11. It was scary and funny at the same time. Then I really got into punk bands like X and Mission of Burma.... I was drinking and smoking and listening to loud music when I was 14, and

Lewd Single (Satz and Blobbo in center)

Below: Inside the Showbox

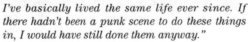

Too many posters

The Enemy meet
future govenor
Mike Lowry

I've basically lived the same life ever since. If there hadn't been a punk scene to do these things in, I would have still done them anyway."

Duds

Fashion among the local Anglophiles evolved as dictated by the UK music papers: gone went the glitter, in came the leather, the torn jeans, the chains, the multicolor hair. Guys who claimed to be radicals or anarchists put swastikas and Confederate flags on their leather jackets, for no apparent reason except they looked cool.

A more indigenous punk fashion supposedly started with kids creatively mixing-and-matching finds from thrift stores and vintage-clothing stores including Danny Eskenazi's seminal Dreamland, originally in the U District and later moved to Broadway. The favorite thrift stores included the giant Goodwill and Salvation Army outlets south of downtown, St. Vincent de Paul on Lake Union north of downtown, the Children's Hospital store in Belltown, and the for-profit Value Village chain.

But what became known as "grunge fashion" had its biggest roots in what some punks called "the Church of the Free Clothes." The Blessed Sacrament Catholic Church, in the U District (near most of the punk party houses), held free-clothing giveaways Wednesday afternoons. Discriminating punks sorted through the offerings every week to get the ingredients for street costumes; a few ambitious types tried to carry out whole grocery bags of garments and sell the best to vintage clothing stores.

Money (too little)

Not only was the scene small, much of it was destitute. Few of the pre-1980 local punks had full-time jobs. Some clerked in bookstores, some waited tables, some hung out at community colleges.

Some lived off food stamps and "crazy money": the state's GAU (General Assistance-Unemployable) program, intended to support those "emotionally unable to fit into society."

A now-thriving contingent of female promoters and managers led from a clique of hard-working women who supported their unemployed boyfriends' musical careers (and, in several cases, their drug habits). Several women in the scene worked at the Amusement Center, a peep show on the ground floor of the Showbox building affiliated with a free-love hippie church. In future years, punk women would work in phone sex and strip joints (lap dancing, the ultimate legal sleaze-sex act, is said to have started here).

Money (too much)

The poorer punks treated bands that had money as posers copping a fake stance, even though most all the punks had middle-class families. The Heats and Cowboys were most reviled, but in the developing punk Puritanism it was a sign of phoniness if a band had a slick poster, a professionally printed picture sleeve for its 45, or even new instruments.

The Enemy got a lot of abuse in this area: because it made well-packaged 45s on its own King Tut label, including its theme song "I Need An Enemy" (produced by Buck Ormsby); because band member Damon Titus had a full-time job as a real estate agent; because it got to play the Bird most every weekend since its manager owned the place; and especially because it had abruptly adopted its punk stance and look. (King Tut also released an LP of trumpet standards by street musician Richard Peterson.) The Enemy toured California and the East Coast in late 1978 and early 1979, traveling in a slick RV and arranging for pickup gigs when they got to a city. Suzanne Grant once got her face kicked in by audiences in Washington, DC.

Back home, one of the group's most devoted fans was a thin, fresh-faced Roosevelt High student, Michael "Duff" McKagan. Grant remembers him as "one of our best little fans, just this little boy who hung around." He'd appear in approximately 30 local bands from 1979 to 1984.

The Lewd also drew its share of detractors. Satz's band printed up fancy street posters, dressed in copies of the latest New York/London punk fashions, and self-released a three-song 45 ("Kill Yourself") that came with a two-color picture sleeve, but was recorded on a cheap home cassette deck. The Lewd broke up when Satz split for San Francisco, taking the name and forming a new Lewd that lasted into the mid-'80s. Some Lewd graffiti was spray-painted on a wall near the Paramount around 1977; it stayed up for a decade. Blobbo moved south with Satz, but soon split to take up his real name, Kurdt Vanderhoof, with a new band, Metal Church, one of the first punk/metal crossover acts. He disbanded that group, returned home to Aberdeen and formed a new Metal Church (see chapter 10). He brought his record collection with him, including a lot of punk discs that had never existed in Aberdeen before. He turned some local kids on to his collection; some of them became the Melvins (named after a much-despised day-job colleague).

Johnny Vinyl: *"The Lewd opened when the Ramones played the Paramount in 1978. I remember a guy sitting down next to me with a shopping bag full of fruit. I asked him if he was going to eat it. He said no, he was going to throw it at the Lewd."*

Robert Newman, *co-founder of the* Rocket, *1985:* *"I found out about the first punk show I ever saw in Seattle from a poster on a telephone pole on Broadway. The show featured the Lewd at a hall I can't remember and it was horrible. I couldn't believe a band could be* that *bad. Little did I realize that bands I would later see would make the Lewd look like technical geniuses."*

Stella Kramer: *"The Lewd was a sucky poseur band, really horrifying. You knew they'd been a bar band that 'went punk' to get a hit."*

Telephone pole art

Street posters were recognized in the scene as a worthy art form, deserving whatever resources a band could put into them (even if, like the Lewd, more care was spent on the poster than on the music). Some were photocopied at commercial copy centers or at musicians' day jobs; others were instant-printed or silkscreened at friends' basements.

One Bird-era band with a definite visual sense was the Cheaters, formed at Nathan Hale High School by brothers Al and Kurt Bloch. The group had a logo of a slash-circle road sign with a "3" inside. The "No Threes" logo was an in-joke: for a poster advertising the first of his career's many drummer searches, Kurt concocted the logo as a way of saying he didn't want to be stuck with a three-piece band. Later, Kurt found a real "No Parking" sign and repainted it as "No Threes." Kurt released a half-dozen singles on his own No Threes Records, including the debut of his subsequent band, the Fastbacks (see next chapter).

Art Chantry, a Western Washington University design graduate from Tacoma, came to Seattle in 1978 and started producing a series of posters that were simultaneously chaotic and clear, with big type (often photocopied out of sample books or found documents) juxtaposed with startling pictures (often cut up from existing images, especially from old ad art, exploitation magazines and hot-rod cartoons). Some of his first work was for the UW student film series, run by future *Rocket* film critic Jim Emerson. Chantry went from there to design ephemeral art for bands, theatre companies and political benefits, always on a low-budget, fast-turnaround basis. He also designed for local rock zines, including four stints as the *Rocket*'s art director; during his last stint in 1991, he started making

reverse-relief headlines on a Dymo Labelmaker, a gimmick he reprised when he designed covers for Rhino Records' compilation series *DIY*.

Emerson left for L.A. in the mid-'80s but still wrote for the *Rocket*. He also helped a fellow UW grad, actress Julia Sweeney, develop the androgynous character "Pat" that she later played on *Saturday Night Live*.

Jim and Mike

Jim Lightfoot and Mike Vraney, owner and clerk respectively at the Time Travelers record and comic book store on Second Avenue, started booking all-ages shows with a Ramones gig at the Norway Center in January 1979. Vraney later said that "we heard a week before the show that the Ramones were going to be playing at the Rainbow Tavern and we thought that was fucked. I knew at least 100 people, myself included, who wanted to see the band but were under 21." The results of their first promotion venture? "Over 600 people came out, we let all our friends in free, made $40 apiece and got to see the Ramones. It was a really successful show."

Seattle's first "poster war" came that June. Lightfoot and Vraney booked San Francisco's Dead Kennedys into Washington Hall on the same night that Terry Morgan, a former promoter of UW student concerts, rented the UW Ethnic Cultural Theater for a show by two bands he was managing, Young Scientist (ambient electronics, with an abstract video-art demonstation) and the Telepaths-spinoff Blackouts. As soon as posters for one show got put up on the Ave, leafleters for the other show would remove or cover them with posters for the other show. By the time the respective camps exhausted their supply of broadsheets, Lightfoot and Vraney invited Morgan to join their new promotion company, Modern Productions.

Mike Vraney *to the* Rocket *on the Dead Kennedys' Washington Hall gig, 8/81:* *"The Communists showed up with flags, and we had made about 50 Kennedy masks for the kids to wear, with little elastics so they'd stay on and with bullet holes and blood. So there were all these kids in the front row with Kennedy masks pogoing around and between sets we showed a silent Kennedy assassination film. It was a real patriotic show."*

The Blackouts had formed about six months after the last Telepaths gig, when Erich Werner, Mike Davidson and Bill Rieflin regrouped along with keyboardist Roland Barker (an Ingraham High pal of Werner's, and James Husted's partner in Young Scientist). Seven years before Public Image Ltd. released its generic-titled *Album*, the Blackouts' debut single (released by Modern Productions) bore the title *Music: 528 Seconds*. The songs on that 45, "Make No Mistake" and "The Underpass," bore a quirky pop-hook sensibility at odds with a just-barely-restrained guitar attack. Some described it as a record the Cars could have made if they'd had

John Keister
bowls a good game

Mark Michaelson,
later art director of Newsweek

"Hershey Bar"
masthead by
Lynda & Mark

Lynda Barry

the guts or the brains.

Bill Rieflin: *"The Telepaths were a punk band with intensity and power. We wanted to get away from the bombast of the Telepaths, into something with dirt simplicity. We were listening to the Gang of Four and the early Talking Heads. All the new stuff was in 4/4 time, with reduced chord changes."*

Rocket roots

After *Stelazine* folded (Stella Kramer's now a photo editor at *Newsweek*), the next local zines included *Boy*, *Strictly Confidential* (edited by Thom Bissett under the pseudonym "Stu Meat") and Robert Bennett's three-issue run of *Twisted*.

Even though the University of Washington had the highest student population of any single campus west of Texas (California's college system is more decentralized), few UW students were part of the early scene. One exception was a tall, prematurely bald Boeing rich kid named John Keister, who'd attended Franklin High School alongside cartoonist Lynda Barry, choreographer Mark Morris, and easy-listening saxophonist Kenny G (Gorelick). A journalism major who didn't care for the department's careerist courses, Keister wrote a column for the *UW Daily* with such topics as "Homosexual Cliff Notes" (envisioning a line of study guides that would help you write a guaranteed-A essay by "proving" every major character of any literary work was really homosexual).

Keister's frequent partner in crime was Charles R. Cross, an Army brat and admirer of Bruce Springsteen and Hunter Thompson (personal motto: "Fuck Objective Journalism"). Cross promoted himself as the real topic of his stories, whether the official topic was the Shroud of Turin or student politics. As *Daily* editor in the spring of '79, he

First issue of
The Rocket

used every device to get his name in the paper, including fake letters to the editor addressed personally to himself. While still in college Cross started *Backstreets*, a national Springsteen fanzine; he hounded Springsteen on tour, to the chagrin of the star and his management, once climbing uninvited into his hotel hot tub. He's edited a *Backstreets* compilation book and co-edited a Led Zeppelin fan book.

Through a quirk of campus politics, the Board of Student Publications named Keister editor for the summer 1979 *Daily*. The journalism professors derided his "punk rock layout" designed by two non-student volunteers, Lynda Barry and her former Evergreen classmate Mark Michaelson. Keister also introduced the first punk/new wave music column in an established Seattle publication, written by Karl Neice under the pseudonym Mad Averros. Nobody at the journalism school figured any of the summer *Daily* staff would go anywhere in the business. Michaelson became one of the *Rocket's* first art directors, then worked at *Vanity Fair* and *Newsweek*, and was the first art director of *Entertainment Weekly*. Barry has a best-selling series of cartoon books and has dabbled in gallery painting, prose fiction, NPR essays, spoken-word recordings and playwriting.

The *Seattle Sun* started a monthly music insert in October 1979. The *Rocket* quickly became known as *the* local commercial rock mag.

The first 16-page issue began with a photo of producer Harry Kool (who left for San Francisco three years later and is now in Chicago) in front of the 8-track mixing board at Triangle Studios, located in the 1900-built Triangle Grocery building on Leary Way in Ballard. Triangle was started in 1976 and owned by engineer Jack Weaver with successive partners Cary Wakely, Eric Betten and Bill Stuber. During Weaver's tenure, virtually every local punk record was made there. Weaver sold his interest in the place to Stuber in 1984; Stuber closed it in 1986, but it was soon reopened by young engineers Chris Hanzsek and Jack Endino.

The first words in the first Rocket, *by **Robert Ferrigno**, 10/79: "Hear that sound? If you listen real close you can hear the recording industry whimpering like a wounded dinosaur. Industry profits are way down, 20 percent or more, according to ABC News. The unemployment offices in L.A. are crowded with dazed Mantanned executives in Guccis who mumble things like 'monster,' 'promo-package,' and 'bullet' as they finger the gold chains that swathe their necks. A plastic surgeon could send ten generations of kids to Harvard on the nose-reconstruction jobs in the information line."*

The fourth *Rocket* cover, an abstract design of flying guitars, foreshadowed the tabloid's future emphasis on flashy graphics above local music coverage. Only six of its first 40 covers depicted local musicians. While most of the staff preferred the new music scene, they felt commercially obligated to put national stars on the covers and folk, blues and metal bands on many of the inside pages. They drew the line at Top 40 cover bands, whom they refused to publicize no matter how successful. The *Rocket*'s Free Musicians Classified became the gathering place for formative bands. Clubs arranged their scheduling around the paper's monthly deadlines.

Evergreen grad Bob McChesney bought the *Rocket* from the *Sun* in 1980, with partial backing by editor Robert Ferrigno, co-editors Bob Newman and Karrie Jacobs, and business manager Greg Feise. John Keister used his UW graduation money to "buy my way into a job there" and became its senior editor. With the *Sun*'s death in January 1982 and the *Weekly*'s solidification into an affluent leisure guide, the *Rocket* became Seattle's only "alternative" paper, without the weekly schedule or political coverage of alternative papers in other towns. Local cartoonists Barry, Charles Burns and Michael Dougan (and Evergreen grad Matt Groening, who moved to L.A. in 1977) made weekly comic strips for national syndication; *Rocket* readers only saw one-fourth of their output.

John Keister: "For the first year or so the Rocket *covered a lot of the Olympia arty bands; that was probably the influence of Karrie Jacobs and Bob McChesney, who were from there. Most of the people and events covered in the early* Rockets *played to maybe 70 people. At the time very little original music was being performed. All the big audiences in town were for cover bands. Their managers were always calling to complain about why we didn't write about them. How much could we have written about Shyanne or Bighorn besides saying they sounded just like Foreigner?"*

Stella Kramer: "The Rocket *was thought of as a piece of shit by the musicians in the center of the punk scene. It was made by these older people who'd been to college, so we thought of them as outsiders to the scene. It was a high-tech operation. It was typeset, it had offices, so it was a mainstream paper as far as I was concerned."*

The first *Rocket* office was in an old storefront church next to the Odd Fellows Hall on Capitol Hill; bands practiced day and night in the other rooms of the building (and still practiced there until mid-1994, under the name Blue Room Music). The second *Rocket* office was upstairs from the Rendezvous Restaurant in Belltown; that restaurant's posh meeting room, the Jewel Box Theater (originally a screening room used by movie distributors) has been used in recent years for bands, performance art, and film screenings, while the old *Rocket* space upstairs became a band practice room and party space. In 1986 the *Rocket* moved to an office on Fifth Avenue, across from the defunct Astor Park nightclub.

A few *Rocket* writers went on to bigger things. Ferrigno moved to L.A. and began a series of thriller novels set there. Karrie Jacobs wrote about

visual design for national magazines and co-authored *Angry Graphics*, a book of political street posters. Ann Powers went to *Rolling Stone* and the *New York Times*, Craig Tomashoff went to *People*, and Dennis P. Eichhorn wrote an acclaimed comic book series of autobiographical vignettes, *Real Stuff*. Ron Hague became a staff writer for *The Ren & Stimpy Show*. McChesney left to persue a Ph.D. in media history in Wisconsin, and wrote a scholarly book on the early years of radio. *Rocket* art directors, artists and contributing designers wound up at *Newsweek*, *Entertainment Weekly*, *The Village Voice*, *Guitar World*, *Metropolis*, Semiotext(e), and Grove Press.

Newman succeeded Ferrigno as editor, then left in 1986 to art-direct in New York. Cross replaced Newman as editor, and bought the paper soon after. Cross initially de-emphasized local bands in favor of covers about national acts like Springsteen and Presley. In the early '90s Cross handed most editorial control to managing editor Grant Alden who quit in early 1994 to open Vox Populi, an art gallery specializing in cartoonists, poster designers and rock photographers.

Rocket radio ad, circa 1983: "The Rocket, *a magazine for today! Lots of* big *pictures, lots of* little *words!"*

Op and company

Washington's slickest rock zine to date was Olympia's *Op* (run by a collective called the Lost Music Network, and so titled because "OP" comes after "LMN"). *Op* was nationally distributed and specialized in short reviews of music of all genres, the only qualification being that a record had to be from an independent label. After the first few bimonthly issues, *Op* added an alphabetical theme section, reviewing bands that started with the letter "A" in one issue, "B" in the next, and so on. *Op*'s art direction, by co-founder Dana Squires, established the inner-childlike cartoon graphics style later made famous by K Records.

Op had grown out of the program guide for KAOS, the Evergreen student-run radio station. *Op*'s editor, Squires's future husband John Foster, had brought his passion for independent music to KAOS in 1975, when he arrived on the campus at age 19 from Connecticut. He'd come to Olympia at the recommendation of pre-med student Stephen Rabow, his ex-classmate at a Quaker boarding school in New York state.

Under the direction of Foster, Rabow and Toni Holm, KAOS's playlist became officially 80-percent indie. Olympia listeners were denied many acts that managed a one-shot deal with a major label but couldn't get on local commercial stations.

Stephen Rabow: "Foster had developed this list of over 1,000 independent record labels in the US and England. This was in 1976, when we were all frustrated with the music business. We made independent music our focus because we wanted to

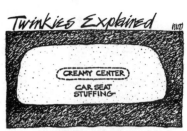

Early Ron Hauge cartoon

Issue "B" of Op

Stephen Rabow

Charles Burns

Issue #4 of Sub Pop

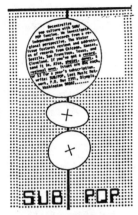

Early Sub Pop ad

"Subterranean Pop"
cover by Lynda Barry

Charles Burns'
cassette covers for Sub Pop

Logo by Wes Anderson
(later art director of
Village Voice) and Dale Yarger

support people who created music out of a love for it, not to get rich.... The KAOS scene, the whole Evergreen campus, dressed as cheaply as possible. We'd all go to thrift stores in Tumwater or Yelm and pick the grungiest things, old Pendleton wool shirts and scruffed out jeans.

"One day in 1976 we got the first Ramones 45 into the station. We played it in the office for review. I immediately fell over laughing and crying. I went into the studio right away; there was a classical program on at the time. I insisted to the DJ that he had to play this and log it. We had to become the first station in the country to play the Ramones. As soon as the Beethoven record ended the DJ introduced me and I said, 'This is the record that's going to change the shape of rock n' roll forever.' "

Steve Fisk: *"In the early punk years, 1979 to '82, Olympia was connected with the rest of the world, while Seattle was still trying to re-create Talking Heads and Killing Joke."*

Foster promised to fold *Op* after the "Z" issue, and kept his word at the end of 1984; two packs of *Op* contributors formed *Sound Choice* and *Option* to take its place. Foster took off on Peace Corps duty after *Op* ended; he now works for Holm and her partner David Rauh, who own a soft-rock FM station in Olympia. KAOS still maintains its strict indie-label quota system, and in 1994 still had a weekly indie-rock show hosted by Calvin Johnson.

Pop goes the sub

One of Foster's Olympia cronies was Bruce Pavitt, an Evergreen student and KAOS DJ who'd come west from Park Forest, Illinois with his friends Hiro Yamamoto, Kim Thayil (who'd been born in Seattle to parents from India), and Stuart Hallerman (who became a live sound engineer and in 1990 started Avast Studios in Seattle). Pavitt be-

gan his own photocopied zine in 1979 as an independent-study project for class credit.

Pavitt's *Subterranean Pop*, like *Op*, was devoted to promoting independent records. Pavitt held the additional emphasis on underground-rock bands that preferably weren't from New York or Los Angeles, believing America's real creative action took place outside the big media cities. In his introductory essays he claimed that the hippie movement had been about taking control of technology; while the next revolution would be all about using technology to take control of culture, away from major corporations and back to the people.

The first cover was hand-colored by crayon on each copy. With issue #2, fellow KAOS DJ Calvin Johnson joined his venture. For issue #3 in 1981, Pavitt shortened the name to *Sub Pop*.

From **Bruce Pavitt's** *"Supreme Statement of Purpose" in* Sub Pop *#8, 1982: "1. Culture is controlled by large corporations. It is bland. 2.Sub Pop combats this by supporting independent means of expression: cassettes, records, publications, video, public access cable television, whatever. 3. We are very big interested in regional trends, movements, ideas, slang, record labels, what have you. We are very big interested in small communities that aren't big time like important N.Y. and L.A. 4. A decentralized cultural network is obviously cool. Way cool."*

In 1983, after six zine issues and three compilation cassettes of his favorite unsigned bands from all over (all in editions of 1,000 or less), Pavitt moved to Seattle and turned *Sub Pop* into a record-review column in the *Rocket*, featuring the now-familiar logo with its "greater-than" and "less-than" symbols between the letters (designed by Wes Anderson, later revised by Dale Yarger). The column's in-your-face design and coverage of music and other entertainment would inspire the tight attitude and look of the later Sub Pop records. Pavitt and his contributing art crew (designers Lisa Orth, Chantry and Linda Owens, photographer Charles Peterson, and illustrator Burns) were all *Rocket* vets. Pavitt self-syndicated his column to rock zines across the country, further establishing his name among the national rock underground. He also started a *Sub Pop* show on KCMU (see next chapter), playing American independent releases.

P.S. O'Neill *on Pavitt's Evergreen days: "He would show up at shows wearing a black jumpsuit with fluorescent traffic-guard stripes and stand in front of the band with his hand in the air like a Nazi salute, with no expression on his face, and then all of a sudden he would start gyrating to the music. There was a very specific type of Evergreen dancing that existed in those days, very free-flowing and improvisational. When the song ended, Bruce would stop and salute again."*

The Showbox

Mike Vraney and Jim Lightfoot (who'd sold Time Travelers) rented out the Showbox Theatre on First Avenue in September 1979. The beautiful decaying big-band ballroom with a spring-loaded dance floor, where Gypsy Rose Lee once stripped and where the first organizational meetings to form the *Seattle Sun* were held, had become a Jewish bingo hall. It still bore the name Talmud Torah when Vraney and Lightfoot's Modern Productions mounted their first show on Sept. 8 starring Magazine (the first British new wave band to play Seattle) with the Blackouts opening. Modern Productions also had a business office in the Terminal Sales Building, one floor below the current Sub Pop office.

The Showbox name was restored to the building in time for the second show, on Sept. 29, starring the Enemy, the Olympia-based Macs Band, the Look and the Dishrags in a benefit for the *Rocket* marking the release of its first issue. Lightfoot and Vraney, with Terry Morgan and Swiss-born theatrical producer Carlo Scandiuzzi as junior partners, soon took a full-time lease on the building.

Terry Morgan: "We could only use the building when the bingo people weren't using it. Then we convinced the landlord that we'd be a better full-time tenant than a part-time tenant. That's when we built the dressing rooms and the stage. Carlo and I went in and 'renovated' the room—we painted it all black, except we kept the art deco patterns on the columns.... It was a great place and there were some great shows, but it never worked out. There were some shows with 800 people and some with just 200. Alternative rock was just not financially viable locally for many years."

The Showbox thrived for a while (popularly if not financially) as a regular stop on the Frontier Booking International bus-and-truck tours run by Ian Copeland (brother of Police drummer Stewart Copeland), which typically went from Boston and New York down the east coast, through southern college towns, up the Pacific coast, across Canada to the upper midwest, and back to New York. Touring bands that played to up to 1,000 pogoing fans included the Police, Devo, the Ramones, Iggy Pop, the Specials, XTC, Tom Robinson, the Dead Kennedys, the Gang of Four, the Plasmatics, 999, Ultravox, DOA, the Jam, the Cramps, Squeeze, and the Psychedelic Furs; all for a cover charge of $7 or less (even then, kids tried to sneak in with forged hand stamps).

Other London and New York bands (including the Raybeats, Mo-Dettes and Delta 5) came to Seattle on "the Eastern Airlines tour." The airline had an offer to fly anywhere in its route system for three weeks for $300, a plan that found a lot of bands crisscrossing the country on flights that all transferred at Eastern's hub in Atlanta.

A 15-year-old high school dropout named Paul Dana was among the kids who hung out at the early Showbox shows. He soon formed a band with himself on guitar, Kyle Nixon on vocals, Tor Midt-

skog on drums and Doug Rockness (his real name) on bass. This group, Solger, was one of the first in town devoted to the new hardcore punk developed by jocks from L.A.'s Orange County suburbs, though compared to them Solger's sound was slower and *a lot* muddier. Solger held a handful of gigs and put out a horrendously lo-fi, five-song 45 that consisted of 80 percent tape hiss, 10 percent guitar distortion and 10 percent unintelligible vocals (titles included "Raping Dead Nuns"). The band was together less than a year, but Dana remains known as Paul Solger to this day. The 45 became an underground collector's item.

Steve Turner, Mudhoney: "The first punk show I saw was Black Flag and Solger at the Showbox. Paul Solger looked as young as I was, about 15. It was so cool to see him up there. I saw Homer (Spence) in the audience and it soothed my nerves a bit: 'that's cool, an old guy is here.' Solger was the first hardcore band I liked. The Fartz were around, but I didn't like them very much, until Paul Solger joined them.... When I was in Green River we opened for Sonic Youth sometime in '85 at the Gorilla Gardens. Thurston (Moore) asked the audience if anybody there had the Solger single, that he'd pay $20 for it. That was the first time I realized the reputation that record had gained."

Rosco Louie

Hippie art promoter Larry Reid and his wife Tracey Rowland started a combined art-music space, Rosco Louie Gallery (named after old local lingo for "right" and "left") in a succession of two Pioneer Square spaces. The first, on South Jackson Street, is now part of the upscale Linda Farris Gallery; the second was on South Washington Street, next to the *Weekly*'s original office (the paper initially joined with other neighbors to try to get the gallery evicted). For most of its four and a half years it was Seattle's only non-yuppie gallery and headquarters for a new kind of installation art. Its shows included a postcard show, an Etch-A-Sketch Invitational, "The Pawn Shop" (the place was turned into a *real* pawn shop), "The Armory Show" (the name was from an historic dada show in a New York armory, but *this* show displayed every kind of gun imaginable on the gallery walls), and "The Video Game Show" (first-generation video arcade games redecorated and sometimes reprogrammed by artists, held before Japan's Nintendo Ltd. established its U.S. division in a Seattle suburb). Reid and Rowland paid the rent from Rowland's job at a clothing manufacturer and by charging admission to opening parties, where museum curators got drunk with punks while hearing bands from here (the Beakers, Rally Go) and elsewhere (DNA, Tuxedomoon, Bush Tetras, Raybeats). Police launched a harassment campaign against the concerts; as Rowland later told the *Rocket*, "they actually accused us of touching off a spontaneous white riot all over town after the Fastbacks and the

First Showbox show

Paul Solger

Below: Larry Reid

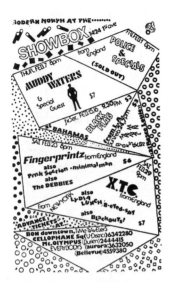

Showbox calendar

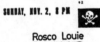

Rosco Louie poetry
reading by Lynda & Jesse

Jesse Bernstein reading

Opposite: Upchuck

Living played in the gallery."

Lynda and Jesse

The first show at the second Rosco Louie space was "The Cheesecake Show," featuring a private collection of Victorian porn; the collector pulled it from the walls in disgust over the opening party-concert that included readings by Lynda Barry and Jesse Bernstein. By this time the poet and former jazz bassist had lived, and looked, well beyond his 29 years. Bernstein held widely attended readings and performance pieces over the following years, based on his experiences with extreme alienation and desperation. He was a maintenance drinker and drug user at the time; he'd been in and out of jail. On any given night he might strip or howl or brandish a gun at the audience. At one Rosco Louie show he reportedly dropped his pants, pulled out a switchblade, and yelled, "If anyone leaves I'll cut my dick off." (He denied the story.) Some members of Bernstein's audiences came hoping for carnage, or at least for a wacked-out display of insanity.

Jesse Bernstein to Grant Alden, 1987: "In our culture, everything is a drug. If it's not a drug, people don't want to buy it. I can make that clearer: People want something done to them. It's a drug effect. You stick a needle in your arm, you press the plunger and it's got heroin in it, say, or good speed, right? It's out of control. Now. There's nothing you can do about it. It's gonna overpower you. Trying to ride it is a big thrill. Take it: Can you take it?"

Bernstein went clean and sober in 1983. He continued to take voluntary stays in the Harborview Hospital psych ward. He'd been to mental hospitals and institutions regularly since childhood; his doctors and his own medical research never definitely found out why his head worked so differently. He continued to write and speak about the demons in his head and in the world around him, but he wasn't a freak show anymore. Some of the trendier kids stopped going to his shows when he got serious.

Music for moderns

In November 1979 there was even a new wave radio station. KZAM, a Bellevue AM/FM that courted the elitist side of the post-hippie market (it was so pretentious, its weather reports were in *metric*), turned its low-power AM station into "The Rock of the '80s," broadcasting in "modern mono." Some of the DJs transferred to the new format clearly didn't know the music at first, but music director Paul Sullivan picked a reasonable mix of Blondie/ Talking Heads, Sex Pistols/Clash, and Knack/Romantics; bands seldom if ever heard on local AOR stations. The station never caught on with advertisers; most of its commercials came from a telemarketing firm that made cold calls to gas stations and shoe stores to "underwrite" safe-driving announcements.

In May 1980, ex-KAOS DJ Stephen Rabow got

an import record store to sponsor a Monday-night show on KZAM. He played three hours a week of "Music for Moderns," import and independent releases closer to music's leading edge than KZAM's regular rotation would allow, based on John Foster's original mailing list of indie labels. Rabow delivered his own variation on the station's driving-tip ads ("Dead people should *not* drive") and lectured his audience on essential themes ("the second law of thermodynamics: Entropy. Everything in the universe is winding down from more activity to less activity. Live with it"). Rabow's car, a Ford Pinto with painted flames on the back and the vanity plate KABOOM (Pintos were notorious for explodable, rear-mounted gas tanks) was pictured in *People* magazine. Rabow gave airplay to numerous unreleased tapes by local bands, while KZAM's regular format publicized local 45s. Rabow hosted two "Local Tape Extravaganza" specials, promising to play everything submitted that didn't have cuss words in it; the first special lasted three hours, the second lasted 16 hours. Rabow launched a poster contest at Rosco Louie that drew almost 500 entries: first- and second-place winners got prizes from station advertisers, the third prize was "a one-way ticket for one to the Tacoma Greyhound station."

Another highlight of Rabow's show was the world premiere of "Ronald Reagan Speaks For Himself," a collage tape by local audio artist Doug Kahn. Working before digital sampling, Kahn manually cut and spliced candidate Reagan's rambling responses from a Bill Moyers TV interview. It was issued on one of Bruce Pavitt's *Sub Pop* tape compilations, and reissued as a flexidisc in Art Speigelman's comix zine *RAW* #4 in 1982. Speigelman had to get the discs pressed in Europe, because the only U.S. flexidisc plant refused it.

New converts heard the music on KZAM and joined the audiences at local shows. The number and scope of bands blossomed. There were grinding Ramones-like bands, experimental art bands, devil-may-care noise bands, tight outfits that aimed for commercial success, manager-driven power-pop bands, openly gay and bisexual singers (and some who pretended to be, in Anglophilic tradition), and bands that bent and blended genres into new combinations.

For a while, it seemed like the punks were going to take over the city.

JOHN CALE

PSYCHEDELIC FURS

HOLLY AND THE ITALIANS

THE EXPLOITED

The Adolescents EQUATORS

Romeo Void

Lou Reed

DEUTSCH AMERIKANISCHE FREUNDSCHAFT Plastics

R A T $ PLASMATICS

STIFF LITTLE FINGERS

THE AU-PAIRS Visible Targets FORTZ

THE BEAT

WALL OF VOODOO

X-15 Heaven 17

PYLON FURIOUS PIG

X E

Everybody knew it but Ellen

DESPERATE TIMES

FASTBACKS DEAD KENNEDYS VAPORS KILLING JOKE

CHAPTER SEVEN: DESPERATE TIMES (1980-1981)

Tony Chu, son of an affluent Taiwanese family, created a band space in the back room of his Chinese restaurant on Second Avenue near Pioneer Square, north of the Smith Tower. Chu's first booker took a haphazard approach, with original bands some nights, biker-blues and cover bands other nights. Then Roger Husbands booked the place for a couple of shows with the Enemy and X-15 (see below). The full houses led Chu to make it a full-time new wave outlet by March 15, 1980. Husbands christened it the Gorilla Room (after the Chinese monkey-face Christmas tree lights decorating the room).

Like almost all the places where punk, post-punk and grunge bands would play, it was small (liquor laws and a lack of investment capital discouraged big showcase clubs). It was a homey, raunchy, delicious place, in various degrees of being trashed. It was adorned with plastic plants and mismatched office-furniture chairs. The back music room began as an all-ages space, with 21-and-overs allowed to drink in the front room.

The Gorilla Room and Bahamas weren't alone for long. Michael Clay, Wes Bradley and Erin McKiernan turned a Belltown leather gay bar called Johnny's Handlebar (on the ground floor of a former brothel) into WREX, a slightly more "respectable" outlet with old car seats in the back, old airline seats in the side area, and the town's first music video system. Some of the old clientele would drop in after WREX's opening on April 4, 1980, expecting the old familiar rite of "being different," only to be disconcerted at the new rite of "being different" that had replaced it. Bands played there two or three nights a week, originally booked by Wes Bradley. Besides almost every local band (starting with the Enemy), Grace Jones, Joan Jett, X, the Fleshtones, Romeo Void and Delta 5 schlepped through there. Upchuck was one of its DJs, alongside British immigrant Dennis White.

While WREX's reputation would be less sleazy than that of the rival Gorilla Room, it still had many nights when spilled beer lay an inch or two thick on the concrete floor, when young couples fucked openly on the back staircase. There and at other venues, restroom sinks regularly became detached from the walls, either from young women sitting on them during sex or from young men ripping them out in drunken rages. That wasn't its only problem.

Dennis White: "WREX was always out of cash. Toward the end I was buying the keg off the truck in the afternoon out of my own pocket, hoping they'd sell enough that night to pay me back."

Bars near WREX on upper First Avenue became punk hangouts. The Frontier Room, an old-timers' greasy-spoon cafe and dive lounge decorated like a ski lodge might look if skiers chain-smoked, became the punks' home away from home; it didn't have live music, because it would have awakened the old people in the residence hotel upstairs, but on a good weekend it did have dozens of scene members swilling cheap hard liquor at half-broken linoleum tables.

On the same block, straight punks started invading Tugs Belltown, a gay disco with an appropriately dark interior and a reputation for danger and fights. While management insisted it wasn't going straight (boy-girl couples were sometimes asked to leave if they behaved too heterosexually on the dance floor), it did cater to the new WREX clientele by offering "new music" nights midweek (sometimes with live bands).

Crest of the wave

The Showbox packed up to 1,200 people into one to eight shows a month. WREX and the Gorilla Room filled their tiny spaces for most of their three-nights-a-week shows. Bars around town started booking bands they'd never have considered before, including the all-ages Mr. Bill's near Northgate (now an electronics outlet), the Athens Cafe in Belltown (now, after a long empty period, the Crocodile), the Hall of Fame in the U District (now the Underground, an 18-and-over dry disco), Pancho's on Fourth downtown (more recently a belly dancing club), Hibble & Hydes in Pioneer Square, the Seattle Concert Theatre (an old church with great acoustics, razed for a *Seattle Times* parking lot), and a few shows at the Rainbow Tavern in the U District, the soft-rock headquarters.

A couple of volunteer DJs at KCMU, a 10-watt FM mono UW classroom station begun in 1971, began to play new music at night, contradicting the station's established soft rock format. The rest of the station's schedule continued as normal: live UW sports, dorm talent shows, journalism-class newscasts, and a few '60s-music shows (including "Beatles Second to None," which played nothing

(above) Alien Boy
by the Wipers (below)

but Beatles, not even other Merseybeat bands).

In the midst of all this fum came the biggest vomit launch in the world, the eruption of Mt. St. Helens in the southwest corner of the state. It rumbled and growled for several weeks before it blew on May 18, 1980; that let officials evacuate residents and loggers. Of the few casualties, the best known was Harry R. Truman, an old codger with 50 cats who refused to leave his home. With few other deaths, the eruption was the best kind of disaster: an event that brought people together and disrupted normal life (due to volcanic ash that rained over Washington and Oregon). A number of novelty 45s were released in its honor, including the somber ambient 45 "Ashfall" by Pete Leinonen's jazz quintet.

The best eruption picture on a record was a truly dark and menacing inner sleeve for the "Alien Boy" EP by Greg Sage's Wipers, based in Portland. Other important bands at this time in the City of Roses included Chris Newman's Untouchables (who learned of a UK Untouchables and became Napalm Beach), Sado-Nation, the all-female Neo Boys, power-poppers Billy Rancher and the Unreal Gods, and Johnny Koonce's Springsteen-esque Distractions.

Hardcore, no wave, art rock, and other rhyming words

The core of the scene remained tight, even if it now numbered several hundred musicians, promoters, zine writers, girl/boyfriends, and assorted hangers-on.

Rob Morgan: *"There may have been only 300 core people in the whole scene, and half of those were the bands. These days, there's more than that at one club."*

Somehow, this center held despite the increasingly disparate music styles these bands were playing. At its peak, there were over 50 bands in a score of subgenres. The Beakers, a no-wave band inspired by England's Gang of Four, could be seen at the same show with the Fartz, a band of Showbox crew members who used the names Blaine Fart (Cook), Steve Fart (Hofmann), Tom Fart (Hansen), and Loud Fart (Lloyd Shattuck III). Tom was replaced by Paul Fart, the once and future Paul Solger.

The Fartz began as the Anti-Toxins; their only trained musician was their first drummer, *Seattle Sun* film critic Tim Brock, who'd composed a piano concerto at age 16 and wore a leather jacket and ripped jeans to attend its premiere performance by the Seattle Philarmonic. The Fartz released *Because The Fucking World Stinks*, a 9-song, 7-inch 45 with such song titles as "Fuck Art Let's Fart;" it got distributed through the Dead Kennedys' Alternative Tentacles label and hit #7 on the British alternative charts. After a self-released tape, *Live to an Audience of One*, the band put out the 16-song opus *World Full of Hate* (the first full-length LP by a Seattle hard-punk band) through Alternative Tentacles' alliance with Faulty Products, the short-lived indie arm of IRS Records. They recorded the whole thing in one night at Triangle Studios and still had money left in their $400 recording budget, which they promptly spent on Dick's Drive-In burg-

ers and cases of beer. It featured such political statements as "Battle Hymn of Ronald Reagan" and "People United," plus a cover of Black Sabbath's "Children of the Grave," presaging the band's forthcoming switch to thrash metal. The cover art was by Steve Fart and Regan Hagar, who'd been in the speedcore band Maggot Brains (with future Accused and Gruntruck member Alex Sibbald) and was by then in Malfunkshun. In 1987, an EP of eight unreleased Fartz tracks (with Duff McKagan, who replaced Loud on drums) came out on the eMpTy label. (Maggot Brains singer Steve Porad and Silly Killers singer Eddie Hewlitt were in the process of forming a new band in the summer of 1993, when Porad overdosed on heroin.)

Recording and touring were the only career outlets for the Fartz, banned from most every club in town due to trendy violence by the neophyte hardcore delinquents. One Gorilla Room show was invaded by a Vancouver hardcore gang called the Fetus Eaters who proceeded to beat up the Seattle punks with tire chains; one woman got thrown against a wall mirror, which broke on her.

The Refuzors—Mike Refuzor (Lambert), Danny Refuzor (Barton), and Roach Refuzor (Dan Bradshaw)—also got banned from the Gorilla Room for attracting the wrong element. They made the daily papers with an infamous gig at Danceland USA (see below), where singer Mike flung a roadkill cat into the audience during a song called "Splat Goes the Cat;" that show, a KRAB benefit, also included the Blackouts, Student Nurse, and the proto-grunge U-Men (see below).

When the Refuzors went on hiatus, Roach drummed in RPA (Raging Peasant Army), with Solger vet Doug Rockness, Randall Mauritzen and Brad Ramels; they released the 1984 single "Shoot the Pope."

Going ape

Tony Chu saw Jean Baptise's success with new wave bands at the Bahamas Underground and asked him to manage the Gorilla Room. Baptise turned down the offer but passed it along to a Bahamas employee, Bryan Runnings. Runnings took over in November 1980 (Roger Husbands moved to the Golden Crown). He booked two or three bands a night, seven nights a week. He "auditioned"

bands by booking them into slow nights. He tore out the partition between the restaurant-bar and the back room, which disqualified it as an all-ages venue. Chu (who lived behind the kitchen) kept the place on a tight financial leash, letting a sleazy looking room get even sleazier looking. Bathroom fixtures were allowed to remain trashed. Grafitti was allowed to fester and breed unchecked. Runnings redecorated the interior at one point by spreading black paint over the walls and all the old posters and decor on the walls and all the furniture.

Runnings's favorite band, X-15, practiced rent-free in the Gorilla Room basement, a dank tall room that (like the basements of many older buildings in the area) had been the ground floor before the downtown streets were regraded. The room was filled with styrofoam boxes and other knick-nacks Chu kept around. One band member lived in that room; Runnings built a loft room for another member to live in, just above the main floor entranceway. Just after a set one night, an employee fell through the floor of that loft and landed on the main floor; she limped off and the partying continued.

Terry and Carlo

The original Showbox partners, Jim Lightfoot and Mike Vraney, broke up over money matters; they sold out many of their shows, but lost big on others, including a disastrous Pere Ubu/Magazine show at the Paramount; besides, there weren't enough shows to pay the rent. The lack of booze sales also hurt. First Lightfoot and then Vraney dropped out of the Modern Productions partnership, having lost $40,000 in a little over a year, leaving Terry Morgan and Carlo Scandiuzzi in charge.

Jim Lightfoot to the Rocket, 8/81: *"The problem with Modern was we grew too fast. For example, we never needed to get that exclusive lease on the Showbox; we could have continued to share rent with the bingo people. They were paying 80 percent of the rent and that would have taken the pressure off us to keep producing more shows, bigger shows with more and more expenses, shows that took a lot of time and energy and didn't make any money. We just got carried away with ourselves. My room! My room! Mostly it was*

The Untouchables

Solger: Raping Dead Nuns

Dead Cat Show

Outside the Gorilla Room

Inside

a matter of ego."

By the start of 1981 Morgan and Scandiuzzi had lost all the money they could, and turned the Showbox's lease to Steve Pritchard, a gifted hustler from the paper-mill town of Longview, who got into booking shows at the Showbox, WREX, the Athens Cafe in Belltown, and the Golden Crown, went broke, managed a few bands, promoted some hiphop battle-of-the-bands parties, and left town in 1984. He soon lost his shirt and turned the Showbox over to a promoter known as Space Muffin (Alfonso Matthew Adinofi), who promptly lost *his*

shirt (he later started a business making handcrafted drums).

Scandiuzzi went into theatrical production, and in 1983 planned to turn the Pike Place Cinema (a former site of the Empty Space Theater) into a multimedia arts and performance center, until the theater's owners balked at the expenses and nixed his plans. He now packages B movies for European video release; he's also acted a little, as mentioned in chapter 10.

Morgan took over the Golden Crown lounge and booked shows there off and on until 1984, when he had irreconcilable differences with its

new manager Charlie Fong (the brother-in-law of original owner John Louie, who was one of 13 people murdered in a gangland slaying at the Wah Mee gambling club in Chinatown).

In September 1981 the Showbox's lease was taken over by Concerts West (Pat O'Day's old arena-rock company, by then owned by national promoter Jerry Weintraub). The new management originally wanted to gentrify the place (one of its first shows starred folk humorist Leon Redbone), but saw the light and agreed to sublet the place out for underground concerts. A handful of independently-promoted shows (X, King Crimson, Public Image Ltd., Nina Hagen, Steel Pulse, King Sunny Ade) took place there through the following year and a half, the last starring the Dead Kennedys with 10 Minute Warning (the Fartz successor band). At that show, as many as 50 fans were jumping on and diving off the stage at once. Terry Morgan co-produced some of the later shows there with Brad Zirckle, under the name Big Z Productions, before he ran out of money again. Morgan went on to promote ethnic music festivals and outdoor jazz concerts, but stayed in the alternative-rock game by managing bands and promoting shows at the Paramount, Moore and Music Hall (a grand downtown film palace, demolished in 1992); he also served as the U.S. booking representative for David Thomas and Pere Ubu.

Vraney went to a stint managing the Dead Kennedys in San Francisco, which ended in animosity between him and the band. Vraney came back to Seattle and now runs Something Weird Video, which packages home-video releases of old sex and gore films.

Lightfoot leased back the record section of the Time Travelers comic book store, doing business as Corporate Records. A couple of years later he turned that operation over to Norman Batley, a North London native who'd been hanging around town since 1979, and who had to deny constant rumors that he'd made up his British accent just to pick up girls. Batley, Jim Anderson, George Romansic and Judy Malmgren co-hosted *Life Elsewhere*, a show on KRAB radio (named from Milan Kundera's book *Life Is Elsewhere*) on which Batley played some of his collection of British independent records. Local photographer Kevin Westenberg *did* make up a fake British accent to get commercial assignments from ad agencies that, like much of the local art and media industries, were prejudiced against hiring local people. Westenberg later moved to England for real.

Men in motion

The Blackouts' next recording, the five-song EP *Men in Motion* for Neil Hubbard's Engram Records, dropped the band's last pop-song elements in favor of what was known in New York as "no wave": screaming dissonance within nontraditional song structures. Mike Davidson left the band at this point, balking at the rigors of no-budget touring. Roland Barker's synthesizer was stolen from the Showbox, where his other band Young Scientist rehearsed, by a hardcore punk. Terry Morgan caught the thief at an Ultravox gig a few weeks later, but the synth had long since been sold off. Barker switched to saxophone. Steve Wymore, from San Francisco's Pink Section, filled in on bass until Roland's brother Paul "Ion" Barker came home from Germany to join the group.

Bill Rieflin: "The Blackouts never really became the Blackouts until someone stole our equipment; we lost Mike at the same time. The sound became more bare-bones, more tribal. Its character became more unique, more condensed."

The Blackouts' live shows were even wilder than its recordings. For one gig at Baby O's, a short-lived club near the former Bird downtown, they found themselves sharing a gig and a dressing room with the despised power-pop Heats. Determined to blow away the Heats, they donned loincloths and drenched themselves (and the dressing room) in pig blood and mud. The Heats' screams upon witnessing the sight and smell of the place were perhaps the only authentic heartfelt sound they ever produced. The Blackouts recreated the flesh-and-blood act in early 1982 for a video production by Robert McGinley. It was shot in a bright white-room installation created by artist James Turrell for a new exhibition and performance group, the Center on Contemporary Art (COCA). They also performed with video collages assembled from found footage by performance artist Alan Lande.

The last preserved products of the Blackouts' Seattle era were the compilation track "Young Man" (see next chapter) and the 45 "Exchange of Goods"/"Industry," released by the U.K. label Situation 2.

Karrie Jacobs in the Rocket on the Blackouts' import 45, 1/82: "The bass sounds draw you in and the trebly stuff (sax and vocals) repel: Listen through headphones to catch the interplay between instruments, listen through good speakers to feel the bass—but Werner's voice will make any speak sound like it's a bad speaker. Listening to his singing feels like having sand in your bathing suit, and the notes that Roland Barker pushes out of his saxophone are often brothers to the sounds that come out of Werner's mouth, making for a double treble yelp."

Big fun

Seattle's first music video (not counting Ze Whiz Kidz' tapes and a few experimental video-art productions by artist C.T. Chew) was directed by KZAM DJ Cyndi Bemel for the minor power-pop ditty "Radio Dance" by the Enemy, who'd abandoned their punk posturings in an attempt at Blondie-like stardom. The video was made before MTV went on the air; it featured Suzanne Grant in perky make-up and new wave hair, pretending to drive a convertible before a white studio backdrop

singing the praises of Top 40 pop radio as if it still existed. The Enemy soon took on a new name to fit their new policy, Big Fun, then broke up in 1983 after several latter-day personnel changes. Grant became a children's music teacher (leading a "Peace Choir" on tours to Russia) and a keyboardist in musical-theater productions. Peter Barnes became a record producer and engineer, and recorded with the techno-pop band Blackwood-Laird. Damon Titus continued his career in real estate. Manager Roger Husbands went to Boston, where he found work in an executive-recruiting firm.

Suzanne Grant: "We started doing more pop and left behind the heavy anger. I was seriously getting bruised and body-beaten at shows. I got my face knocked open at the Showbox.... When I quit, I'd never made any money on the band. We had backers at that point who said, 'Do you want to make money or do you want to make music?' That's no question to ask me; I care about music too much. I'd had enough of seeing talented people going around and around and never getting out."

Big Fun

Pink Section

The Refuzors have agreed to musically entertain for a Biker's Bash December 7, 1979 9pm-2am at Kennydale Hall 2424 NE 27 Renton
they made us an offer we couldn't Refuze *signed*

The Blackouts

sued a stream-of-consciousness prose work, *Personal Effects*, through a small Vancouver press.

More street art

With the British influence, striking visuals were always a part of the scene; street postering reached epidemic proportions, especially on Broadway and the "poster wall" on First and Yesler. Poster designers (sometimes band members) became influential in the local graphics world (and, through the *Rocket* art staff, in the New York graphics world). They became the bane of polite society, more than the bands themselves because their work was in full public view. Merchants and politicians routinely decried the practice. Posterers were arrested and jailed. The City Council almost passed an anti-postering law.

Fashion was also a major part of the scene (even the hardcores at the time primped their rainbow mohawks carefully, using plenty of Knox gelatine to make every strand stand up straight). A new crew of local designers tried to turn apparel into an expression of fun. One of the first local showcases for new wave fashion was Judi Stay and Ralph Becker's store Kitchy Koo, across from Roosevelt High. Stay and Becker sold black miniskirts, pink and purple striped tops, glitter make-up, and Crazy Color hair dye. They kept their poodle Kitty tressed in the latest hair colors and styles, including a mohawk (either before or just after Lynda Barry published her "Poodle With A Mohawk" T-shirt). Kitchy Koo mounted fashion shows at the Showbox and other local venues. The store also had America's only punk rock post office, a real U.S. Postal Service contract station where you could make your outgoing mail *really* outgoing with fanciful rubber stamps and colorful envelopes and stickers. The store lasted from 1980 (when Stay was 34) to 1990.

Judi Stay to the *Post-Intelligencer on public reaction in malls to her red-and-blue hair and purple make-up, 4/82: "At Northgate, it's everybody giggling. One time at Penney's, this little girl was real cute, she said, 'Mommy, look at the clown lady.'"*

Ironically, it was the anti-fashion look of the hardcore punks, in part a reaction against new wave primping and in part a necessity of youthful poverty, that became the eventual darling of the New York fashion world. The Ramones had worn leather jackets, dingy T-shirts, black boots and pre-torn jeans since 1975. Hardcore pioneers like Vancouver's DOA had worn flannel shirts since 1979—in a 1987 video covering Bachman-Turner Overdrive's "Takin' Care of Business," the band played a flannel-shirted hockey team (with the song's co-writer Randy Bachman as its coach) overtaking a business-suited team to win an old milk can instead of a Stanley Cup trophy.

Penis oriented rock

Some legendary/infamous parties took place at this time, some fueled by an assortment of drugs.

Patio Table

Student Nurse's Eric Muhs joined Audio Leter (named after Texas conspiracy-theorist Peter Beter's "Audio Letter" mail-order rant tapes), an anti-rock band formed by Rosco Louie co-owner Tracey Rowland and Rally Go's Danielle Elliot. Its line-ups included Sue Ann Harkey of Children of Kellogg, James Husted of Young Scientist, and Jeff McGrath of Fred. Muhs played tape loops and homemade instruments (particle-board guitar, wire book racks with electric violin bows, et al.). Poet-dancer Sharon Gannon became its singer, chanting recitations based on the philosophies of Michael Foucault and Jacques Derrida. Her catch phrases included "Sex Is a Dis-Ease" and "Freedom Is a Psycho-Kinetic Skill."

Elliot and Rowland left Audio Leter when they began Little Bears from Bangkok, with bassist-singer Jim Anderson (the *Rocket* called his voice "Big Bird meets David Byrne") and guitarist Joan Maneri. After the local art zine *Spar* published a glowing tribute to Gannon written by her then-boyfriend, Elliot wrote and Anderson sang a song about a "fictional" art critic called "(I Just Wanna Fuck) Sharon Gannon." Elliot's last band before moving to California in 1984 was Circle 7 (with bassist Sabina Miller and singer-guitarist Randy Pepprock). She later performed several times with Johanna Went in L.A.

Gannon, Harkey, and writer-conceptual artist Deran Morris published two issues of *Patio Table*, a photocopy literary zine. Under the name Patio Table Press, Morris (who later took the name Deran Ludd, after English industrial saboteur Ned Ludd) published two short novels by Jesse Bernstein, *The Wraith* and *Hermione*. Bernstein also is-

Cocaine (powder, freebase and injected) and speed were common, and chemical drugs were starting to become popular. Heroin was only beginning to catch on, initially among the hardcore kids. Several people started on the road to addiction and/or police records.

But *the* drug of choice among the crusters, besides cheap beer and hand-picked mushrooms, was MDA, a variant of the better-known "designer drug" ecstasy (MDMA). Made in home labs from commonly available chemicals, it was easier to hide, transport and distribute than pot, cocaine or opium products, and it wasn't mob-controlled. It was even legal until 1985. It worked by scrambling incoming sensory signals. Its effect of heightened intensity influenced the aesthetic of the scene, among users and non-users alike—an aesthetic of unabashed noise and rage. The drug first showed up at the party houses in 1980-81, and became ubiquitous by 1987.

Nils Bernstein on the MDA experience: "It made you want to be hit. It charged you up mentally, emotionally and physically. It was a whole body high, of love and throbbing gut feelings."

In the midst of this applied chaos were grumblings that the scene was already becoming stale. Nobody was breaking out beyond the local underground; only a few were getting big followings even there. And there were already grumblings that the "alternative" scene was just a different version of the same old rock-star mentality.

NY Rocker *scene report by* **"Lawrence Gersham" (Jim Anderson)**, *11/80: "As Seattle new-music fans continue to withhold support from their own best bands, what was once a strong and thriving scene is now a mess. New bands constantly form and re-form, searching for the elusive chemistry that will attract these recitent listeners.... Seattle listeners suffer from a socialized addiction to POR (Penis-Oriented Rock) and refuse to embrace cockless groups.... There are practically NO women involved in Seattle's new rock. One enjoyable exception is a two women/one-man pop trio called the Fastbacks. Portland's Neo-Boys, an all-woman band, recently played to a near-empty house in Seattle—perhaps another manifestation of the POR complex. Seattle rockers want it bigger, harder, and faster—not smarter.... Local groups aiming for the moon realize that their first stop is anywhere out of Seattle. Others who just want to play continue to chip away at the indifference of their audience."*

Punk had always contained a parody of juvenile delinquency; with a new subgroup who admired the speedcore of L.A.'s Black Flag and Circle Jerks, it began attracting true delinquents. Rampant drunkenness, drug excess, space-trashing, and overall cruster behavior abounded. A few shows got held in the auditorium of St. Joseph's Catholic Church on Capitol Hill, before the punk sinners were ousted from the lord's house. Before long,

people wouldn't rent halls to rock shows because of the disreputable looks, uncouth behavior and material damage.

In retrospect, the hardcore kids' sleaze could be seen as a precursor to more serious waves of youth violence in America. Punk was losing its stance as the righteous opposition to American excess, and was becoming just a more self-destructive version of a consumption-oriented lifestyle. The early punks had insisted on creating their own culture; the newer punks were all too willing to let L.A. tell them how to live.

Commentary by **Mish-L in** Punk Lust: *"A lot of club owners have refused to allow good hardcore to play anymore. The reason given is that hardcore is 'oh god too violent and fucking our places up.' It doesn't help the owners to have sinks torn out at gigs.... If we don't start shaping up, Seattle is going to be stuck with asshole bands such as No Cheese Please and the Pudz."*

The Fastbacks

Rougher than the middle-class punks, and with no Bellevue daddies to bail them out, were a gang of street teens derisively called "donut holes" by the punks, after their chief hangout, the International Donut House next to the Showbox (shut down when its owner was convicted of masterminding a teen burglary ring). These kids, who included some suburban metalheads and some genuine homeless kids, reacted with great hostility at the presence on First and Pike of make-believe delinquents from the U District. This animosity led to at least one mini-riot at a Dead Kennedys Showbox gig, which started when some punks scrawled graffiti with felt markers on a car owned by Donut House metalheads.

The street kids became the subject of the 1983

The Fags

BABY NEVER SCREAMS
9:00 $2.50

STARRING
FAGS AND THE REFUZORS
(Parental Discretion Advised)

Sat. Feb. 28th

Danceland U.S.A. 1st and Pike

A VERY QUEER PROD.

the FAGS

SAT. MAY 30th 9:00
at DANCELAND
1st & Pike
LAST SHOW!

Life magazine piece "Streets of the Lost," by Mary Ellen Mark and Cheryl McCall, and the 1984 film *Streetwise*, by Mark's husband Martin Bell.

Dark glitter, light glitter

Another subgroup was into a gothic, dark sound and image, the pale skin and pale tones of Joy Division and Public Image. Upchuck's newest glam-gothic band, the Fags, played a series of ethereal/improvisational gigs starting in late 1980 in the Belltown Ballroom, the Enemy's practice space in an old restaurant-supply warehouse at 66 Bell St. (The Lincoln Arts Center later hosted bands in another space in the building.)

The Fags' lush decadence attracted an audience of MDA-heads who began to engage in the now-standard punk violence, even though the band didn't play speedcore. The band's gigs got regularly trashed by intolerant hardcores who held an increasingly narrow definition of what was and wasn't real punk rock. The Fags soon got banned from WREX and the Gorilla Room. Fags manager Mark Brewster, needing a venue for his group, rented Danceland USA (a gorgeous old upstairs ballroom-dance studio across from the Showbox) for a weekly series of all-ages gigs, until Brewster tired of having to spend almost all the cover proceeds to fix the repeatedly punk-trashed bathrooms. Brewster also mounted several shows at the United Commercial Travelers Hall north of Seattle Center. The UCT hall became an off-and-on punk site throughout 1980-81, until zealous cops started harassing the patrons and hardcore boys started wrecking things.

The Fags' romanticized outrage was executed by a core group of Dahny Reed, Ben and Barbie Ireland, Paul Solger, and Jane Playtex (Brownson); some gigs also featured ex-Meyce drummer Lee Lumsden. A typical gig might see guitarist Reed dressed like a vampire, lying on his back, scratching his guitar strings with long, day-glo fingernails. One Danceland show saw 20 people lying in a heap in front of the makeshift stage, high on MDA just like the band; Solger got sick during the set and started convulsing with his head against an amp.

The group was also known for a series of exquisitely lurid street posters (Upchuck later told the *Rocket* that because of the posters, "The Fags started getting hassles from religious groups and grandmothers").

Pete Leinonen on the Fags: "They had a good momentum rolling, a forward energy. Ben Ireland's timing was fantastic. They were really pure, good musicians. They played with an energy that's essential. They got in and out of their material a lot more musically than a lot of other bands of the time."

Barbie Ireland on a typical Fags show at Danceland USA: "During one action-packed evening, the rival band, the Fartz (whom Paul later joined), threw rotten vegetables at us, splattering our skin with what felt like weird squishy animals from a late-night, low-budget horror flick; Chuck ate vomit that had been captured in a huge leaf of rotten lettuce—now it consumed his face; I sang "Why?" with a wet vomit rag wrapped around my waist while beer cans whizzed past, just about hitting Ben's face. Luckily for him the MDA had created an effect of slow motion in his awareness, so he had lots of time to move his head away from the line of fire."

Paul Solger and Jane Brownson left in mid-1981 (Jane says "we wanted to play rock, not Las Vegas") and next appeared in the hardcore DT'z with Duff McKagan and Mike Refuzor. Retiring the Fags name, Upchuck began the slightly more beat-oriented Sleeping Movement; that line-up included Reed, Gordon Raphael, the Irelands, Gordon Doucette, and co-singer Pony Maurice. They recorded several tracks, all unreleased.

Jane Brownson: "Duff played in every band he could. He had the drive as well as the talent. There always was the talent in Seattle, but he had the ambition to make a career of it."

Some of the romantic/decadent musicians who worked with Upchuck also dallied in Pro Noia and in Gordon Doucette's next band, Red Masque. The latter included over a dozen members over its three-year life, including KZAM DJ Mike Stein (previously in the Accident and later in two neo-pop harmony bands, the Young Executives and the Holidays), Gordon Raphael, Scott Boggan and Shawn Allen (the latter two later in Room Nine).

A different glam-revival take was offered by Malfunkshun, formed on the affluent suburban Bainbridge Island in 1980 by 16-year-old Andrew Wood (a.k.a. "Landrew the Love Child," a name taken from a *Star Trek* villain). By the time the group started taking the ferry boats in to play Seattle, Wood was assisted by his brother Kevin and neighbor Regan Hagar. They took the influences of the Fags and other early local punks into a different dimension, from gothic to cartoony. Wood wore a silver lame cape, feather boa, painted platform shoes and white make-up; some unsuspecting audience members thought he was a girl and tried to hit on him. Wood described the band in 1986 as "a deranged gypsy hard rock band" influenced by T. Rex, Kiss and Cheap Trick; in contrast to the play-acting Satan worship of metal bands like Black Sabbath, Wood wrote "anti-devil songs" and called his outfit a "333" band instead of 666.

Malfunkshun only had a handful of headlining gigs in its eight-year life, but opened for almost everybody. The band appeared at an April 1982 Showbox "punk fest" with the Fartz, England's Discharge and other bands; Discharge was held up at the border after a Vancouver gig and the show had to be delayed a night; almost nobody showed. Wood also did solo shows (with taped backing) and emceed other bands' gigs.

Tor Midtskog, ex-member of Solger, Sleeping Movement, Red Masque, Pro Noia and Violet Caste: "The difference between what Upchuck was doing and what Andy was doing is that Upchuck and his bands were influenced by the darker side of glam, like the Pretty Things and the Velvet Un-

derground. Andy glorified the kid '70s, the lighter side of glam, the fun/scary bands like Kiss and Alice Cooper that were less dangerous to middle America. The Fags and Sleeping Movement were darker, with more decadence and theatrical excess. Malfunkshun was more fun."*

Waiting for the clampdown

If the winter of 1979-80 saw the new music subculture seemingly on the verge of triumph, 1980-81 was its winter of discontent. First came the election of President Ronald Reagan, the personification of everything bohemians held in contempt: militarism, big business, cultural repression. Then came the assassination of John Lennon, the real father of rock n' roll as it was known to anyone born in the late '50s. Then the mainstream media began to exploit punks as A Menace To Be Stopped, culminating in a hilariously exaggerated scandal segment on KOMO-TV's talk show *PM Northwest*.

KZAM-AM died in February 1981, when its out-of-state owners sent orders to pull the plug on those rock rebels. The station signed off with an evening-long epic show of record-smashing and tearful goodbyes by all the DJs; despite the attention given it in local media and the successful promotions and concerts it sponsored, the Arbitron rating service claimed it had too few listeners to even merit a ranking.

A group of listeners tried to lobby the owners to reconsider by forming a group called Rescue the Rock of the '80s. They gathered 10,000 names on a petition to the station's owners, who held by their decision. KZAM-AM's frequency now hosts an automated country station.

Rescue the Rock of the '80s put on what may have been the greatest of the Showbox's many great shows, starting at 2 p.m. on March 15, 1981. For nine hours a full house rocked to 15 bands, including Sex Therapy, the Spectators, Student Nurse, the Shivers (with John Keister's brother Paul) the Visible Targets, the Pudz, the Enemy, the Cowboys, X-15, and Jonathan Poneman's Rockefellers. The group published five issues of a newsprint zine, *Rescue*.

Daina Darzin in Rescue, 4/15/81: "I have no desire to streak my hair, but I respect the guts it

Below: Epp

FASTBACKS
every day is saturday

Dear Captain Clark:

I hate Mr. Epp & the Calculations! Pure grunge! Pure noise! Pure shit! Everyone I know loves them, I don't know why. They don't even wear chains and mohawks! They all look different, yuk! And they have no sense of humor. In fact, they have no sense. They're all pretentious, older than the Grateful Dead, and love Emerson Lake & Palmer (my mother's fave).

I love Phillip Glass! While my frineds listen to Mr. Epp & the Calculations, I listen to Mr. Glass. His music is repetitious, redundant, and repetitive. Pure art! It's soooooooo intellectual, like me. I love to listen to Phillip Glass over and over and over and over again etc. ad infinitum.

Mark McLaughlin
Mark McLaughlin
Mark McLaughlin
Mark McLaughlin

(Ed. Note) Mark McLaughlin does guitar & vocals in Mr. Epp and the Calculations).

takes to do it. It isn't too hard to be weird in New York, either because they were weird so they moved to New York, or because they grew up in New York and are therefore weird. It's harder to be weird in Seattle: it's more of a commitment. So. Punks. Purposely disgusting behavior and all. What is a more rational response to TV, nukes, and the Moral Majority? And 21-and-unders, if you aren't rebelling, what the fuck is the matter with you?"

Three months later, Rescue the Rock of the '80s rechristened itself as the Association for Alternative Arts and turned its *Rescue* zine into a fashion-oriented tabloid, *Neon Circuit*, that lasted one issue. Stephen Rabow went to work as the national program director for Yesco, a local company that compiled "foreground music" tapes of existing records as mood music for stores and restaurants. He was still there in late 1982 when he found a job for a fellow ex-Evergreener, Bruce Pavitt.

A six-letter word

The first alternative to the *Rocket* was the hard-core-oriented *Desperate Times*, a tabloid pasted from typewriter type and press-on-letter headlines, full of snide remarks about bands the writers loved and snider remarks about bands the writers hated. Ex-*Rescue* volunteers Daina Darzin and Maire Masco and WREX DJ Dennis White ran it from a U District party house, one block south of Thomas Pynchon's last Seattle address. Generally, *Desperate Times* paid more attention to touring acts than to local ones. When it mentioned locals, it loved the Refuzors and hated the Heats. *Desperate Times* published six tabloid issues, before Darzin returned to New York with her new husband, singer of the local hardcore band Joe Despair and the Future. Darzin has since written for *Rolling Stone*, the *L.A. Weekly*, the *Hollywood Reporter* and the *Village Voice*.

I wrote a piece in the first *Desperate Times* inviting readers to nominate the most overrated band in Seattle. The second issue featured the following response:

"I hate Mr. Epp and the Calculations! Pure grunge! Pure noise! Pure shit! Everyone I know loves them, I don't know why. They don't even wear chains and mohawks! They all look different, yuk! And they have no sense of humor. In fact, they have no sense. They're all pretentious, older than the Grateful Dead, and love Emerson Lake & Palmer (my mother's fave). While my friends listen to Mr. Epp and the Calculations, I listen to Mr. Glass. His music is repetitious, redundant, and repetitive. Pure art! It's sooooo intellectual, like me. I love to listen to Philip Glass over and over and over and over again etc.

Mark McLaughlin
Mark McLaughlin
Mark McLaughlin
(Ed. note: Mark McLaughlin does guitar & vocals in Mr. Epp and the Calculations.)

Mr. Epp and the Calculations was originally a hoax by McLaughlin and Jeff Smith, students at the suburban Bellevue Christian High School who put up posters and graffiti announcing fake gigs by their "band" (named after a math teacher). Smith called it "like a Dungeons and Dragons-y thing; we just pretended it was real." It became real one night when Dennis White and Maire Masco, who'd started booking shows, were walking toward the Gorilla Room saw McLaughlin and Smith putting up one of their posters.

Maire Masco: "We'd seen their posters before. We really liked their sense of humor. When we saw them putting posters up we chased them down. At first they thought we were going to attack them. We finally convinced them that we were real promoters and we wanted to put them in a show. We found out that they didn't play instruments. For their 'practices' they'd been getting together in Jeff's basement, banging on pots and pans. They finally agreed to open up at a show."

Mark later told *Goldmine* that his first response was, "Gee, I guess we'd better get some instruments."

After their first real gig was officially canceled, according to *Desperate Times*, "because one of the band members was grounded by his parents," the group managed to stumble onstage as part of a Washington Hall rental show. By then, Smith was known as Jo Smitty and McLaughlin was known as Mark Arm.

Arm's letter is the earliest known reference to a Seattle band as "grunge." Bruce Pavitt claimed to have popularized (but not to have invented) the word as a musical label in a 1987 Sub Pop promo blurb for Arm's later band Green River as "ultra loose grunge that destroyed the morals of a generation." A 1988 Sub Pop PR release described Arm's current band Mudhoney as "ultra sludge, grungy glacial, heavy spacial, dirty punk." English journalist Everett True and Cat Butt/Girl Trouble singer David Duet also claimed coinage of the term; though Lester Bangs and other writers had used it in the '70s, to describe everything from Kiss to Neil Young to California punkers Flipper.

Fastbacks forever

The Fastbacks, formed at the start of 1980, combined alternately-keyed female harmonies with punchy-anthemic guitar chords. Their lineup included singer-bassist Kim Warnick, singer-guitarist Lulu Gargiulo, and guitarist-songwriter-producer Kurt Bloch (previously in the Cheaters). Kurt was the band's first drummer (out of 13 so far, counting a couple of guys with two tenures each). The second was Duff McKagan, who by now (age 16) had also served in the Vains (led by Chris Crass) and the Living (with Greg Gilmore). McKagan briefly left town with Chris Harvey's hardcore Silly Killers when they moved to San Francisco; he came back and played guitar in Cannibal and drums in the last version of the Fartz.

Bloch's No Threes Records produced 45s for the Fastbacks, the Accident ("Kill the Bee Gees"), the Cheaters, Vains and Silly Killers. Vains singer Chris Crass (Utting) was later in Little Bears from Bangkok, the local hardcore No Compromise, and the L.A.-based Muffs; he's now back in town drumming with the Rockinghams. Kurt's brother Al Bloch played guitar with the Cheaters, Weenus, the Deans (with Utting and Pam Lillig), the power-pop Bombardiers, and LA's Concrete Blonde; he's now in the L.A. band Wool, with the brothers Franz and Pete Stahl (they used to be in the Washington, D.C. band Scream with singer John Corabi, who later joined Nikki Sixx in Motley Crue, and drummer Dave Grohl, who we'll meet in chapter 11).

The Fastbacks stayed together through times thin and thinner—a year could go between shows, they never had a permanent drummer, Gargiulo took a couple of hiatuses to concentrate on a film-making career, and Bloch wrote far more material than they could release. They got out the 45 "It's Your Birthday" and the EPs …*Play Five of Their Favorites* (1982; featuring the anti-Reagan anthem "In America") and *Every Day Is Saturday* (1984) on No Threes. The DeDbeet label put out a three-song 45 (mostly recorded in 1983, released in 1985). The group teamed up with PopLlama for the LP …*And His Orchestra* (recorded in 1985-86, released in 1987), which became a darling of the U.K. music press and spawned the British single "Wrong Wrong Wrong." They returned to self-releasing for the tape *Bike Toy Clock Gift* (reissued by Lucky Records in 1994), released the album *Very, Very Powerful Motor* (PopLlama, 1990), went with John Matheis's Steve Priest Fan Club label (named for the Sweet's bass player) for the EP *In the Summer* and a split single with Gas Huffer (both in 1990), then moved to Sub Pop for the double 45 *The Answer Is You* (1991), the old-stuff collection *The Question Is No* (1992, with art direction by Bloch) and the albums *Zucker* (1993) and *Answer the Phone Dunny* (1994). The latter included the band's first pop epic, the six-minute anthem "Meet the Author." They've also been in compilations on Engram, K, Green Monkey, PopLlama, and Sub Pop. While they still have other jobs (Warnick as a Sub Pop office slave, Gargiulo as a cinematographer, Bloch as a Young Fresh Fellow and producer), they've endured. With the final breakups of Red Dress in 1990 and Fred in 1991, the Fastbacks became the longest-running punk band still based in Seattle.

Kurt Bloch *in a fax to Sub Pop, 3/93: "I was just looking at* The Question Is No *Japanese CD (licensed to Sony) and thinking…. Nowhere among our timeline could I have ever imagined that these strange recordings would be released and scrutinized in such a worldly fashion…or that my countless hours in front of (behind?) a drafting table with a Sharpie, scissors and some crazy rubber stamps would be issued by one of the biggest conglomerates in a country as awesome*

as JAPAN. Or music we made 10 years ago would be desirable today. WOW…. I wrote those songs. People still like them. How can I complain about anything?"

The Fastbacks played their first gig in March 1980 during a rental-hall show at a community center in the posh lakeside Laurelhurst neighborhood; it was also the debuts of the Vains and Psychopop. The latter group became Popdefect, which shared the Fastbacks' exploration of the lighter side of cynicism. Charlie Hutchinson, Alan Anderson and Nick Scott played straightforward, happy-go-lucky pop-punk tunes (including the self-released 45 "Rococo Crispies") in Seattle until 1984, when Anderson entered USC film school and the rest of the

DESPERATE TIMES

$.25
JULY 8
VOL.1 NO.1

ADOLESCENTS
CLASSIX NOUVEAUX
DTZ
EQUATORS
EXPLOITED
FAGS
FARTZ
HOLLY & THE ITALIANS
MAGAZINE
MAGGOT BRAINS
PLASMATICS
PSYCHEDELIC FURS
RAPID-I
RATS
RED DRESS
REJECTORS
SHATTERBOX
URBAN VERBS
VAPORS
VISIBLE TARGETS

VANCOUVER REPORT • HARDCORE NORTHWEST

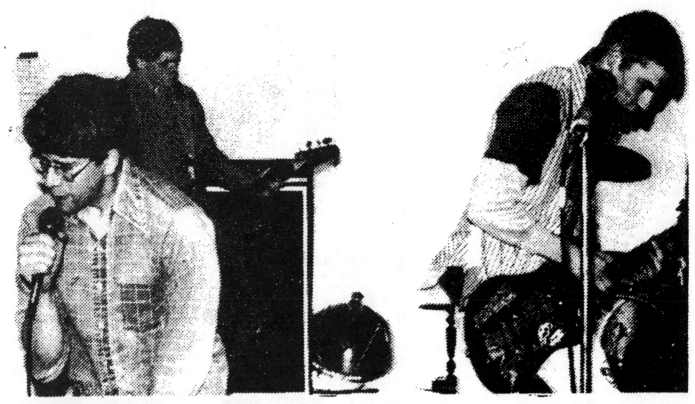

Mr. Epp and the Calculations

band followed. They still launch months-long van tours out of L.A., shown in the 1993 video documentary *Live With This*. They now record for the Flipside label, and contributed a track for the *Beverly Hills 90210* "tribute" CD *I Hate Brenda*.

Verna Doherty in Desperate Times, *7/81:* "Popdefect satisfied my need for something wonderfully tight and fast. They were more fun than your average pissed-off band and easy to dance to. They were energetic, the kind of band that gets you 'up.' "

The birth of the dirge

Amidst all this were a few bands, including the Melvins and the U-Men, who (inspired partly by Flipper and the Cramps) experimented with slowing hardcore down to a loud drone. At the time, it was seen within the community as another variation on the L.A. surf-punk noise, not as a harbinger of the future.

The Melvins formed in Montesano, a lumber town near Aberdeen. They started by playing a lot of basement/backyard gigs attended by friends. Guitarist-singer Buzz Osborne (a.k.a. King Buzzo), bassist Matt Lukin and original drummer Mike Dillard (replaced by Dale Crover) played a lot of open practices and impromptu outdoor shows in their hometown, including one in back of the Aberdeen Thriftway supermarket where Osborne worked. They began as just another teen metal cover band (named after a hated co-worker of Osborne's), but soon got the punk religion thanks to their exposure to the record collection of Aberdeen prodigal son

Kurdt Vanderhoof, and became a punk cover band performing heated-up recreations of Who and Hendrix tunes. By 1983 they'd created their own sets of distortion-full originals. One of their first Seattle gigs was a Metropolis-sponsored show at the Mountaineers Club in 1984, opening (with the U-Men) for Minneapolis's Minutemen. Shortly after that they switched from one of Washington's fastest bands into its slowest, performing noise dirges that couldn't be danced to, only viscerally experienced. They gigged for nearly five years before setting foot in a recording studio (see chapter 9).

The U-Men were named after a Pere Ubu bootleg LP, but had little in common with Pere Ubu's joyous dissonance. Instead, they were slow, harsh and (in the early days) clumsy players. They invoked a Dionysian orgy of mutual aggression and abandon that no cartoon-devil metal band could approach. They were also extremely loud, playing tiny rental halls with the PA at near-arena levels.

The U-Men's first entourage included a gang of leather-jacketed teen alcoholics and druggies who hung out at a U District convenience store where it was easy to score underage beer. Renton High School grad John Bigley (previously in the hardcore Social Deviates with Steve and Loud Fart), Jim Tillman (whose mother Heather managed a Pioneer Square jazz club), Tom Price (previously in Psychopop, the early Popdefect), and Charlie Ryan (previously in Upchuck's Wad Squad) partly cleaned up their act over the years and gathered a slightly more respectable clientele. By their first recordings in 1984 they'd augmented their frontal assault with mixed-up time signatures, vocal and studio effects, and garage rock.

The first lineup also included bassist Robin Buchan, a 16-year-old waitress at Steve's Broiler downtown; another Steve's waitress, Susan Catherine, used her experiences there for a series of cartoon books, *Overheard at America's Lunch Counters.* Catherine and Buchan also worked as strippers to support their artistic work.

The first U-Men gig was at the UCT Hall, with the Fastbacks and a band led by Johnny Vinyl, Jeff Larson and ex-Cheater Dave Shumate that had a logo of a graph line inside two diamonds instead of a written name and a guttural shriek instead of a spoken name. Most club listings referred to that band as Aieee!, an approximate transliteration of the shriek. They played off and on until 1992.

Lust for punk

Perhaps the most beautifully written punk zine ever was Wilum Hopfrog Pugmire's *Punk Lust.* Pugmire (alternately spelled Pugmyr) put out 11 issues from 1981 to 1983, supported by his dishwashing job at the Bon Marché department store. Pugmire, a self-described "hardcore punk horror fag," was a gentle balding man in his late twenties who lived with his grandmother in the south end and loved hardcore punk for its celebration of darkness. He'd worked as a teenager at Jones Fantastic Museum, an amusement arcade in Seattle Center; he wore a Dracula suit and frightened the tots who came to play coin-operated games (including one where you had to maneuver a "poison pill" into Hitler's mouth). Pugmire's last regular

Punk Lust (he made one comeback issue in 1985 and resumed publication in 1993) commented on the de-evolution of punk with a Lee Ellingson cartoon of fascist skinheads pummeling longhairs in the street ("Last week I saw Van Halen at the Kingdome! This week I shaved my hair and bought this funny T-shirt! Now I'm a Punk Rocker! Ha-ha-ha! Kill! Kill!"). Pugmire has also contributed short stories to horror anthologies and collaborated with cartoonist "Triangle Slash."

From the last regular issue of **Punk Lust***, 1983: "When I saw the Accused at the fabulous club, the Metropolis, I had a reminder of why, two years ago, I became a punk. Great Cthulhu, this band is so good, so tight, and they have such a great attitude. That is the magic word: ATTITUDE.... When John, the (original) singer of the Accused, took the stage, we knew at once that he was one of us. It wasn't Him the Singer and Us the Audience. We were united in hardcore. He paced the stage like a wild animal, made jokes, really got into his music, and made us feel good.... Thanx to old bands like Fartz and RPA, and new bands like the Accused and Extreme Hate, I became a punk and found a whole new lifestyle. Punk gave me the guts to be myself, and for this I shall be eternally grateful."*

Riding a new(er) wave

With KZAM gone, a few specialty shows on KRAB and the UW classroom station KCMU constituted new music on Seattle radio. That changed in July 1981, when UW budget cuts threatened to

AIEEE...

Wilum Pugmire

The Vains

close KCMU. A dozen student DJs started a Committee to Save KCMU, petitioned the administration to let them run the station, and got a $22,000 grant from the student government. Needing a unique format that would attract listener donations, they junked the soft rock and adopted the slogan "Riding a New Wave." The station went silent for 10 days in August before the new regime took over. The new crew organized fundraisers, recruited volunteers, and contacted record labels (who didn't all have college-radio marketing departments yet). Seven months after Rescue the Rock of the '80s pleaded for somebody to "Save the Wave," some kids went ahead and saved it themselves.

Mike Fuller, *first KCMU music director, recalling early fund drives in* Wire, *8/91: "Our first record giveaway consisted of me going down the hall to the KCMU archives (the junk sister station KUOW didn't want) and digging through treasures like a history of the Royal Canadian Mounted Police marching band and a Social Security Administration-sponsored radio series of old show tunes hosted by Carol Channing (both of which I'm proud to say I still own), until I found enough stuff like David Bowie and Garland Jeffreys 45s to justify a giveaway. Not having any money for postage meant winners had to come to the station for their prize. As a result, somewhere in the studios KCMU probably still has four out of the five packets we tried to give away."*

Meanwhile, in Greenerville...

Live alternative music began in downtown Olympia in December 1980, when local jazz buff Gary Alan May booked shows at a downtown bar called the Gnu Deli. It featured several bands that had formed among the KAOS community, including Bruce Pavitt's Tiny Holes and John Foster's Pop Philosophers. KAOS DJ Calvin Johnson (one of the few Evergreen students *from* Olympia; his father had been press secretary to early-'60s Gov. Albert Rosellini) was supposed to have played there with a band called the Cool Rays, but declined after the Liquor Board said the place couldn't let under-21s in.

Ex-Olympians Jim Anderson and George Romansic formed the Seattle-based Beakers with Mark H. Smith and Francesca "Frankie" Sundsten. They played a passionately cold art-funk sound with sax, inspired by England's Gang of Four. They were led by the ambitious Smith, who used his middle initial to distinguish himself from the Fall's Mark E. Smith, whom he was sure he'd become as famous as. The Beakers broke up after releasing one 45 on the Mr. Brown label (named for James). That label was co-run by Toni Holm, John Foster, KAOS DJ Dave Rauh, and Steve Fisk, a 27-year-old music student and KAOS engineer from Lakewood, California who'd come to Evergreen from Central Washington University in Ellensburg.

Jim Anderson: "I was acccepted into Evergreen in 1976. I went down to look for housing. On the bus from downtown to the campus I saw this tall white guy with a big Afro, talking reverently into his hands. He was barefoot on a wet day. I decided I couldn't go to any college where this guy went. He turned out to be Steve Fisk.

"George Romansic and I were both on KRAB at the time. I had a jazz show; he was playing alternative music, he had connections with John Foster and got into all these bands really early. George got me hooked up with Mark, who was one of the most confident people I've ever met, a real self-promoter. Mark broke up the Beakers because he felt hamstrung. He thought Frankie and I were too crude. He had a hard time giving up on his dream of becoming big."

Sundsten went into Children of Kellogg, Anderson into Little Bears from Bangkok (and more recently the Gardenias, with May), and Romansic into Danger Bunny. Smith's next band was the even more Go4-sounding Three Swimmers (a four-piece band with Romansic, Fred Chalenor and Colin MacDonnel), whose left-leaning lyrics ("The Worker Works to Live," "Safety for China") led from an art-school fascination with British socialist theory, not from any fondness for the American working class. Smith spoke in interviews of wanting to record LPs in Montreaux for British labels and to kiss hick-town Seattle goodbye forever. The Swimmers got as far as to tour in California with Gang of Four. After recording two 12-inch EPs, Smith split town to try to break into filmmaking in L.A.. Chalenor went on to join Craig Flory and Myles Boisen in Face Ditch, described by Eric Muhs as "groovy fast cool rock/jazz instrumental improvisations."

P.S. O'Neill: "Supershaft, my duo with Jim Anderson before adding double drummers, played at a show at Rosco Louie with Face Ditch. Right after our set, Calvin Johnson, who was about 17 or 18 at the time, showed up outside and asked me if he could play. I'd known him in Olympia because he was the youngest DJ in history at KAOS. I said yes, and he got up in front of the mike and started singing in his low, frog voice. It wasn't long before the guys in Face Ditch got pissed and turned the mike off, told him to hit the bricks, 'cause they were next and wanted to protect their playing time, and Calvin started having a slight breakdown and Jim and I took him outside to calm him down. I think it was his first performance in Seattle, and he'd gotten fired and didn't know how to act."

Children of Kellogg (named after a PBS documentary about birth defects in the silver-mining town of Kellogg, Idaho) were as unpretentious as Three Swimmers were pretentious. They included Sundsten, Sue Ann Harkey from Audio Leter, and Virginia Inn bartender Annie Mulcahey. Nobody at

The Beakers

3 Swimmers

Little Bears from Bangkok

Mr. brown records

the time thought they were freaks for being Seattle's first all-female band to perform at advertised gigs. They were neither sex objects nor anti-sex objects, just pals who got together to play some cute dissonant anti-pop tunes.

Mr. Brown Records also put out 45s by MacDonnel's Macs Band, Westside Lockers, Fisk and Jim Stonecipher's band Anonymous (also known as Conch), the EP *Life Elsewhere* (with Fisk's band Customer Service, the Beakers and Foster) and the compilation tape *Absolute Elsewhere* (the latter two named after Romansic and Norman Batley's KRAB show).

Westside Lockers, led by P.S. O'Neill and Judy Schneps, were first called Larry and the Mondellos, until four other Mondellos bands were discovered in different towns; their A-side was the Lene Lovich-like "(I Want to Live and Die In) Fuscia Rayon." O'Neill later directed videos, including "Ever So Clear" by Houston rappers the Geto Boys and a clip for one of Fisk's electronic-pop projects, Pigeonhed. Schneps served time in the hippie-R&B band Annie Rose and the Thrillers, then went new-wavy again with O'Neill in Tse Tse Force (with ex-Rally Go bassist Heidi Sutter, who died of a heroin overdose in 1985) and the Chains of Hell Orchestra (whose drummer, Peter Blecha, became a historian of the 1960s Northwest Rock). Both latter bands recorded EPs on O'Neill's label, Dr. Stimson.

Anonymous, described by O'Neill as "a bitches brew of Genesis and Frank Zappa," released the scathing no-wave noise 45 "Corporate Food," that ended with the sound of a hamburger frying in a pan. It was reissued on the Jello Biafra-curated compilation *Let Them Eat Jellybeans.* Some Anonymous gigs (but not the record) featured drummer Philip Hertz, who played in Pavitt's Tiny

Holes, Foster's Pop Philosophers and other Oly bands before moving to Chicago and starting Cargo Records (a sometime distributor for Calvin Johnson's K label).

The B-side of the Anonymous 45, "Snake Attack," was one of Fisk's first solo tracks, built around electronic effects, tape loops and sampled sounds. He persued this further on *Kiss the Day Goodbye*, the first of his solo albums. He began assembling tracks for *Goodbye* in Olympia in 1982, then finished it after he left to join Pell Mell, a Portland-born electronic band that had moved to San Francisco (it signed to a major label at the end of 1994). While there, Fisk helped out on early Negativland tracks.

If the early Olympia bands had one primary inspiration, besides Gang of Four, it was Rough Trade Records, the most widely distributed British independent in the U.S. and the most-played label on the KAOS rock shows. The Olympians, particularly Calvin Johnson, admired the way many of Rough Trade's bands (the Raincoats, the Slits, Delta 5, Young Marble Giants) abandoned punk's vestiges of hard-rock machismo in favor of homespun charm and human-scale emotions. A few of the Oly scenesters were reportedly upset when Rough Trade released a distinctly bad 45 by the Smashchords, a studio-only hardcore slop band from Edmonds. Gary Alan May recalls that "the Smashchords record was like Rough Trade's attempt to prove that American bands weren't any good." Rough Trade later released a couple albums by Johnson's band Beat Happening; after Rough Trade folded, Stuart Moxham of Young Marble Giants, co-produced Beat Happening's album *You Turn Me On.* Johnson's pal Kurt Cobain was later involved in getting the Raincoats' old Rough Trade records reissued.

The Gorilla dies

The Liquor Board shut down the Gorilla Room in September 1981 over repeated violations. Underage musicians were getting in to play, which was legal under certain restrictions, but they were getting their underage friends and siblings in, which wasn't legal. Two of the under-21s caught on the premises were Duff McKagan and DOA drummer Chuck Biscuits (later in Black Flag, the Circle Jerks, and Danzig). The great seedy punk living room was gone. Gorilla Room manager Bryan Runnings went on to run sound boards for several bands and sound companies, including one co-owned by future RKCNDY partner Thomas O'Neil.

Rental-hall all-ages shows continued. A few shows took place at Washington Hall;, which was available less often due to the increasing schedule of its main occupant, the performance-art booking group On the Boards;. Other sites included the Mountaineers; Building (the renamed Norway Center;) and a couple of old ethnic meeting sites on Capitol Hill;, the Polish Hall; and Serbian Hall;.

The Laurelhurst Community Center was booked for an all-ages show with the Silly Killers, the U-Men, and Johnny Vinyl's band. Between sets, 100 UW fratboys showed up to kick punk butt. The riot led police to close the show, ending the Laurelhurst center as a venue.

Dawn Anderson in Backlash, 11/88: *"There were two types of rock n' roll in 1981: New Wave and Rawk. New wave was thought to encompass punk; rawk was thought to encompass heavy metal. I realize how difficult this is to believe, but I swear it's true—heavy metal and punk were thought to have nothing to do with each other at all."*

Nils Bernstein: "There used to be all these fights and animosities between the punks and the rockers. These days the punks are the rockers. Everyone's complaint now is that the dirtheads from the suburbs have taken over. But that's exactly what it was like in 1986."

With the end of the Gorilla Room, the Bahamas, and (in February 1982) WREX, the Golden Crown and Astor Park became the leading "new music" rooms by default. The original-material bands that had begun to infiltrate mainstream venues and radio stations found themselves shut out again, as oldies and other predictable formats regained their stranglehold.

John Keister in the Rocket, 8/83: *"The established clubs began to tighten their playlists again. Local music was eliminated from the airwaves and the rock stations tried formats of either mixing 15-year-old music with a small selection of commercial hard rock bands or, claiming that rock radio had 'grown up,' some stations began pumping out so-called adult oriented pablum at an unheard of rate. The repressive retrenchment of all this has-been crap went on as if the new music scene was some momentary aberration. And at the low point it started to look that way."*

Jodi Larusson, ex-tour manager: *"Seattle had a great scene in the old days, but not that many great bands. I liked Mr. Epp a lot, but most of the time the best shows I saw in Seattle were by touring bands. We had nobody like X, nobody like Fear. Gradually that changed."*

Plenty of gigs took place in unadvertised clubs and private party spaces, some known by the Prohibition-era term "speakeasy." One of these was located on the main floor of the Strand Hotel, an old workingman's dive on First Avenue (the space is now Casa-U-Betcha, a yuppie restaurant and disco), where promoter Bob Jenkins ran shows with Audio Leter and Hell's Smells for $3 (cash or food stamps accepted).

Meanwhile, in timber country…

In Aberdeen, a lonely 14-year-old whose uncle had just given him a guitar for his birthday had been reading in *Rolling Stone* and *Creem* about the international punk revolution. But young Kurt Cobain still hadn't had the chance to hear much of

the stuff. He'd spent his first seven years absorbing the Beatles, then had gotten into the standard '70s metal universe. There hadn't been a national punk show in his town since the Ramones' fiasco in 1977, when he was 10. The recordings on hundreds of turntables in Seattle's U District weren't sold in Aberdeen's chain stores. His only exposures to the new music came from the occasional Blondie or B-52's appearances on *Saturday Night Live.*

Finally, the local public library saw fit to add the Clash's *Sandinista* triple LP to its record collection. Cobain checked it out, only to find six sides of fake reggae. Cobain went back to the same metal gods all the other local kids were listening to, until he was briefly transferred into Matt Lukin's high school and entered the Melvins' entourage. He later said that he signed with a major label, despite his affinity towards the indie-rock scene, because he wanted his music heard in towns like Aberdeen.

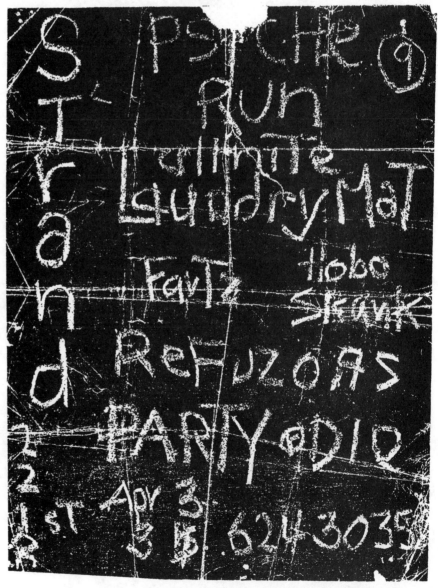

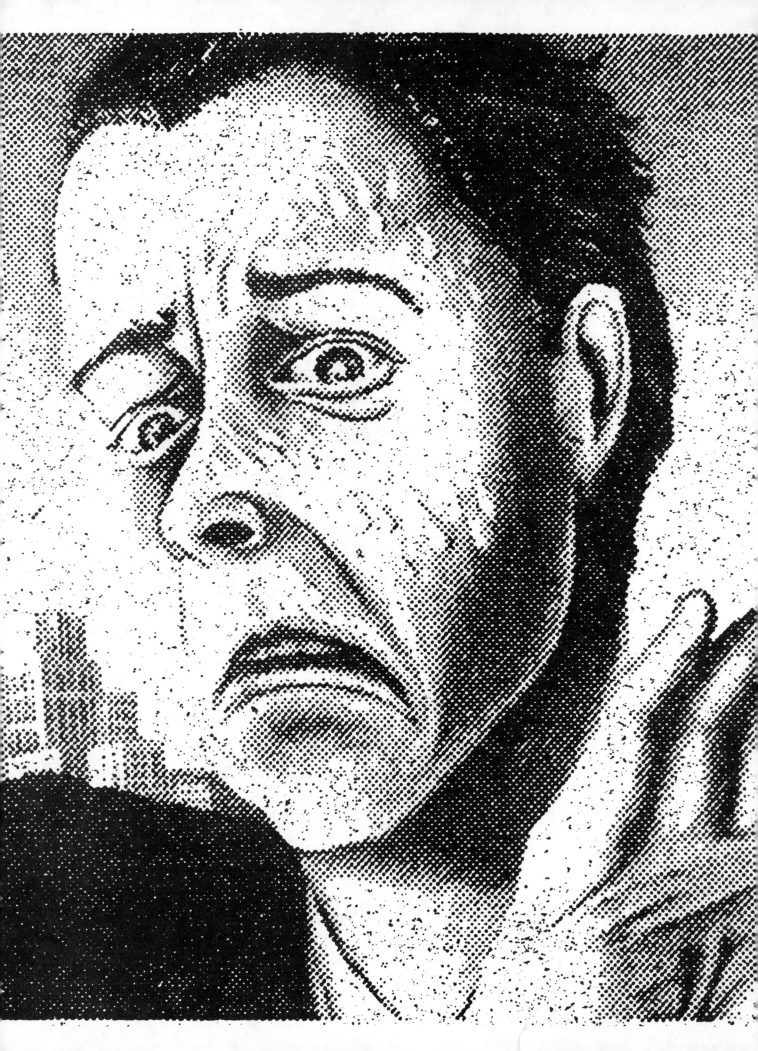

CHAPTER EIGHT:
THE SEATTLE SYNDROME (1982-1984)

The Seattle Syndrome Volume One was the first defiitive document of the Seattle new-music scene. It came out on the Engram label at the end of 1981, produced by Neil Hubbard and Homer Spence, bankrolled by Spence's pal Danny Eskenazi, and recorded mostly by Jack Weaver at Triangle Studios in late 1980 and early 1981. It was a souvenir of a time that was already moving on (eight of its 15 bands had broken up by the time it came out).

The "Syndrome" of the title, according to Hubbard, was that a Seattle band could produce stunning renditions of highly original tunes, to little or no support. You could do anything here, good or bad, and nobody would care.

The LP's 15 cuts included the pop-hit-that-should-have-been "(I Wanna Be) Vaporized" by Kelly Mitchell's X-15 (who changed their name to Life in General after another X-15 was located), the killer Blackouts track "Young Man," ambient electronics by Eskenazi's K7SS (with Roland Barker and James Husted; named after Eskenazi's ham-radio call letters), thrashcore by the Fartz and Refuzors, a peppy Jim Basnight cut, Rob Morgan's Pudz with the killer pop ditty "Take Me To Your Leader" (also released as a 45, backed with a hilarious cover of "Take A Letter Maria"), the Macs Band, Audio Leter side project Body Falling Downstairs (named after a track on a sound-effects record, which *wasn't* used in their song), and a rockabilly bar band called the 88s (previously the Magnetics, with ex-Moberlys bassist Steve Grindle and the same go-go dancers who also worked with the Frazz; the band went to L.A., added a female singer and made an LP for a European label).

Life in General, the renamed X-15, released a self-titled EP in 1982 with "Vaporized" and other tracks that combined new wave dance beats with intense words and serious attitudes. Mike Davidson took over the bass spot after the EP's release, replacing Kenny Wooding who replaced first bassist Tim Loller. Cyndi Bemel directed a "Vaporized" video, with stock footage of politicians and wars culminating in a mushroom-cloud shot superimposed over the Seattle skyline. LiG played until 1987, a year after their last 45 came out, breaking up after they were booked into that fall's Bumbershoot festival; Mitchell kept the gig with a pick-up band. Guitarist Eric Alton now has a new band, Planet Gunn.

Kelly Mitchell on Life in General's early days to the zine Subcharge, 2/85: *"The scene was more tightly knit, everybody knew each other; there weren't that many people that would show up at shows.... There might be like 500 people tops that would come to shows and you pretty much knew everybody."*

Changing economics

The local economy was changing. The post-Vietnam military slump finally hit Boeing in the early '80s (before Reagan's military boom and airline deregulation led to another temporary up cycle). Microsoft, founded in 1975 by local rich kid Bill Gates, bought an existing disk operating system and sold a revised version, MS-DOS, for the new IBM PC. Microsoft became a Fortune 500 company within five years and eventually employed over 8,000 people (including some 1,000 stock-plan millionaires) in a labyrinthine office park deep in the Eastside suburbs. Local clothing companies (Generra, Unionbay, Shah Safari/International News) filled the malls of America with big, bright, Asian-made jeans and sweats; their formula of brash design, costly advertising and cheap overseas labor also turned an Oregon shoe company, Nike, into a global institution.

The new Reagan Administration pushed through the biggest corporate tax cut in history. One tax change, however, adversely affected the music business. Record companies could no longer apply their write-offs on money-losing releases against profits on successful ones. The major labels closed many regional offices (including the CBS and Arista offices in Seattle) and fired hundreds of employees. All of the mid-level national labels like Motown and Chrysalis got sold to or affiliated with the majors, or folded. Most of the regional one-stop distributors that serviced these mid-level labels also folded; leaving a clear demarcation between the six majors and the remaining independents, who now had access only to specialty record stores and the more progressive chains like Tower. Low-selling acts were dropped, and few new acts were signed.

Among the casualties was one of the Northwest's first major-label acts since Heart, which began as a Portland hippie R&B band called Seafood Mama. They were signed by ex-Moberlys manager

Mike Davidson

Blackouts leave town

Life In General

NO CHEESE PLEASE!

Jay Isaac and promptly shipped off to L.A., where groomers replaced several band members, imposed a new commercial sound on the revamped group, gave it the name Quarterflash, pushed one hit through the industry's network of freelance promoters, and dropped it when its second record flopped.

The power pop bands' backers quickly faded from the scene; the bands themselves faded away a bit more slowly. When the Heats fizzled out in 1983, singer Steve Pearson formed the bar-band Rangehoods with ex-Red Dress member Billy Shaw; their career height came when Miller Beer signed them as one of its sponsored bands in 1986. They recorded the EP *Rough Town* in 1985 and the LP *Long Way Home* in 1990. The Cowboys gigged until 1986, three years after the Heats and No Cheese Please closed up shop. No Cheese Please singer Steve Aliment joined San Francisco's Yanks, then returned to join Pearson in the Rangehoods. Cowboys singer Ian Fisher now paints houses for a living.

Steve Pearson to the Post-Intelligencer *on the Heats' 1983 breakup, 1/94: "We were having a meeting to decide what we were going to do in the next few months, and Don Short, who was the other guitarist and songwriter in the band, said, 'I'm bailing, it's over.' After all these years I don't have the slightest idea what bugged him. It was an inauspicious ending for a fairly auspicious band."*

Moving Parts gathered record-biz attention and made a series of demo deals with CBS. The band ended up wasting three years in contract negotiations and attorneys' fees when, on the verge of finally signing, CBS Records was sold to Sony, all the executives the band had dealt with were fired, and

the new guys expressed no interest in them. Co-founder John Irwin now does PR for bands.

The Eagles flies again

The decline of the Showbox highlighted Seattle's disadvantage in attracting low- and mid-budget touring acts. We were 17 driving hours from San Francisco and 33 from Minneapolis. If a band couldn't land a reasonably-priced space in Seattle, it often would bypass Portland and Vancouver, or vice versa.

Because mid-level touring bands needed Seattle stops to make Vancouver stops feasible, Vancouver's Perryscope Productions reopened the Eagles Auditorium. The hippie rock palace remained an all-ages space; Perryscope was succeeded in March 1982 by Art Bernstein and Jean Baptise, who named it the Eagles Hippodrome. Acts that played there from October 1981 to June 1983 included Siouxsie and the Banshees (Sleeping Movement opened), the Ramones, DOA, Simple Minds, Lene Lovich, and the Psychedelic Furs. An all-ages disco with occasional bands, the Eagles Nest, was in the basement.

Siouxsie Sioux to a slam-dancing audience at the Eagles: "Don't you know all that shit has been over for two years now? I'm very disappointed in you."*

Steve Pritchard promoted an Iggy Pop show at the Eagles. The singer invited fans to climb up the speaker stacks; the speakers toppled and injured several fans. As part of the legal settlement, Pop was ordered to give the victims a portion of his proceeds from any future shows he gave in Washington. The single biggest influence on Seattle punk didn't come back until March 1994.

The final Eagles show starred the Damned; guitarist Captain Sensible screwed up a riff at one point and shouted toward the ceiling, "Sorry, Jimi." The room closed when the building was incorporated into the new Washington State Convention Center next door; plans are now afoot to reopen the auditorium for stage plays.

The Eagles (and the briefly-revived Showbox) closed around the time the Moore Theatre dropped movies and started booking a few rock shows, in between booking regional beauty pageants and bodybuilding contests.

Splitting

The Blackouts held their last show as a local band at the Odd Fellows Hall in August 1982 (the U-Men opened). They moved to Boston, looking for a scene that would properly appreciate them; Erich Werner was particularly convinced that the band would find its proper audience once it hit the east coast. There, they recorded the WaxTrax Records EP *Lost Souls' Club* plus a few unreleased tracks with producer Al Jourgenson at the Cars' studio. Managed by Patty Marsh (Jourgenson's future wife), they continued to make outrageous stage shows, including a few shows in New York and

Philadelphia. At one gig, they all dressed as Hassidic Jews except for Roland Barker, who dressed as a Nazi brownshirt. From there, the Blackouts moved to San Francisco in 1984; following Bill Rieflin's future wife, ex-Children of Kellogg member Frankie Sundsten, who was going to art school there.

Bill Rieflin: *"The idea was that we'd play New York but have a lower cost of living in Boston. It was just horrible. We only played New York two or three times. We were all in a tiny apartment with 50,000 times more cockroaches than us. I was making $60 a week selling muffins in Harvard Square with some teenagers. We probably wrote a total of five songs the whole time we were there."*

Rocket graphic designers (including Helene Silverman, who married punk cartoonist Gary Panter) landed more successful careers in New York than ex-Seattle musicians, many of whom succumbed to drugs, poverty or burnout.

Fuck art, let's Warn

Shortly after the Fartz' *World Full of Hate* LP came out (and drowned in the domestic market when Faulty Products folded), bassist Steve Fart (Hofmann) dropped out from a California tour to stay beside his pregnant wife, former Fags member Jane Brownson. Blaine Cook, Duff McKagan, and Paul Solger chose to make Steve's vacation permanent. They also abandoned the Fartz name, with its reputation for fan violence, becoming 10 Minute Warning.

Steve Fart to the *Rocket*, 7/82: *"Violence is just a phase of people new to the scene who think it's cool. We're working against that. You've got your macho fucking idiots. My girlfriend had three of her ribs broken by one of them at one of our shows. Macho is our worst enemy."*

The revamped group concentrated on what McKagan, in the zine *Backfire*, called "tunes for groovin', not tunes for anti-this or anti-that"; abandoning the anarchist politics, all-black clothes and what McKagan called "raw smash, stage dive and shit." Paul Solger recalls the band as "melding punk rock with more psychedelic '60s stuff; not so much heavy metal yet, except for early Black Sabbath."

Cook, the last original Fartz member, soon quit. He resurfaced in 1984 in the Accused. His replacement as 10 Minute Warning's singer, Steve Verwolf, poured silver paint over himself at one show. This version of the group recorded tracks for an unreleased EP in early 1984. The only released Warning tracks were on homemade tapes (see below).

McKagan switched to guitar when the band added drummer Greg Gilmore. Hofmann was replaced on bass by David Garriques, in turn succeeded by Daniel House. House, who came here from Berkeley, Calif. in 1981, was originally in the gothic concept band Death of Marat with KCMU DJs Chris Loathesome and Brad Matter (who took the stage name Alfred Butler when he started the avant-pop Vexed with Eric Muhs in 1984) and Chip Doring (later in Couch of Sound and Crypt Kicker Five). House later told *Goldmine* it was "the suckiest band *ever* in Seattle. We were art fags, we couldn't play, we blew!"

Under House and Verwolf, 10 Minute Warning evolved further from hardcore toward a semi-improvisational gothic feel that Henry Rollins reportedly compared to "a punk version of Hawkwind." This lineup cut an album's worth of material, unreleased, before it drifted apart at the beginning of 1985, playing its last official gig at Lincoln Arts. In its last months it was the target of a "tribute" song, "10 Minute Fart" by the hardcore purists Aerobic Death, whose leaders Tim Larsen and Scott Larue apparently believed the Warning had sold out its punk integrity.

**Below:
Moving Parts**

Pravda

More splitting

The end of 10 Minute Warning marked the end of Duff McKagan's Seattle career. He and Greg Gilmore drove to L.A. in January 1985. Within days, they answered a want ad by a guy named Slash who was forming a band. Gilmore and McKagan started practicing and partying with the nascent band. Gilmore got turned off by these guys' drunken-decadent personas and drove back north.

Duff McKagan to Backfire, *11/83: "Basically what the whole quote-unquote 'punk scene' was about was getting away from the cliques and the peer pressure. Now it's just regressed back…to what I was trying to get out of."*

Blackouts

Paul Solger joined Upchuck's re-formed Fags. This lineup, including Dahny Reed and Ben Ireland, soon split to New York where it played increasingly dark shows (some involving vampire rituals, with real bloodletting by Upchuck and Reed), changed its name to Scarecrow, added some new members, appeared as a shocking freak act on Jane Whitney's TV talk show, and broke up. Reed entered a career in zoology, eventually moving to Africa. Upchuck found scattered session work in New York, recorded tracks for a proposed solo album with Brian Briggs producing, and appeared in a video for the studio-created band Goon Squad. Upchuck, Reed, Ireland, and Solger all appeared as extras in *Desperately Seeking Susan*.

Solger came back to Seattle just as black tar heroin was starting to show up on the streets; it took him three years to kick the habit and start playing again.

Paul Hood, guitarist for the Meyce and the last

**Below:
Loud Fart**

version of the Enemy, joined San Francisco's Toiling Midgets; later joined by the Blackouts' Erich Werner. Erich's brother Curt Werner wandered between Seattle, Paris, New York, Italy, Portugal, New Orleans and Chicago before returning home in 1993. Pam Lillig, guitarist of the Girls (and later of the Deans, with Al Bloch and Chris Crass), became an L.A. record-company executive and is now an assistant vice president in charge of music at Universal Studios. Girls singer Rick Smith formed the Lonesome City Kings, then went to Texas and joined the Austin Lounge Lizards; he's now in Oregon. He's written songs recorded by Stevie Ray Vaughan and other stars.

Back home, party houses were disbanding or getting seized by landlords; a couple were demolished. Some people moved into apartment buildings together (especially Belltown's Rivoli and Cornelius) or sought artist studios.

Pravda product

Mr. Epp and the Calculations put out a five-song EP, *Of Course I'm Happy, Why?* All the songs were sung by Jo Smitty except for "Mohawk Man," a hilarious low-key ditty about a nice young delinquent entering the hardcore-punk lifestyle, with lyrics and deadpan vocals by Mark Arm. It was released by former *Desperate Times* writers Dennis White and Maire Masco, doing business as Pravda Records (no relation to the later Chicago label of that name). It got heavy airplay on the L.A. radio station KROQ, but White and Masco couldn't afford to press more than the original 1,000 copies. Around this time Arm entered the UW as an English lit major.

Charles Peterson, *photographer: "I was living in the Terry-Lander dorm when I saw this guy with short hair and a CRASS T-shirt in the cafeteria. He said his name was Mark Arm and he had this band called Mr. Epp. He invited me to take some pictures at their shows. The year after that we started living together. I've been taking pictures of bands ever since."*

Pravda also released 45s by Student Nurse (with Helena Rogers singing the A-side, "Recht Op Staan" (stand up straight), in her native Dutch), Steddi-5, the Beat Pagodas and Byron Duff's Spectators (a.k.a. the Byrons and Idiot Culture), plus the cassette *Pravda Volume 1* (with the above bands plus Joe Despair and a Johnny Rubato solo track). Dennis White promoted shows on his own and with The Swedish Housewife (Paula Sjunsseon) under the name White Boy International, and designed "close to 1000" band posters. He later moved to L.A. and managed the Blue Yonder Sounds label, home of the Fibonaccis and the Del Rubio Triplets, then came back in 1989. Masco produced shows through 1985 (see next chapter).

Mr. Epp played its brand of loud, stupid "snide rock" until February 1984, appearing at 24 gigs in 28 months and releasing the 27-track noise-and-feedback cassette *Live As All Get Out*. Its songs in-

cluded "Mac Truck from Mars," "The Ballad of John and Jodie" (Reagan assailant John Hinckley and his idol Jodie Foster), "Wild Youth on Money," and "Stairway to Heaven." The latter wasn't the overplayed Led Zep tune but what Smitty told *Goldmine* was "a collection of bad rock cliches." The hardcore punks treated the slow-droning Mr. Epp as "art fags." Even more unrespectable by the punks' standards, the guys were learning to play their instruments. The lineup on the album included Jo Smitty, Arm, bassist Todd Morey (later in the Portland art/thrash band Atomic 61) and his drumming brother Darren Mor/x (later in San Francisco's Steel Pole Bathtub). Smitty's Dog Tapes and Box Dog labels have continued to issue old Mr. Epp demos, live recordings and video footage.

Mr. Epp's final incarnation included guitarist Steve Turner, then a high-school senior at the private Northwest School. He'd started his career inauspiciously in the short-lived Ducky Boys ("we practiced a lot but never appeared anywhere"), with classmates Jeff Covell and Stone Gossard (son of a prominent Seattle attorney, and cousin of ex-Clone member Jeff Gossard). Stone went from the Ducky Boys to the speedcore March of Crimes, with 15-year-old guitarist Pete Droge (now a Portland-based singer-songwriter) and Bainbridge Island kid Hunter "Ben" Shepherd. Turner went on to Spluii Numa, a melodic-punk band that looked like preppies, with singer/painter Harold Hollingsworth (later in the bands Blanket and Snoboy), bassist Keith Strobel (now Mudhoney's accountant), and sometimes kilt-clad drummer Alex Vincent (Shumway).

Steve Turner to Goldmine *on the Ducky Boys:* "Stoney and Jeff [Covell] were like heavy metal kids. They were into Motorhead, and Stoney was really into Kiss. I was into the California hardcore, but I also liked the Clash, Devo and 999."

Turner had also practiced (but not performed) with Arm and flailing singer Dave Middleton in Limp Richerds, a deliberately bad knock-off band based in Federal Way (the forlorn south-end suburb where the Spanish Castle had been). Their logo was the male symbol with a drooping arrow. They released "My Dad Forgot His Rubber" on Bruce Pavitt's last *Sub Pop* compilation tape in 1983, and made a joint cassette with Portland's Rancid Vat with a slam at Seattle's most beloved restaurateur, "Death to Ivar."

Green River, part one

By then, Arm and Turner were already working on a "real" band, Green River (named for a local riverbank where several serial-killer victims were found), with Alex Vincent and Jeff Ament. Ament had moved here from Missoula, Montana with a band called Deranged Diction; its singer Rod Moody later played in Swallow and in the '90s started the band Spike and co-founded Y Records with Ron Middleton). Journeyman punk musician Ben Thompson described Deranged Diction as "speed metal-cowpunk-Circle Jerks type stuff." Arm reportedly wanted Ament because he could "jump real high" while playing and was the only guy he knew who owned a working distortion box. After six months, Arm stopped playing guitar to concen-

See pg. 93

trate on his sneering vocals; Turner's pal Stone Gossard joined in as second guitarist.

Debuting in June 1984 at a private party on Capitol Hill with retro-psychedelic band PMA (Positive Mental Attitude), Green River expanded on the Melvins/U-Men big noise sound, at a steady-assault pace faster than the Melvins' new dirge sound but slower than speedcore; on any particular tune, all four instruments could be playing lead, sometimes all at once. The *Rocket* said their "hardcore/metal/greasy rock fusion is a double-bareled attack of audio destruction."

Arm's lyrics usually had to do with combinations of sex and/or violence. Arm, Turner and Vincent originally wore preppy costumes onstage, including Oxford shirts; Arm soon grew his hair and donned ripped spandex or black lingirie.

Ament had big, billowing hair; he wore pink tank tops with scarves, or satin shirts with vertical-striped pants, or white Kiss make-up with glitter paint. He played a big Destroyer bass with scarves tied to it in the style of Aerosmith's Steve Tyler. Gossard once created his own platform shoes by nailing 2 x 4s to a pair of Capezzios.

Ament also started to develop serious career ambitions, pushing the band into recording and touring. Arm also pushed the band, writing its praises in scene reports under a pseudonym in the Berkeley zine *Maximum Rock n' Roll* and also in his own short-lived zine, *Attack*, whose mailing list included members of the Butthole Surfers and Sonic Youth.

Jeff Ament *in the Mother Love Bone home video* The Love Bone Earth Affair: *"I think a lot of us grew up listening to Black Sabbath, or Aerosmith and Kiss and stuff. I think a lot of us got into the punk scene, from a playing standpoint, because we could relate to the Ramones. We could play along to 'Blitzkrieg Bop.'"*

Dead air, live air

KRAB-FM found a few hours on its schedule for new-music shows: *Expressions of Critical Timez* (with Audio Leter's Deran Ludd and Sharon Gannon), *Stephen Rabow's Unpopular Hit Parade*, and *Life Elsewhere* (by now hosted solely by Norman Batley). These shows brought some new life into a schedule dominated by "progressive" mellow music for old hippies (blues, jazz, and the mellow foreign music later known as "world beat"); with some classical slots, foreign-language talk shows, and feminist talk shows mixed in.

The station was facing identity problems with its slapped-together schedule, its amateurish DJs (some had a hard time finishing their own sentences), and internal dissentions. Faced with mounting debts, its parent Jack Straw Memorial Foundation imposed a mainstream schedule and a higher emphasis on fundraising; the moves alienated longtime listener/donors, and failed to attract enough new converts. Jack Straw tried to take over a frequency on the 88-92 noncommercial FM band, so they could sell their existing frequency on the 93-108 commercial band. They tried to take over the frequencies of KCMU (when it was a classroom-lab operation) and the Seattle School District's KNHC (home to the only black-music programming in town), but were rebuffed. In April 1984, faced with declining revenues and an insurrection of disgruntled listeners and volunteers, KRAB left the air and sold its frequency at 107.7 FM to a commercial station that ran it for seven years with little success, until it moved to a new format in 1991 (see Chapter 11). Jack Straw started a recording studio and in 1991 launched a station in the northern suburb of Lynnwood, unhearable in much of Seattle.

KCMU's new collective volunteer management soon set up pledge drives and benefit concerts to improve the station's facilities and record library. In May 1982, the station moved up from 10 watts in mono to 182 watts in stereo, heard over most of the city. Stephen Rabow made a guest appearance on the station that month; he derided the "fraternity consciousness" he found in the station's power-pop playlist, initially full of Duran Duran and the B-52's. Soon after, they started planning for a boost to 400 watts, which would cover most of the area.

The station's playlist and consciousness quickly changed. Over the next 11 years, KCMU became the constant in an ever-changing scene, the gathering place for everyone who cared about the music. Its volunteer DJs went on to form bands and zines and record labels. The station grew to the point where it could hire a full-time manager. Ex-KZAM DJ Kerry Loewen and world-beat concert promoter Jon Kertzer had the job for short terms, before a national search led to the hiring of Chris Knab, a former partner in San Francisco's 415 Records.

From the fourth issue of KCMU's first newsletter, **News Wave***, 5/82: "A crazy new thing called MTV (short for Music Television) jumped onto the ca-*

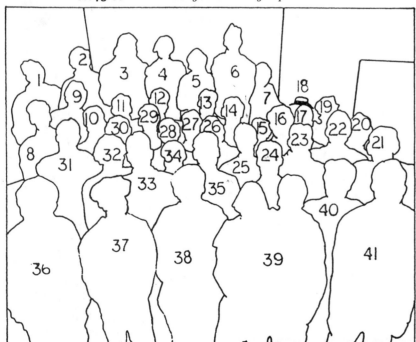

ble-waves last month. They show video singles from groups like Human League, the Psychedelic Furs and the Police. Plus, for a few extra buckeroonies they'll hook your STEREO up to the TUBE for some wild times."

Because its hilly contours interfered with TV reception, Seattle was one of the first major cities to be significantly wired for cable. Hence, it was one of the few big cities to witness some of the early days of MTV. The channel's early programming was heavy with new wave bands, who at that time had more and better videos. The new exposure given to bands like Madness made some businesspeople begin to reconsider new music.

On Memorial Day weekend 1982, two months after MTV came to Seattle and two weeks after KCMU went citywide, the local owners of AOR station KZOK turned their AM signal into KJET, a low-budget commercial operation that served a mildly eclectic blend of modern rock (Bowie, Modern English, Devo). The DJs, led by Bill Reid and Damon Stewart, knew their stuff but were hampered by the weak signal, restricted playlist and low budget. They didn't even have live DJs except during Reid's morning-drive shift; for the rest of the day, the station ran on a tape-automation system (nicknamed "Otto Matic") that frequently broke down so that DJs were heard introducing the wrong songs. Reid was joined (and later succeeded) on his morning shift by "news god" Thad Wilson, who resurfaced in 1992 as The Psychic Guy, giving readings and public essays about the spirits who talked to him.

KZOK-FM promoted a fundraising campaign to put a Jimi Hendrix statue in a Seattle park; when the Parks Department refused to participate, the station had to settle for a "hot rock" monument in the Woodland Park Zoo's African savanna exhibit, near the giraffes. Tourists preferred to flock to Hendrix's grave in Renton's Greenwood cemetery, where they still lay flowers and steal sod today. In 1992, Microsoft co-founder Paul Allen launched a drive to build the Jimi Hendrix Museum/Experience Music Project at Seattle Center.

More professional production than KJET's (if less-knowledgeable DJs) could be heard on KYYX, a commercial FM station that inaugurated a "Wave" format in December 1982 under local radio legend Pat O'Day and his son Gerry. Stephen Rabow resurfaced that February as its afternoon DJ. The station promoted its launch with "The Wave Spectacular," a throwback to O'Day's old KJR Teen Spectaculars. The three-day expo at the Seattle Center Exhibition Hall included gigs by the local Visible Targets, Life in General, Big Fun, Allies, Dynette Set and Frazz; California's Oingo Boingo, Wall of Voodoo, Berlin and Missing Persons; plus fashion and hair shows, video games, booths by station advertisers, and a heavy-metal show.

As these commercial stations played the new wave hits on the national "college radio" charts, KCMU moved further underground with more independents and imports. As KJET emphasized R.E.M. and the Smiths, and KYYX ran toward A Flock of Seagulls and the Motels, KCMU was more likely to play Nick Cave and Danielle Dax. Contrary to commonly-held notions in the broadcasting industry

KCMU staff

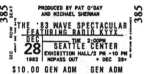

The Allies

(even in the "public" broadcasting industry), KC-MU's listenership and donations *increased* as its music became more intense and more obscure.

Peeling

The first local video to get MTV airplay was "Emma Peel," made in early 1983 by the Allies, a power-pop band formed out of Bighorn, a Top 40 cover band dating back to 1972 (its early line-ups included ex-Viceroys drummer Fred Zeufeldt and Jr. Cadillac bassist Garey Shelton), recording one poor-selling Columbia LP along the way. The group's manager, real estate investor Scott Soules, decided there could be money in new wave, so he fired Bighorn's singer, promoted position player Dave Kincaid to the lead spot, got them new haircuts and skinny ties, and commissioned an EP that sold 10,000 copies. The band's line-up eventually settled with Kincaid, Carl Funk, Andy Pederson and Larry Mason. The video (about a loser whose only joy is watching *Avengers* reruns) made the finals of an MTV "Basement Tapes" contest. Kincaid soon left to New York and formed the Brandos, who recorded a couple of albums and won a couple of New York Music Awards in the late '80s. The director of the "Emma" video, Brad Huskinson, continued to make videos between more lucrative assignments on commercials and industrial films; he became nationally known for Sir Mix-A-Lot's breakthrough clip "Posse on Broadway" (see chapter 11).

Mainstream reactions

The most visible "punk band" in Seattle in 1983 was *Angry Housewives*, a yuppie novelty stage musical by Ann Marie Collins and Chad Henry about four frustrated suburban moms who make a hit record called "Eat Your Fucking Cornflakes" under the guidance of a promoter named Louie Fingers (based heavily on Larry Reid). The show ran for six and a half years, spawned brief productions in Lon-

don and New York, and subsidized its producer, the nonprofit Pioneer Square Theatre. At one point, PST had three stages and a restaurant, all supported by *Housewives*. In an average week, more people saw *Housewives* than saw all real local punk shows combined. The local mainstream media adored these fake punks, while continuing to ignore or repress the real punks. *Housewives* finally died after almost 1,900 performances to over 300,000 people; PST collapsed with it.

KING-TV tried to get in on the music video craze in 1983 with *R.E.V. (Rock Entertainment Video)*, the first local rock n' roll TV show since the mid-'60s. Ex-KZAM DJ Mariane Seymour and ex-Heart guitarist Roger Fisher hosted the weekly hour, which alternated national bands' videos with local dance-pop bands (Allies, Visible Targets, Mondo Vita) taped live at Astor Park. The show also had a mock newscast by *Rocket* co-editor John Keister (whose brother Paul, former singer for the new wave/ska Shivers, had gone to San Francisco and married Romeo Void singer Deborah Iyall) and comedy sketches by the Off the Wall Players (including Joe Guppy, who sang with the comedy-rock Dick Everson Trio and Acoustinauts). The show was canned after one unsuccessful season; Keister and the skits were carried over to *R.E.V.*'s replacement, a comedy-talk show called *Almost Live*.

The last Syndrome, the first Fresh Fellows

Engram Records issued the *Seattle Syndrome Two* compilation in March 1983: four months after its scheduled release date (due to a breakdown of talks with KYYX, which was to have co-released it), almost two years after the first record. The 14 acts included the cream of local pop and sort-of-pop combos: Rally Go, 3 Swimmers (with new singer Lya Badgley), Mr. Epp, Beat Pagodas, Moving Parts, the Dynette Set, Sue Ann Harkey, and Phil Otto and ex-*Desperate Times* writer Corinne Mah's Steddi-5 (who appropriately shared several gigs with 3 Swimmers). More important for historical purposes was Norman Batley's cover of local street photos, including a famous band-poster wall on First Avenue near Pioneer Square (demolished by the time the record came out).

The Dynette Set, a vocal trio formed by Leslee "Penta" Swanson (an ex-girlfriend of Telepath Curt Werner), Riki Mafune and Christy McWilson to sing girl-group covers, put out its own *Rockers and Recliners* LP of covers and originals later that year. Swanson left the group before the record was made (replaced by Shelley Stockstill); she settled in New York with experimental-theatre director Carlo Altomari, who moved here with her in 1991. McWilson later joined with Leroy Sleep in a pair of punk-rockabilly bands, the Power Mowers (with KCMU/KJET DJ Marshall Gooch) and the Picketts.

One of the Dynette Set's male backing musicians, and author of many of the band's original tunes, was McWilson's husband Scott McCaughey, who'd come up from Saratoga, California in 1979. He and Chuck Carroll, a pal who'd come to town with him, decided to make their own record. They asked Carroll's cousin Tad Hutchison to come up from Colorado to drum for them. Within days of their first practice, the jovial Young Fresh Fellows recorded their first LP, *Fabulous Sounds of the Pacific Northwest* (the name and cover art came from a phone-company promo record made in 1962). *Fabulous Sounds* featured the quirky "Young Fresh Fellows Theme" and the big-beat "Rock and Roll Pest Control."

Based on demos McCaughey and Carroll cut in California, the group recorded the LP in a week (with McCaughey doubling on bass) on a used 8-track deck and some borrowed monitors in the garage of Uncle Cookie/Pink Chunk veteran Conrad Uno, who'd met McCaughey while running the sound board for a Dynette Set gig. After the Cookie crumbled, Uno had played with attorney Don Kellman and sometime Cowboys member Ernie Sapiro in the power-pop Nu Vitations. He also used his share of the Cookie's old PA to run sound for a lot of bands. Uno called his new makeshift recording setup Egg Studios, after his proudest performing achievement—getting pelted with eggs by ex-Telepath Geoff Cade at the Pink Chunk's only live performance.

The *Fabulous Sounds* album came out in early 1984 on Uno's PopLlama Records (so-named, according to Uno, "...because the llama is the goofiest animal we could think of"). Uno had already used the label to release Red Dress and Moving Parts singles and *Astray in the Manger*, a cassette of various singers fronting the New Flamingos, all covering Christmas rock classics. Initial response from an album mailing to college radio stations (packaged with autographed paper plates) led to the Fellows' first national tour (which also comprised its first live gigs). The band needed a separate bass player for the tour, so Hutchison called on Colorado pal Jim Sangster, who'd previously lived in Seattle and played in the 1979 punk band

Blunt Objects (with future Living singer John Conte and future Thrown-Ups leader Leighton Beezer). Hutchison and Sangster moved into a U District house with Jeff Ament.

McCaughey later took over the *Rocket*'s indie-record column from Bruce Pavitt; he renamed it "Searchin' USA," after a song from the Fellows' 1985 second album. That album, *Topsy Turvy*, also featured odes to the Alderwood Mall and B-movie actor John Agar and a musical search for the elusive "Groovy Town." It garnered a long, gushing review in *Rolling Stone* that brought the band to the attention of L.A.'s Frontier label. *Topsy Turvy* took nearly a year to record; one big delay came when Uno's old tape deck broke down. The band performed a Christmas 1984 benefit concert at the Rainbow to help him get another deck. Uno, meanwhile, kept his day job, mowing lawns for elderly homeowners. He cut grass until 1988, when he started getting enough paid production work to quit.

*From the **Young Fresh Fellows**' "Searchin' USA": "And my friends all think that I'm so funny, 'cuz these things that I do are bizzare/But they haven't really got me too far."*

The Fellows also served as a backup band to ex-Pudz yukster Rob Morgan, performing '70s schlock covers under the name Ernest Anyway and the New Age Urban Squirrels. Morgan spent the next decade fronting a number of Squirrels bands with assorted names (Squirrels Live Unit, the Mighty Squirrels, 23 Squirrels 5) and assorted musicians—more than 30 at last count, including Joey Kline and Mark Nichols from Prudence Dredge (see next chapter), members of the Posies and Flop, the Dynette Set women, a horn section, a

Above: Uno
Below: Fellows

Tom Dyer

LOCAL PRODUCT

0 71520 09354 4

SUPER BOSS ROCK

POP LUST 2

Below: The Squirrels

five-year-old boy playing a Slinky, a vegetable-percussionist, a Cabbage Patch doll named Baby Cheevers (voiced by Kline), and ex-Tubes singer Re Styles. Their original tunes included the Kline-penned "Pope on a Rope," "Television On My Leg," the McCaughey-penned "Demise of Ricky Nelson," and the doo-wop hay fever ode "Gotta Be A Reason." The Squirrels' finest hours came with the cover of their 1985 *Five Virgins* LP, with the band members baring their rears *a la* John and Yoko (one whole side covered UK rock pioneers Johnny Kidd and the Pirates), and with "Oz on 45," a 1988 medley of *Wizard of Oz* songs set to a spunky beat. They've since released the PopLlama CDs *What Gives?* and *Harsh Toke of Reality,* the latter with a Morgan-designed logo of a yin/yang Happy Face. *Rolling Stone* described the band as "extremely silly…. Imagine the Flaming Groovies on a weekend pass from Bellevue." The "Bellevue" the reviewer referred to was the New York psychiatric hospital, not the affluent Seattle suburb. Morgan also published the hand-lettered zine *Pop Lust/Super Boss Rock,* featuring his comic strip "2 Katz and a Toaster."

Meanwhile, in another studio...

The Fellows' early success turned local bands onto the idea of making a record or tape as soon as they could afford to. Some were already onto the concept.

The ethereal stylings of the Visible Targets (three Yakima sisters with the stage names Pamela Golden, Rebecca Hamilton and Laura Keane) were captured on two EPs put out by their manager Bob Jeniker on his Park Avenue label (named for his record stores in Portland and Seattle). The Targets' second record, *Autistic Savant,* was produced in Vancouver by David Bowie's pal Mick Ronson. Both discs featured the haunting harmonic ballad "Life in the Twilite Zone." The group opened a national tour for Simple Minds before breaking up in

1985. Golden returned in the '90s with the solo record *Happens All the Time.*

One of Seattle's first ambient-synth-noise bands, Enstruction (typical song title: "Keep Out of My Body Bag"), set up Dues Ex Machina Records to release its own EP, *Force of Movement,* plus tapes by the Fartz, 10 Minute Warning, Mr. Epp, and Solger. It also sold a compilation tape, *What Syndrome?,* with 10 Minute Warning, Silly Killers, Limp Richerds, Solger and one big-loose-grind Enstruction cut that seemed lost amidst the big-beat guitar feedback. Enstruction also passed out pamphlets at its live shows, citing such influences as Schopenhauer and Nietzsche.

Ex-Mr. Epp member David Kulczyk issued a two-volume cassette compilation, *Sounds of Young Seattle.* The tapes documented art-rock, folk-rock and neo-psychedelic outfits, including Lee Lumsden's Celestial Pygmies, the Walkabouts, A Western Family, and Clay Alien.

Tom Dyer, a veteran of the no-wave bands Adults, Colorplates and Icons (he recalls them as "art-noise" combos that did original "weird stuff" and "unrecognizable cover songs"), launched Green Monkey Records with two cassettes: his own *Truth or Consequences* (backed up by Al Bloch and Peter Barnes) and the compilation *Local Product,* both duplicated at his home in 300-copy editions. The latter included tracks by Dyer, the Fastbacks, Mr. Epp, Group Sex, fellow ex-Colorplate Bob Blackburn Jr. (son of the SuperSonics' first radio announcer), and 10 other acts. The *Local Product* cassette label featured a supermarket bar code for generic beer. Green Monkey (named after his favorite childhood stuffed doll) remained a part-time venture for its eight-year life, between Dyer's night production work in his bedroom studio (later moved to a basement) and his day job at a lumber yard.

One of Dyer's first production jobs at his home studio was a Mr. Epp session, with Mark Arm and Darren Mor/x unsuccessfully attempting to play saxophones. It was released on Dog Tapes (renamed Box Dog), a label started by Jo Smitty and partner Paul Usitalo. It released tapes by Mr. Epp, Fred's Crashshop (a "difficult listening" noise band named for a sign on a local garage), Irish Potato Famine (described in Box Dog's catalog as "what John Cage would sound like if he put his sense of humor in his music"), and Smitty's own subsequent band with Seattle's most politically correct band name to date, Lapses In Grammar (Afforded To Avoid Sexism). Box Dog later released a Melvins videocassette, taped live in Olympia after the group had become a touring band from California. Smitty, sometimes using his real name Jeff Smith (no relation to the local TV chef of the same name), also produced music shows for public access cable, published the zine *Feminist Baseball,* and contributed to his girlfriend Nancy Ostrander's zine *Hip Clown Rag.*

Metal refuses to die

In the Eastside suburbs across Lake Washington from Seattle, Led Zep bombast still ruled. The city punks may have still abhorred corporate heavy metal with its cliché chords and rote macho posturing as sold by conglomerates and bought by redneck dirtheads; but some were learning to tap into a new generation of headbanger music, with devoted fans and indie labels that could actually sell records, with a defined career path that could take the right band out of the garage and into the stadiums.

The Lake Hills Roller Rink (later renamed the Crossroads Skate Center), a stop on the Pat O'Day '60s teen-dance circuit, had reopened to bands in 1979 with "Battle of the Bands" contests booked by Unicam, one of the big local cover-band circuits, essentially serving as on-stage auditions. In 1982, former Unicam staffer Craig Cooke (a white guy with Jerri-Curls) took over the band nights at Lake Hills. Every week Cooke booked local metal bands like Shadow (with Chris and Rick Friel and guitarist Mike McCready), Culprit, Mace, Heir Apparent, Rottweiler, DC LaCroix, and Soldier (no relation to Seattle's hardcore Solger) into all-ages shows. Cooke built the scene into a circuit of Saturday night shows at nine skating rinks, all outside Seattle; fading out in 1985 when some of the rinks folded for real estate development.

Rick Friel, Shadow/Easy/Give: "Lake Hills was great. The place was packed: 300 or 400 people, most of them under 18. There was a stage at each end of the room; as soon as one band was done with its set, the next one started. No waiting. Everybody would rush out to the other end of the hall. The same people went to every show and loved every band.... We were about the only band in that scene that was from Seattle. Most of the others were from the Eastside, and they were a lot heavier, a lot darker. We were more rock, more fun. We included Kiss and Alice Cooper covers, where the other bands were more into Scorpions."

One of the top bands on the Cooke circuit was TKO, formed by ex-Whiz Kidz Brad Sinsel and Rick Pierce. Its best-known LP was *In Your Face*, done in 1984 for the Combat label and featuring guitarist Adam Brenner (who later formed his own band, Adam Bomb). Sinsel played with various lineups under the TKO name (including ex-Culprit members Scott Earl and Kjartan) from 1975 to 1988. In the '90s he formed Black Is Black, which split off into the punkish Sleep Capsule and the metalish War Babies the latter band released one Columbia album before Sinsel left and the other members formed a new Black Is Black. Pierce and other ex-TKO members formed Q5, which recorded the 1986 PolyGram LP *When the Mirror Cracks* and later evolved into Nightshade.

The ten-year-old Bellevue metal band Rail (Terry Young, Rick Knotts, Andy Baldwin, Kelly Nobles) won a Basement Tapes contest for unsigned bands on MTV in 1984, and got a one-record contract with EMI; they made three moderate-selling LPs for the Passport and Dynasty labels and toured with the likes of Van Halen. Rail's career finally wound down by 1986, around the time a grittier flavor of metal began to emerge (see next chapter).

John Keister in the Rocket, 6/84: *"The way it is now, the only music young people are legally able to see is the traveling arena shows which are heavily oriented towards hard rock and heavy metal. As a result the vast majority of young bands in this state (and perhaps others like it) try to duplicate the only live music they are exposed to. They put on their own heavy metal concerts in fields, school gyms, roller rinks, etc. And they look like almost the real thing with the standard leather uniforms, flash pots, and their very own T-shirts and albums on sale in the lobby, all at the tender age of 16. And that's fine. It's fine that we've got a hundred or so teenage heavy metal bands around here.... But I somehow think it would be a better place if there were, in addition to all those metal bands, another hundred bands of 16-year-olds who played music of different genres."*

Queens of the ryche

The biggest Eastside metal band never depended on the roller rinks. Five kids from well-to-do suburban families (Jeff "Geoff" Tate, Chric DeGarmo, Michael Wilton, Eddie Jackson, Scott Rockenfield) started in hard-rock cover bands with names like Tyrant and Myth. They got together as the Mob in 1982. Rockenfield's brother slipped a demo tape to Mr. Kim Harris, who in 1980 had closed the U District punk hangout Campus Music (he later told *Billboard* that Campus Music's landlord was "tripling the rent every week") and opened the Easy Street store in Bellevue. His new store was home to the "Wall of Death," Washington's largest import metal selection. Harris suggested the band change its name to Queensreich; after a song on its demo called "Queen of the Reich." The name was finally altered to Queensryche so as not to imply Nazi sentiments.

Harris sent a copy of the demo to the European

Visible Targets

Rottweiler

Mace

Northwest Metalfest

Jeff Gilbert's KCMU show

METAL CHURCH

Below: Shadow

metal magazine *Kerrang*, which gave it a rave write-up. The band's self-titled EP for Harris's 206 label (named for Western Washington's area code) promptly sold out its 3,500-copy first printing and got them a major-label contract after they'd played locally under the Queensryche name only once. EMI reissued their debut and followed it with *The Warning*, recorded at Abbey Road Studios in London. It was one of the first hard-rock LPs with political and environmental commentary.

Harris and his wife Diana continued to manage the band and run the store until 1987, when they went into the management biz in California; they moved back in 1991 and now run a new Easy Street in Kirkland. Diana's son Matthew Vaughan owns a separate Easy Street store in West Seattle.

Jeff Gilbert: "Queensryche was an anomaly. They came out of nowhere, exploded into the big time, and disappeared from view. They were off conquering the world while the rest of us were back here scratching our heads."

Mark Hale on Queensryche in the book Head-Bangers, *1989: "The premier U.S. 'class' metal act...superb vocals, excellent musicianship, intelligent lyrics, well-produced LPs."*

Kurdt and Kurt

Willy McCay and KCMU DJ Jeff Gilbert started the metal label Ground Zero in May 1983. They applied punk rock marketing techniques to hard rock bands, including the concept of local-compilation records. Their debut release, *Northwest Metalfest*,

may have been the first local speed-metal compilation in the country. It featured Rottweiler, Sado, the Bondage Boys, Mace, Overlord, Strike, Koda-Kahn, Lipstick and Open Fire. McCay and Gilbert supported its release with a joint concert in the Moore Theater: 10 bands for $7. The sold-out crowd got to see future members of Alice in Chains, Faster Pussycat, the Pleasure Elite, Mistrust and Crawl; along with one band that got famous under its original name, Metal Church.

Metal Church rose from the suburban metal circuit to major-label status by 1985, after selling 50,000 copies of its debut album on Ground Zero without major radio play; it sold 100,000 more copies after it was picked up by Elektra. Singer Dave Wayne (replaced by Mike Howe) and company made the jump to the majors without adopting cock-rock or dregs-of-Led-Zep clichés; instead, they kept their black clothes and played vehement songs about terrorism, nukes, and neo-Nazis. The group moved from Aberdeen into a garage in the working-class Boeing suburb of Kent, away from Seattle's higher rents and close to the street-level metal audience. Band leader/guitarist Kurdt Vanderhoof still lived in Aberdeen, and commuted the 100 miles to practices. Even after two major-label LPs the band members still had day jobs; Vanderhoof worked in a Hoquiam fish market, while bassist Duke Erickson worked in a shake mill.

The Metal Church debut also launched the career of its producer, the Idaho-raised Terry Date, who started in the scene by running the Cowboys' sound board. Date went on to record the Accused, Sanctuary, Soundgarden, and Sir Mix-A-Lot.

Terry Date to the Rocket *on his production aesthetic, 6/88: "I think that if they've ever heard a train wreck, it would be similar."*

Kurdt Vanderhoof to the Rocket *on the Metal Church concept, 1/84: "My first initial impression in forming the band was to combine the aggressiveness and obnoxiousness of the punk movement with the technicalities and speed of such bands as Judas Priest. I had no idea anything was going to happen, though."*

Ex-Lewd member Vanderhoof had moved to San Francisco with the Lewd in 1980. He split from Satz's band (which released one album in 1983) and formed the first Metal Church there, hoping to mesh the power of punk with the populism of metal ("the metal thing wasn't happening; the punk thing was happening but it didn't look like it would ever get out of the clubs"). After recording a demo tape that became an international bootleg hit, he moved back to Aberdeen and started a cover band that served as an ongoing tryout for local musicians. He gave this group the Metal Church name just in time for the first Moore Theater Metalfest show.

Vanderhoof ceased performing with the group in 1988, his guitar part taken first by Mark Baker and later by Metallica vet John Marshall. Vanderhoof still wrote and produced for the group as it recorded for Elektra, Epic, and Joan Jett's Blackheart label. He later returned to the clubs with Hall Aflame, which gigged heavily in the early '90s and put out one record on IRS, before launching Buzzing Room at the end of 1993.

But long before that happened, Vanderhoof inspired an aspiring singer-guitarist from his hometown to change his stage name for a time (at the suggestion of the Melvins' Matt Lukin) from Kurt Cobain to Kurdt Kobain.

Cobain had started to hang out at practices and outdoor parties with the Melvins; sometime in '83, he'd asked Buzz Osborne to make him compilation tapes of punk records that had never been in Aberdeen stores. Before long the 16-year-old Cobain had gotten a spiked hairdo, started practicing with the 18-year-old Chris Novoselic, and started going through a succession of drummers and band names. Osborne took Kurt up to see his first punk shows: the first with DOA, the second starring Black Flag at Seattle's Mountaineers Hall. Cobain also got to drive the Melvins' tour van. It was the first real "family" he'd had; after his parents' divorce eight years earlier, he'd been shuttled among various relatives' homes. He dropped out of high school; his mother soon kicked him out of the house, and he started sleeping on friends' couches or in their vans. For a short time he slept under an Aberdeen bridge. He'd grown up to hate the macho logging culture of Aberdeen, a world that had not been kind to him or those around him. Three of his male relatives had committed suicide.

Buzz Osborne to the Times, *3/92, on meeting*

Cobain: "He looked like a teenage runaway. Still does, in fact."

J'Accuse

Back in Seattle, a rising gothic/metal/thrash scene began to coalesce around SGM and the Accused.

SGM (which stood alternately for Shot Gun Mama, Such Good Music, and many other things) was formed by Cole Peterson, Rich Albrecht, Chris Quinn and Adam Czeisler, students at the affluent private Bush School. Peterson had started performing in a band called Apex that did mostly Hendrix covers; Albrecht began in the hardcore Skank Puppies. As several members went off to college over the years, the band evolved away from punk toward metal; releasing the album *Aggression* on Medusa/ Enigma. In the early '90s Czeisler, Peterson and Albrecht re-emerged as Sweet Water, taking the punk/metal crossover the rest of the way.

Adam Peterson: "We figured this band was going to only go as far as playing parties. But then (in 1985) Rich got us a gig at the Gorilla Gardens. We thought it was great to be there, even if we were getting only $5 and it was really just this big dump. We were all in the seventh, ninth and tenth grades. Soon we were playing in bars we were too young to be in, opening for Green River…. Medusa gave us $14,000 but didn't really promote

Culprit

The Accused

the record. We bought a brown van and went on little tours to California and Nevada, sleeping on floors and playing punk dives. On the day of a show in Vegas, we got to the club and the guy told us it had just closed that day. He tried to pay us off in drugs; some guy next door tried to shoot us."

Adam Czeisler: *"We'd play at Legends, an all-ages space in Tacoma, and it was all packed. Then we'd do a show at the Vogue and nobody'd be there. If there was a better party that night, nobody'd go to our show. We didn't have any real fans.... We thought if we just got out of Seattle, we'd make it. It quickly became boring and repetitive. It soon wasn't that much of an adventure anymore."*

Tommy Accused (Niemeyer) and Dana Collins formed the Accused in 1981 in the Navy town of Oak Harbor. The group helped further the evolution of Seattle punk away from the frenetic purity of fast hardcore and into the realm of feedback, distortion, minor keys, and spiked leather. In 1984, original singer John Doleen was replaced by Fartz/10 Minute Warning vet Blaine Cook; the group's core line-up solidified soon after with Alex Sibbald, previously of the hardcore bands Maggot Brains (named after a George Clinton song), Itchy Brother and Cheating Death.

The Accused adopted a cartoon mascot, Martha Splatterhead (designed by Niemeyer and Cook), who appeared on its record covers, in its lyrics, and in a one-shot comic book based on the band's songs. They got onto vinyl with a "split" LP in 1983: their own suite (*Please Pardon Our Noise, It's the Sound of Freedom*; named after a sign near Tacoma's McChord Air Force Base) on one side, the Burien-based Rejectors (with Tom Fart) on the other. Then came the self-released *Martha Splatterhead EP, The Return of Martha Splatterhead* LP on Subcore, and *More Fun Than An Open Casket Funeral* on Combat Records. Their second Combat release, *Martha Splatterhead's Maddest Stories Ever Told,* included guest appearances by Vanderhoof and Sir Mix-A-Lot (see next chapter). The Accused then made a split 45 with West Seattle band Morphius and the album *Hymns for the Deranged* on eMpTy, followed by *Grinning Like an Undertaker, Straight Razor* and *Splatter Rock* for Nastymix. They continued to play gothic thrash-rock until 1992, by which time every original member had been replaced (Niemeyer was the last to split). Cook now works at a day care center; at the end of 1994 he started a new band, Black Nasty.

Alex Sibbald *on Martha Splatterhead: "It was a violent thrash image, but we were still from the politically correct punk rock school, so we had a female mascot who punished wrongdoers."*

Another gothic/metal/punk band of this time, Extreme Hate, was far less lucky: One member overdosed, another hanged himself, and a third became an accountant.

Rocket writer Dawn Anderson published five issues of *Backfire*, a Lynnwood-based zine intended to encourage a metal/punk coalition. She sprang for slick color covers, inside of which she covered both cool local bands and national bands that locals considered very uncool, like Def Leppard and Bryan Adams. While the magazine didn't last, the punk/metal crossover eventually caught on. Anderson held a benefit for the magazine at an old Fremont Masonic lodge (it later became a performance-art space, and is now the fifth home of the Empty Space Theatre). It starred Eric Wilson and Uncle Cookie vet Mark Sargent's power-pop outfit Mondo Vita (their self-released LP *Fins de Paris* featured the peppy "That Darn Pope"). The eight people who showed up saw a freak accident, when Mondo Vita's wireless guitars flew off the stage on their own power.

The new clubs

In the pre-PopLlama days, the Seattle scene had developed an ideology that was almost antithetical to practical business principles. Bands were treated as sellouts if they had the money to make 45s with decent-looking covers, or if they had managers who knew what they were doing, or if they appealed beyond the inner circle of true punks. It wasn't only that you had to leave town to make a career out of your music. If you even thought about music as a route to material sufficiency, you were treated as a pariah who ought to leave town and keep the local scene pure. Wanting to be a Bigtime Rock Star was the ultimate sign of selling out. This animosity peaked in 1988-89 with disgust over Mother Love Bone's drive for stardom.

The career paradigm for bands was to play and play until you got discovered. The problems with that were (1) there was nobody in town to discover you, (2) there was no organized touring circuit to take you to where you could get discovered, and (3) even starting at the bottom was problematic, because even hole-in-the-wall clubs couldn't stay open. Still, people tried.

The Rainbow picked up a few more new-music gigs; by 1983 it was hosting a midweek New Music Night, as booked first by P.S. O'Neill and later by Jonathan Poneman, who'd also become a KCMU DJ and held day jobs as a janitor and a cook.

Ex-Tugs employees Alan Lucier and Ted Ladd joined with former WREX partner Erin McKiernan to revive WREX as the Vogue, opened on Jan. 15, 1983. Terry Morgan and Carlo Scandiuzzi helped design the space, turning the new wave video bar into a blue-neon intimate disco with DJs on the weekends, bands on the slow nights of Tuesday and Wednesday. The place had a door policy on non-band nights, refusing people who weren't "dressed nice" (including much of the old WREX crowd). By September, it became dominated by the yuppie crowd on Fridays and Saturdays. Also briefly open were Baby O's near the original Bird (now a deli), the Dragon Palace (the lounge in Ru-

by Chow's Chinese restaurant on lower Broadway with Bruce Lee's old bedroom upstairs), and Dez's 400 (a tavern north of Seattle Center, demolished for a parking garage).

The Backstage, a big showcase bar, opened in Ballard in 1983. It booked a few local and touring alternative bands within a schedule dominated by baby-boomer nostalgia and progressive-acoustic acts. The 500-capacity basement space faced high expenses, particularly for touring acts; in 1990 owner Ed Beeson had to ask bands to donate their time for a benefit show to keep it open.

Also in early 1983, the Central Tavern in Pioneer Square (billed as "Seattle's Only 2nd Class Tavern") added some alternative-rock gigs to its normal (for the area) jazz/R&B fare. It soon became the city's top rock club by default, with Jan Gregor of Next Exit and Variant Cause (see next chapter) and other promoters booking bands nobody else would, three or four nights a week. Not quite as intimate or as decrepit as the Gorilla Room, it was still a dark, musty, beer-stenched, smoky, fine place. Owners Mike and Donna Downing held on until late 1990, much of that time almost alone in town.

Sean Kinney, Alice in Chains, to Rolling Stone, 2/94: "(The Central) would sell these cheap pitchers and cram 2000 people in here, with (an inch) of beer on the floor, and people were killing each other. It was great."

Soozy Bridges: "The Central had a great vibe. It was on the Square, on a busy street with lots of foot traffic. People were just hanging out, milling around."

Scene people grumbled at the time about perceived favoritism in liquor, fire and noise-ordinance enforcement. Alternative-club owners and bookers were outside the networks of business and political influence, and didn't have the connections or cash

to muscle in. The Central frequently faced harassment, including selective enforcement of noise ordinances. The staff once went out with noise-measuring devices and found louder sounds emanating to the street from yuppie-blues and meatmarket bars that weren't being threatened with shutdowns.

The Liquor Board also claimed the right to censor entertainment at bars. In 1984 the board was rumored to be looking for excuses to shut down every rock club. The board also threatened comedy clubs where people said cuss words on stage and gay bars where male-nude pictures were displayed. And the Seattle Parks Department tried to ban rock groups from playing in city parks.

Gathered for the Feast

Among the top-drawing acts in the Central's early years were Feast and Bundle of Hiss. The former was a gothic/metal/dirge unit formed in Snoqualmie (Charles Peterson called them "a cross between the Cure and Led Zeppelin") with Tom Mick, Danny Blossom, and Jane Higgins (who later did design work for Sub Pop); ex-Fags member Pony Maurice sang with them for a while. Their only released recording (aside from a track on the compilation LP *Lowlife*) was a self-released tape, cheaply recorded but packaged in a custom cardboard box with a gold-embossed logo. Mick more recently was in a band called Sissy; Stone Gossard wore its T-shirt when Pearl Jam appeared on *Saturday Night Live*.

Bruce Pavitt in the Rocket on Feast's tape, 7/87: "It says here that 'Feast reside in a musical world of murky shadows alternating with powerful shrieks of light.' Whoever wrote that should be embarrassed. A bit pretentious. They should have said, 'Feast rock like motherfuckers.'"

Jack Endino: "By 1986, for a couple of months Feast was the biggest band in Seattle. Ben (McMillan) was going out with Jane Higgins at the time

Overlord

Metal Church

and wondered why his band (Skin Yard) wasn't as popular as Feast. They made as much as $1,000 a show, even at a place as small as the Vogue. But they never managed to make a good recording."

The Stanwood-formed Bundle of Hiss (originally Bold Pandas) churned out eerie, beautiful, loud rock (early song titles: "Leprosy," "Mass," "Random Torsos"), as performed by Jamie Wayne, Russ Bartlett, Dan Peters, and UW poetry grad Kurt Danielson. Its last lineup included guitarist Thomas A. "Tad" Doyle, a 350-pound ex-butcher and college music major from Boise who came here in 1986 as the drummer for the acid-pop band H-Hour. (Doyle had also been in a high school jazz band that played the Nixon White House.) Besides its club gigs, Bundle of Hiss played powerful practice-space parties to hundreds of fans.

Nine's lives

Ron Rudzitis's Room Nine (named after their first rehearsal space, inside a former Grandma's Cookies plant) debuted at the Golden Crown opening for Student Nurse. Originally Rudzitis performed a few quasi-neo-psychedelia originals augmenting sets of old Johnny Thunders and rockabilly cover tunes, as executed by guitarist Michael Laton, bassist Scott Boggan and drummer Scott Vanderpool (replaced by Shawn Allen, who with Boggan had been in Gordon Doucette's Red Masque).

Ron Rudzitis on Room Nine's early material: "We played early punk songs, late '60s stuff, old soul songs; anything that was under three and a half minutes long.... It was about getting into punk rock and believing I could do it. I didn't have to be John McLaughlin to be in a band."

Baby O's booker offered a regular Tuesday night slot to Rudzitis's band if it could perform a rockabilly dance set. They accepted, and for a couple of months played under the alternate name

Hick-Ups. After that ended, Room Nine concentrated on building an all-originals set, with light shows. Rudzitis took the stage name Ron Nine, and kept it with his subsequent band Love Battery (named after a Buzzcocks song), in which he sang textured, tortured love wails that critics labeled "psychedelic grunge."

Tim Chamberlain on Room Nine in Yeah!, 8/87: "Shawn Allen keeps a good heavy no-frills beat through most of a song and saves the wind contra-rhythms and two-measure fills for the end, where guitar-vocalist Ron Rudzitis goes bonkers on some bizarre, squiggly lead line, and holds it till it feeds back, where Shawn finally beats it to death with a few last savage slams on his skins.... The ultra-simplistic chord structures and the repetition of their songs fits in well with the chic and gritty mood of the Vogue—still definitely one of the hippest places in town despite its commercial success and its often dispirited clientele. (C'mon kids, this is supposed to be a fun place.)"

Keeping all-ages music alive

All-ages shows were held briefly at the Meatlocker, a real former meatlocker on the fourth floor of a decrepit Central District warehouse building that also housed the sound company of future RKCNDY partner Thomas O'Neil. It was dark, smelly, and foreboding; the perfect place for MDA-oriented rock. The beer kegs were kept in a freight elevator, so they could be transported out of sight when the cops showed up.

The Paradise Loft (renamed the Kit Kat Klub) was a performance art co-op with bands at an old bicycle repair shop in Fremont, co-founded by Sharon Gannon. Its regular performers included Johanna Went's younger sister Mary Humble, who read postmodern fairy tales with unhappy endings at the space's weekly cabarets. One day in early 1983, after she'd compiled her tales into a self-published booklet, she asked her friend Jesse Bernstein to give her a haircut, specifying that her neck be made completely hairless. Bernstein, apparently thinking that was the newest punk style, complied. That night Humble took some sleeping pills, put a plastic bag over her head, and sealed the bag with a rubber band around her neck.

The Metropolis

In mid-1983, Gordon Doucette and French college dropout Hugo (Hughes Piottin) co-founded a very cool all-ages space in Pioneer Square. The Metropolis was cooperatively run with a healthy DIY spirit. During its nine-month life it was more like a community center than a commercial club. People volunteered to mount shows, create and distribute posters, run the door, serve pop, and clean up. Doucette's then-girlfriend Susan Silver helped run the place; she and Doucette advised Hugo on what bands to book, as his musical knowledge ran more toward Euro-pop than to punk.

It was a tall, spacious room with a wooden floor, a sandbox in the center, galvanized walls and good acoustics. Maire Masco booked many of the touring-act concerts with DSML member Tony Godbehere (Anthony Rhodes, now with a major local promoter, Monqui Presents), under the name Holy War Cadet Productions. Out-of-town Metropolis visitors included the Violent Femmes, Gun Club, DOA, John Cale, Shockabilly, GBH, and Bad Brains. Local talent there included Red Dress, Student Nurse (in its last incarnation as The Nurse), the U-Men, the Accused, 10 Minute Warning, Life In General, Beat Pagodas, Room Nine, Mr. Epp, Gordon Raphael's Colour Twigs, Red Masque (with Doucette, Raphael, Mike Stein, and Scott Boggan), Colin MacDonnel's Cinema 90 (one show found him singing original lyrics to opera records, another found him wearing only gold body paint and a sash), and one of the first gigs by Soundgarden (see below). Hugo and Doucette used midweek nights to present performance art events, film shows, and DJ nights.

Hugo: *"The Metropolis was my first creative venture. I was 23 at the time. I came from the background of a frustrated artist without knowing it. I was studying math and physics in Europe; I quit, and became a commercial fisherman in Alaska. In the winter I was teaching skiing in the Alps. I moved to Seattle and really decided to create something to bring people together. I had ideas but they were really fuzzy ones. The space came together out of my control in a way. It had a life of its own, very strong. I loved the shows, getting together in a club. I wanted a nonoppressive environment, a non-alcoholic environment. The kids needed a place to go and be safe and not be exploited. I never had a show that cost more than $4 (except for touring acts). I had a strong desire to give, in a creative place where people could meet friends, and maybe get exposed to ideas in art and music that inspired them. I think it worked."*

Partly because no booze was served and because nobody was trying to get rich, the Metropolis fostered a nice atmosphere where everyone had fun while they learned to create their own culture.

Hugo

Holy War Cadets

Left: Mondo Vita

Room Nine

While there were a few scattered fights outside, the atmosphere inside the building was safe and supportive. Of course, that was something the Powers That Be had to stop.

The space closed when developers of a condo next door pressured its landlord to kick it out (it's now a tile store). The last show, on March 6, 1984, starred touring act Alien Sex Fiend with Red Masque. Hugo and Silver promoted shows at other sites under the Metropolis name through mid-1985. These included some of the first concerts at the Moore Theater, plus shows at the Odd Fellows Hall, the Mountaineers, the Golden Crown, and one Violent Femmes gig at the Gorilla Gardens (see next chapter). Hugo then left music for the restaurant business.

To many of the original punk/wave community, the end of the Metropolis marked the end of the all-ages, no-bullshit spirit they'd loved. After that, things got druggy and macho, small and commercial, then big and commercial.

Silver moved on from the Metropolis to book some shows at the Golden Crown, then quit due to disputes with manager Charlie Fong, who continued to make life miserable for many bands and bookers (including Terry Morgan and Steve Pritchard) who switched the upstairs room between alternative-pop, punk, funk and hippie blues before the building was razed for a downtown mall in 1986. Fong opened a new Golden Crown on Second Avenue that operated, without bands, until 1991.

Punks who liked metal, or metalheads who liked punk?

North Seattle native Chris Cornell had lived a rough-and-tumble life after getting a GED from the Seattle schools at age 15. He'd been a drug dealer, a burglar, a car thief and a journeyman drummer in several short-lived bands by the time he made his singing debut at age 17 in the Shemps, a 1982 cover band specializing in dead rock stars' songs, with

guitarist Matt Dentino and bassist Hiro Yamamoto. Within weeks of Cornell's arrival in the band, Yamamoto backed out; the latter's old Illinois chum Kim Thayil stepped in. Cornell soon took on Yamamoto as a roommate (Cornell later shared a house for a while with Andrew Wood). Cornell, Yamamoto and Thayil shared both a punk sensibility and a lingering fondness for '70s metal. In 1984 the three formed their own band.

The new band, Soundgarden (sometimes erroneously spelled Sound Garden, named after the art installation near Magnuson Park) premiered in November 1984 as an opening act for the U-Men at the Top of the Court, a short-lived all-ages space upstairs from the Back Court Tavern in the industrial Interbay neighborhood. Their second show, part of a rental-hall gig at the Langston Hughes Cultural Arts Center near Garfield High, ended when the band got booed off the stage for not being hardcore enough.

Cornell first tried to sing and drum simultaneously, until the group decided it needed him as full-time frontman. Scott Sundquist took over on drums; he was replaced in 1986 by Matt Cameron, who'd played with Daniel House in Feedback and Skin Yard (see next chapter) and recorded with Amy Denio in the jazz-rock Tone Dogs.

In the fall of 1985, Thayil invited his other Illinois chum Bruce Pavitt to hear his band at the Rainbow, a gig booked by Jonathan Poneman.

Bruce Pavitt, *introducing the Soundgarden home video* Louder Than Live: *"I said Identity Crisis (Thayil and Yamamoto's Illinois punk band, with Pavitt's brother) wasn't so great, but I'll check out your new band. I thought they were great. At the time, at least in the punk scene that I was a part of, you really weren't supposed to slow down your songs at all. After a while it became one big contest to see who can play faster.... Soundgarden was one of the first Seattle bands to reject that philosophy and say it's OK to listen to Black Sab-*

bath, for example. They had a very unique sound at the time. It was definitely a kind of a punk/metal crossover. People in the punk community hated them at the time, and the metalheads were all living out in the suburbs and didn't even know about Soundgarden at the time."

Back in Oly…

Downtown Olympia finally got an all-ages venue in March 1984, the same month the Metropolis closed in Seattle and the over-21 Gnu Deli closed in Olympia. The Tropicana was owned by Chris Pugh (later in Swallow), Larry Roberts and Brad Sweek. But, like the Metropolis, it operated as a semi-cooperative. Scene members fixed and painted the place, designed and posted flyers, worked the door, and ran the PA. It finalized the shift of Olympia's music scene away from the Evergreen campus to downtown. It also made an important link between the local Olympia kids and the Evergreen art-rockers, many of whom were affluent kids from out of state who stereotyped local kids as redneck idiots.

Calvin Johnson played the Tropicana several times with his new band Beat Happening (with co-singer Heather Lewis and drummer Brett Lundsford) According to Johnson, the roots of the Tropicana began long before it opened: "Me and a few other people were sitting around complaining about why there weren't any all-ages clubs in Olympia." The only place underage Olympians could play or see music was in a floor of adjoining apartments where Bruce Pavitt and Gary Alan May

had lived. Johnson continued to argue for all-ages shows after he turned 21.

Then in 1983 the Wipers came to town. They were invited by the Young Pioneers, a band of Evergreen students including ex-Room Nine member Scott Vanderpool.

Scott Vanderpool: _"We were trying to put on rock shows, but they wouldn't let us do any rock shows on the Evergreen campus. If there was anything else going on the campus a particulalr night, like a Deadhead poetry reading, we couldn't have a concert on campus. So we rented a storefront and put on our own shows."_

Calvin Johnson: _"They just looked around downtown for a vacant storefront, called the landlord and offered to rent it for one night. Up to this point we'd all been accustomed by the KAOS and Op people to do things the Evergreen way: Set up a non-profit organization, form a board of directors and write up a mission statement. These guys just came into town and did it. We were all going, 'All right, let's do more shows like that!' But that space was rented the next month and there wasn't any other place that seemed to be available. We ended up putting on 'acoustic punk' shows once a month in the alley behind the Martin Hotel. It was great, it was rocking, it was a totally new thing._

"Then after four months of those shows we moved into the Tropicana. It wasn't supposed to be just punk rock. We had plays and art shows. Then we

Above: John Foster
Below: Soundgarden

METROPOLIS
$3 Sun. Jan 15 2:00

Generic Skate Team

TINA
HIGH THERE!

Tina Chopp is God

K

Olympia, Wash.

Below: Beat Happening

got lazy and it was just bands…. By the end it had become just another formula."

Johnson believed you shouldn't try to keep one venue (or concept for a venue) open permanently. To him, most spaces that lasted a year or less still lasted too long:

"It's like something's new and nobody knows what to make of it. You have bands, you have performance artists, you have films or slides or whatever, and it's great. But you do anything for six months and people start to have expectations—'OK, it's a punk rock show, entertain me.'

The U-Men played their first non-Seattle show there; Johnson's Beat Happening played an average of a gig a month. As the only all-ages space in the state for much of its brief life, it attracted under-21s from as far as Bellingham.

The Tropicana shows were great, but they had troubles with local jocks who liked to harass the place and its patrons, driving by and tossing bricks through the windows. After eleven months, the Tropicana had to close when anti-punk merchants bought up the building's lease. Thurston County authorities tried to prevent similar spaces from opening by rushing through a strict anti-noise ordinance that exempted virtually every source of noise except music. It was thrown out by a district court.

By that time, Johnson had started the K (for "knowledge") label, initially a cassette-only company. The logo, a crayon-esque drawing of the letter K inside a shield, was redrawn by Johnson every time it appeared (up to a dozen different renderings in a single flyer). In addition to Johnson's own band, he put out cassettes by the Supreme Cool Beings and *Op* editor John Foster, plus several compilation tapes of unsigned bands along the lines of Bruce Pavitt's original Sub Pop tapes.

Calvin Johnson: "The origins of a lot of the things that came out of Olympia had to do with demystifying the tools of media so access was not restricted due to fear: learning to make your own recordings, your own radio shows, your own performance spaces. It's all tied up in the idea of punk rock breaking down the barriers between the performers and the audience. It fosters an atmosphere where people feel empowered."

Chopp schticks

With more punks around, punk graffiti became widespread. Confused Seattleites began to stare at the obscure logos for the *Patio Table* zine and Jak's skateboard team, and at such spray-painted epithets as THE URGE TO BUY TERRORIZES YOU. Most mysterious of all was a phrase painted, scrawled, etched and drawn seemingly all over town: TINA CHOPP IS GOD. The phrase appeared everywhere from overpasses to trash bins to street-corner electrical boxes. Larry Reid exploited the mystery with a Rosco Louie gallery show starring local graffiti artists, *Who Is Tina Chopp?*

Reid tracked the name down to a Mercer Island High School graduate who went to Western Washington University for one year, then returned home. While there, she dated and then left a DJ at the WWU student station KUGS. He tried to get back at her. He drew, painted and carved libelous statements about her all over Bellingham. Copycat graffitists took up the cause of scrawling statements in her defense, culminating in the "…Is God" line. Chopp graffiti spread to Seattle, and from there around the world. The real Chopp had nothing to do with it, or with the two groups that took her name: a Seattle band led by Pete Spotts called Tina Chopp (its self-released 1993 CD *Nebbish* featured the tune "God Is My Co-Dependent"), and a parody religious sect in Bellingham called the Church of Tina Chopp.

The leather triangle

Visual artists looked for alternatives to the commercial gallery world, which even in Seattle was oriented to big-money collectors. (This is not a town noted for old-money grandchildren with free cash and the willingness to spend it on art.) Two Belltown dive bars were cleaned up into art spaces with beer, the Virginia Inn (where Homer Spence and Annie Mulcahey tended bar) and the Two Bells. In 1982, they served up some of the first local microbrewery beer, one of the yuppies' few worthwhile inventions (made possible when the Liquor Board rescinded an old rule against strong brews). The higher profits from high-test beer (at $2.50 to $4 a glass) boosted the survival potential of beer-and-wine venues. In 1983, the Two Bells exhibited a show of paintings and drawings by Lynda Barry, one of her last shows before she left town.

Other artists organized in the second half of 1983 around the corner of Second and Washington east of Pioneer Square, site of the We B Art, Ground Zero, and Graven Image (successor to Rosco Louie) galleries; the latter two also hosted

LOSER

bands on Friday and Saturday nights.

Peter Mumford's Ground Zero Gallery (no relation to the Ground Zero record label) hosted shows by many local bands, including the Fastbacks and Mr. Epp (a Blackouts homecoming show with the U-Men was closed by city authorities). It was also home base to the Jesse Bernstein Band, formed by Bob Jenkins and featuring Pete Leinonen, Jeff Greinke, Rob Angus, and Jeff McGrath of Fred. Jenkins reportedly recruited Bernstein by telling him that he was going to perform with a band called "Jesse Bernstein" whether Bernstein wanted to be in it or not. Bernstein agreed; he played acoustic guitar and sang beautiful/tortured love songs over the band's jazz-rock soundscapes. Bernstein and Leinonen also recorded the 1984 cassette *Words & Music*, in which Bernstein performed his poetry and prose, Beat-style, over Leinonen's mood-settings. Bernstein and Leinonen continued to perform and record together (amassing scores of unreleased tapes) throughout the decade.

Jenkins dabbled in many other performance and music concepts, before and after the Bernstein Band. He created post-modern rock operas that featured choreography by Kathleen Hunt and Sharon Gannon. He performed with Fred, the Mexicans, Steve and the Soft Guys (with Bernstein on vocals), the New Art Orchestra, Hell's Smells and most recently with Officer Down. In 1987 he began a movie that would star some of his music friends, *Gorefest* (see chapter 10). More recently he hung out with the people who created Rathouse Records (see chapter 11).

Ground Zero hosted the final gig by Audio Leter, just before Gannon and Sue Ann Harkey split for New York and formed a new Audio Leter (Gannon runs a yoga center there; Harkey did graphic design for Grove Press and Autonomedia before moving back in 1994). Eric Muhs went on to compose electronic scores for choreographer Pat Graney; he moved to California in 1985 (where he and fellow ex-Seattleite Myles Boisen made the ambient-noise CD *Notochord*) and returned in 1991.

Eric Muhs *on Audio Leter's last show: "The floor of the space was all filled with rusted metal junk. Most of us were on acid when we arrived. We cleared enough space to stand and to place our equipment. The audience members had to clear spaces where they could stand. We found ourselves in separate mindsets, separated by the metal parts on the floor. We became more and more noisy, apocalyptic. It rose to a crescendo of unimaginable loudness. We stopped playing. The noise was absolutely unabated. People had picked up pipes and stakes and started banging them on the hoods of cars and the other pieces of junk. It was SO LOUD; it was like having your head inside an oil drum and having people beat on it."*

Larry Reid and Tracey Rowland's Graven Image Gallery was named in honor of an old man who walked around in front of the Pioneer Square galleries holding a sign bearing the Old Testament pro-

hibition "Create No Graven Images." It was a dank, musty basement space with a sooty coal-burning stove. Bands played amidst hanging pipes and bare green light bulbs; the perfect setting for some of the gothic death bands of the era. Its first art show was *Trouble in Bedrock* by Tony Horn, known at the time for stencil graffiti of a paranoid Fred Flint-

stone.

Graven Image hosted the record-release party for the U-Men EP *Blight*, the only release on Bruce Pavitt's Bombshelter label (named after the Bombshelter Records store on Broadway, which he managed at the time).

Tracey Rowland: *"One of the wildest things that I remember at Graven Image was the U-Men record release party, the 'Urban Picnic.' We got all these hamburger patties and chicken wings from a wholesale outlet, all frozen. I'd gotten a recipe for a barbecue sauce with Coca-Cola that sounded so bad that I had to try it out. The barbecue was held in the alley behind the gallery; the barbecue was horrible and the burgers and chicken were still frozen in the middle when they were served. People still come up to me and ask me if I've been barbecuing lately."*

The U-Men next recorded the 1985 *Stop Spinning* EP on Homestead Records, the first Seattle punk record with national distribution since the

WORDS & MUSIC
steven jesse bernstein
and pete leinonen

Audio LeTer

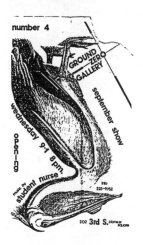

number 4

GROUND ZERO GALLERY
september show
wednesday 9-1 8 pm
opening
made by student nurse
info 722-9752
202 3rd S. pioneer square

≡BOMBSHELTER≡ RECORDS

Eric Muhs

Lincoln Arts Center "Riot"

Big Brother

Fartz album three years before. When the Bombshelter store folded, Pavitt's fellow Bombshelter employee Russ Battaglia started another Capitol Hill outlet, Fallout Records and Skateboards. Pavitt took other day jobs, including stints as a restaurant cook and an engineer on Yesco's canned-music service.

Ground Zero, Graven Image and the Metropolis formed a viable punk circuit, a "black leather triangle" uneasily sharing Pioneer Square with the baby-boomer blues bars. The three spaces collaborated on a "Welcome to 1984" New Year's party with the Fastbacks, Room Nine, Student Nurse, 10 Minute Warning, DSML (fake-Hebrew for "dismal"), Popdefect, the U-Men, and Fred. The year of Reagan's recoronation (and its royal jubilee, the L.A. Olympics) was ushered in by nearly 2,000 kids in black roaming Pioneer Square and upsetting the blues-bar yuppies. Flyers for the event featured an anonymous artist's illustration of George Orwell's Big Brother that had been plastered as a poster all over town.

Alan Pruzan, ex-911 Media Arts staffer: "There were three all-ages clubs at the same time, within blocks of each other. At the time, I didn't think it was a special thing. I didn't know what an exception it turned out to have been. But when I turned 21 I didn't care about that anymore."

Graven Image became headquarters to the Buzz Scooter Club, a bunch of kids devoted to fixing, riding, and re-fixing old Vespa motor scooters, some of whom wore the mod fashions that had been revived in England by the Specials and the Jam. The

highly un-mod U-Men became the scooter club's official band.

Don Cooper, a member of the early U-Men entourage, tried to keep the Gorilla Room spirit alive with the Grey Door, an unlicensed private club with an unadvertised location in the basement of We B Art's building. He opened it with settlement money after he fell of a two-story roof during a construction job. Starting in the winter of 1983, the Grey Door was by far the sleaziest corner of the black-leather triangle. Instead of working restrooms, it had one porta-potty in the back that was never emptied. In the main room, bands like the Refuzors played L.A.-style fast hardcore, while bands like the Melvins instructed people in the new, slow hardcore. In the halls, patrons openly shot up coke and/or heroin, or swallowed hits of the ubiquitous MDA. It was home to a teen-punk skateboard team, the Boppo Boys. Larry Reid described its clientele as "the outcasts of the scene; the people who were 86'd from the Metropolis." The Grey Door was evicted in the spring of 1984. Cooper went clean and sober, and dropped out of the music scene.

A mile north of all this, all-ages punk shows took place regularly at the Lincoln Arts Center, a black-box theater space inside the old warehouse loft at 66 Bell St., until a DOA show was shut down by the cops, leading to a brief riot (bottles thrown, fires lit). Somebody spray-painted circle-A anarchy symbols on some parked police cars.

One last chance
On Aug. 11, 1984, fire marshals shut down

Graven Image before an over-capacity show by Youth Brigade and L.A. hardcore band Jody Foster's Army, leading to a brief riotous scuffle by the black-clad rebel throng. The punks started a bonfire in the street with papers and wooden crates, and used it as a skateboard-jumping obstacle. The leather-studded kids demanded their money back; Reid tried to placate them by promising a free make-up show the next day at Ground Zero. Reid was cited for "posing a serious menace to human life;" he kept the space closed, except for scooter club meetings, until his lease ran out at year's end. By that time, Ground Zero and Metropolis also closed, leaving no regular all-ages space between Olympia and Canada. Ground Zero became Here Today, a co-op gallery/performance space run by a collective that included Jesse Bernstein and A.S. Loris. They held shows by arty performers like Jeff Greinke, Rob Angus and Fred; when they lost their lease, they booked performance-art shows at other spaces through 1985, while Pioneer Square was made safe for blue-eyed blues bars again.

Hardcore punks tried to establish the all-ages Spider's Web (renamed Barricades), an old movie theater in the south end, in the fall of 1984. The effort died shortly after a DOA Halloween show was stopped due to flying beer bottles. Similar shows at Munro's Dance Palace, a ballroom-dance studio in Interbay, ended after a riot at a Fartz reunion show. (Barricades reopened in 1993 for occasional private parties.)

*From a **Spider's Web** poster, 10/84: "This is our last chance! No alcohol! No assholes!"*

Some advocates tried to start SOS: Save Our Scene, a benefit group to keep independent clubs going; it didn't last much longer than the clubs. Someone else put up a street poster around that time saying simply, "SEATTLE SCENE FOUND DEAD."

Key to Diagram on page 76

1. 0.	11. Johnny Smoke	21. George Sinfield	31. Mark Backer
2. Aaron Taylor	12. Kerry Loewen	22. Andy Taylor	32. Sarah Stanley
3. Ben McMillan	13. Craig Nelson	23. Lance Rieck	33. Bruce Pavitt
4. Abby Staten	14. Peter Curry	24. Ray	34. Mary Gillespie
5. Snoopy	15. Debbie Letterman	25. Kris Lall	35. Eric Tollefson
6. Neil Sussman	16. Jon Wright	26. Jimi Plant	36. Gary Action
7. Chris Loathesome	17. Kevitch Stanton	27. Bianco Piaggio	37. Mali Sarriutarte
8. Alfred Butler	18. Marsh Gooch	28. Greg Phipps	38. Leslie Foster
9. Jeff Smarr	19. Norman Bately	29. David Pinkis	39. A Couple of Girls
10. Jah Bernard	20. Mike Larson	30. Charles Cutter	40. Lisa Aqabian
			41. Cyrus Chen

VOGUE

SEATTLES FOREMOST
AND MOST BELOVED
CITIZEN

CHAPTER NINE :
AIN'T NOTHIN TO DO (1985-1986)

In the winter of 1984-85, a start-up software business completed its first product at a small third-floor office in Pioneer Square. Aldus Page-Maker soon revolutionized the world of publishing, especially the world of self-publishing. Self-made music was waiting for its own next revolution. It seemed far away at the time, if not impossible.

At the midpoint of the Reagan presidency, the so-called "rock of the '80s" seemed to be winding down to a stop. Only a couple of small bars still welcomed original-rock bands. KYYX shut down its "Wave" format after Pat O'Day ran into fiscal problems and had to sell. Most of the original party houses closed; their residents dispersed around town, across the country, or into junkiedom. In January 1985, the *Rocket*'s year-end pick of "best venue" was "Your Living Room."

Some people were working to change that.

Gorilla Gardens

Ex-Gorilla Room owner Tony Chu joined with Dave Stone, Douglas Mays and ex-Funhole promoter Ed Shepherd to open the Rock Theater, an all-ages space in an old Chinatown movie house. It had two auditoriums, the 305-capacity Gorilla Gardens (specializing in punk) and the 335-capacity Omni Room (specializing in metal); most people just called the whole place Gorilla Gardens. The rooms were connected by a common lobby. It was a big step in bringing the kids with big hair and leather together with the kids with short hair and leather; to this point, metalheads from the suburbs had been driving into town to bash punks. Maire Masco, Tony Godbehere, David Portnow, Susan Silver and Hugo booked many of the shows there. The venue also published its own zine, *Subcharge*.

Art Chantry to Fiz, *12/93: "Metal and punk bands started playing at Gorilla Gardens, the kids would meet in the lobby and realize that the only difference between them was their hairdos. I think that's when this melding that became the 'big grunge sound' really started."*

As he had with the Gorilla Room, Chu put as little money into the space as he had to. The result looked rickety in a friendly way, but was far below code. Fire marshals tried to shut the Rock Theater down just before the Masco-promoted opening show by Austin's Butthole Surfers on Pearl Harbor Day 1984, due to a shortage of exits. The staff im-

mediately moved to make the place legal by chain-sawing a six-foot-tall hole in the back wall. Hugo built an exquisitely decorated dressing room, which was promptly trashed by the touring Replacements.

Susan Silver: "Hugo and I had booked the Violent Femmes for two shows on the same night; they both sold out. Hugo thought it would be convenient for them to stay near the club, so he made reservations for them at the Bush Hotel (a dingy Chinatown flophouse, since upgraded as low-income housing). So even before the show started, the band and their road manager almost got into a fist fight with Hugo... During the first show ceiling fans started falling on people on the floor. Some guy was running around on the false ceiling; he'd been stealing equipment. Hugo went up there chasing after him. Meanwhile there were about 20 cop cars and a fire marshal outside, along with the 500 people waiting for the next show. Tony Chu was nowhere to be found, and Hugo was chasing this guy, so it was up to me to show the police that we had our proper occupancy permits and all these things the place was supposed to have and didn't. I opened the first door into a hallway that was supposed to be clear; it was piled up almost to the ceiling with carpentry stuff. I was trying to convince them not to shut us down. I opened up the emergency exit door that was supposed to lead to the alley; the exit way was completely boarded up with 2 x 4s.

"I convinced them that they should let the second show go on because there would be a riot if they didn't. It was already 10:30, the first show was still going on, and the police gave orders to clear the building by 11:30. I had to plead with Richard Peterson to cut his opening act for the second show down from 45 minutes to his three best songs. Somehow we got the show in."

Fastbacks-Silly Killers-Vains-Fartz-10 Minute Warning vet Duff McKagan returned from L.A. to perform one show at the Omni Room. It was the first show on the first tour by his new band, first called Hollywood Rose but by then known as Guns n' Roses (the Fastbacks opened). The band hitch-hiked part of the way when its van broke down on Interstate 5; the guys only received $50 of their promised $250 fee for a gig ony 13 people saw.

Richard Peterson

Below: Renee Refuzor

Refuzors redux

Among the bands that played the Rock Theater's first weeks were the Refuzors, once a loud and angry three-piece, now a loud and angry six-piece with Mike Refuzor sharing vocals with Renee Refuzor (sister of Look veteran Rob Vasquez) and guitar duties with Ward Nelson. This new lineup, like the original, treated punk rock as a cultural, not a political, rebellion, and emphasized assault chords over intricate fingering.

On April 9, 1984, after several months' worth of noise complaints concerning Mike's Capitol Hill apartment-practice studio, police showed up and started carting his gear away. While his lawyer negotiated to get his stuff back, Mike and the band painted NO NAZIS and POLICE STATE on bedsheets, which they hung out the windows. Cops showed up again and told the band if they didn't take down the sheets they'd go to jail. "Let's go," Mike said; the police left without him. The band got their returned equipment and an eviction notice. The group also got in trouble with the cops for putting the words EAT SHIT on a street poster for a show at the Graven Image.

From "I'm A Refuzor" by **Mike Refuzor***: "I don't believe in books, don't believe in school; I brush my teeth with beer/If I've ever had a dollar to my name, it must have been last year."*

Renee Refuzor was not our first female hardcore singer. There had already been Tina Bell of Bam Bam (also the first black punk singer in town). The *Rocket* described their 1984 single "Villains Also Wear White" as "slap in the face punk that sounds safe confined on vinyl while being very battering in a live setting." After Bell left husband-bandmate Tommy Martin, he turned Bam Bam into an instrumental unit (with Nicholas Rhinehard and Mike Peterson) and made the self-released tape *Pollywog*. Martin also played in the "psycho industrial punk funk" band Mommy, with singer Brad

Mowen from Portland's Sweaty Nipples.

Return to the Odd Fellows

In June 1985, a new band called Skin Yard opened for the U-Men (still in their scooter-thrash phase as managed by Larry Reid) at a self-promoted show in the Odd Fellows Hall. The show was a "going away" party for the U-Men, one of the first Seattle bands of its time to make even a regional tour (just eight shows).

It was nearly a decade since the TMT Show; the scene that show had spawned had become harder and even more cynical. The early punks were serious about having fun. These punks were having fun about being serious—"Loud ugly pop," Skin Yard's PR called itself. Singer Ben McMillan stood motionless at the mike as he droned on in gloom-n'-doom territory—not the whimpering cry-in-your-beer gloom of the Smiths, but a passionate depressiveness that said things *are* shitty but they sure as hell shouldn't be. The band's assorted line-ups contained future scene stars Jack Endino, Daniel House, Greg Gilmore, Jason Finn (later in Love Battery), and Matt Cameron (later in Soundgarden). It also featured drummers Scott McCullum (aka Norman Scott) and Barrett Martin (later in Screaming Trees) and bassist Pat Pedersen over its seven-year life, evolving from psychedelic gloom (the *Trouser Press Record Guide* called its self-titled debut "positively glacial in both temperature and speed") toward straightforward defiance (Cameron told *Goldmine* it was a "dissonant, angular kind of dorky prog-rock").

Hanmi Hubbard *in* Backlash *on* Skin Yard's *start: "They were an artsy band: dramatic vocals, guitars that resembled whales copulating, some weirdo trying to play guitar on the bass (just kidding Daniel—really) and a drummer who wanted to be in Soundgarden."*

Flaming and rioting

The U-Men continued to perform outrageous, beer-sodden gigs, some featuring porno movies as opening attractions.

For the Bumbershoot festival in September 1985, the U-Men were booked to perform at the Mural Ampitheater, an old World's Fair structure with a reflecting pool separating the audience from (and continuing beneath) the stage. The band and Reid devised an untoppable ending. During the gig, singer John Bigley pretended to drink from a vodka bottle; he really just held the bottle around without ingesting from it. During the last number, he poured its contents (really lighter fluid) into the pool, set fire to a broom, then dumped the broom in the pool. The pool went ablaze. Flames spread to the creosoted bottom of the concrete stage, bringing smoke everywhere. Sound man Tom O'Neil rushed to get his equipment off stage. Cops, believing the excited audience to be rioting, billy-clubbed people. Mark Arm called it the greatest show he'd ever seen. It enhanced the U-Men's reputation for

LOSER

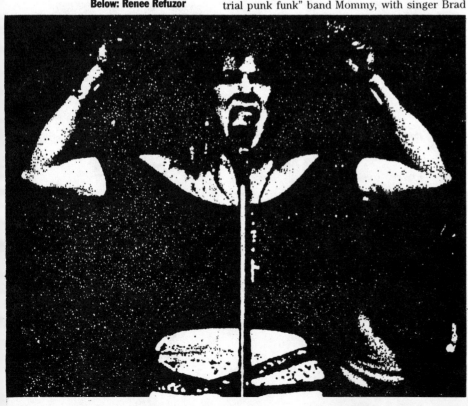

unstoppable mayhem. At one point they had 13 consecutive shows canceled and were banned from every club; they booked one show under a pseudonym, MiG Motto and the Ubongo Sound Shapists. Police seemed to know when they were to appear at private parties, and moved faster than normal to shut those parties down.

Silencing the all-ages scene

Skoochies, an all-ages disco in the former Jesus People coffeehouse near Seattle Center, became the site of a wild parking-lot scene in 1985, including one shooting incident. The event gave more PR fuel to sensational media campaigns, shouting that Our Children were in danger and that all-ages entertainment, especially discos like Skoochies and the Monastery, was a menace.

City Attorney Doug Jewett proposed an evening curfew for minors. That didn't pass, but under Jewett's lobbying, City Councilman (now Mayor) Norm Rice introduced a Teen Dance Ordinance, which effectively banned all-ages disco events by for-profit promoters with over 150 patrons. Dance shows could only be 21-and-over with alcohol, 18-and-over without alcohol, or for ages 16-20 within the law's excessive insurance and security requirements.

Club Broadway, a fancy disco in a Capitol Hill warehouse, tried to comply with the ordinance and lost its shirt. The Retro (a short-lived dance/band/video space at Eighth and Olive) and City Beat (a disco with occasional bands, in a once and future gay club on Boren Avenue) imposed an 18-and-over policy, and went under without the 17-year-olds' patronage. Jewett (who also wanted to ban street postering) and Rice faced off in the 1989 mayoral race; the youth vote helped Rice win handily, but he remained dedicated to the Teen Dance Ordinance.

The rock community paid little attention to the Teen Dance Ordinance as it was rushed through the City Council. Most people assumed it wouldn't apply to live concerts. But soon after it took effect at the end of August, authorities cracked down hard on the Rock Theater, citing Chu and independent promoter Anthony Triage over underage dancing at a Husker Du show (the space was flooded, with patrons crowded onto a small dry patch of carpet) and notifying the venue's landlord that he was leasing the space to "a known teen dance promoter." The landlord promptly revoked the Rock Theater's lease, effective the end of October. Its closure left no place in Seattle for touring bands too big for the Central, too small for the Moore, and too punk for the Backstage. The building became a warehouse, and is now vacant. The Mountaineers building also stopped booking rock shows when the ordinance took effect.

Ed Shepherd tried to mount shows at Le Club Hit on Westlake Avenue (batting-practice cages by day, bands by night). Its most famous "show" was a no-show: John Cale didn't get his promised advance and never left his hotel room, while several hundred fans milled impatiently and were shooed away. Shepherd moved to Hawaii, where he ran a record store and managed reggae bands.

Maire Masco quit the business when the Rock Theater closed. She'd lost a lot of money, and was tired of the atmosphere and attitudes that had infiltrated the scene. She entered the booming computer software industry.

Maire Masco: "I got tired of people being such jerks. People just wanted the opportunity to be irresponsible. The lack of regard for each other, for property, for other people's efforts is what destroyed it. You could work in the Seattle music scene until your face turned blue, but unless you had the right band and the right break, you could just keep struggling forever.... Susan Silver was able to take her promotion experience and move up to the next level, booking bigger shows in bigger places. I'd work up to three months getting a show set up and maybe net $100 after the band, the space, the sound man, and everything else.

"Boy, it's great having a regular paycheck. It's nice being a grown-up. People are supportive; they don't spit on you. I like having a house."

Tony Chu and Tony Godbehere booked a few shows at the Golden Crown after the Rock Theater's demise, then tried to open a second Gorilla Gardens in an old auto-parts warehouse on Nickerson Street, south of the Fremont Bridge. Again, Chu didn't renovate it enough to become a legal public auditorium. On Nov. 26, 1985, during one of Seattle's rare snowfalls, L.A.'s Circle Jerks were about to take the stage when the Fire Department showed up with the usual orders to cease operation. Chu agreed to stop the concert. He was trying to get people to leave 15 minutes later, when 24 cops stormed in and ordered the 350 patrons to disperse without saying why. Several patrons threw rocks, bottles and snowballs at the cops, who beat up patrons with nightsticks. Three cop-car windshields were broken. Neighborhood property was trashed. Chu (who locked himself in an office during the riot) and seven others were arrested.

The U-Men held a New Year's party for 200 people at a downtown art studio run by former Zero Deals member Brook Lizotte (Skin Yard opened), hoping to skirt the Teen Dance Ordinance by promoting it as a private party. Some time after the gig ended and the doors were locked, the last remaining patrons on the street were attacked with nunchucks by a Filipino street gang, who apparently mistook the leather-clad punks for a rival gang trying to encroach on its turf. Dozens suffered broken bones and other injuries. Rick Lewis, singer for the Olympia bands Idol Worship and Immoral Roberts, was knocked into a coma for six months and ended up with permanent paralysis and brain damage; he died in August 1993 in his hospital room.

Tony Chu's bad luck continued on Jan. 26, 1986 when he tried to re-stage the Circle Jerks gig at the

The U-Men

United Commercial Travelers hall. When the Circle Jerks didn't show up, about 50 of the 150 patrons got fired up and rioted along Fifth Avenue North. Cops claimed that four Molotov cocktails were thrown into the street, beer bottles got thrown at passing motorists, and a phone booth got trashed. An inflammatory *Times* editorial used the riots as examples of why all-ages concerts should be heavily regulated if not banned altogether. Chu left the music business and returned to Taiwan.

Lois Pierris's Soho Restaurant and Clothing, a small 1985-86 space up the street from the old Athens Cafe, was the first place in town to experiment with a Liquor Board rule that allowed minors in a separate booze-free area of the room. It also sold clothes on the stage and dance floor during the day. Soundgarden opened for Soul Asylum there in one of the loudest shows performed anywhere. The place still lost money and closed after less than a year. Natasha's (renamed Natacha's), a 1963-built dance hall across the sound in Bremerton, was open for a while as an all-ages space until some rowdy teens started causing trouble on the ferry back to Seattle.

Some teens formed the Youth Defense Council, a political movement proclaiming the right of underage citizens to low-cost entertainment. The group gathered 5,000 petition signatures in a futile effort to get the Teen Dance Ordinance overturned. It also booked a few shows into the Lincoln Arts Center, until that group was evicted from its 66 Bell space by developers in the spring of 1987.

Washington Hall stopped booking bands after what the *Rocket* called "600 maniacs" stormed the place during a show by touring act Agent Orange. Windows got broken, doors got taken off their hinges, holes were smashed into walls, stair railings were busted. The place didn't hold another rock show until 1991.

A few free all-ages shows were held in 1987-88 in the basement of Luna, a designer shoe store on Broadway; they included the first all-cover gigs by Lords of the Wasteland, the soon-to-be Mother Love Bone. The space was small enough to be exempt from the teen-dance ban. For larger shows, under-21s had to go to Tacoma's Community World Theater (see chapter 10).

L'affaire Guzzo

KIRO-TV geezer editorialist Lou Guzzo (a former *Times* art critic and crony to ex-Gov. Dixy Lee Ray) spoke in favor of the repressions: "Who needs teenage punk rockers anyway?" The hardcore Dehumanizers sampled his remarks in their blistering 45, "Kill Lou Guzzo" ("Hey Lou, I'm dating your daughter, she's kind of cute.… I'm going after your wife next"). Guzzo and the station sued to stop distribution, and reached an out-of-court settlement that allowed the record to stay in print with revised lyrics. Singer-guitarist John "Mort" Mortensen left the band before its 1987 album *The End of Time*; he joined Bellingham's garage-pop Mono Men. Bassist Marcus Membrane became a trumpeter in Rudy Yuly's ska-revival Tiny Hat Orchestra. The Dehumanizers reunited for a 1992 EP, featuring "Grandma I'm A Drug Feind."

"Kill Lou Guzzo" was on Subcore Records, also home to sides by the Mentors, the Accused, and New York's self-proclaimed "violent and obscene rock performer" G.G. Allin. It was run by local entrepreneur David Portnow, who started at age 18 with the first of four *Metal Meltdown* compilations. He'd issued tracks by 30 artists before he was old enough to see any of their bar shows. He promoted Gorilla Gardens shows and worked for Victor Hayden's Alchemy label (which issued the Melvins' *Gluey Porch Treatments*). His other labels were Ever Rat (metal and thrash by Coven, Dumt and Lethal Dose; named after Portnow's hometown of Everett), Ever Rap (hip-hop), Ever Dread (reggae), and Ever Rus (Russian rockers The Prepinaki).

David Portnow to Backlash *on the KIRO/Guzzo suit, 11/88: "At first, he didn't even know about the record. People from out of state started calling information, to find out who he was, and his number was listed. Finally he went out and bought the record. Then they (KIRO) sent a threatening letter telling me not to press any more copies. So I immediately pressed another 1,000. Then they got really hard about it, so I put out a 12-inch single of it and really pissed them off. Now they are suing for $2.25 million."*

No place like home

While the all-ages scene was dying, the 21-and-over venues weren't too robust either. Clubs closed faster than new ones opened; those that opened were often smaller, or less dedicated to the harsher kinds of music, than those that came before.

Bands still formed and practiced in basements, warehouses, and commercial rehearsal rooms carved out of old manufacturing buildings. Just like in the Klondike gold rush, the only people making money were suppliers. The *Rocket*'s top advertisers in these years were demo-tape studios and instrument stores.

The scene retreated back toward party houses. One was the Room Nine House, north of the Rainbow, where Ron and Tracy Rudzitis lived with Charles Peterson and Dan Peters. "We held 'small' parties," Peterson recalls, "with never less than 200 people." On the same block was the Green Barn (and, next door, the Green Barn Annex). Tammy Watson, later of Kill Sybil, described life in the

Green Barn as "a wild, crazed, hippie-punk-MDA freakout. You never knew who'd be playing in the practice room, blasting some rock you'd never heard before."

Peterson was at another party house in the U District on a night when "some bands, including Feast and Green River, were to play a back yard gig up in Stanwood that got canceled because of rain. It moved to a basement at 50th and 11th. There were 250 to 300 people in a five-bedroom house. Around 2 a.m. a paddy truck showed up. Someone said there were at least 11 cop cars and some police dogs. I didn't see it, because me and eight other people were hiding in one of the bedrooms."

The Ditto and the new folk-rock

Hank Ivan opened the Ditto Tavern in Belltown at the end of 1984. He first played dance tapes, then (at the suggestion of Johnny Rubato) switched to bands. One gig had Andy Wood (opening for Skin Yard) singing solo to tapes, then preparing a bowl of Count Chocula and milk, chatting up the utter coolness of cereal, before throwing it at the crowd.

Partly because his wife worked there, Ron Rudzitis found frequent Ditto bookings for his band Room Nine. They also appeared on one of the *Sounds of Young Seattle* compilation tapes, and made the finals of an MTV Basement Tapes contest with the Cure-esque "Seas Without a Shore" from the *Voices of a Summer's Day* album on the Louisiana label C'est La Mort.

Ron Rudzitis to the Rocket *on Room Nine's brushes with fortune, 6/92: "Unfortunately, the*

THE SOUND OF
YOUNG SEATTLE

Below: Skin Yard

Below: Pure Joy

Seattle scene wasn't quite what it is now. We had so many good things almost happen to us that it destroyed us."

Charles Peterson: *"The Ditto was just swimming in cheap beer. The floor was covered in beer. When Faith Henschel (a KCMU DJ) and Tracy Rudzitis were tending bar, free beer was flowing like you couldn't believe. It always seemed crowded, even when there were really just a few people in there."*

Hank Ivan *to the* Times, *1986: "I couldn't stand the noise. I was driven out of my own club. And I'd have to paint the bathroom walls every week because they wrote all over them, and they didn't even buy any beer—they were already high on drugs."*

By late 1985 Ivan turned the booking chores over first to Earl Brooks and then to Dean Wartti. They shunned some of the lowlife hardcore outfits but booked the emerging grunge acts, alternating with art-rock bands like Laura Weller and Bonnie Hammond's Capping Day (see next chapter), the Walkabouts, Rusty Willoughby and Lisa King's Pure Joy (originally the Dwindles, renamed after a Teardrop Explodes song), and John Massoni and Liz Wick's neo-psychedelic A Western Family (which evolved into Weather Theatre), plus fun-rock bands like the Young Fresh Fellows, Johnny Rubato and Phil Otto's No News, Nancy Clarke and George Romansic's Danger Bunny, KJET DJ Jim Keller's Different Ones (with his brother David, both formerly in the New Flamingos), and Wartti's own bluegrass-parody Center for Disease Control Boys (Chris Cornell drummed on their self-released 45, "Who We Hatin' Now Mr. Reagan?"). Ivan turned his black-painted walls into a forum for local photographers.

Still, paid attendance seldom exceeded 40; bands like Soundgarden often played for fewer than a dozen people. Richard Pauletti bought the Ditto in 1986 but closed it in 1987. He reopened it in late 1989 with bands on Fridays and Saturdays, hippie poets on Sundays.

The Walkabouts formed when Carla Torgerson and Chris Eckman met in an Alaska cannery. For their first gig, they got paid $35 to open for the Refuzors at Gorilla Gardens. They grew from a duo into an acoustic/electric melange with keyboardist Glenn Slater (from the art-pop Melting Fish) and Eckman's brothers Grant on drums (replaced by Terri Moeller) and Kurt on bass (replaced by Michael Wells); violin-mandolin player Bruce Wirth came aboard in 1992.

The early Walkabouts recorded the EP *22 Disasters* and a couple of compilation tracks, then spent $3000 in a 24-track studio recording a never-released album for an out-of-town indie label. While that company kept promising to put the record out, the band self-released the 45 "Linda Evans (This World Is Your Mistake)," an ode to one of the Hollywood celebrities who'd moved to Washington. Once they gave up on that label, they signed with PopLlama and recorded the 1988 LP *See Beautiful Rattlesnake Gardens* (described in *Backlash* as "balancing dreamy, introspective songs with spritely rockers, both acoustic and electric") on Conrad Uno's 8-track board for less than $1500; they claimed it sounded much better than the more expensive spread.

Tom Phalen *in the* Times *on the Walkabouts, 3/93: "Listening to them is like staring at a lava lamp. The colors and light are beautiful and bright, sometimes amusing, often soothing, but the movement never stops; the flow, bounce, and change is constant. The shapes and sizes are forever metamorphosing. Just when you think you have something identified, it changes and rolls or floats away."*

While these more "mature" bands found gigs at the U District bars (including midweek shows at the Rainbow), life remained tight for the heavier bands, largely stuck at the Central, the Vogue, the Ditto, and private parties.

Exit the Blackouts

Down in San Francisco, the Blackouts finally broke up in 1985 after producing biting, innovative music in three cities and going nowhere commercially. The band's last year was marked by internal dissentions, few gigs, and fewer new songs. Erich Werner stayed behind and later joined ex-Meyce member Paul Hood in the Toiling Midgets.

Paul and Roland Barker and Bill Rieflin called Ministry founder Al Jourgenson, now based in Chicago, to offer their performing services. As the Blackouts had evolved from avant-pop to experimental noise, so had Jourgenson evolved from synth-disco to in-your-face speed noise, hardcore rock with electronics instead of feedback. He'd recorded the album *Twitch* by himself, and needed a band to perform it on tour.

LOSER

Black Cat Orchestra

K. Leimer

After the tour Paul Barker became Jourgenson's senior partner in the new Ministry, with Rieflin as its permanent drummer. Paul also recorded a 1990 solo CD for WaxTrax, *The Age of Reason*, under the band name Lead Into Gold. Roland Barker continued to tour with Ministry but wasn't a credited participant in its studio recordings. He *has* recorded with one of Jourgenson's side projects, Revolting Cocks; he's also composed background music for a series of meditation tapes.

Roland and Bill Rieflin again live in Seattle. In 1991 they and fellow ex-Blackout Mike Davidson were invited to China by Dennis Rea, a former guitarist with Fred and Color Anxiety whose girlfriend had a teaching residency there. Their pick-up band, the Vagaries, was one of the first US bands to tour in China. They played to community centers and youth groups, and gave a lip-sync performance on a TV variety show seen by an estimated 600 million people, one tenth of the Earth's population.

More art rock and non-rock

Rea was one of a growing number of Seattleites who took a more experimental-compositional approach to music, including composer David Mahler, Stuart Dempster, the New Art Orchestra, Bob Jenkins, binaural-soundscape creator Norman Durkee, guitar/tape composer Wrick Wolff, cellist Brent Arnold, keyboardist Charlie Rowan, vocalist Jay Clayton, tape/sampler artist Your Host bObYY, percussionist Michael Shrieve, Ron Fein (who composed pieces played simultaneously on 20 boom boxes), sampled-voice assembler Blackhumour, and the pseudo-Eastern European sounds of the

Black Cat Orchestra (with composer Kyle Hanson, cellist Lori Goldston, painter-musician Friese Undine and screech-vocalist "Detonator Beth" Lawrence). Members of the New Art Orchestra wound up in rock and art-rock bands including Color Anxiety, the Catabatics, and Some Velvet Sidewalk.

Jeff Greinke (a former Penn State meteorology student) issued a series of ambient-synth recordings that explored the texture of environment and pure sound: *Cities in Fog*, *Lost Terrain*, *Crossing Ngoli*, the latter with his sometime partner Rob Angus (who also led the ambient-rock band Color Anxiety).

K. (Kerrie) Leimer released his and other people's ambient discs on his own Palace of Lights label, including the one-off project *Savant* with himself, ex-Young Scientist member Marc Barecca, and Jim and David Keller. Leimer also composed the soundtrack to a documentary film about Jamaica, *The Land of Look Behind*.

The ambient scene gained a foothold at Incubator, an unadvertised party space in an old bottling plant in the south end, later moved to the former Kalberer Hotel Supply warehouse (one band that practiced there took the Kalberer Hotel Supply name as its own). In 1992 the rhythmless noise produced by these groups showed up at an aboveground venue, Re-bar's Monday night "Seven Beats Per Minute Ambient Industrial Lounge."

The more upscale art-music composers performed at On the Boards' Washington Hall and other culture spaces. Some of their shows were booked by Soundwork, a performance series run by ex-KRAB DJ Herb Levy.

The Melvins

Across the Cascades

Steve Fisk came back from "a dying scene" in California in late 1984 and spent the next four years at Sam Albright's Velvetone studio (named after the Velvetones, one of Jimi Hendrix's teenage bands) in Ellensburg, where he'd gone to college before transferring to Evergreen. He made more cut-up records ('Til the Night Closes In and One More Valley), involving TV and movie samples, tape loops, and electronics. At Velvetone he recorded two Beat Happening records, two Girl Trouble records, Pell Mell and Soundgarden remixes, Damon Romero's Olympia band Treehouse, and a number of Eastern Washington hardcore bands including Moses Lake's Moral Crux (originally with Dustin Warren, later in Olympia's Fitz of Depression). The Columbia Basin Herald said Moral Crux "played at a tempo a hummingbird might envy." Moral Crux's bassist's dad had played in the Bards, a '60s Jerry Dennon-produced pop band.

But Fisk's most famous early productions were the first sessions by Screaming Trees, a local neo-pop band that incorporated both melodic and punkish elements into its textures of neo-psychedelic noise. Screaming Trees evolved into a strong yet delicate mix of big beats, interweaving guitar lines by Gary Lee Conner and moody lyrics by Mark Lanegan.

Lanegan first met Gary Lee's brother Van Conner in a high school journalism class in Ellensburg, where they discovered that both were regularly taking two-hour bus trips into Seattle to shop for punk records. A few weeks later, according to the band's official bio, Van and Mark separately crashed the same college kegger. "I was unwelcome there," Van said; "I had no hair and looked different from everybody else." Seeking out a familiar face, he ran into Mark. "He bit me on the ear and said, 'Let's start a band.'" They started practicing cover tunes in a garage behind Conner's par-

ents' video store, with Van on guitar. Mrs. Conner reportedly hounded Van to let older brother Gary Lee sit in on bass. A couple of months later, after the Conners had switched instruments, Gary Lee got a four-track tape deck and, according to Lanegan, the group "actually started writing things that sound like songs."

The band, with drummer Mark Pickerel, made a six-song tape at Velvetone Studios in 1984 (released as the SST EP Other Worlds in 1988), which included the enveloping textural trip "The Turning." Their vinyl debut came with the 1986 Clairvoyance LP on Albright's Velvetone label, then joined SST Records with Even If And Especially When. There were separate Screaming Trees bands in Canada, England and Holland. Some of them may have been named after the Screaming Tree, a popular guitar pedal; our Trees weren't. They also appeared on the compilation tape Ellensburg—Where Cows Live, with cuts by Fisk, Albright, the "hardpsycherockcore" King Krab, MDL (Bif, Baf, Blare and Dave Lenin), and Greensuit (with the youngest Conner brother, Pat).

The Inland Empire's first important band started as Sweet Madness, a power-pop combo formed in Spokane by Jan Gregor, Mark Fenton, and Jeff Tzara. In the winter of 1981, right after John Lennon's murder, they tried to stage a gun-control benefit concert at a Spokane armory where the Sonics had headlined 15 years before. Gun fans tore down their posters and pressured the building's landlord to cancel the show. The band put up new posters with an apolitical image and were allowed to go ahead; but the affair persuaded them to move to Seattle, where they took the name Next Exit. Under that name they made a 1982 album with the novelty anthem "Static Cling." Gregor then put together an instrumental no-wave album under the name Koo Dat Tah in 1983; then Gregor and Fenton reformulated themselves as Variant Cause. They recorded two Variant Cause LPs and assorted 45s on their KDT label until 1991 with various players mixing up saxes, pianos, Farfisa organs, guitar effects, and wailing vocals. Gregor also booked shows at the Central Tavern and the Off Ramp (see chapter 11), and worked as road manager for the Jim Rose Circus Sideshow.

Reid redux

Larry Reid resurfaced as the 1986 season director at the Center on Contemporary Art (COCA), an organization that staged installations and performances at a succession of different sites. Reid mounted a group show called "Feminists and Misogynists, Together at Last": The artists invoked so many of the same images of aggression and martyrdom, it was hard to tell the feminists and misogynists apart. Reid revived his punk opening parties by flying in the team of Lydia Lunch and Jim Foetus for that show (Foetus performed with a real pig's head).

Reid published a one-shot COCAzine with an essay by Gary Heffern, formerly of San Diego's

Penetrators, who'd been living in Seattle since 1984:

"People everywhere seem to think that there are greener pastures. I've seen and known the extremists in nearly every town I've been in, and I've been studying Seattle like a hawk. I know it's just like San Diego, Portland, Vancouver, L.A., San Francisco. You see, there's a small-mindedness that has got to change, and I'm not talkin' fashion bullshit—I'm talkin' thought...

"One thing that's impressed me is people fighting snow and rain to go to shows, paying the cover, and supporting local bands. However, I feel the punks need their own place. Someone has got to go to the cops and say, 'Look, man, give us our turf, let us run it our way, and you can come in periodically to check it out, but give us our place and leave us alone.'

"...Heavy metal kids hang out with the punks, it's fuckin' great. You have KCMU playing local music. Going to see James Brown and seeing the acceptance of punks there, as well as at poetry readings, even at Richard Thompson at the UW. Bumbershoot was packed with punks as well as hippies and old folks, and I didn't see one fight.... I think people really care about each other. Their 'scenes,' whether it's hardcore, metal, psychedelic, gloom, or whatever...you can see the hurt in their eyes when an injustice is done, or a place is thrashed, or people are getting beat-up (i.e., the U-Men show on New Year's Eve). I think the people (here) are genuine, sensitive and respectful of not stepping on or crossing over unknown territories. However, that's not to say they're not the first to cry Bullshit or fight when it's needed.... Seattle is a proud city."

With Reid working full-time at COCA, he couldn't manage the U-Men anymore. Susan Silver took over, launching a career running bands instead of just booking them. She still held a day job until one of her acts, Soundgarden, got a record deal.

A lot of other early punks dropped out at this point; not only were they aging beyond the noise and smoke of a bar scene, but the increasingly homogenous music turned them off.

Calvin Johnson: *"I went to some of the early Seattle shows at the last version of the Bird at the Odd Fellows hall. They were friendly, they were great. But by the mid-'80s the scene sucked. The bands were assholes; the audiences were assholes."*

Steve Fisk: *"I had some problems in Olympia, but overall it was a great creative center. But going to Seattle was like going to a bank. Seattle was run by people with stuck-up fake New York attitudes. If you were at dinner and you said the wrong thing they'd eat you alive. Or they'd send you back totally humiliated. It's much friendlier now."*

Some of these guys and gals had tried to lift

rock beyond heavy metal clichés; to them, the Soundgarden/ Green River bands were just a different kind of monotonous hard rock, Black Sabbath clones in Black Flag clothes. They didn't notice that these bands used some of the metal vocabulary, but to express different messages. Your generic corporate metal band was obsessed with self-indulgent paeans to the rock-star lifestyle. Seattle bands often eschewed that in favor of gritty dirges affirming rage and cynicism. Even Bellevue's Queensryche, the local band that most loyally adhered to the big-hair metal aesthetic, saw its 1986 release *Rage to Order* damned with faint praise as "thinking man's metal," too esoteric for arena stardom.

Metal still refuses to die

The suburban metal circuit entered a new phase in 1985-86; the roller-rink circuit died down and the music moved into bars (most notably the Riviera in Lynnwood) and rental halls. With the new spaces came a new set of thrash-speedcore outfits, many of whom signed with majors or national indies.

Sanctuary (Warrel Dane, Lenny Rutledge, Sean Blosi, Jim Sheppard, Dave Budbill) signed to Epic in 1987. Its shearing debut disc *Refuge Denied* included the Anne Rice-inspired vampire tale "Veil of Disguise" and a revision of the Jefferson Airplane's "White Rabbit" in which Alice dies of an overdose. It was followed by *Into the Mirror Black* in 1990, featuring "One More Murder" and "Taste Revenge."

Forced Entry (Tony Benjamins, Brad Hull, Colin Mattson) played what they described as "heavy, bone-crunching death" on the 1989 Combat release *Uncertain Future*, followed by the Relativity CD *As Above So Below* (featuring "Bone Crackin' Fever").

Coven (Jay Clark, Paul Hash, Garry Peebles, Dean and Neal Babbit) introduced their cartoony death metal with 1988's *Blessed Is The Black* on Ever Rat (distributed by Medusa/Enigma), followed by *Death Walks Behind You* (with "Ministry of Lies" and a tribute to executed local serial killer Ted Bundy) and *Boneless Christian.*

Bitter End (Chris and Matt Fox, Harry Dearinger, Russ Stefanovitch) put out *Harsh Realities* for Metal Blade in 1990. Panic (Jeff Braimes, Martin Chandler, George Hernandez, Jack Coy) recorded *Epidemic* for Metal Blade in 1991 (songs included "Hypochondriac" and "Devil's Night Out"). It was followed by *Fact* in 1993. By the time Panic and Bitter End signed, the suburban metal scene was fading out. The hard-rock center moved to north Seattle, at the New World and Far Side (later Mad Dog's) bars.

For a while there was a complementary scene of redneck-thrash bands in south King County, including Strychnine, My Remains, Tramp Alley (with Johnny Wright, who went on to the Seattle band Bathtub Gin and Kurdt Vanderhoof's Buzzing Room), and one band that got scandalous TV coverage for its name, Date Rape.

i dont smoke dope chew rope dance france romance fight fart fuck shoot the shit or drive a truck i been to maine spain spokane round the world three times ten worlds fairs and i even seen goats fuck in the marketplace...

...but i aint never seen no shit like this

Jack Endino

Deep Six, House, and Endino

Chris Hanzsek (an old Penn State classmate of Jeff Greinke's) came here from Boston in 1983, the week the Blackouts moved in the other direction. Hanzsek got some work as a recording engineer and briefly ran his own studio in the Interbay area, Reciprocal Recording. After that studio folded, Hanzsek booked some sessions at Ironwood Studios with the U-Men, Skin Yard, Soundgarden, Malfunkshun, Green River, and the Melvins. Those tracks became the compilation LP *Deep Six*, issued in January 1986 on Hanzsek and girlfriend Tina Casale's new C/Z label (a play on letters in their names; no relation to the cheap jewelry product Cubic Zirconia). Nobody involved with *Deep Six* has anything nice to say about its recording job. The 2,000-copy run took three years to sell out. Hanzsek and Casale put out a self-titled Melvins EP that May. Then Casale split for Pittsburgh and Hanzsek got tired of the hustle of moving units, so he turned the label over to Skin Yard's bassist, ex-10 Minute Warning member Daniel House. Hanzsek sold House the remaining *Deep Six* and *Melvins* inventory at a discount, and threw in the C/Z name for free.

Marc Ramirez reminiscing in the Times *on* Deep Six, *4/92: "The guitars were slow and ponderous, monster trucks sloshing through syrup. No Patsy Cline cover tunes here, just a Northwest sound that developed organically under the Seattle rain, nurtured by radio station KCMU, in clubs like Squid Row, Gorilla Gardens and the Rainbow Tavern, away from the L.A. and New York spotlight."*

When he assumed control of C/Z, House had already put out a 250-copy cassette, *Pyrrhic Victory: A Goal Attained At Too Great a Cost*. Its ten tracks included current bands (Skin Yard, Soundgarden, Vexed) with unreleased tracks by long-gone groups (10 Minute Warning, Gordon Raphael's Colour Twigs, the Horrible Truth, the Probes, Mental Mannequin, the 1984 version of the Fags, and House and Matt Cameron's instrumental band Feedback).

House used C/Z to put out records by his band and his friends' bands: My Eye, Coffin Break, Vexed, Slack, and the party/art band Crypt Kicker Five (led by singers Jamie Caffery, Rhonda Pelikan and Chip Doring; named after a line in Bobby Pickett's "Monster Mash"). He also put out a series of *Teriyaki Asthma* compilations, seven seven-inch EPs each with four different bands. Skin Yard moved to the Arizona-based Toxic Shock label for the 1988 album *Hallowed Ground*, and from there to SST's sister label Cruz for the albums *Fist Sized Chunks* (1990), *1000 Smiling Knuckles* (1991) and *Inside the Eye* (1993; recorded after the band had essentially broken up).

The drummer for Crypt Kicker Five was the guitarist for Skin Yard, Jack Endino (Michael Giacondino). He'd previously played bass in the Ones, fronted by a ponytailed stud-folkster from Yakima

via Texas, Terry Lee Hale (who later formed a "hard-acoustic" solo act and booked bands at the Squid Row, the Crocodile and the Weathered Wall).

Endino, a UW electrical engineering grad and former employee of the Bremerton Naval Shipyards, set up a four-track recording facility in his Seattle basement in early 1985, and soon attracted a steady stream of bands coming in for demos. In June 1986 he and Hanzsek reopened Triangle Studios in Ballard as the new Reciprocal Recording. Hanzsek soon bought out Endino's share of the business; Endino remained as its in-house engineer.

From the same control room photographed on the first *Rocket* cover, Endino became *the* producer (though he preferred the less pretentious credit "Recorded By") for Sub Pop, C/Z, and a bevy of other labels. He's worked on some 90 albums and compilations, 40 EPs and 110 singles in the past seven years. The raucous sound in his early productions came from the bands' common desire to rock extremely hard (and his workaholic drive to schedule as many sessions as possible by skimping on set-up changes). The results often resembled Kearney Barton's old, unpretentious productions for the Kingsmen and Sonics.

Jack Endino to the Rocket, *6/92: "I had a pretty good notion of how to record a grungy sloppy guitar 'cause that's the kind of guitar I played myself. I realized early on that I had a terrible guitar sound and how was I going to record it? Then I ended up recording about a hundred bands that had equally terrible guitar sounds and a new aesthetic was born. What sounded horrible back then is now a standard."*

Endino to the UW Daily *on his early work, 9/93: "It was more a function of the lack of money and time, really. Most of the recordings were done on an eight-track. And there it is; you can't do ten layers of backing vocals. You get it right and there it is. It's nice. It makes the band have to get a good live-ish performance. And you can't get all indulgent, so that's cool. But when time is available, I use it. I don't necessarily like doing albums in four days. It's like cramming for exams, trying to learn a textbook the day before the test. That's like the crazy intensity you can get into, trying to mix an album in one day. You drink coffee, get incredibly wired, and concentrate for 14 or 16 hours, then you go home and collapse for a few days."*

Rich Hinklin took over Reciprocal in 1991, changing its name to Word of Mouth. It's now run by Stuart Hallerman and John Goodmanson as John and Stu's Place. Hanzsek opened a new studio, Hanzsek Audio, just up the street from his old one.

Green River, continued

Bruce Pavitt was inspired by *Deep Six* to make his own commitment to recording local bands. But

before he got to that, he revived the Sub Pop label with *Sub Pop 100*, released in the fall of 1986. The LP (subtitled with the slogan "To K-Tel With Love") was a dillentantish collection of acts from the art-pop wing of college radio, with Sonic Youth, Steve Albini, Naked Raygun, Vancouver's dissonant-noise masters Skinny Puppy, Shonen Knife (with a song from a K compilation tape), and only two local acts: the U-Men and Steve Fisk.

Spine copy from **Sub Pop 100***: "The new thing, the big thing, the God thing: A multi-national conglomerate based in the Pacific Northwest."*

Sub Pop's first taste of fame would come from Green River, who had already recorded the six-song EP *Come On Down* in late 1984 (released on Homestead in December 1985) before appearing on *Deep Six*. After that came a self-released 45, "Together We'll Never" backed with a cover of the Dead Boys' "Ain't Nothing To Do" (rewritten with local references). It was recorded in March 1986 and released eight months later on green vinyl with production credited to "J. Perry"—it was really recorded by Endino and Gordon Raphael, not Aerosmith's Joe Perry. The fake credit referred to rumors that started when Perry appeared at a Green River gig in New York (it was one of the first Seattle bands to head east), leading to an erroneous *Rocket* comment that Perry would produce the group's next record.

Leighton Beezer *on* Come On Down*: "It opens with 20 seconds of pure noise, then Mark yells YOW! It always sends chills up my spine."*

Before the first of three Green River van tours in August 1985, guitarist Steve Turner quit. His punk/garage leanings were increasingly out of step with Jeff Ament and Stone Gossard's growing dreams of arena stardom, as the band evolved from post-L.A. hardcore toward mid-'70s revivalism with punk volumes and punk self-mockery. Ament's old Deranged Diction bandmate Bruce Fairweather replaced Turner, who took time off from music to study at Western Washington University. Fairweather, who later worked alongside Arm at the Seattle FilmWorks photo-processing lab, played on the *Dry as a Bone* EP, recorded in June 1986 and released 13 months later as the first single-band record on the Sub Pop label.

From **Green River's** *"P.C.C." (Pest Control Corporation): "I've crushed a hundred ants/And I've flushed a thousand spiders/I never even knew their names/Never let it bother me."*

The Green River tours were not wild successes. They played the punk equivalent of the Palace, CBGB in New York, but the audience consisted solely of two employees and four Japanese tourists. A Detroit gig ended when a punk purist in the audience grabbed the longhaired Ament by the ankle and pulled him down off the stage; a cop showed up to stop the fight.

Green River got banned from the Central after a show where the band threw Spam and bread at the audience, some of which got thrown back into the monitors. At later gigs, band members tossed out cooking oil and other goodies from the stage.

Around this time, Turner started gigging in the

Screaming Trees (with Donna Dresch)

Below: Steve Fisk

Thrown Ups, a deliberately sloppy group with Leighton Beezer and Limp Richerds drummer-guitarist Scott Schickler. Arm and Australian-born UW art student Edwin Judah Fotheringham joined it later. The group never practiced, but prepared elaborate visual concepts for each gig. The guys appeared in cardboard daisy-head costumes, or with mud and dirt all over themselves, or for a Christmas show as three wise men and a sheep (the sheep was Fotheringham in a costume covered with cotton balls). At the "Zit Bag Show" the members fashioned pants out of garbage bags, into which Fotheringham loaded whipped cream that they shot out 20 to 30 feet to the audience. The group recorded three EPs for Amphetamine Reptile (*Felch*, *Smiling Panties* and *Eat My Dump*), followed by a self-titled 45 box set, *Melancholy Girl Box* (released as an LP in Europe).

Ed Fotheringham to the zine Fiz, 12/93: "(The Thrown-Ups records) became like a joke on every band in town, every band in the country that was struggling. It was like, no, actually, guys, it's really easy to put this shit out. This is the worst thing you'll ever hear, and it's out. It became a really convoluted joke."

Leighton Beezer: "I invented barf rock, the forerunner to grunge rock—loud and sloppy. The Thrown-Ups evolved from a bunch of one-time bands at parties from February to August 1984. A lot of people played with a lot of different people; we felt free to experiment. We used to have rave-ups that were longer than the songs; we'd just jam in A endlessly, break into buildups, dynamics, leads. I had the idea to cut out the songs and just do the rave-ups.... Our goal was to be just good enough to be considered bad. I had the militant idea that the less you practiced, the better. I'd rather have a conversation than listen to a speech."

The first few Thrown Ups gigs (before Arm, Turner or Fotheringham were involved) featured Beezer, Mike Faulhaver, and UW dropout Steve Mack, who soon left to study in London. Once there, he was working in a pizza joint when he heard that Damian and Sean O'Neill, formerly of the Undertones, were holding auditions for their next band. Mack went to the audition on a lark just to meet his Irish alternative-pop idols, and ended up the lead singer of the O'Neills' new poltically-charged band, That Petrol Emotion (biggest U.S. albums: 1988's *End of the Millennium Psychosis Blues*, 1990's *Chemicrazy*). Mack and Damian O'Neill recorded under the Petrol name until mid-1994, though most of their latter albums weren't released in the U.S.

Fun rock, love rock

Tom Dyer's Green Monkey label released the *Big Ellen* LP by fun-rockers Prudence Dredge (led by Joey Kline, who'd come here from Montana in '82 with the band Boy Toast), plus releases by folkster Jon Strongbow, Tony Driscoll's Purdins (self-described as "Wimp Rock for Losers"), Bob Blackburn Jr.'s Liquid Generation, and the compilation *Monkey Business* with the Fastbacks, Al Bloch's Bombardiers, Danger Bunny, the Walkabouts, Prudence Dredge, Arms Akimbo (a reggae-ska band with Kline's ex-Boy Toast mates Charles Wheeler and Jeff Mosier), Melting Fish (with future Walkabout Glen Slater), Pip McCaslin (now of the Haps), and the group that became Dyer's principal interest, Green Pajamas.

Led by the delightful acid-pop vocals and lyrics of Jeff Kelly (with bassist/co-songwriter Joe Ross (later in 64 Spiders), Steve Lawrence, Bruce Haedt and Karl Wilhelm), the Pajamas first made the self-released tape *Summer of Lust*, then hooked up with Dyer and scored a regional hit in 1984 with the dreamy love-ode 45 "Kim the Waitress," clocking in at over six minutes of ethereal innocence. (Dyer mixed a shorter version for airplay on KJET, whose automation equipment couldn't play tapes longer than five minutes.) The Pajamas followed it up with a live-in-the-studio tape, the lapsed-Catholic-themed single "Sister Anne" (no relation to the MC5's "Sister Ann" or Flop's later "(Sister) Anne"), and the singer-songwriter-y *Book of Hours* and *Ghosts of Love* LPs, the latter released through L.A.'s Bomp label. The group broke up during the *Ghosts* sessions. Kelly next recorded solo material, sold only on self-released tapes. The Pajamas reunited in 1994, after Seattle's Sister Psychic and Chicago's Material Issue issued simultaneous covers of "Kim."

Calvin Johnson moved his K label into vinyl with a 1985 45 by his own goodtime-punk band Beat Happening. Johnson and new business partner Candice Pedersen also started the "International Pop Underground" series of 45s with such bands as Vancouver duo Mecca Normal and Tacoma garage-punkers Girl Trouble (see chapter 10). Over 50 IPU Series singles have now come out, by bands from across North America, Britain, Europe and Japan.

Before its first discs came out, K had already started a series of compilation tapes. *Danger Is Their Business* and *Dangerous Business International* covered acoustic bands from the U.S. and abroad; while *Let's Together, Let's Kiss* and *Let's Sea* documented local and international punk bands from the Melvins and Fastbacks to Japan's Shonen Knife. Sales barely cracked 100 copies per release, until Johnson and Peterson began to take marketing seriously. The label started a tabloid mail-order catalog that sold its own releases plus those of like-minded indies. The label's 1993 catalog bore the slogan "Superpunk's Not Dead."

Mixing a lot

Rap emerged nationally as the statement of disaffected youth that punk wanted to be. The first local hip-hop team, the Emerald Street Boys, played with what the zine *Flavor* later called "really no signature type of style that one could call their own." But they got a lot of press in the *Rocket*, partly because few others were performing what was still a New York regional sound. Seattle had a relatively small African American population, which initially had few connections to the Northeast urban hip-hop universe. The only regular spaces to hear recorded rap were Lateef's and Club Broadway, which both closed by 1984.

The first big rapper from here, Sir Mix-A-Lot (1981 Roosevelt High graduate Anthony Ray), applied the same career strategy that the rockers were using; he promoted his own DJ shows at the Central District Boys and Girls Club, made records in a home studio (including the novelty "Square Dance Rap") and released them on the Nastymix label set up by his manager Ed Locke (named for Mix-A-Lot and Locke's other client, KCMU DJ Nasty Nes Rodriguez). Ray hadn't been into the early New York rappers; he was a computer-electronics buff who listened to Devo and Kraftwerk instead of Kurtis Blow. He came into hiphop as a black version of electronic pop. He moved his live act downtown in mid-1985 at the Mountaineers Hall. It was one of the first local hip-hop shows to a mixed audience. A prior such show, at the Bumbershoot festival in September 1984, starred Afrika Bambatta and a full band. Bambatta returned the next year with a DJ and tapes at Gorilla Gardens; the largely white alternative-rock audience felt cheated by the lack of live musicians, and nearly rioted.

Sir Mix-A-Lot to Backlash, *3/89: "In the '70s, there was nothing for me but basketball and Parliament-Funkadelic. All these Teddy Pendergrass ballads and disco were nowhere. (Rap label) Sugarhill comes along and all these guys were saying, 'That's what got me into rap.' Not me; I hated it. Rappers sayin' 'I got this, I got that;' it was boring. It motivated me to do something better."*

Clubs keep opening, closing

Capitol Hill's Five-O Tavern, the Attic in Madison Park, Jilly's East in Montlake, and the U District's University Bistro and Scoundrel's Lair served up bands to the over-21s for a while in '86-'87. The Five-O was forced to stop booking amplified bands by residential neighbors' noise complaints; the Soho lasted a few months longer.

Scoundrel's Lair (the old Llahngaelhyn, where Jesse Bernstein debuted in the '60s) was booked by KCMU DJ Jonathan Poneman. Poneman also had his own band, the Treeclimbers, who recorded a self-titled EP; the band's changing line-ups included Amy Denio (see below), Peter Barnes and ex-Sex Therapy singer Cha Cha Samoa. Guitarist Gary Thorstensen wound up in TAD (see next chapter). Poneman also appeared in the knockoff band Sick Man of Europe with Kurt Bloch, John Sutherland and Rusty Willoughby; they once appeared at the Vogue with an all-Cheap Trick set.

P.S. O'Neill: "I left for L.A. in 1984 to persue a filmmaking career. The scene here was at an all-time low.... I came back after about a year and Poneman asked me to sing in the Treeclimbers. We went to the rehearsal house and I walked in and here were the guys from a band we opened for at the Bahamas five or six years before. And I looked in the mirror and I said, 'I don't think I can do this anymore.' 'Cause I felt like the huge burst of energy that my hometown boys in the '70s had had was it."

Jonathan Poneman to the Rocket, *12/86: "The town right now is in a musical state where there is an acknowledgment of a certain consciousness. A lot has to do with our geographic isolation: for once that's paying off in that the bands here are developing with their intentions staying pure. In bigger cities, that all gets diluted because so much is going on.... Something's gonna happen."*

By this time the Central booked bands every night, though audiences seldom approached its 199-person capacity on weekends and usually dwindled below 50 midweek.

Hangouts and day jobs

Ex-Metropolis promoter Hugo opened the Free Mars cafe on Western Avenue in September 1985, with reasonably priced ethnic-veggie cuisine and outrageous art exhibits and relief murals. The Urban Nomad Collective, a successor to the Here Today gallery, booked acoustic music and spoken-word shows at Free Mars once a month. Performers included Jesse Bernstein (singing his original folk songs and cooking omelettes), Greinke & Angus, a *packed* acoustic U-Men show, and Entropics, the first local band of a guitar-sax-accordian-voice virtuoso from Detroit via Amherst, Mass., Amy Denio. Denio and her Entropics partner David Stern soon joined Fred, participating in some of that group's last Red Square jams (the hardcore crowd started showing up and throwing bottles at UW po-

Emerald Street Boys

**Jesse Bernstein/
Free Mars ad**

AUG. 20   AUG. 30   SEPT. 11
RAINBOW   BUMBERSHOOT (BREWHAUS)   VOGUE

Green River

Joey Kline & Tom Jones

lice cars during some of the last midnight sessions). Stern soon went back east and Denio tired of Fred's dumb lyrics and sloppy playing; she went solo and also had a series of long- and short-term bands, some running concurrently: the Tone Dogs, Couch of Sound, DeDuo, the Nudes (renamed the (EC) Nudes, as in European Community, to avoid a lawsuit from a Florida Nudes), Blowhole (an industrial-noise combo organized by *Rocket* writer Patrick Barber), three solo CDs, and the Billy Tipton Memorial Saxophone Quartet (a four-woman combo named after a woman who led a Spokane lounge trio for decades while passing for male).

Hugo sold Free Mars in 1987; it was renamed Café Mars and is now owned by Gina Kaukola as Cyclops, with largely the same food and art concepts but without the performances. Hugo went on to lead motivational courses for office workers, and now leads men's consciousness-raising groups.

Free Mars was situated on the ground floor of SCUD Towers ("Subterranean Cooperative of Urban Dreamers," named years before the Gulf War), a two-story co-op artists' space. Its residents over the years included Steve Fisk, Skin Yard singer Ben McMillan, graphic designer Art Chantry, conceptual artist Diane Sukovathy, band photographers Cam Garrett and Arthur S. Aubry, *Punk Lust* editor Wilum Pugmire, S&M chain-mail artist Louie Raffloer, and his then-wife "Triangle Slash," an illustrator and tattoo designer who signed all her work with a logo of a triangle bisected by a diagonal slash. She made two limited-edition, hand-bound art books, *Faux Pas* and *Discrete Ephemera*, and collaborated with *Punk Lust* zine author Wilum

Pugmire on a series of gothic-horror tableaux in the *Rocket*. A room on SCUD's ground floor became a band practice space. Nastymix Records' first office was in the building right behind SCUD.

Leading day-job employers at this time included catering companies, house construction, vintage clothing stores, the *Auto Trader* ad magazines, the Seattle Film-Works photo-processing lab, the American Passage campus marketing company, and the fast-growing espresso bars. Joey Kline, head of fun-boy band Prudence Dredge, opened University Coffee in 1985; his first location featured the Video Lounge and Toast Bar, plus weekly acoustic sets by his favorite musicians.

In late 1986 the locally-owned Yesco Foreground Music merged with the New York-based Muzak Corp. The combined company moved all its operations here. Several of Seattle's hardest-rocking people got office, engineering and editing jobs at the elevator-music giant, which also operated in-store music video services and Yesco's tapes of familiar hits for stores and restaurants. Ex-Yesco employee Bruce Pavitt got a job in the Muzak shipping department after he sold his half of the Fallout Records store. Others who toiled at the firm included Poneman, Denio, Mark Arm, Ron Rudzitis, Feast singer Tom Mick, and Tad Doyle.

DJ Stephen Rabow, who loved to warn his radio listeners about the inevitability of entropy, quit Muzak and left town in 1987 after four of his six successive radio outlets (KZAM, KRAB, KYYX, and the short-lived KHIT) folded. His final local gig was on KNHC, the Seattle School District station. Rabow moved to Sarasota, Florida, where he's been a TV personality, nightclub promoter, publicist, and a publisher of tourist guides.

Punks on TV

At the time of Lou Guzzo's anti-punk tirade, the new-music scene had received little attention on local TV, aside from KING's short-lived *R.E.V.* The Visible Targets had lip-synced one song on KING's morning talk show. PBS affiliate KCTS had aired a short newsfeature segment taped at a Lincoln Arts show with Feast and Bundle of Hiss. Local music videos were still rare, though a few enterprising bands (Red Dress, Bellingham's Applied Science, the Metaphonics) made clips without releasing records for the clips to promote. That was about to change.

Spud Goodman (Bruce Walkup), a Tacoma probation officer and Evergreen grad, started booking bands in February 1985 at the Bedrock Lounge in Tacoma's Prosito restaurant, the first commercial alternative bar in the Wailers' and Sonics' hometown. He and the Bedrock concept were kicked out by Prosito's management after the Liquor Board objected to the after-hours performances and the graffiti on the walls (Prosito returned to alternative bands on an off-and-on basis in later years). He also bought airtime on a Tacoma cable system for a parody talk show, featuring band segments taped at the Bedrock with the U-Men, f-Holes, Refuzors, Life in General, Sir Mix-A-Lot and Portland's Napalm Beach. Holding a spatula in one hand and an open bottle of Pepto-Bismol in the other, the deadpan, stubbled Goodman interviewed both real and fictional guests and bantered with blank-faced co-host Chick Hunter (Tim Hoban). Goodman moved to Seattle's public access channel the next year. The public access channel soon attracted other hip-minded people to create local music shows (*Bongo Corral*, *Music Inner City*, *Dave's Dimension*, *Cathode Café*, *Dr. Shorts*), more fake talk shows (*Call Us Now!*), real talk shows (*The Government We Deserve* and *Political Playhouse*, whose host Philip Craft once performed a whole episode nude), homemade sitcoms (*Gavin's Howse*), and performance-drama-whatever (*International TV*, *Heart Attack Theater*).

Goodman's act caught the attention of Lani Edenholm, an administrator at the public access studio. She volunteered to produce the show for a commercial cable channel. A more elaborate Goodman show premiered on UHF station KTZZ in 1992. In this version, Goodman became the straight man for brief tirades by fictional relatives. His sister was played by Julie Cascioppo, a cabaret singer whose act consisted of outlandish costumed novelty characters. Spud's musical guests included TAD, the Best Kissers in the World, the Young Fresh Fellows, Common Language, and a lounge-act medley of Nirvana songs.

Exit Melvins, enter Nirvana

The Melvins' next recording after *Deep Six* and their self-titled C/Z EP was their full-length debut,

Gluey Porch Treatments, recorded in San Francisco in late 1986 and released on the California label Alchemy in early 1987.

First Buzz Osborne and then Dale Crover relocated to the Bay Area after *Treatments*' release, leaving Matt Lukin temporarily bandless. Subsequent Melvin bassists included ex-Clown Alley member Lori Black, Olympia native Joe Preston, Billy Anderson, Bill Bartell, and former indie-label distribution exec (and Black's ex-Clown Alley bandmate) Mark Deutrom. Black was the daughter of film legend Shirley Temple and businessman Charles Black; Temple's previous husband, B-movie actor John Agar, was tributed in a couple of Young Fresh Fellows songs.

The Melvins signed to Boner for the *Ozma*, *Bullhead* and *Lysol* albums and the *Eggnog* EP, before moving to the majors (and a more mainstream-rock sound) with the 1993 Atlantic release *Houdini* (the CD version includes the closing sound effect of a tape rewinding). They also put out Osborne, Crover and Preston solo EPs on Boner, whose covers looked just like the Kiss members' four-pack of solo albums. In 1990 they covered Malfunkshun's "With Yo' Heart (Not Yo' Hands)," for an Amphetamine Reptile 45. C/Z recently issued the CD *10 Songs*, with old unreleased tracks and alternate takes of the songs from the old *Melvins* EP. Under the name "Slivlem" the band released *Prick*, a 1994 album of noise experiments, tape samples and two actual songs, through the indie Amphetamine Reptile, just before its second Atlantic effort, the somewhat more commercial-sounding *Stoner Witch*. The Melvins also played on one track of former MC5 guitarist Wayne Kramer's 1995 solo album *The Hard Stuff*.

While the Melvins lived in Washington, they played frequent Seattle gigs to moderately-sized audiences; their subsequent, occasional "welcome home" shows packed the clubs. In interviews, Osborne attributed this to the idea that Seattle fans

Bundle of Hiss

KCMU welcomes from NYC

SONIC YOUTH
U-MEN
GREENRIVER
SAT. JAN. 19 $5
Gorilla Garden's OMNI ROOM
FALLOUT   ALL AGES

MELVINS
EASY AS IT WAS
NOW A LIMO
GRINDING PROCESS
#2 PENCIL
AT A CRAWL
DISINVITE
SNAKE APPEAL
SHOW OFF YOUR RED HANDS

Below: Malfunkshun

Above: Rainbow R.I.P.
Right: The Treeclimbers

were trendy poseurs who wouldn't support a band that didn't have the cachet of being from ouside. This belief was shared by his fellow emigrant, ex-Blackout Erich Werner. Daniel House has a more practical explanation: "When you play local clubs too often, you dilute your audience base. All your fans can't see you every week or every other week, or they don't all want to. Coffin Break found out that they couldn't even play some of the same places on tour too often."

At a Melvins Tacoma show in 1990, the venue management cut the power to stop stage diving. The band played Kiss covers until the promoter plugged back in.

While Crover was still in Aberdeen, he doubled as one of the early drummers for Kurt Cobain and Chris Novoselic's band, which eventually became Nirvana.

Cobain's father once broke his guitar for playing too loud; he left home soon after and stayed at friends' houses, until those friends' moms kicked him out over such offenses as trashing bedrooms. Like many of the early Seattle punks, he was a voracious and curious reader (especially about poetry and philosophy) who had little patience for school. After dropping out of high school he held a series of brief jobs.

The early rockers had been white guys appropriating the hip-outcast status of blacks; Cobain was a straight guy appropriating the hip-outcast status of gays. He took the glam fascination with gay culture into the realm of teen vandalism, spray-painting "God Is Gay" and "Homo Sex Rules" around town just to infuriate the local rednecks. He was arrested after one graffiti spree (with Osborne and Novoselic, who eluded the cops) and fined $180. In 1985 he and Crover made a cheap demo in Aberdeen under the name Fecal Matter. He played the tape to everyone he knew, hoping to attract collaborators. Novoselic got to hear it repeatedly, and eventually agreed to join him.

Novoselic had spent even less time in Weatherwax High than Cobain, before he too left to study life on his own. Born in Compton, California (future home of rappers NWA) to immigrants from Croatia, his family moved to Aberdeen in 1979, when he was 13, to join the town's sizable Croatian-American community. The next year, he went to the then-Yugoslavia to spend a year with relatives; he spoke Croatian from childhood. When he came back, he worked as a house painter and started a band called the Stiff Woodies; Lukin introduced him to Cobain, who became the Woodies' drummer. The two tried a number of bands with friends as the Sellouts, Bliss, Ted Ed Fred, Throat Oyster, Windowpane and Pen Cap Chew; interrupted when Chris and his future wife Shelli moved to Arizona for a year. He came back and resumed playing with Kurt. They wrote a set of songs in a week, reuniting the poppier and heavier sides of the punk tradition.

Kurt Cobain to the Chicago Tribune, *10/91:* "*Around 1985, '86, the hardcore scene seemed exhausted to us.… It was boring, so we just started accepting the fact that we liked the music that we grew up on: Alice Cooper, the MC5, Kiss. It was almost taboo to admit something like that in '85, but we grew our hair long and said, 'Fuck what everybody else thinks, we're going to do what we want.'… We're paying homage to all the music we loved as kids, and we haven't denied the punk-rock energy that inspired us as teenagers.*"

What goes up must come down

John Lydon (the former Johnny Rotten), who'd had a hand in starting all this worldwide, wrote a song in his hotel room after a late 1986 gig at the Paramount by his band Public Image Ltd. The local mainstream media couldn't understand why he'd call a song "Seattle" that wasn't about bright perky lifestyles but instead about disposable buildings and equally disposable people. But *we* understood, and loved it. The song's vision of Seattle was the one that the "alternative nation" would come to believe.

In interviews at the time of its release, Lydon said the song wasn't specifically about Seattle but about urban alienation in general. The events of the evening might suggest otherwise. Opening act Green River had trashed Lydon's dressing room and walked off with his La-Z-Boy recliner chair. At the close of Green River's set, Mark Arm announced to the audience, "If you want to see what happens to somebody who's completely sold out, just wait."

End of the Rainbow

The venerable Golden Crown, Astor Park and Rainbow all closed by the end of 1986. The Rainbow's last hurrah came as the site of Robert Cray's breakthrough video "Smoking Gun." Cray promptly moved to L.A. and soon thereafter married a fashion model. The Rainbow space became a strip joint

LOSER

and is now an upscale Irish-style pub. The Rainbow's last owner, Rhoda Mueller, tried to open a new site in Wallingford, across the freeway from the old Rainbow, but was thwarted by neighbors who opposed live music in their newly-yuppified district.

At one point, there were no regular venues except midweek gigs at the Vogue, weekend gigs at the Central and the Ditto, gigs by the lighter or artier bands at U District bars, and occasional shows on the UW campus and in rental halls. Of those main bars, only the Central could legally squeeze in more than 100.

In theory, the scene might have withstood the forces against it had it achieved a larger audience base. With more revenue, clubs could have met building codes (or bribe the same people that richer restaurants and bars bribed) and pay escalating liquor-liability insurance premiums (which rose for some clubs in 1986 from $7,000 to $44,000 per year). With a steady clientele, club owners might have been able to get bank loans instead of relying on their own resources. Bands might have been able to bankroll LPs. But despite frequent admonishments to "Support Local Music," the scene stayed too small to stand on its own. Besides, the very concept of "support" seemed contradictory to punk nihilism. "Support" sounded too much like dressing for success. Some people blanched at the thought of commercial marketing tactics, even changing their bands' names as soon as they approached familiarity.

Kurt Bloch reflecting on his career in Yeah!, 8/87: "Things haven't changed that much. There are places to play, and tons of good bands. If there is one major problem with the scene, it's a lack of audience support for live music. It's hard to get people out to see bands."

Calm before the storm

This seemingly final decline of new music was repeated nationally; local scenes in most non-media cities contracted. The second breath early MTV gave new music faded, as labels backed videos for their top stars. The conversion to the CD format gave labels less money to promote new acts, and trashed small labels and stores that had depended on long-term LP inventories. CDs speeded the consolidation of the business: the majors bought out the last big independents, and turned smaller indies into product-supply slaves. The early CD aesthetic favored sterile, slick product, produced in large quantities. The first CD plants wouldn't even handle indie labels. Commercial radio remained under the thumb of MBAs and consultants.

And in retrospect, Seattle may not have been the best setting for music tied to art-school conceits, New York/London fashion primping, and middle-class fantasies of the *demimonde*. It remained to develop a punk rock that *did* speak to the frustrations of average American youth, a punk rock that didn't presuppose familiarity with the latest fads in the U.K. music papers. Punk to this point was the work of people whose earliest musical memory was "I Wanna Hold Your Hand." The punk to follow was the work of (or for) people whose earliest musical memory was "Stairway to Heaven."

Above: Chick Hunter and Spud Goodman

Below: Inside the Omni Room

CHAPTER TEN:
SUB POP ROCK CITY (1987-1988)

Kurt Cobain, Chris Novoselic and drummer Aaron Burckhard were to have played their first gig together at a house party in Olympia, but it got shut down before they showed up. They did get to play weeks later at a party in the Grays Harbor County town of Raymond; Cobain later proudly told Michael Azerrad that "we got everyone so scared of us that they were in the kitchen hiding from us." The Melvins connection helped the band (then called Skid Row; no relation to the New Jersey band of that name) get its first public gig in the spring of 1987 at Tacoma's Community World Theater, to 13 people. It was followed a couple of weeks later by a show at Olympia's GESSCO booked by Matthew "Slim" Moon, a Seattle punk fan who'd just moved south. Burckhard was replaced by the Melvins' Dale Crover (who appeared on a demo recorded by Jack Endino at Reciprocal on Jan. 23, 1988) and then by Aberdeen native Dave Foster. Burckhard came back briefly before getting kicked out for unprofessional behavior.

During Burckhard's second tour of duty, the group held its first Seattle gig in a Sub Pop-sponsored show on April 24, 1988 at the Vogue, opening for Blood Circus. Cobain had turned 21 two months before. Cobain moved to Olympia at this time, while Novoselic moved to Tacoma and set up a basement practice space. They played Seattle clubs as often as they could, often to little response (one gig at the Central was canceled when nobody showed up). They took day jobs, Cobain as a janitor in a dental office and Novoselic as an industrial painter.

Dawn Anderson in the Rocket, *12/94, on Nirvana's first Seattle show: "It was a regular promo night that Pavitt put on, where you could pay a $2 cover to see an unknown band. Later, folks who were present that night estimated the 'crowd' as anywhere from 10 to 50 people—I think it was about 20. Kurt Cobain was so nervous he was shaking in his flannels. I went with some friends who were casually acquainted with him as a fellow Melvins fan and they all thought it was real cute that little Kurt had a band."*

Veronika Kalmar in the same Rocket *issue on the same show: "We all went 'to be supportive' and ended up scraping our blown minds off the club's cement floor."*

Gimme a Break

Seattle's drought of venues eased slightly when the Moore Theatre stepped up its schedule of shows, having backed off during the darkest days of hall-trashing. It became a rival to the bigger Paramount for larger touring concerts, as booked by Dustin Waln of the folk-rock band Somebody's Daughter. Waln's band was part of an acoustic subscene of people who either hung out or worked at the Two Bells Tavern in Belltown and played that cramped space on the odd Sunday or Monday night, including painter Whiting Tennis's bands Random Splandom and Big Tube Squeezer, Tony Matthews and Doug Creson's punkabilly f-Holes, and Nick Vroman and Earl Brooks's Blood of the Lamb Band. Brooks was the first person to promote rock shows at the Rendezvous Restaurant's Jewel Box Theater. He also booked shows with his friends' "Belltown bands" at the Ditto and at the Five Point Cafe near the Space Needle. He produced the monthly public-access cable show *Bongo Corral*, with all-live bands and goofy comedy segments.

The Moore was a great place for touring concerts, but it was too big for all-local gigs. The locus for all-ages shows moved to Tacoma, in 1986-87 at the Crescent Ballroom (one of the old Pat O'Day teen dance spots) and from February 1987 to July 1988 at the Community World Theater, an ex-porno cinema taken over by Gary Alan May's brother Jimmy. It became home to a second generation of hardcore thrash bands (the Derelicts, Subvert, Jesters of Chaos) and Malfunkshun's last gig, opening for Skin Yard. When the Community World got shut down after its landlord raised the rent, the Reko-Muse art gallery in Olympia became Washington's only regular all-ages venue, while Seattle's OK Hotel struggled to get and stay open.

Kurt Bloch: "The Community World was a neat place. We were supposed to play there one night with five other bands; I imagine it was late in (the theater's) history. Just before we were supposed to come on, I looked around and it was fairly obvious that nobody who worked there was there. The people running the place, the people who took the money, had just left. The soundman started pulling mikes before the show was over. I said there were still bands who were supposed to play; he said it looked like we wouldn't get to play.

Nirvana's cancelled show

The f-holes

World Theater

At the time no one was forming a band to get rich, mainly to travel and get your music out. You formed a band because you wanted something to do. For a while my pop tunes melded well with Peter's metal songs. We got tour diaries from bands that had done it, got numbers, begged for dates, and worked a lot of shows for free. We did it the one-fan-at-a-time method. At that time the network wasn't as established as it is today."

Chris Cornell to the Post-Intelligencer, *5/94: "All the other scenes that were happening—Athens and Minneapolis and Austin and New York and all that—had these bands that were really cool. It seemed that if any of those bands came to Seattle, you'd open up for them no matter how good your draw was.... There was a perception that things were cooler outside of Seattle. We didn't realize until after one or two tours how special the Seattle scene was."*

In a similarly cynical vein was My Name, formed in Tacoma in 1986 by Abe Brennan, Trevor Lanigan, Robb Williamson and Dave Gleza. They set tales of what a *Rocket* review called "personal issues like child abuse, awkward crushes and the problems of living in an overpopulated world" to melodies that toyed with time signatures and tempos, ever-so-gently subverting the predictability of punk words and rock music; as revealed on the C/Z CDs *Megacrush* and *Wet Hills and Big Wheels*.

Neil Rogers's Tacoma-based Derelicts stayed true to the ear-crushin', hall-trashin' concept of "a straight-across punk band," on the Penultimate Records single "Bullet for Fifi"/"Sharon Needles" and album *Love Machine* (recorded 1989, released 1991), and a Sub Pop EP. Rogers went on to Zipgun and from there to Blazed.

Pure and Fresh

After a self-released EP, Pure Joy (Rusty Willoughby, his brother Randy, Lisa King, Craig

Coffin Break

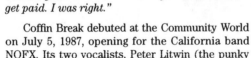

I said I guess this meant none of the bands would get paid. I was right."

Coffin Break debuted at the Community World on July 5, 1987, opening for the California band NOFX. Its two vocalists, Peter Litwin (the punky one) and Rob Skinner (the poppy one), mastered the art of being alternately sarcastic, perturbed, and unintelligible. One lyric written by Litwin and sung by Skinner began with the prosaic scene, "I'm so happy, it's sunny outside/I'm so happy, it's snowing today," before the singer's reasons for happiness get more perverse and we finally hear the title line, "(I Want to) Kill the President."

Coffin Break recorded three singles, four compilation tracks, the album *Rupture*, the EP *Psychosis*, and the compilation album *No Sleep 'Til the Stardust Motel* for C/Z one single for Sub Pop, and the *Crawl* and *Thirteen* albums for Restless/Epitaph before disbanding at the end of 1992. Litwin went on to the hard-rockish Softy (with Mark Arm's wife Emily Rieman). Skinner formed Pop Sickle, an outlet for "my more poppy songs, not as political or confrontational as Coffin Break." Skinner's idea of light pop apparently includes "Adrian," the lead track on Pop Sickle's C/Z debut *Under the Influences*, about the self-defense slaying of a wife beater.

Coffin Break was also one of the first Seattle underground bands to tour extensively, crossing the U.S. 12 times and Europe twice, logging in 100 to 200 road shows a year. Coffin Break (along with Soundgarden, the U-Men and Skin Yard) spread the Seattle rock gospel along a developing "grunge trail" of tour stops in Oregon, California, Montana, Utah, Colorado, Arizona and Texas.

Rob Skinner: "We went out and through Daniel's (House) help put out our first couple of releases.

Right: Chemistry Set

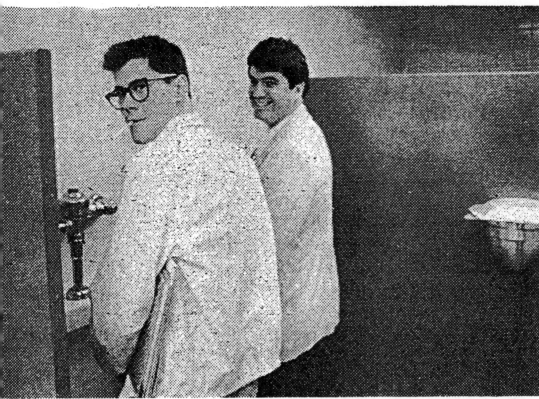

Montgomery, Jim Hunnicutt) made the synth-laden 1986 KJET hit "Ocean" (the *Rocket* said it walked "a fine line between being hard-edged and brittle, modern pop songs with Randy Willoughby's synth wading through them like a computer virus through a software program"), only to get into serious debt to make a second pressing. They next made the LP *Welcome to My New Psychotic Dream* for Clint Southerd's No Big Business label, which folded without releasing it. (Flydaddy Records, a Sub Pop affiliate run by Kevin O'Leary and Adam Silverman, issued it in 1994 as *Unsung.*) Then the band took a more stripped-down sound with just Willoughby, King and new drummer Andy Davenhall, shorn of past psychedelic embellishments.

Early Pure Joy guitarist Scott Sutherland formed (The Fabulous Stinking) Chemistry Set, with Bill Campbell (later in Willoughby's Flop), Silly Killers vet Bryan Learned, and Room Nine vet Scott Vanderpool (who'd become a DJ on KXRX, the AOR station that replaced KYYX); its peppy, melodic nightmares were captured on a self-released EP recorded in Ellensburg by Steve Fisk. Vanderpool played short stints in Jonathan Poneman's Treeclimbers and the Best Kissers in the World, and is now forming a band with Sutherland and Capping Day's Laura Weller.

Bryan Learned: *"We kept trying to get Sub Pop to put out a Chemistry Set EP. They finally said they'd put 50 copies on the shelf and accept orders, but they wouldn't push it. We put it out ourselves. When we did a 45 on green vinyl after that we called our label Fatbald, because John (Poneman) was fat and Bruce (Pavitt) was bald. We also put out a Pure Joy 45; Rusty Willoughby named his publishing company Fatbald Music."*

The Young Fresh Fellows moved from PopLlama to the California indie Frontier for their third album, 1987's *The Men Who Loved Music*, featuring odes to such pop-culture footnotes as Amy Grant, Karen Carpenter and the Solid Gold Dancers. They've since released *Totally Lost* (1988), *This One's For the Ladies* (1989), *Electric Bird Digest* (1991), *It's Low Beat Time* (1992), and the EP *Temptation on Sunday* (PopLlama, 1994); plus the old-stuff collection *GAG Fah* (PopLlama, 1990), a live CD recorded in Spain (where the band curiously found its biggest market), assorted one-off singles and compilation cuts.

Original guitarist Chuck Carroll left in 1989 and was replaced by Kurt Bloch, concurrently in the Fastbacks. Bloch's addition was immediately present on *This One's for the Ladies* with "Still There's Hope," a definitive Fastbacks song with Scott McCaughey singing instead of Kim Warnick. *It's Low Beat Time* included one serious song: "99 Girls," a disillusioning look at the world-weary prostitutes on Highway 99. The band also released a series of 45s under Jim Sangster's label, The Cruddy Record Dealership. McCaughey made a solo LP for PopLlama, *My Chartreuse Opinion.* Sangster's brother Johnny formed the Sharing Patrol, who moved to Denmark and released a translation of the Fellows' "Rock n' Roll Pest Control."

McCaughey took a day job as second-in-command ("the guy in charge of losing money") at PopLlama under Conrad Uno. Uno kept PopLlama going with the Fastbacks LP *...And His Orchestra*, the Walkabouts' debut LP *See Beautiful Rattlesnake Gardens*, Joe Guppy's wacky-folk Acoustinauts, the Squirrels, British Columbia's Smugglers and Bum, and trumpeter Richard Peterson (who also got sampled on the second Stone Temple Pilots album). PopLlama celebrated its 10th anniversary in 1993, the first Northwest label to be continuous-

Early Sky Cries Mary

**Right:
The Posies**

ly active that long.

I'll always love you

PopLlama's biggest act since the Fellows was a pickup release: *Failure* by the Posies, the power-love harmony duo of Bellingham kids Jon Auer and Ken Stringfellow (who later married Fastback Kim Warnick), self-described "music nerds" who'd hung out together since their early teens and toyed with everything from classical piano to metal and a punk band called the Stinkbugs, before settling on what Stringfellow called "the good thing about all these kinds of bands—good songs."

Ken Stringfellow: "We got burned out on bone-head music. We got into clever songwriters like Squeeze, Elvis Costello and XTC; grainy book-worm music crafted by writers who had some-thing cinematic about what they did. We set about making clever wordplay-infused pop songs. At first it was without a lot of pre-conceptualization, but but we quickly realized it was setting us apart. It was something that was deliberately un-cool; that made it cool for us."

Auer and Stringfellow made *Failure* by them-selves in early 1988 at a fancy home studio in Auer's dad's basement and self-released it on tape. After PopLlama picked it up, it quickly attracted major-label attention. Tom Ensign, a young Belling-ham filmmaker, volunteered to create a video for their ode to relationship confusion "I May Hate You Sometimes (But I'll Always Love You)." They then

became a full band with bassist Rick Roberts and drummer Mike Musburger (a distant relative of Brent Musberger, a TV sportscaster disliked by Su-perSonics fans for belittling the team during its 1979 championship season).

Auer and Stringfellow also played in an indus-trial-noise ensemble, Sky Cries Mary (named after the Hendrix song "Wind Cries Mary"), led by a UW drama student known as Roderick (he changed his last name of Wolgamott to Romero when he mar-ried working partner Anisa Romero). He recruited Stringfellow (another UW drama student) and Auer to co-score a play he created as a senior project, *Until the Grinders Cease.* He went to Paris that summer and dropped off a tape of the score at the New Rose Records store. Three weeks later, he was signed to New Rose's label. He flew back to Seattle and got Auer, Stringfellow and guitarist Stephan Byron-Salit to improvise in the studio; these tracks formed the basis of the EP *Don't Eat the Dirt.* The trio made a few live gigs and an hour-long home video before Auer and Stringfellow backed out to become full-time Posies. Roderick's stage antics included cutting off his dreadlocks with a chainsaw. The album and the video (pro-duced by Alan Pruzan) each cost $500. After Auer and Stringfellow left, Roderick rounded up other players (including Alfred Butler of Vexed) to finish the *Dirt* record, then formed a new Sky Cries Mary with a revamped concept of "tribal ambient love rock" (see chapter 12).

Theatricals

Prudence Dredge/Squirrels keyboardist Mark Nichols created a punk-musical concept album on PopLlama, *Little Boy Goes to Hell.* It featured a rock band, string and horn sections, lead and back-up singers, and a narrator, crowded into every odd corner of Uno's home studio. It was released as a boxed set of four seven-inch records, like the old Golden and Disneyland kids' records. The musical was performed live for a four-month run, with Uno's wife Emily in the cast. It was the first hit for Annex Theatre, a cooperative troupe in a former Fred Astaire studio downtown. Annex also housed a few all-ages concerts, including one of Nirvana's first Seattle gigs.

Uno staged annual "Night of the Singing Dead" live revues at the Backstage, with local musicians imper-sonating their favorite dead rock stars (Bon Scott, Sid Vicious, Hendrix, Lennon, Jackie Wilson, Andy Gibb). Uno stopped the shows before we started getting dead rock stars of our own.

Other comedy-rock crossover artists in town included Peggy Platt (who performed with Lisa Koch in the political-rock band Dos Fallopia and the parody-country Spudds) and ex-Sympathy Cards singer Cathy Sorbo (who developed standup routines about the philosophical aspects of shit and straight women who apologize for not being lesbian).

The Fastbacks' Lulu Gargiulo, the Walkabouts' Carla Torgerson and ex-Fag Barbara Ireland were

Left: Scene
from "Shredder Orpheus"

COCA
JULY 3

Pat Seabeck

Demolition Films

Below: Karl Krogstad

among the scene members who entered careers in Seattle's growing film and video industry. They worked on TV commercials, industrial films, location shoots for Hollywood productions, and in-store compilation tapes of music videos. Ex-KZAM exec Paul Sullivan co-founded Miramar Productions, which released several home videos of nature scenes and soft instrumental music (the firm never uses the term "new age"), then struck gold with *The Mind's Eye*, a compilation of computer-animation shorts made around the world; its profits supported a Miramar record label, which recorded several easy-listening artists and one rock band, Symon-Asher.

Local filmmaking was an even smaller and less-supported scene than local music-making. Portland and Vancouver produced several popular cult directors (Marv Newland, Gus Van Sant, Will Vinton); Seattle was known in the film world only as an art-film exhibition market and a location site for Hollywood productions. Still, many people worked at developing a real filmmaking scene, shooting and editing in spurts as money allowed. A spin-off of the old and/or arts-support organization, 911 Media Arts (named after its first street address, on the ground floor of the Odd Fellows Hall), became a main local home to screenings and editing facilities.

Janice Findley spent four years on one ten-minute film, *Beyond Kabuki*, working as grants became available. Findley was one of nearly 100 local film and music people who collaborated in 1988 on *Shredder Orpheus*, Robert McGinley's skate-punk retelling of the lost-love epic (one of at least *four* revisionist Orpheus stories made by local filmmakers). McGinley and Megan Murphy starred, with Jesse Bernstein as a paralyzed veteran of "the Contra drug wars" with a skateboard instead of a

wheelchair. Ex-Showbox promoter Carlo Scandiuzzi played a Satanic televangelist; the role led to other movie and TV gigs, including a bit part in the *Untouchables* film. Roland Barker created the score, with Amy Denio and the Metaphonics (an industrial percussion band with homemade instruments, in the manner of Einsturzende Neubauten). It was released on video by a tiny firm that specialized in B cop movies.

Bernstein appeared in Lynn Wegenka's *Birthright*, a one-hour eco-feminist dystopia similar to (but much less sleazy than the film version of) Margaret Atwood's *Handmaid's Tale* (Jeff Greinke supplied the gothic-industrial score); and in Peter Voght's *Windows*, a three-part short that chronicled one man's life in childhood, adulthood and old age (with music by Amy Denio and Steve Fisk). Bernstein also performed his poetry in Chuck Iffland's documentary film *The Unseen*, and shot scenes for *Gorefest*, an unfinished horror spoof started in 1987 by Bob Jenkins.

Ireland made a 30-minute surrealist Alice-in-Wonderland update in 1986, *Secrets*, with Upchuck as a punk harassing the Alice substitute (Elizabeth Ruiz) by mooing.

One local filmmaker, Karl Krogstad, funded some of his shoots by charging crew members up to $300 to work for him; he called these arrangements "internships" or "filmmaking laboratories." Even then, Krogstad had a hard time getting his works finished, edited and released. He's still sitting on a music video he produced without a song to accompany it (the cast paced around to the accompaniment of a click track). Krogstad did finish music videos for the Visible Targets and Red Dress.

Hollywood bigshots started scattering across the western states in the '80s. Known actors,

Frank Harlan

Above: Kevin Seal
Below: Crisis Party

screenwriters an directors moved into million-dollar "cabins" on Puget Sound islands and had nothing to do with the local community. Director Alan Rudolph made a local camp/thriller, *Trouble in Mind*, with a non-drag Divine as a mobster living in a mansion (shot at the Seattle Art Museum) full of works by Seattle decorative artists. (Another *Trouble in Mind* location, the old Union Station railroad depot, became a brief all-ages venue in the winter of 1988.)

Writer-director Cameron Crowe married Heart's Nancy Wilson and made a straightforward teen romance, *Say Anything*; like most features shot in Seattle, it's full of geographically impossible scenes (leisurely afternoon strolls between beaches that are really 10 miles apart).

Bill's bored

Frank Harlan, a musician/zine publisher/street mime from Anchorage, came to town in September 1987 and launched *Bombshelter Videos* (no relation to the earlier Bombshelter Records store or label), airing first on KSTW and later on KTZZ. The show specialized in what Harlan called "underground-garage-band-art-thrash-noise music"—national punk and postpunk bands, some too rough for MTV's *120 Minutes*. He aired bands on local commercial TV that were considered too weird for local commercial radio. Harlan bought the airtime, selected the videos from independent labels, sold and shot the commercials (mostly for local record stores and coffeehouses), and hosted the show under the name Bill Bored, taping the VJ segments in his apartment.

Harlan later claimed that his Bill Bored costume introduced the "fashion" of denim cutoffs above longjohns. Others credited that look to Pearl Jam road manager Eric Johnson, or to a clique of musicians and fans who moved here together from

Arizona. In any event, it was a costume of convenience and cheapness, not of Greenwich Village preening. Some of Seattle's Arizona transplants included the Supersuckers, the Best Kissers in the World, performance artist Jim Rose, promoter Jeff Holmes, and singer Kelly Canary of the female punk band Dickless (also with Kerry Green and Jana McCall; tour slogan: "Castration Across the Nation;" Canary went on to the 1994 band Teen Angels).

Harlan directed a few videos by local bands. He shot them on freely-available locations with simple staging, with portable video cameras or Super 8 film. While the results might not have met MTV's slickness standards, he got bands onto videotape for less than a real production company would charge just for lights, fulfilling the promise of his corporate name—No-Budget Production.

Harlan's other ventures over the years included a videocassette of skateboard stunts (with Nirvana and the U-Men donating songs for the soundtrack), a children's-activity video series, and *Northwest Bands and Labels* trading cards, mainly featuring independent and unsigned bands. Sir Mix-A-Lot offered to be on a card in 1992, but had already sold the rights to his likeness to a national card company. As a compromise, Harlan issued a card showing Mix-A-Lot's limo, torso and gun but not his face.

Frank Harlan: "In 1987 all the clubs were shutting down, there were no all-ages venues, there were only a couple places you could see bands. All of a sudden you started to be able to see (touring) bands whose names were on the flyers before they came to town. People in the suburbs could tell if they wanted to drive into town to see somebody. Within a year, I think things were opening up again."

Bombshelter Videos' *opening disclaimer: "Attention late night viewers. Portions of the program you are about to see may seem strange, unusual or unsanitary. Just sit back and relax. You can't change it."*

Seal of disapproval

UW drama major Kevin Seal won a nationwide talent search to become an MTV VJ; he shaved himself on-camera for his audition tape. From 1987 to 1991, he goofed around on the air and made a total fool of himself in interviews, occasionally also performing the valuable service of making fools of the stars he interviewed. For two years he hosted *120 Minutes* and *Postmodern MTV*, the channel's late-night ghettos for major-label "alternative" bands; he often inspired audience ire for treating cult heroes like Depeche Mode with the same irreverent sarcasm he gave during his regular shifts to Winger and Nelson. After Seal's contract wasn't renewed, he stayed in New York, auditioning for industrial videos. He reappeared in 1993 on the syndicated series *Music Scoupe*.

LOSER

Kevin Seal reading a viewer letter on 120 Minutes: "'Dear Kevin Seal: You suck.... Why don't you go back to Seattle and impale yourself on the top of the Space Needle?' It would be very hard to do that. You see, it's got this round aircraft beacon on the top of it, so to try to impale myself on it would be even more difficult and more painful, which of course is what you want anyway."

Lashing back

Dawn Anderson revived *Backfire* in November 1987 as *Backlash*, "Seattle's Only Local Music Magazine": all band interviews and reviews, no flashy graphics. Held to a tight budget by her publisher Terry Denton, Anderson struggled to cram as much coverage as possible into 8-page and 12-page tabloid issues. The first issue already referred to something called "the so-called Seattle Sound"—in an article about a band that (like 90 percent of Seattle's bands) didn't play whatever that sound was, the hardcore Crisis Party, with ex-Joe Despair/Refuzors guitarist Ward Nelson, ex-Bonehead member Tommy Bonehead (Simpson), and ex-Joe Despair member Quiet (Jim Norris).

Dawn Anderson's opening editorial, 12/87: "Yeah, we're an alternative (to the *Rocket*) all right. But you'll find when you open this rag that we're every bit as pompous and opinionated as that other magazine. We're just a different kind of pompous. And this town needs all the diversity it can get."

Anderson reviewing the Mr. Epp/Mudhoney/Melvins video collection Hoop Skirt/Loop Yarn: "I do not want to mislead any art school types who may be reading this and thinking it's art and therefore I don't understand it—I do understand it and it still sucks, OK?"

In 1987 Wendi Dunlap, a former Prudence Dredge backup singer and neice of Frantics drummer Don Stevenson, started the photocopy zine *Yeah!*, focusing on the Green Monkey/PopLlama fun bands. She turned it over to Christopher Rimple and Holly Holman, who kept it going until 1989. Other late-'80s zines included *Swellsville*, KCMU's *Wire*, *Zero Hour* (literary decadence co-run by photographer Alice Wheeler, writer Jim Jones, and Audio Leter/Patio Table guy Deran Ludd), and the slick literary poster-zine *Four Five One*.

The publication that least accurately represented the Seattle rock milieu was Matthew Aird's *City Heat* (1988-92), full of gratingly "upbeat" hype for "hot" bands about to break into the bigtime. The newsprint monthly improved after Aird stopped printing photos by clothing store owner Jim Hadley, who believed in women with big hair, big boobs and small clothes. For a cover story about "Women In Rock," Hadley shot a kneeling busty woman in low-cut tights, giving fellatio to a microphone.

More in tune with the local punk zeitgeist was

Jeanne Wasserman's *Slur* (originally *SLR*), a photocopy zine of post-postmodern visual art and lowlife culture.

Jeanne Wasserman in Slur #2, winter 1988: "In our Sham and Glam Department: We find a band whom the *Rocket* says 'may singlehandedly revive Seattle's listless rock n' roll scene,' and who has had its name relentlessly splashed across the pages of *Backlash*. Well, you won't find it here. And as for a revival, forget it. This insipid band could put an insomniac to sleep. Please, dear God, let this dull exercise in pretension get signed to some major (i.e. wimpy) label in the hope that they will find a hole to bury their 'bone' in L.A., that enchanted village of every wanna be rock god's dreams."

OK by me

Visual art was dominated locally by an upscale version of decorative crafts. Its top supplier was Tacoma native Dale Chihuly, who sold prosaic glass bowls to Microsoft's stock-option millionaires. But some visual and performance artists wanted to do more than high-priced fluff. They gathered at COCA, Art/Not Terminal (a co-op gallery in an old Trailways depot with bands once a month), Galleria Potatohead (a DIY space for installations and monthly performances that wandered between three locations), AFLN ("A Frilly Lace Nighty," a co-op gallery in an old Capitol Hill

Left: the Georgetown Steamplant

'zine crazy!

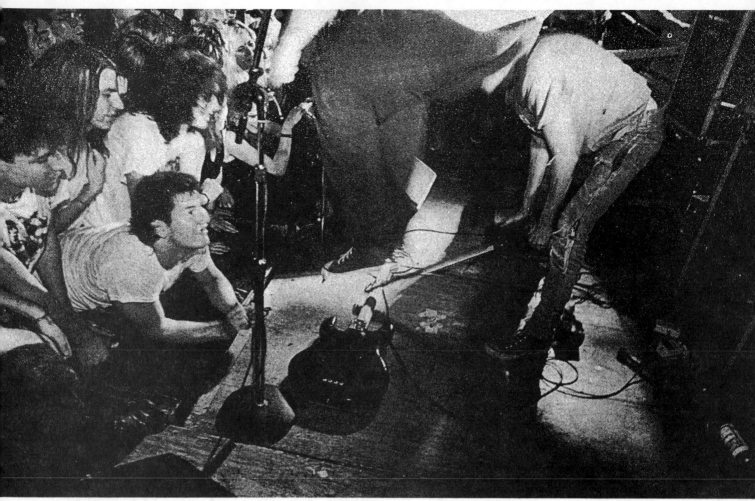

medical office), and the OK Hotel Cafe.

Steve and Tia Freeborn and many volunteer helpers converted the OK, an old waterfront flophouse, into an art space with food and performances downstairs and exhibits in the tiny hotel rooms upstairs. Shortly after the place opened for private parties in 1988, cops hounded Freeborn under the Teen Dance Ordinance. He closed briefly to install additional fire exits, then reopened as a cafe with performances.

The OK opened up an old back ballroom for bands in January 1990, small enough to be exempt from the Teen Dance Ordinance. The room was the ultimate moshing space: no booze, no windows, just loud bands on stage and tightly packed teens and young adults on the floor, shoving and stagediving. Insurance restrictions put a stop to the stage diving; shortly after that, the Freeborns' desire to appeal to more "artistic" tastes put a stop to the OK's all-punk schedule. Hard rock bands still played there but less often and with strict no-moshing rules; more of the schedule was devoted to world-beat, improvisational, industrial, and folk acts. In 1993 the OK became the first full-time local space in years to offer both all-ages music (in the back room) and beer (served in the front cafe area only). But that would prove to be just an interim step toward making the whole place 21-and-over.

Showbox revisited

Until the OK's beer experiment, the last shows

to offer all-ages music with a separate drinking area were two shows at the Showbox Theatre, produced by Larry Reid for the Center on Contemporary Art. Reid produced performance events for COCA in 1987 and returned as its director from 1988 to 1991.

Under Reid, COCA sponsored two of the last three shows at the long-closed Showbox in March 1987 and April 1988, a hardcore concert starring Steve Albini's Chicago band Big Black and a video screening by English industrial-noise makers Psychic TV. The Big Black show (with the U-Men opening) was a major influence on the scene. Albini showed how a band could be "alternative" without abandoning the larger-than-life passion of hard rock, preserving the heroics and volume levels of metal without the hairspray clichés. COCA brought Big Black back later that year for its farewell show. It was held in the abandoned Georgetown Steam Plant, the perfect match of noise and atmosphere; 1,000 people got their hearing permanently shot and loved it.

The final rock show at the Showbox was an AIDS benefit with Mudhoney and a host of other bands in February 1990. The Empty Space Theater planned to take over the space, but flinched at the cost of bringing it up to new building codes. It ended up as a franchise of the Improvisation comedy-club chain. The franchise owner was a former executive with Casablanca Records in L.A., who walled off the big ballroom into a showroom and a cocktail lounge. The walls of the lounge were decorated with gold records and other memorabilia from corporate-rock bands that the Showbox patrons had loathed. In late 1993 live music briefly returned to the space with hiphop and R&B shows co-booked by Rob Brewer and Sir Mix-A-Lot's business associate Ricardo Frazier. They provided a rare outlet for contemporary black music in a city where "R&B" still meant white John Lee Hooker impersonators. In October 1994 new owners renamed it the Showbox Comedy and Supper Club.

Reining in the airwaves

Albini made a third trip to Seattle in June 1988 for a show at COCA's new permanent space with his new band, Rapeman (named after a violent Japanese comic-book "hero"). KCMU management refused to let Rapeman's name be included in promos. It was the first hint that the station's programming would be reined in.

KCMU had boosted its signal from 182 to 400 watts, after years of fundraising and paperwork. The station adopted the slogan "listener powered," and dramatically boosted its audience and its fundraising. It spawned a listener guide, *Wire*, which DJ Denis Twomey later bought out and turned into an independent arts zine. The final FCC application was pushed through with the help of Wayne Roth, manager of KUOW, the NPR station down the hall in the UW Communications Building. Roth became involved in behind-the-scenes station planning. He advised the new paid KCMU manager, Chris Knab, to make KCMU more "professional."

Knab abandoned the station's collective management system, with Roth's blessing. He decreed the station would cease to play what he called "harsh and abrasive music." He was forced to back down on that one after local press reports led to a public outcry, but over the next four years he gradually revised the station's mix to include fewer all-rock sets, more old blues, folk and "world beat" curated for upscale baby-boomers. He fired longtime volunteer DJs whose programming tastes veered from his decreed softer direction.

Modern music became the sole local franchise of KCMU with the end of KJET, the AM commercial new wave station. Its local owners sold out to one of the out-of-state station groups that began speculating in the buying and selling of broadcast properties (with little interest in their long-term operation) after Reagan deregulated the industry. KJET tried to stage a show of support with a mock sign-off on April Fool's Day 1987. It died for real on Sept. 23, 1988, when new owners suddenly switched it to an automated oldies format. *Sub Pop 200* was weeks away from release; KCMU's monopoly on new-music airplay abetted the local dominance of bad-boy guitar rock over the friendly pop bands KJET had championed.

KJET's last program director, Damon Stewart, tried to start a station that would be carried only on cable TV audio channels. KJET's FM sister, the AOR dinosaur KZOK, also went to oldies. In February 1990 the renamed KZOK-AM became an outlet for the Dallas-based Z-Rock network's pop metal format. Former KCMU *Brain Pain* DJ Jeff Gilbert took over the station weekday afternoons, playing local music hours on Fridays. As other AM stations turned to oldies, country and right-wing talk, Gilbert became Seattle's last AM rock DJ. Gilbert signed off for the last time on Oct. 1, 1993, when KZOK-AM switched to simulcasting KZOK-FM's oldies. For the first time since 1958, there was no new rock on Seattle AM radio.

Dissonant trances

Squid Row, a tiny ex-dive bar on Capitol Hill, opened in late 1986 with music by a jazz-fusion house band; six months later, as booked by Terry Lee Hale, it invited punk/noise bands (which were now being referred to by the "grunge rock" moniker). Tiny (patrons tripped over bands' monitors just inside the door), dark and smoky, it was a perfect place to sway with a sardine-pack of bodies while sharing in the big-beat MDA trance music of the U-Men, Soundgarden and Cat Butt; alternating with the softer sounds of the Walkabouts, ex-San Franciscan folkster Jimmy Silva (who wrote songs recorded by the Young Fresh Fellows and the Smithereens before dying of severe chickenpox in December 1994), Gus Mustand and Sylvan Smith's Paisley Sin (self-released tape: *It's Not Just a Hobby, It's a Hassle*), and John Massoni's understated and melancholy Weather Theatre, which released an EP, two self-issued singles and a European LP. Massoni later led Maxine, which made a CD for England's Blast First.

John Massoni to Backlash, *12/88: "In Seatle, you're playing with the likes of Soundgarden. Then people come and see us and say, 'They didn't move around much.' It's kind of screwed. We're*

Galleria Potatohead

Left: Steve Albini in Rapeman at COCA

Terry Lee Hale

bands that <u>will</u> make money

**Below: inside
Squid Row**

just here to play and if people want to sit down and listen to us, that's cool."

Squid Row was the first successful rock club in the neighborhood where most of the punks now lived; all previous punk spaces on the hill had lasted less than a year. But even Squid Row's full houses didn't keep owner Scott Wild from being overwhelmed by speculative landlords, complaining neighbors (he tried to reduce noise emissions by only letting people in or out between songs) and rising costs. In mid-1990 the space was taken over as the new Tugs Belmont, a more specifically gay dance club than the original Tugs Belltown, which had closed the year before. In the fall of 1994 bands began to play the room again, now called Beatnix.

J.A. Anderson, Backlash *writer and booking agent: "Squid Row was a weird scene. Three hundred people crammed into a 100-person space. It was nuts; it was this incredible, inebriated, massive craziness. Total substance-abuse days."*

Going "pro"

In the winter of 1987, some club owners and the *Rocket* formed the Northwest Area Music Association (NAMA). The group intended to make Seattle a professional music center, by holding business seminars, showcase concerts and annual awards banquets. The group collapsed five years later, partly because many of its original organizers had become too busy. A rift immediately developed between those members who wanted NAMA to help preserve the DIY-level scene and those (including KCMU manager Chris Knab and Backstage owner Ed Beeson) who wanted a bigger scene: venues big enough to meet fire and liquor codes and stable enough to stay in business, managers and promoters smart enough to build support; bands savvy enough to build marketable images. In advocating this direction, Knab cited his experience in San Francisco. The early California punk bands weren't courted by major labels, but had supportive promoters and indie labels with national distribution, advantages Northwest punks hadn't had.

From NAMA's first PR release by **Andy Aldrich**: *"Seattle has fallen on hard times for performing musicians: We can no longer hold the best and brightest, the established acts don't have full bookings, there are no strong agents selling NW acts to buyers, musicians can't work enough to spawn vibrant new acts, clubs have given up on live music. Apathy prevails. Except for certain people..."*

Backlash *review by* **Michael Cox** *of NAMA's first convention, 4/89: "I wanted to sit in on 'What We Can Do About Washington's Stupid Liquor Laws,' 'How We Can Win Seattle Back for the Youth' and 'Postering—Get Around the Stupid Ordinances.' Instead, all I saw were people telling me how I can do it right and be a big star and rake in the dough. This is* not *what NAMA said they'd be when they first asked for musicians' hard-earned moolah!"*

KCMU DJ Faith Henschel compiled a two-tape series of local bands, *Bands That Will Make Money.* Recorded with support from a major label, Henschel sent the tapes to agents and record companies; they weren't released to the public. They included Soundgarden, H-Hour, Green River, Skin Yard, Pure Joy, Fred, Vexed, and Portland's Napalm Beach. Henschel herself became a major-label exec in New York, as the industry was staffing up with hipsters to attract "mainstream alternative" stars.

Alice lives here anymore

One glam-metal band saw more potential in the Seattle club circuit than in the suburban metal circuit where it formed, and which was also fading by this time. Guitarist Jerry Cantrell and singer Layne Staley played their first gig as Diamond Lie three weeks after their first practice in January 1988. They changed their moniker to Mothra and then to just Fuck, before Staley renamed the band after a previous project of his, Alice 'N Chainz; the name was later amended to Alice in Chains. Staley's band (with bassist Mike Starr, later replaced by ex-Ozzy Osbourne sideman Mike Inez, and drummer Sean Kinney, son of a homicide officer who'd investigated the Green River serial killings) initially dressed in what Staley called full glam regalia ("Total spandex, huge hair"), but traded that for flannel and long straight hair (Staley was among the first in town to grow a goatee) and got gigs at the Central

Left:
Alice 'N Chainz

My Sister's Machine

Above: Gordon Raphael
Below: The church fire

and the Vogue.

They got Soundgarden manager Susan Silver to oversee their transition from glitter to grit. They rented a practice space at the Music Bank in Ballard; a couple of record-business people overheard them on a visit to another band. Eight months later they were negotiating a contract with Columbia. They self-released the EP *We Die Young* in early 1990. Months later came their Columbia debut *Facelift*, a slicked-up blend of heavy blues-rock guitar solos, plodding beats, and downbeat lyrics as exemplified in "Man in the Box" (in interviews, Staley said it was about "government censorship and eating meat as seen through the eyes of a doomed calf"). If Soundgarden's first releases stripped the celebratory spirit of hard rock down to a pure force of power, *Facelift* stripped the negative energy of heavy metal down to its core, shedding the cartoon Satan worship and leaving serious tormets about very personal hells.

Columbia PR copy for **Facelift**: *"A cutting-edge thing, a cross between King's X and Soundgarden."*

Layne Staley to Backlash, 8/90: *"My mother hated it when she first heard it: 'Oh Layne, can't you call it something else, that's just terrible. That's demeaning to women'. 'Aw mom, it's just a name.'"*

A member of Staley's previous Alice 'N Chainz,

Nick Pollock, formed the hard-rock combo My Sister's Machine in 1989 with Chris Ivanovich, Owen Wright and Chris Gohde (the latter two from another Eastside metal unit, Mistrust). They recorded what the *Post-Intelligencer* called "hard-edged, discordant metal" on the Caroline album *Diva* and the Elektra/Chameleon album *Wallflower*. The band was in the middle of a national tour in November 1993 when it was informed that it would receive no further tour support because Chameleon had just folded.

Church services
The "No Future" described by the Sex Pistols in

Blood Circus

Primal Rock Therapy

greatest collection of creativity Seattle had ever seen." He wanted to hold concerts, performance art, films and poetry readings in the sanctuary, to form a co-op household upstairs, and to record his favorite bands in the basement studio for a record label he wanted to start. He negotiated with Soundgarden, the U-Men, and other bands about recording for his label, and with Jonathan Poneman about investing in it.

Instead, Raphael recalls, The Church "degraded into a bohemian flophouse" with the standard punk party atmosphere. "There were empty cases of beer rising to the ceiling where poetry readings should have been. Infighting among the residents was a chief feature. The first public event we held was closed by the police." Cops were regular visitors; the place was cited for noise violations almost weekly.

Pete Leinonen: "When the police raided [the Church's] *Halloween show, I played the responsible adult role, talking the police down, and completely forgetting until after the fracas that I was dressed as a dog."*

After nearly a year as punk-party headquarters, an electrical fire of unknown origin struck The Church one night in October 1987. The place burned down, melting Raphael's recording equipment and audio and video tapes of Soundgarden and Green River. Neighbors stood outside and applauded as firefighters took their axes to the stained glass windows. Disillusioned, Raphael went to New York for two years; he failed to make it in the music business but succeeded at getting hooked on heroin.

Gordon Raphael: "I went to New York in 1988. I saw TAD on the cover of a copy of Melody Maker *that was lying in the street. That was my first inkling that things were changing in Seattle.... I suddenly started seeing all these bands I'd worked with in Seattle getting shows in New York. Almost nobody from Seattle had played New York before this. All these bands I'd worked with were now on Sub Pop."*

Open for business

In the months since *Sub Pop 100*, Bruce Pavitt had released Green River's *Dry as a Bone* EP and Soundgarden's *Screaming Life* EP and "Hunted Down"/"Nothing to Say" 45. Then he had to hold off on further releases, including another Green River record, while he raised more money.

Pavitt and new partner Poneman incorporated Sub Pop as a full-time company with national distribution in April 1988. They started with $43,000, half of that from a bank loan. They used the money to release three records, hire seven staffers, and lease an office in the penthouse of the Terminal Sales Building, across from the Virginia Inn and the Vogue. Over the next six months they put out 45s and EPs by Green River, Soundgarden, Blood Circus, Swallow, the Denver-based Fluid, Nirvana and

pre-Thatcher England had come to pass in Reagan's America. The media didn't notice at first, being concerned mainly with upscale baby-boomer audiences. Magazines and TV ads ran endless images of smug middle-aged boomers enjoying the good life to soundtracks of '60s oldies. The movie business treated young people as instinct machines, to be exploited with mindless orgies of violence. The news media treated teenagers as a problem to be curtailed or an inferior species to be ridiculed. The L.A. music industry still cranked out scads of pop-metal bands relentlessly aping 15-year-old clichés of power chords and misogyny. Chief among these offenders was Duff McKagan's Guns n' Roses.

The time was ripe to recapture the rebellion of early punk, adapted for a nation of disenfranchised mall rats. Industry crackdowns against import records and government visa restrictions against foreign performers had inadvertantly aided American independent acts by crippling the ability to launch British bands in this country, though the American underground still depended on the British music press to tell it which American bands to support. "Alternative music" was becoming an industry, with its own *Billboard* chart and its own New York conventions. There were finally CD plants willing to work with indie labels; by 1989 the manufacturing cost of a CD would be less than that of an LP. The electronics revolution had made recording cheaper; digital 8-track decks appeared in basements and rehearsal rooms all over town.

Gordon Raphael rented a former church in Ballard for a performance space to be called simply The Church. It had a sanctuary with pews seating 150, ten bedrooms (Ben Ireland and Walter Leinonen were among the residents), and a five-room recording studio. He intended it to be "the

TAD (originally just Tad Doyle, playing all the instruments), as well as T-shirts printed with the simple slogan "Loser" (later the title of a TAD single), a statement of defiance against the yuppies' obsession with "winners."

*TAD guitarist **Kurt Danielson** in the* Rocket, *circa 1990: "The loser is the existential hero of the '90s."*

Photographer Charles Peterson was on the early staff, doing graphic design as well as "picking bands up at the airport and opening boxes…. It was an informal, family kind of atmosphere at the time." Peterson shot most of the live photos of the bands, including his trademark "hair shots" of long-haired musicians bobbing their heads around. Michael Lavine took most of the studio shots, with bands looking scruffy and pensive in front of drenched psychedelic color backgrounds.

Pavitt and Poneman boasted publicly about making Seattle the music capital of the world. It's no exaggeration to say few people believed them at the time.

***Bruce Pavitt**, 8/89: "If we play our cards right and get the records out on time it's going to be an invasion of unheard-of proportions. Seriously."*

***Calvin Johnson** to the* Times *on the early Sub Pop: "So many people involved in underground music are almost apologetic. Sub Pop comes right out and says, 'We're the greatest. Give us your money.'"*

***Parody Sub Pop logo street poster**, circa 1990: "Soda Pop—Super Sugar Big Buzz."*

***Parody Sub Pop logo T-shirt** commenting on the label's massive debts, 1991: "Sub Plop—What Part of 'We Have No Money' Don't You Understand?"*

***Parody Sub Pop logo T-shirt** issued by C/Z Records, 1991: "Bruce Pavitt Gave Me Head."*

Blood Circus (Colorado-raised frontman Michael Anderson, Geoff Robinson, Doug Day, T-Man), one of the forgotten components on the early Sub Pop roster, offered up what Anderson called "just meat-and-potatoes rock and roll" on the single "Six Foot Under" and the 1989 EP *Primal Rock Therapy*. They then undertook a six-week national tour in a beat-up station wagon, got on one another's nerves, and broke up. Robinson and Day shuttled into other bands; Anderson went to work at a hardware store. Three years later, Sub Pop reissued *Primal Rock Therapy* as a full-length CD with five unreleased 1989 tracks, and the group briefly reunited.

***Geoff Robinson** to* Backlash, *6/88: "We don't really have a Seattle sound. We think of it as primal rock. If the cavemen were playing rock n' roll, this is what it would sound like."*

Times *freelancer **Phil West** reminiscing in 1992 about the Blood Circus single "Six Foot Under": "Starting with a simple, plodding bass line, the song locks into a tight, guttural pattern, with lines about white-trash teen alienation growled over low notes and pounding drums. If it were any closer to epitomizing grunge, it would be parody."*

Another casualty of the early Sub Pop era was Swallow (Chris Pugh, Rod Moody, Andy Scheen, Scott Schickler). Sub Pop issued the Olympia collegiate-punk group's mid-tempo thrash on the single "Guts"/"Trapped" and its self-titled first album, both in 1988, but its follow-up *Sourpuss* got released only in Europe. The group broke up in 1990. Pugh and Dani Kelly formed a band called Creep that released two singles through local indie Blatant Records and Sub Pop, before Pugh went to teach English in Taiwan. Swallow and Blood Circus reunited for joint "Grunge Nostalgia" gigs in 1993 and 1994.

***Stuart Hallerman**, Avast Studios: "I remember Chris Pugh saying with glee that every Sub Pop*

Above: Sub Pop ad
Left: Swallow

Mudhoney

called the Scream opening for Jane's Addiction, who I think is one of the worst bands I've ever heard in my life. We're at the Scream and there's 2,000 people waiting for someone to look at them without looking at anyone else. Everyone thought they were a star.... A crowd like that is not going to get into anything unless they're told it's cool. They just go by what their friends like and if it sounds similar to what they're used to listening to."

The other Green River members (except drummer Alex Vincent, who later moved to Japan) and their entourage held weekly meetings in the Camlin Hotel Cloud Room, a beautifully decrepit penthouse piano bar across from the Paramount, to drink and to plan strategies. Tor Midtskog was at some of these schmoozing sessions and says they "reeked of L.A.-ism, and of chicks who smelled money." Ament, Gossard and Fairweather started rehearsing with Malfunkshun's Andrew Wood and Regan Hagar, originally with a set of '70s covers under the name Lords of the Wasteland. If Green River had partly been a low-budget parody of '70s rock excesses, the new band would treat those excesses with near-total sincerity.

Roderick, *Sky Cries Mary:* "I was studying drama at the UW and working at Raison D'etre (a restaurant on the ground floor of the Terminal Sales Building). Andy worked there and so did Jeff Ament. We were always fighting over what to play in the kitchen. Andy would put on his Kiss tapes, Jeff would put on his hard rock and I had my industrial bands. When Malfunkshun broke up I was bummed. When Green River broke up I was disappointed. But then Mother Love Bone started happening, and that was something new and exciting."

Jim Basnight: "One of the biggest turning points in the scene was when Duff McKagan hit it big in Guns n' Roses. A lot of the people here who knew him started thinking they could get that big. That's when you started to see people grow their hair long and try to become guitar gods. Mother Love Bone wanted to be the next Guns n' Roses."

Former 10 Minute Warning/Skin Yard drummer Greg Gilmore came back to Seattle after spending a year traveling around Asia. On Dec. 22, 1987, he was walking up Broadway with one dollar to his name when Gossard spotted him and asked him to jam with himself, Wood, Fairweather and Ament. Gilmore was promptly in the band and Hagar was out, while the band forged its own tunes. Wood came up with the name Mother Love Bone and stubbornly convinced the other members to accept it. For the band's first T-shirts, old Green River shirts were re-printed with Wood's face superimposed where Arm's had been.

Hagar went on to Mo'Lasses, one of a new spate of white funk-dance bands, then joined singer Shawn Smith to form the electronic-ballad

completist would have to buy the Swallow album, even though it sucked."

Green River dries up

Green River's eight-song record *Rehab Doll* (with a title cut co-written by Paul Solger and a "howling" guest appearance by Sonic Youth's Kim Gordon, mostly taken out in the final mix) came out on Sub Pop in April 1988, nine months after the band broke up, due in large part to Mark Arm's reluctance to get serious about persuing fame and fortune, about dropping the drag and glam costumes and the food-throwing for Pure Rawk. Among the factors that led to the split was Jeff Ament and Stone Gossard's suggestion that Arm take singing lessons.

Nils Bernstein to Goldmine, *8/93:* "Green River was one of the first bands to merge metal and glam into punk rock. Jeff and Bruce dressed like joke glam, while Mark wore ripped spandex; it was all very tongue-in-cheek."

Mark Arm to Slur *on Green River's final show, 1988:* "Jeff and Stoney want to be rock stars and I think Bruce (Fairweather) does too. And I think they realized that they could not get as famous as possible with a singer like me. I don't have a commercial voice; I thank God for that.... The last Green River tour was a five-day thing down to L.A. It was great until we played L.A. at a place

combo Satchel (originally titled Bliss), which signed to Epic in early 1994. The third Malfunkshun member, Wood's brother Kevin, eventually wound up in the Fire Ants (what he called "a loud, crushing rock band") with yet another brother, Brian, and Chad Channing, Nirvana drummer #4. They recorded a single and EP on Ed Dekema's self-named label before Kevin and Brian formed the rock-funk Devilhead, signed to Stone Gossard's Loosegroove label.

The week after the last Lords of the Wasteland gig in early 1988, Arm fronted a one-off gig under the name Wasted Landlords.

The land of mud and honey

Arm next reunited with Steve Turner to form Mudhoney (named for a Russ Meyer softcore movie), with ex-Melvins bassist Matt Lukin and ex-Bundle of Hiss drummer Dan Peters. The band debuted in July 1988 with two shows at the Vogue, opening for Blood Circus. For a July 8 show with Blood Circus and Swallow at the Seattle Boxing Club, a gay private club next door to the Comet Tavern on Capitol Hill, the band members wore blue beads and played all-blue instruments. In early interviews, Arm and Turner described their new band as an outlet for the stripped-down lines and satirical attitudes that had become out of place as Green River got more conventional. As recorded by the increasingly-busy Jack Endino, Mudhoney's early tracks switched effortlessly between raucous indignation and pop burlesque. As the chief stars of

the initial Sub Pop hype campaign, Mudhoney was among the first Seattle underground bands to play Europe, performing at a big German music festival later that summer.

(Another local kid also named a band after a Meyer movie: Gus "Taime" Down from the Bellevue metal band Bondage Boys, who left for L.A. in 1983 and formed the glam-metal band Faster Pussycat.)

Before its first show, Mudhoney had already recorded the garage-classic 45 "Touch Me I'm Sick," perhaps the first and purest evocation of the sludge-punk ethos (and almost a measure-by-measure copy of the Sonics' "The Witch"). It helped establish Sub Pop with college radio outlets nationwide, and was extensively hyped on John Peel's BBC Radio show. It was rewritten as "Touch Me I'm Dick" for the movie *singles*. Its follow-up EP, *Superfuzz Bigmuff* (named for two of Turner's favorite distortion pedals) spent a year on the UK alternative charts. The band released five more singles (one split with Sonic Youth, covering each other's songs), two albums (*Mudhoney* and *Every Good Boy Deserves Fudge*) and another EP for Sub Pop, one split single (with Halo of Flies) for Amphetamine Reptile and another (with Gas Huffer) for eMpTy, and tracks for seven compilations, before signing with Warner-Reprise in 1992. Along the way, Arm managed to complete a UW English degree.

The wonders of Tacoma

Sub Pop's first full-length, single-band LPs were

Below: Mother Love Bone

"We had our first big success at the Tropicana in Olympia. They thought we were a nice little garagey band. They thought Kurt was cute. But then came Dave, who was a bit more rude. He'd get drunk and fall onto girls. The PC people in Olympia didn't like that. But he was a lot better than we were at talking people up, so he helped us get better known in Seattle."

Girl Trouble followed *Hit It* with the PopLlama album *Thrillsphere*, the Northwest Rock cover EP *Stomp and Shout and Work It On Out* on the L.A. label Dionysus, a double EP of Elvis movie songs on Sympathy for the Record Industry, the eMpTy album *New American Shame*, and singles and compilation tracks for K, PopLlama, Estrus, Cruddy, eMpTy, and the Issaquah-based Regal Select.

Girl Trouble started its own zine, the Wheelie-edited *Wig Out*, which in addition to band news discussed such fun topics as Sea Monkeys, the career of William Shatner, clothes made from beer-can pulltabs, and "The Seven Wonders of Tacoma." Twenty-one issues have been photocopied since 1985.

Backlash headline about **Girl Trouble**: "They live in Tacoma. They watch television. They eat meat. They practice sometimes."

Bon Von Wheelie to the Times on choosing prizes to throw to the audience, 2/91: "If I see something we can use as a prize, I hit myself over the head with it a couple of times to make sure it's OK."

Henderson to the Times on Girl Trouble's early days: "We weren't doing what was expected, and having Bon in the band was especially uncool. First off, she was a girl drummer. On top of that, she was my sister. Plus, she was 10 years older than me."

The Seven Wonders of Tacoma, according to **Wig Out**: *Felix & Wolf, a car-dealer sign combining Felix the Cat and a cartoon wolf; the B&I Circus Store, Washington's last independent discount store and home until 1994 of Ivan the caged gorilla; Clinton's House of Music, a piano store with a red neon piano sign; Neverneverland, a display of fairy-tale statuary at Point Defiance Park; the teapot-shaped Java Jive restaurant; the Frisko Freeze drive-in; and the Bostick Apartments, site of a plaque honoring the man who first made school kids stand for the Pledge of Allegiance (and more recently a main location in the Tracey Ullman film* I Love You to Death*).*

Clear Black Paper, a German Glitterhouse co-release by the Fluid, and *Hit It Or Quit It*, a K co-release by Girl Trouble. The latter was billed in Sub Pop PR as "a murderous assault of purebred rock'n'roll from Tacoma's foremost going-nowhere crew."

Girl Trouble was formed in 1984 by guitarist Bill "Kahuna" Henderson, his drumming sister Bon Von Wheelie, vocalist Kurt Kendall and bassist Dale Phillips. Their stage antics included throwing variety packs of cereal or cans of root beer at the audience. Their early gigs featured a lot of Cramps covers; their later gigs featured a lot of covers by early Northwest Rock bands like the Frantics, the Viceroys and Tiny Tony. Girl Trouble blazed the trail of fun-punk that Mudhoney and others followed: Kendall growled schlocky tongue-in-cheek lyrics, backed by tight, swift, serious riffing. Granny Go Go, an 80-year-old go-go dancer still featured at Tacoma's Java Jive bar, grinded away at a 1991 Seattle gig (their excuse for covering the Viceroys' oldie "Granny's Pad" on a 1993 45). They've remained dedicated to songs about (as Scott McCaughey described them) "girls, coffee, dancing, rock n' roll, girls in jail, Indians, trains, sex, dream girls, voodoo girls, you get the idea—important things."

By the time *Hit It* came out, following two K singles, Kendall had left the band and come back. His interim replacement, Texas native David Emmanuel Duet, went on to form Cat Butt.

Bill Henderson: "We started playing just for ourselves. Bon got a $75 drum set from Sears; I had a guitar I'd made in shop class in high school. When I asked Kurt to sing he said he couldn't; I said that was OK 'cuz we couldn't play."

The Sub Pop Sound

The compilation *Sub Pop 200* was scheduled for release in September 1988; it didn't show up in local stores until December. It was a boxed set of three 12-inch EPs with a total of 20 cuts, including Nirvana ("Spank Thru"), Mudhoney, Beat Happening, Cat Butt, Girl Trouble (covering "Gonna Find a

Cave" from the *Banana Splits* kiddie TV show), Green River, Screaming Trees (covering Hendrix's "Love or Confusion"), Soundgarden ("Sub Pop Rock City," with a title inspired by Kiss's "Detroit Rock City" and sampled phone calls by Poneman and Pavitt), TAD, the Thrown-Ups, a Jesse Bernstein rant about eating oranges with Jackie Onassis, Terry Lee Hale, Blood Circus, Chemistry Set, ex-Look leader Rob Vasquez's Nights and Days (named for the Wailers' song "All Of My Nights and All Of My Days;" Vasquez later mutated the band into the Night Kings and now leads the Man Tee Mans), Swallow, the Fluid, the Walkabouts, Steve Fisk, and the Fastbacks (doing Green River's "Swallow My Pride," also covered on Soundgarden's *FOPP*; Pavitt was trying to promote it as a grunge answer to the oft-covered "Louie Louie") plus a promotional booklet of Charles Peterson's band photos. All the acts were local except the Fluid. At least half the acts couldn't be identified with any homogenous sound; but that didn't stop the BBC's John Peel, praising it to high heavens in the weekly London *Observer*, from hailing it as a singular document of a singular music: "It is going to take something special to stop *Sub Pop 200* being the set of recordings by which all others are judged."

Sub Pop 200's cover art (of a tortured scrawny guitarist with a *real* monkey on his back) was by local cartoonist Charles Burns, who'd illustrated Pavitt's three earlier *Sub Pop* compilation cassettes. Burns had left to pursue illustration work in Philadelphia, but continued his adult comic strips and books (*Big Baby*, *Dog Boy*, the masked-wrestler parody *El Borbah*). He designed visuals for *The Hard Nut*, a revisionist "Nutcracker" ballet by former Seattle choreographer Mark Morris, and wrote a live-action *Dog Boy* serial for MTV's *Liquid Television*. He's now writing a live-action *El Borbo* movie.

The label promoted the boxed set's release with showcase nights at the Vogue and an official release party at the Underground (the 18-and-over disco in the Hall of Fame's old U District space).

Pavitt and Poneman recruited Daniel House as "sales czar;" he built an impressive wholesale-retail network reaching independent record stores and hip chains like Tower. (House was also running C/Z on the side and recording with Skin Yard for Cruz Records). Self-distribution meant the label got its money from stores sooner (in many cases COD), but it also meant it didn't have a big distributor's crew or money.

Meanwhile, across town...

C/Z released its own sampler two months before *Sub Pop 200*. *Secretions* proved a last off-time-signature bleat for post-new-wave artiness released just in time for KJET's demise, before the metal-crossover guitar gods took charge. As curated by Patty Herlevi of the band Vertigo Bus, it featured the aforementioned Pure Joy track, three cuts with Amy Denio (including trombone-punks

Fred's only vinyl appearance), Skin Yard, Rob Angus's Color Anxiety, Weather Theatre, Capping Day, Vexed, Crypt Kicker Five, and H-Hour (whose drummer Tad Doyle had already gone solo). The LP's only hint of big bad noise came with Coffin Break's "Just Say No (To Religion)."

Besides Doyle, the two records shared the production services of Jack Endino. Both were modest sellers in their original (and, in *Secretions'* case, only) release. They differed in their attitudes. *Secretions'* two-page insert, written by Endino, moaned on about how the scene was dying, there wasn't anyplace to play, cops kept trying to shut everything down, censors were trying to ban things, and the bands on the record had to hold benefit concerts to get the thing out. *Sub Pop 200's* booklet insert, bold art, and box-set packaging promot-

**Below:
Girl Trouble**

ed a "Loser" image but did so with unapologetic pride, promoting Seattle as a hotbed of rockin' action. The former more accurately portrayed the real scene; the latter created a more lucrative myth.

Also in September 1988 came a compilation of top-40 bar bands from the North End suburbs, *Ready for the Majors*. Its cover showed three spandex bimbos crouched as a baseball umpire, catcher and batter (swinging a guitar instead of a bat). The 20 bands on that record all wanted to be Rock Stars; none did. None of the *Sub Pop 200* bands officially wanted to be Rock Stars except for the already-defunct Green River; six have gone to the majors.

After the U-Men

Under House, Sub Pop became a distributor for K, C/Z, and Black Label (run by Russ Battaglia of Fallout Records and Skateboards). Black Label released a U-Men album, *Step on a Bug: The Red Toad Speaks* (described in the *Rocket* as "an unbridled, post-graduate exercise in highly articulate noise") before the oldest dirge-rock band in town finally expired in 1988. After they broke up, an import sweatshirt company stole the U-Men name.

The final U-Men gigs included bassist Tom Hazelmeyer, a veteran of the Minneapolis punk scene who'd joined the Navy and got stationed at Oak Harbor. While still enlisted, Tom started the Amphetamine Reptile record label as a weekend project; it recorded several Washington bands and released a posthumous U-Men 45. Shortly after his

discharge, he moved the label with him back to Minnesota and formed the band Halo of Flies (named for an Alice Cooper song). AmRep and Sub Pop are planning to jointly reissue the U-Men's back catalog.

U-Men singer John Bigley next formed the garage-punk Crows (no relation to the national Crow, Black Crowes or Counting Crows), with Charlie Ryan and ex-YBGB (Young Boys Gone Bad) member Garth Brandenberg; they made two singles and a video in 1991 but didn't release an album until mid-1994. At the time of the U-Men break-up, Tom Price and Ryan already had another band, Cat Butt, with ex-Girl Trouble singer David Emmanuel Duet and 64 Spiders vet James Burdyshaw (who went on to Yummy and the Sinister Six); guitarist Danny Bland joined toward the end of its two-year life. The noise-sleaze group released a Penultimate Records single and a Sub Pop EP, the latter promoted as a "derelict clan of hillbilly raunch." In November 1994 Duet and Birdyshaw reunited in the Rain Dogs.

Danny Bland *to the* Rocket *on Cat Butt: "It was an exercise in self-destruction. We were born to destroy ourselves and we did. It was really fun. What I learned was uh—uh—nothing."*

Bland had moved to Seattle from Phoenix with a power-love band, the Best Kissers in the World, which played U District bars in 1987-88 and snared attention from Capitol, PolyGram and Columbia

Right: Cat Butt

before breaking up. After Cat Butt's demise, Bland re-formed the Best Kissers with original band mate Gerald Collier and new recruit Dave Swafford. With Bland writing the lyrics Collier sang, they released a 45 on Lucky Records and a self-titled EP on Sub Pop. Bland left again (to the San Francisco-based Dwarves) before the Kissers put out the EP *Puddin'* and the album *Been There* on MCA. Their 1994 lineup included. Collier (the only remaining original member), Swafford, Jeff Stone and Tim Arnold. Jimmy Paulson played guitar on *Puddin'*, then quit to form the Kent-based Lemons (described in *Pandemonium* as "three-chord, man-on-top rock" playing "cool, calculated, premeditated submission"), releasing the yellow-vinyl 45 "Just Happy to Be Here" on C/Z.

Price's next band, the retro-garage-rock Gas Huffer (with singer Matt Wright, ex-Vexed drummer and poster artist Joe Newton, and bassist Don Blackstone) released singles, EPs and compilation cuts through Black Label, Amphetamine Reptile, Rathouse, Estrus and Sub Pop ("Beer Drinkin' Cavemen From Mars"), as well as the albums *Janitors of Tomorrow* and *Integrity, Technology and Service* on eMpTy (the LP versions included comic books starring the band). In mid-1994 they signed with Epitaph.

*From **Gas Huffer's** "Sandfleas": "They hop around and eat and screw, they're a little bit like me and you."*

More new labels

Gas Huffer became the top-selling act on eMpTy, started by Blake Wright in 1987 ("I moved to Seattle just in time"). Prior to that he had a California cassette label, Masking Tapes, then moved to Germany and started the Musical Tragedies label (which still exists as eMpTy's European licensee). The odd capitalization of his new company's name was a tribute to his earlier ventures, and had nothing to do with a popular bumper sticker deriding MTV as "eMpTyV." Partly because it didn't advance cash to bands, kept expenses down (at his peak, Wright put out a CD a month with only two employees) and shared mastering and art costs with its German affiliate, eMpTy could turn a profit selling as few as 5,000 copies of a release (through California distributor Mordam).

Dave Crider of the Bellingham band Roofdogs started Estrus Records in 1987, named after a dictionary word for female arousal. Crider's next band, the Mono Men (with Mort Mortensen, Ledge Morrisette and Aaron Roeder), debuted on vinyl with the 1989 45 "Burning Bush"/"Ratfink." They merged the coolness of Ventures-style early Northwest rock with the rawness of '80s punk; Dawn Anderson called them "the aural equivalent of a giant insect ricocheting off the walls, refusing to die." Estrus's first LP (a joint venture with PopLlama) was *Here Ain't The Sonics*, a compilation tribute to the late local band all the punks loved but none was old enough to have seen. It's also released 45 box

The Mono Men

**Right: Gas Huffer
on Spud Goodman**

Slam Suzzane

Lisa Orth

sets (*The Estrus Lunch Bucket, The Estrus Gear Box, Tales from Estrus*) with trash-rock combos from across North America. The label's covers and ads let designer Art Chantry indulge his fascination with '60s trash culture. Its other releases included Stumpy Joe and the Fall-Outs (no relation to the Fallout Records store), a 10-year-old mod-rock inspired act with Dave Holmes, Dino Lencioni and Shannon McConnell; Holmes also played in the Calabros, named for current SuperSonics announcer Kevin Calabro. The Fall-Outs also recorded for Steve Turner's Super Electro label, home to Rob Vasquez's Night Kings and the teen-beat revival Statics (with Zack Hoppenrath and Diane Kitaro).

Estrus championed the new garage bands in its releases and its Garageshock festivals, which brought small, enthusiastic numbers of bands and fans from the U.S. and Japan. To Crider, what made a band "garage" wasn't a specific sound but an attitude of fun and direct action.

Dave Crider to Option *on the neo-garage aesthetic, 9/93: "Anybody with the right attitude can do it. Being technically trained can actually be a hindrance. Music is all about communication, and I think it's best when it's done on a basic level. The band Supercharger recorded a great album for us, and you know, I'm not even sure that they know how to tune their guitars."*

More Monkey business

Capping Day began at an open mike night at the University Bistro with Laura Weller (Scott Vanderpool's future wife) playing guitar, Bonnie Hammond playing xylophone, and a drum machine playing itself. The women added a succession of

rhythm players (including Skin Yard drummer Scott McCullum, their manager Terry Morgan, and the Posies' Mike Musburger) to become a "real" band that could play their introspective songs of alienation at the Squid Row and the Attic. Their 1987 Green Monkey Records 45, "Mona Lisa" (not the Nat King Cole song), won them first place in a national "best unsigned bands" contest. The prize was to have been an EMI recording contract, but contract hassles and dealings with shady promoters left the band with nothing but some unfinished tracks produced by Jon Auer (eventually released on a PopLlama EP) and big legal debts. The group slogged on, but Weller and Hammond's haunting dreamscapes of religious imagery never again landed the big name attention; the two still perform occasionally as an acoustic duo.

Green Monkey also recorded the only LP of the Life, led by Jim McIver (the *Rocket* called it "buoyant pop-ability with compelling Ventures-inspired guitar work") and the first album of garage-thrashers Slam Suzanne (typical lyric: "So this party, it went on and on/I saw this couple, they were fucking on the lawn"), before label boss Tom Dyer ended the label in 1991 to teach at the Art Institute of Seattle, part of a national chain of for-profit colleges that enticed kids on the promise of lucrative fun careers in the music, video and commercial-art businesses. The school deposited a steady stream of young graduates in Seattle with massive student loans, few traditional career opportunities, and some knowledge about making records and videos. Some put out records and videos as class projects; some kept at it after leaving the school, increasing the local talent pool.

The importance of color vinyl

Sub Pop soon got overextended and had to cut back to its own material, dropping its distribution ties to smaller labels. Pavitt and Poneman's forte wasn't shrewd financial management. It was image and hype.

Pavitt knew a record was a document, a physical object that made a contact point between a listener and an idea. He also knew the importance of collectibility. Every Sub Pop product, even a one-off single by an unknown band, was treated as a precious object: limited press runs, picture sleeves, vinyl in colors not found in nature. *Goldmine* estimates some early Sub Pop 45s as now worth $200 or more.

The sound of most of its stuff was hard and muddy. The art direction (by Linda Owens, Lisa Orth and Jane Higgins) was slick and direct; identical bold-type titles above identical bouncing-hair photos. Bruce and Jonathan knew how they wanted to achieve world domination, even if they didn't have the capital for the task. They became darlings of the British and American-underground music press, at a time when none of their releases had sold 10,000 copies.

In October 1988 they launched the Sub Pop Singles Club. You paid in advance for collectible 45s, most on color vinyl. The first 1,000-copy club release was Nirvana's first 45, with the Shocking Blue's "Love Buzz" backed by the original "Big Cheese." Nirvana also cut "Mexican Seafood" for C/Z's first *Teriyaki Asthma* EP.

Eric Amrine, ex-Color Anxiety: "Poneman came over to my girlfriend's flat one evening, brandishing a cruddy cassette. He had barely gotten Sub Pop off the ground, and boasted about these guys from Aberdeen with the world's worst name for a rock band. They had somehow gotten a tape to the guy. What Jonathan said will live with me for a long time—'Eric, listen to the character in this guy's voice! It's kind of like Paul Westerberg, but much more so. And those songs, man—if I have my way, this band will go all the way up!' I didn't always agree with him; his pure pop, marketing, and packaging instincts and my eldritch leanings were an inspiring but strange pairing. For example, we went to see Green River and I really thought they sucked. I still do…. But I was eager to admit there was something there on that cassette tape, a vocal quality that crept inside you and made you listen, and I always have preferred raspy vocals. It seemed quite likely that Poneman would finally succeed as far as the industry would allow."*

Tending a new garden

Soundgarden had left the label by the time of *Sub Pop 200*'s release, following the *FOPP* EP. The split, according to all parties, was amicable.

Kim Thayil to the Times, *10/89: "Sub Pop is this huge hunk of indigenous Seattle culture that is getting attention nationally and internationally. It's like Seattle's got something home-grown that isn't rent-a-culture. That's a fact that got recognized in New York and London and L.A. before it got recognized here. I think it's the best time to be in Seattle."*

In the fall of 1988 Soundgarden released *Ultramega OK* on SST Records, a lush melange of hard-rocking riffs and psychedelic wails which furthered its reputation among the hard-rock cognoscenti. It included a minute-long segment of studio noise after the last track, billed as "One Minute of Silence" and attributed not to John Cage but John Lennon.

SST promo copy for **Ultramega OK**: *"Twisted metal from the magnetic north with wailing vocal gymnastics punctured by razor-edged guitars, served atop hypno-erotic rhythms. Some mighty good eatin'."*

By the time *Ultramega OK* and *Sub Pop 200* came out, Soundgarden was already negotiating with A&M, a company known for signing and discarding regional bands (from Seattle R&B pioneer Dave Lewis to Portland rockers Johnny and the Distractions) without giving them a real chance in the national marketplace. Many fans were proud of Soundgarden's achievement but didn't seriously expect anything big to come of it beyond the band's reported $175,000 advance.

Fopp

Below: Soundgarden

CHAPTER ELEVEN:
MORE NOISE PLEASE (1989-1991)

Mother Love Bone signed to PolyGram after playing only 14 gigs, many to fewer than 50 people. The group released the EP *Shine* in early 1989, in advance of a tour devised to establish the band nationally. They wound up opening for Dogs D'Amour, described by Jeff Ament as "English drink rock."

Andrew Wood fronted his new band in bell bottoms, berets and flowing blond hair. He set aside the white hair dye, velvet coats, pale makeup and Elton John glasses from his Malfunkshun days. He sneered and preened on stage like the Rock Star he believed he was, even with only a couple dozen people in the room, many of whom believed a Rock Star was not something to be. He played the total cock-rock god ("I'm the instigator of the me generation/the official seminator of the female population") laced with just enough self-parody to make it palatable. The band churned out hard rock riffs behind him, with durable Van Halenesque wailing guitar solos.

Andrew Wood in the Mother Love Bone "video press kit," released on home video as The Love Bone Earth Affair: *"We were all influenced by the same stuff gowing up, everything from King Crimson to Kiss and in between. It was a product of growing up in the '70s and listening to the same bands. I don't think there's any signature sound to Seattle.... Getting signed is just a step and it's not a big deal 'cuz you've got to sell the records once you've made them.... Touring in a van is not what I want to do. I need a bus! Now!... No one is as anxious as me to get in an arena. I want to go on an arena tour with anyone, even Warrant...That's the kind of crowd I like, an easy crowd. You could say your mother smells bad people! and they'd just yell Yeah!"*

The band circulated demo tapes and recruited former Heart associate Kelly Curtis, by then a partner with ex-Heats member Ken Deans in Mark Alan Management (named for their middle names), to help them work up the best possible deal. Capitol, Island, Atlantic, A&M, and Geffen negotiated with the group before PolyGram offered a $250,000 advance (an unprecedented sum for an unknown band) and the band's own subsidiary label, Stardog (from its song "Stardog Champion"). Curtis left his old company to manage the group. He then became Susan Silver's business partner for a couple of years, then started his own management firm.

In real life, Wood was a *very* shy boy from the upscale suburb of Bainbridge Island. He augmented his introversion via heroin. Even in the Malfunkshun days he was on and off the stuff, trying to break the habit that fueled his sense of self-importance. He went cold turkey while the band recorded the album *Apple* in late 1989. About half of Wood's lyrics dealt obliquely with his and his girlfriend's attempts to stay off the stuff. He'd already known one local musician who'd died of an overdose in 1988, Jim Norris of the punk-thrash bands Crisis Party and YBGB.

Jonathan Poneman to Melody Maker *on Wood: "He was a total Rock Star, though he was the only person who thought so."*

Chris Cornell to Rip *on Wood: "He totally created his own personality as a rock star. He was a total rock star before anybody knew who he was.... Eventually, it became a really efficient escape, because he was really scared. Anyone who's a musician or a songwriter and/or a performer can be pretty insecure.... And it was moving really fast for him. It was an easy way to forget about it. He was probably a lot more scared about simple things—living socially and working. He was probably just more afraid of being alive than anybody would realize, because he was so outgoing that you never saw that side of him. He was guarded. He was always on. At his worst times, he was laughing about it. He was like a game show host."*

Mother Love Bone's blatant pursuit of stardom led other local musicians to name a side band in its "honor": Daddy Hate Box, with Coffin Break singer Peter Litwin and TAD drummer Steve Wied, which played a few unapologetically-sloppy club gigs and made a couple of C/Z 45s and an EP on *Rocket* writer Adam Tepedelen's New Rage Records.

Ad copy for New Rage Records, 1/91: "Our competitors: Limited edition, singles club, boxed set. Us: No gimmicks, no hype, big music."

Ticking away

After over a decade of hundreds of bands trying, for a Seattle underground group to get onto a Big Six label was a welcome feat; but people here,

Mother Love Bone

used to the comfort of defeatism, didn't think it'd amount to anything really big. A *Rocket* article in June 1989 predicted this national interest in Seattle bands would quickly fade: "The clock is ticking away on Seattle's 15 minutes of fame."

Amid the Mother Love Bone/Soundgarden industry mania came a last batch of record deals from the declining Eastside/South End metal circuit and the West Seattle thrashcore bands: Brad Sinsel's War Babies, Bitter End, Forced Entry (song titles: "Bludgeon," "Foreign Policy," "Kaleidoscope of Pain"), Panic, My Sister's Machine. The post-Jim Norris version of Crisis Party (Kenny Dope, Tom Fart/Hanson, Tommy Bonehead/Simpson, Whiskey Ward/Ward Nelson, Erick E., and a succession of bassists) made one album through Capitol affiliate Metal Blade, then got tossed aside in one of Capitol's periodic restructurings.

Veronika Kalmar in the Rocket *on Crisis Party, 4/90: "It's that Johnny Thunders/Guns n' Roses "love me, want me or fuck off and die" attitude which can't be faked, though millions try, that reaches under your belt and grabs the rock n' roll arrogance hidden demurely beneath your neatly pressed trousers."*

C/Z, meanwhile, released *Another Pyrrhic Victory: The Only Compilation of Dead Seattle Bands*, with tracks by Green River, H-Hour, Malfunkshun, My Eye and 64 Spiders (with James Burdyshaw and ex-Green Pajama Joe Ross). The LP played at 33 r.p.m. but had a 45-size hole.

A wide variety of unheard music continued to be developed by local bands, from the haunting melodies of Capping Day, Pure Joy and Common Language, to the bubble-grunge of Gnome (with ex-Treeclimber Loren Evans), to the electric punk-folk of Beat Happening to the acidic (musically and lyrically) tunes of Love Battery, to the tight witty garage-pop of Stumpy Joe (John Ramberg, Mark Hoyt, Christian Wilson, Scott Russell; named for

one of Spinal Tap's dead drummers and described in a *Wire* review as "stomping, rocking, jeering fun"). After Stumpy Joe's breakup, Ramberg formed Model Rockets (described in the *Stranger* as "an ooey, gooey, rich and chewy confection: pop music straight from the cookie jar").

But few people in Seattle bothered to hear them, and the national underground came to believe that Seattle produced one and only one kind of music. By mid-1989, national zines like *Option* and *Factsheet Five* started reviews of any non-grunge Seattle recording with remarks like, "This isn't a typical Seattle band, but…"

The *big* irony was that the scene of MDA-fueled, loud slow dirge bands playing to crowded moshpits in tiny bars had already peaked. The Melvins had left town; the U-Men, Green River and Cat Butt had broken up; Mudhoney was veering toward fun-punk, and Soundgarden was veering toward straight-ahead rock. Of the clubs that spawned the development of this sub-scene, only the reopened Ditto and the Vogue (now owned by former plumber Matt Basta) would be around at the end of 1990.

When the folk-rock Walkabouts did regional tours for their second LP (and Sub Pop debut) *Cataract*, reviews treated them like freaks for being from Seattle and not sounding like Soundgarden. Sub Pop's contrived attempts to promote them with goofy PR copy didn't help; by 1993's polished-yet-rustic CDs *New West Motel* (followed by the equally impressive *Satisfied Mind* and *Setting the Woods on Fire*), the Walkabouts were dropped by Sub Pop in the U.S. They became an import-only act, holding out on domestic releases while trying to land a major-label deal. They didn't land it until the end of 1994, when the Cargo affiliate Creative Man announced it would domestically release the group's three Euro-only records. The group was also negotiating a contract for new material with the MCA affiliate Fort Apache.

Bruce Pavitt PR copy for the Walkabouts' Cataract: *"Sensitive hippies with big amps.... Strumming, churning, electrified 'folk' music that gets all the tie-dye people moshing in the pit. Enlightening."*

From the Walkabouts' "Feast or Famine": *"A trailer park with hungry dogs eat stolen bread from a stolen credit card."*

Love songs

Financial deep pockets were still considered a sign of inauthenticity in the scene. Scott Barr's band Boom Boom GI (named after a siren call of Saigon hookers) attracted ill-feelings simply by finding the wherewithal to make its own videos, a half-hour TV special, and a mini-CD. The group began in 1987 as Faye West and the Bleeding Hearts, before Barr replaced West with Laura Love, who billed herself as "octoroon" (mixed ancestry; in her case including African-American and native American blood). Love belted out Barr-written tunes criticizing everything a "political" rocker was supposed to criticize: TV preachers, materialism, suburbs, foreign dictators.

Love then went solo with her own "Afro-Celtic" acoustic band. She won rave reviews for her segment of the New York Singer-Songwriters' Festival at Carnegie Hall in October 1994. *Billboard* named her one of the year's top 10 unsigned acts.

Louder than Sub Pop

Soundgarden's first A&M album, *Louder Than Love* (alleged original working titles: *Louder Than Fuck, Louder Than Meat*), was recorded for $80,000 (a previously unheard-of figure locally) by producer Terry Date The psychedelic and experimental influences of the band's indie work were, for the time being, gone. Date and the band cleaned up the churning sea of noise so you could hear every nuance of every chord.

The band ground out a purer grade of metal than most corporate metal bands. The lack of pop-metal trappings made the sound seem even harder. Just grinding guitars, pounding drums, feedback, screeching-wailing vocals, downbeat subject mat-

ter (including environmental destruction in "Hands All Over") and flaying long hair, all at moderately-slow to gratingly-slow tempos. No acoustic ballads (yet). No self-indulgent guitar solos. No videos with butt-cleavage bimbos. No tall hairdos. No laser lights. No stage explosions. No tributes to the rockstar life. Not even groupies: at a Philadelphia tour stop, a woman snuck backstage demanding to fuck Chris Cornell (who often appeared on stage in tight short pants and no shirt); his manager-wife Susan Silver led her away and politely chided her for being a bad role model to women. The closest thing they did to a love song was "Big Dumb Sex," a parody of stupid heavy-metal sex anthems. It was misinterpreted *as* a stupid heavy-metal sex anthem by people who didn't listen closely to the tight, clever/cynical lyrics on it and the album's other songs, like the parody-bombast "Power Trip."

The album's home video version, *Louder Than Live,* was filmed in black and white at L.A.'s Whiskey A Go Go, and included sincere renditions of Spinal Tap's "Big Bottom" and Cheech & Chong's "Earache My Eye," closing with a ritual guitar-destruction.

Chris Cornell, introducing "Gun" in Louder Than Live: *"This is your chance to tell the band to fuck off.... C'mon you can do better than that.... All right, fuck you too. When I say fuck, you say fuck on this song."*

Los Angeles Times *critic Robert Hilburn liking Soundgarden for all the wrong reasons, 11/90: "This young Seattle band may become the arena-rock band of the '90s.... Chris Cornell is a sexy lead singer who could win more female hearts than Bon Jovi, and the group's rhythm section—without losing the hardcore edges that appeal to hard-rock males—plays in a sensual groove that, too, should win a mainstream following."*

Kim Thayil to New Musical Express, 5/90: "Being an important thing to music is like inventing a more sturdy trash liner."

Hiro Yamamoto quit the band after *Louder*'s release, to pursue UW studies in science and chem-

Below: Soundgarden

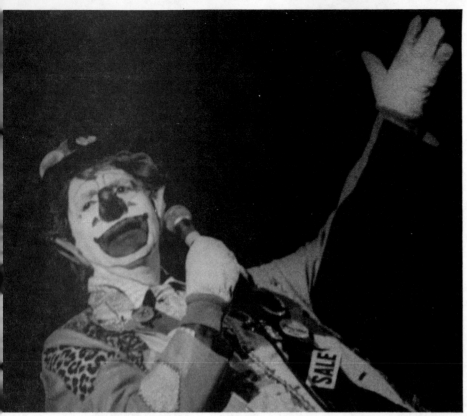

J.P. Patches introduces
Soundgarden

istry. He ended up teaching at Western Washington University. On the side he teamed up with former Screaming Tree Mark Pickerel in the band Truly, which released two Sub Pop EPs before signing with the Capitol affiliate Revolution. Soundgarden's next interim bassist was Jason Everman, who'd previously played second guitar for Nirvana; he was replaced in Soundgarden by Ben Shepherd, who'd played with Stone Gossard in the high school band March of Crimes.

Bleach and cyanide

Bruce Pavitt and Jonathan Poneman tried to put Sub Pop into the big time, with little capital save the steady income from their Singles Club (which peaked in 1991 at 7,000 members). Their spring 1989 release schedule listed LPs by Swallow, Nirvana, and TAD. By now Tad Doyle had a complete band, with ex-Treeclimbers guitarist Gary Thorstensen , ex-Bundle of Hiss bassist Kurt Danielson, and successive drummers Steve Wied (Wiederhold), Rapeman vet Ray Washam, and Accused vet Josh Sinder. The first TAD album, *God's Balls*, featured such non-mainstream songs as "Sex God Missy, "Pork Chop," "Satan's Chainsaw," "Cyanide Bath" and "Nipple Belt" (about one of serial killer Ed Gein's fetishes).

Kurt Danielson to Backlash *on the TAD sound: "...like one big, loud, unoiled machine that was about to explode."*

Nirvana, with Bainbridge Island native Chad Channing assuming the drummer's slot, released its debut album, *Bleach* (reportedly named after the anti-AIDS campaign asking drug users to clean their needles between uses). It was an amalgam of scorching anthems, the Ministry-like assault "Negative Creep" (which could be interpreted as a rape

nightmare, as narrated by the criminal), the pumping hardcore churner "Blew," and the near-perfect pop-punk ditty "About A Girl"; plus the two songs from their first single and two tracks from their original demo tape with Dale Crover drumming. The eight new songs (plus two outtakes) were recorded by Jack Endino in three 10-hour sessions for a little over $600. (No, Endino won't record *your* band for that little now.) The band borrowed the money from temporary second guitarist Jason Everman, who didn't even get to play on the sessions. It broke into the national college-radio top 20 and sold a respectable 30,000 copies over the next two and a half years, much of that after the band opened on tour for Sonic Youth.

They fired Everman after a few gigs because he wanted to incorporate some of the power-blues heroics Mother Love Bone was pursuing. Everman went on to Soundgarden, was soon kicked out of *that* band, then joined the New Jersey band Mindfunk. Continuing Everman's hard-luck streak, Mindfunk hired Terry Date to record its second album just before Epic dropped the band. The album later came out on Megaforce under the title *Dropped.*

Kurt Cobain told Michael Azerrad that he felt pressured to conform to a "Sub Pop Sound" on *Bleach* by toning down his pop-songwriting sensibility. When he enveloped his angst inside beautiful melodies on *Nevermind*, some *Bleach* fans mistook it for a sellout. He also claimed the minimalist lyric to "School" was based on the cliqueish immaturity he saw in the Seattle scene. He was right to some extent: after more than a decade, the egghead kids from the North End were still at odds with the stoners from the South End and the crusters from West Seattle, who were all at odds with the jocks from the suburbs.

Within the next year Nirvana cut the Sub Pop single "Sliver"/"Dive," a degenerate cover of Kiss's "Do You Love Me" released on C/Z's *Hard to Believe: A Kiss Covers Compilation* (from a 1989 Olympia show with Everman), a cover of the Velvet Underground's "Here She Comes Now" for the Communion label compilation *Heaven and Hell Vol. I,* and two songs recorded by Steve Fisk for a British "Blew" EP. "Sliver" was an upbeat yet melancholy reminiscence of a part of Cobain's childhood, when he was living with his grandparents; the side also included an answering-machine tape of a call between Poneman and a hung-over Chris Novoselic. "Dive," with the screaming refrain "Dive with me!," was recorded in Madison, Wisconsin by producer Butch Vig, in sessions for a planned second Sub Pop album.

Because they were always driving up the 75 miles from Cobain's place in Olympia and Novoselic's place in Tacoma to gig in Seattle, they were the first Sub Pop band with its own equipment van.

Sub Pop catalog copy for Bleach: *"Hypnotic and righteous heaviness from these Olympia pop stars. They're young, they own their own van, and they're going to make us rich!"*

Nirvana T-shirt, 1989: "Fudge-packin' crack-smokin' Satan-worshippin' motherfuckers."

Nirvana T-shirt, 1992: "Flower-sniffin' kitty-pettin' baby-kissin' corporate rock whores."

They opened for the Melvins at a 1989 "Welcome Home" gig in Aberdeen's twin city of Hoquiam. Cobain took to the stage with his neck painted bright red; Novoselic just wore underpants, and danced by jumping up and down on one foot.

Lame Fests, lamer critics

Nirvana opened for Mudhoney and TAD at Sub Pop's first "Lame Fest" on June 9, 1989 in the Moore Theater. The sold-out show (the first over-1,000 audience for any of the bands) was lowlighted by frequent scuffles between stagedivers and overzealous bouncers. Tad Doyle mooned the crowd. Mark Arm tried to kick one of the hated bouncers into the pit. The Swedish Housewife climbed on stage, not to dive but to flash peace signs and plea for calm.

Paul deBarros, Times *jazz critic, reviewing the first Lame Fest:* "The war between the slam-dancers and the bouncers upstaged the music, particularly during the show by Mudhoney, who stopped playing three times to calm things down. At one point, four clever guys managed to suddenly fly from backstage, out over the monitors and bouncers and into the crush of dancers, easily the most memorable moment of the evening. Beyond extra-musical distractions, the whole point of this show seemed to be based on the perverse, reverse notion that grungy, foul-mouthed, self-despising meatheads who grind out undifferentiated noise and swing around their long hair are good—and 'honest'—by virtue of their not being 'rock stars.' How confounded this primitivism is, which defines bands in the reverse image of someone else's

market position, rather than music. And how sad, because the young, enthusiastic and clearly intelligent crowd at last night's show apparently could not tell the difference.... If this is the future of rock n' roll, I hope I die before I get much older."

In August 1989 there were two nights of concerts featuring most of Sub Pop's bands at COCA's new space on First and University, a block south of the old Showbox and next door to the relocated Amusement Center peep show (now the Lusty Lady). The concerts accompanied *Modern Primitives*, a touring exhibit of human oddities, including pictures of tattoos, body piercings and freak show acts. At one of the shows, one of the tattoo artists flung powdered sugar at the members of Nirvana.

The COCA showcases included the second Seattle gig by a former Tucson band, Black Supersuckers (later just Supersuckers). Eddie Spagetti, Dan Bolton, Ron Heathman (replaced in 1995 by ex-Didjit Rick Sims) and Dan Siegel's three-minute songs of beer, hot rods, horror movies, bad sex, pot, and more beer quickly endeared the band to the cramped audience (sample titles: "Retarded Bill," "I Say Fuck"). They cut a series of singles for Sympathy for the Record Industry, Lucky, eMpTy, and Sub Pop ("Like a Big Fuckin' Train") before issuing the Sub Pop albums *The Smoke of Hell* and *La Mano Cornuda.*

Future Lame Fests were produced by Terry Morgan at the Moore in 1990 and 1991, and one Ultra Lame Fest invaded the Paramount in April 1992. That show symbolized a transition for Sub Pop, with Mudhoney (who'd already left the label) headlining after new signees Seaweed, the Supersuckers, Earth and Pond.

Across the pond

Pavitt and Poneman kept their bands on short purse strings, instead paying for major promotion. (As was the case with other indies, Sub Pop's bands originally paid their own studio costs; big la-

Sub Pop at COCA

Left: Mudhoney at Lamefest

Charles Peterson

bels typically fronted recording costs but charged them against future royalties.)

Savvy marketers always, they developed a clear identity for their label: postpunk noise as an apolitical lowbrow lifestyle. With Soundgarden, TAD and Mudhoney as their leading examples, Bruce and Jonathan (and their staffers and friends) devised a distinct image for the label: Long hair, flailing heads, slam dancing and stage diving, beer, cynicism, male bonding, feedback, ear damage, smoke. No politics, no intellectualism, no fashion, no sincerity, no R&B, no women in sight (not even as video models). The image was exemplified in Charles Peterson's concert photos, which typically showed singers and guitarists flailing their sweaty long hair right in front of slammin' crowds at tiny bars. Not only was this image an inaccurate portrayal of all Seattle bands, it was an inaccurate portrayal of all Sub Pop bands. But it sold, particularly to the image-hungry British music press.

Britain itself was never a large market for records. The U.K.'s value was as an axis of style and influence. House music was invented in Chicago, but most Midwestern disco-goers heard British ripoffs of it before they heard the originals. In American alternative-record shops, British labels held more cachet and stronger distribution than American indies.

And without an equivalent to our commercial AOR radio with its rigid formats, it was easier to break a new band in Britain—especially if it could supply good visuals and provocative text for the weekly music tabloids. The U.K. music press would take novelty in the idea that world-class music could come from what they seemed to think was a backwoods territorial outpost that barely had electricity or paved roads.

Knowing that the best way to gain credibility in the American underground market was through the British music papers, Sub Pop hired London press agent Anton Brookes to promote a handful of bands playing in a few tiny bars in a far-off port city as the potential saviors of rock. They played up an image of the label's acts that exploited British stereotypes about non-Manhattan Americans as ugly and stupid. They paid the weekly tabloid *Melody Maker* to send reporter Everett True out here to cover the "grunge" explosion, a term he falsely claimed to have invented. In a March 1989 cover story on Mudhoney, True called Seattle "one small, insignificant, West Coast American city" producing "the most vibrant, kicking music scene encompassed in one city for at least 10 years." Over the next three years, True and *MM* hyped the Seattle scene more enthusiastically than any of the jaded media outlets here.

Mudhoney, Nirvana and TAD were sent to perform at a London "Lame Festival" (not "Fest") in the fall of 1989. It was one of several "Seattle Invasion" tours by various promoters that year, including Soundgarden, Beat Happening, Metal Church and Green Pajamas. Some of these acts played festivals in 1,500-seat halls in Germany and Italy, then

went home to slog it out for 50 to 100 fans at the Central Tavern.

Cobain had a rough time on the TAD/Nirvana European tour, for which both bands (including the tall Novoselic and the large Doyle) tooled around in a tiny Fiat van. They got to Germany in time to witness the hoopla over the fall of the Berlin Wall; but Cobain ended his set there by smashing his guitar and walking out after six songs. Pavitt and Poneman flew out to see the tour-ending show in Rome. Cobain was four or five songs into the show, as Pavitt told *Rolling Stone*, when "he·quit playing and climbed up the speaker column and was going to jump off. The bouncers were freaking out, and everybody was just begging him to come down. And he was saying, 'No, no, I'm just going to dive.' He had really reached his limit. People literally saw a guy wig out in front of them who could break his neck if he didn't get it together." He climbed from the speakers up to the rafters, walked from there to the theater balcony, and walked out. He threatened to quit the band that night, but within weeks was performing again.

Mudhoney, continued

The international hype didn't translate to sales right away. Mudhoney's *Superfuzz/Bigmuff* EP was a U.K. alternative-chart topper but sold only 6,000 copies overseas through Sub Pop's British and German licensees. Mudhoney's members still all lived off day jobs, including Steve Turner's gig parking cars and pouring soda pop at A Contemporary Theatre.

Mudhoney's self-titled, first full-length album came at the end of 1989. Billed by Pavitt as "LOUD ballads of love and dirt," its highlights included the ultimate answer to every come-on song, "You Got It (Keep It Outta My Face)." For the "You Got It" 45, Charles Peterson photographed the guys in mud and loincloths, aping a famous LP cover by England's Slits. As Peterson recalls, "Tad was living out by Northgate at the time. We did it in his back yard, then we went up to Northgate in a pickup and walked around the mall's parking lot. A lot of heads were turned that day."

Mark Arm and Steve Turner still dabbled in Leighton Beezer's Thrown-Ups until 1990. Artist Edwin Judah Fotheringham sang, usually about sex and more sex; everybody else played instruments they didn't normally play (Arm drummed). Fotheringham also performed in the knockoff bands Sad and Lonely(s), Love and Respect, and Icky Joey (named for Peterson's high school nickname), and posed for several other people's record cover photos.

Arm covered Bob Dylan's "Masters of War" on a Sub Pop solo single titled *The Freewheelin' Mark Arm* (Eddie Vedder played the same song at a Dylan 30th anniversary show in New York) and recorded with Australian emigres Blood Loss; he and Turner recorded a side project, Monkeywrench, with Gas Huffer's Tom Price, Tim Kerr of the Austin band Poison 13 (no relation to Port-

Left: Black
Supersuckers

land's Tim/Kerr Records), and Martin Bland of Blood Loss and Monroe's Fur.

Sub Plop?

Sub Pop's proposed distribution deals with Columbia and the Disney-owned Hollywood Records fell through, leaving the still-tiny label with tens of thousands of dollars in legal fees. Had Sup Pop gained access to the majors' marketing muscle, it might have lost its street credibility but it might have kept some of its original bands. Instead, Sub Pop's releases remained accessible only through mail order and a few hundred hip stores in big cities and college towns. In some areas, imports from its European licensees were in more stores than its own product. Sub Pop started shelling out money for bands, more than the label could recoup at its market position. By the beginning of 1991, the company was in serious trouble and nearly folded. It was late paying pressing plants, late paying its landlord, and very late paying its bands. A *Rocket* headline from the summer of 1991 said it all: "Sub Plop?"

Daniel House came back from a Skin Yard tour to learn he'd been laid off from Sub Pop. House and Pavitt still have slightly different stories about the firing: Pavitt says he needed a full-time sales czar who wasn't moonlighting with both a band and his own label; House was quoted as saying Pavitt wanted someone "who would work for $2.50 less an hour and be a girl." House took advantage of the free time on his hands to turn his moonlighting project, C/Z Records, into a full-time enterprise.

To make matters seemingly worse for Sub Pop, a drunk Chris Novoselic came to Pavitt's house one night and demanded a long-term contract for Nirvana, something Sub Pop had never sprung for. Later, when David Geffen wanted the band for his DGC label, he settled with Sub Pop for some cash, a Sub Pop logo on the next two Nirvana CDs, and a

2 percent royalty in the unlikely event that the band's sales topped 200,000. That (along with Mudhoney's *Every Good Boy Deserves Fudge*, 1992 sales of *Bleach*, and an infusion of capital from new distributor Caroline Records) saved the company.

New visions

KING-TV's *Almost Live*, begun in 1984 as a talk show with comedy sketches, switched to all comedy in 1989, a year after John Keister took over as host from Ross Shafer (who went to L.A. to be the last host of the Fox *Late Show*). The show's acting tended toward the goofy-guy side of standup comedy (typical running sketch: "The High Fivin' White Guys"), but the camera work and editing (both by Darrell Suto, who starred in the kung-fu parody sketch "Mind Your Manners with Billy Quan") were superb. The writer/actors freely milked local references ("The Ballard Driving Academy," "Cops In Wallingford"). Soundgarden's Kim Thayil, members of Forced Entry, and DJ Jeff Gilbert appeared in a sketch called "The Lame List," which alternated Keister's listing of "what's weak this week" with leather-clad members of "America's Heavy Metal Community" shrieking "Lame!" The sketch was still being used in 1994, with the same old shrieks intercut with new announcements of lame things, including designer grunge. Thayil, Mike McCready and Dave Grohl appeared in an October 1994 sketch about a "Rock Star Fantasy Camp."

In 1990, sketches from the show were used on the Fox show *Haywire*. In 1992, re-edited *Almost Live* reruns aired nationally on the Comedy Central cable channel. Cast member Bill Nye ("The Science Guy"), descendent of turn-of-the-century humorist Bill Nye, took his Rube Goldberg-like physics demonstrations to the Disney Channel's *New Mickey Mouse Club*, and in 1993 to his own Disney-backed show.

In February 1989, David Lynch filmed the *Twin*

Right: Sub Plop?

The Swedish Housewife

Riz Rollins

Peaks pilot in east King County's Snoqualmie-North Bend area. Star Kyle McLachlan was a UW drama grad who had grown up in the eastern Washington town of Yakima (described in *The Fortean Times*, a British UFO magazine, as "like a Twin Peaks on Earth" for its unexplained phenomena in the night skies and its wealth of Indian heritage). Lynch himself knew a lot about mysteries of the woods, having grown up in Eastern Washington and Montana with a father who worked for the U.S. Forest Service. Most of the show's characters were only slightly exaggerated versions of real types you'd see in a Washington town. After a successful premiere in April 1990, the series was quickly done in by network interference, reduced budgets, and writers who forsook Lynch's reality for self-parody.

Shortly after the *Twin Peaks* premiere came the more commercial *Northern Exposure*, a light-comedy series set in Alaska and filmed in the Cascade foothills town of Roslyn. Roslyn and Snoqualmie became tourist meccas for the "Northwest lifestyle" glamorized on the shows.

End of the old clubs

In Seattle, Tugs Belltown and the Watertown (known for its slide shows projected onto the wall of the Apex Belltown Cooperative across the street) were situated on the ground floors of old residential hotels that got renovated as part of the city's too-little, too-late drive to preserve low income housing. The nonprofit agencies that now ran the buildings decided music downstairs was incompatible with living spaces upstairs.

Letter to the Rocket *by The Swedish Housewife, 1/89: "This week I said goodbye to an old friend, a place that I've haunted since 'new wave' started, when 'Rock Lobster' was still a fun song to hear.*

The first time I went there in my leopard-print Capri pant suit, toilet paper for a hair bow and way too much eyeliner. I danced like a wild fool until two. You put up with me all these years, gave me a place to be my wild and obnoxious self and turned a cheek to most of my growing pains for close to a decade. I just want to say thank you. I'll miss you when you're gone and I'll always keep you close to my heart. Goodbye, Tugs."

Slide projected by Watertown owner Keith Robbins onto the Apex Belltown Cooperative across the street, 9/89: "Dear God. Please save the Watertown."

Start of the new clubs

New clubs opened in 1990 to take the place of the dead or dying ones. The heretofore unusual part is that most of the new places *stayed open.*

In January 1990, performance artist Steve Wells (he sang lounge songs in a fat-man suit under the name Everett Mall Jr.) and Pit Kwiecinski opened Re-bar, a dance club intended to draw a gay/straight crossover patronage. It succeeded with the Vogue format of mid-week bands and weekend DJs. On opening night, the line to get in stretched up to two hours. It was decorated in a moderate-budget version of thrift-store chic, with tacky murals, a plexiglass bar and heating duct pipes painted to resemble eight-foot cigarettes. A *Weekly* cover story on the club scene led to a rash of BMW-driving snots barging in and complaining out loud about all the faggots around. Wells was forced to put a sign at the door, in the boldest type available: "We welcome our gay and lesbian patrons. Bigots keep out!" The Vogue put up a similar sign a few months later.

In Belltown, the Vogue had disco competition from the intimate Belltown Club (opened 4/90) and Downunder (opened 3/91). Downunder attracted entire groups of tuxed and prom-dressed rich kids, some of whom came downtown in charter buses from the Eastside. The yuppies' drift toward new clubs allowed the Vogue to be more adventuresome, scheduling fetish, industrial-rave, and gay nights. The Swedish Housewife promoted Seattle's first acid-house nights at the Vogue, and brought record-store clerk Riz Rollins as the DJ for Re-bar's funk nights.

Capitol Hill briefly had the awkwardly named "1501, aka The Club," across from Fallout Records. 1501 tried an L.A.-style "pay to play" system where bands had to rent the stage and sell their own tickets; many bands and fans chose not to cooperate.

Re-bar was situated a few blocks west of the Off Ramp Cafe on Eastlake Avenue, a 1908-built bar that had served as the Galaxy R&B club (where the teenage Hendrix is rumored to have once played), a '60s go-go club where Sonny and Cher once played (with dancers in cages suspended from the ceiling), a mob-controlled topless club, and most recently a lesbian bar under male owner

Lee Rae. Rae opened the Off Ramp to bands on weeknights in the fall of 1990 with three or four bands a night in a large but intimate, appropriately-seedy room with full liquor service (the liquor board had relaxed its booze-food requirements; a restaurant/lounge could derive as little as 30 percent of its cash flow from grub and not get shut down).

Amazingly it worked, after a rough first year. It worked thanks in part to the perserverence of its original bookers, band manager Soozy Bridges and Variant Cause vet Jan Gregor. Its next booker, ex-Arizonan Jeff Holmes (who booked the Vogue before and after his Off Ramp stint) never realized his initial dream of all-ages nights (a legal practice in some Portland clubs), but did help establish it as the first of a wave of successful spaces. Jan Morgan started working there shortly after the start of the rock format; she and her daughter bought the place in August 1993.

Soozy Bridges: "We started just doing shows on Tuesdays, Wednesdays and Thursdays, and gradually got more nights as we built up an audience. The first rock group we booked into the Off Ramp on a Friday night was Alice in Chains. We didn't know if the lesbians were going to kill us or not over taking their weekend dance nights away, especially for a band with that name."

While the Off Ramp looked like a sloppy dive, it was managed with much more precision than the Gorilla Room or even Squid Row ever were. The showroom opened promptly at 9 p.m. Most nights, three opening bands took 40- to 45-minute minute sets starting at 9:30, 10:30 and 11:30. The headlining acts started at 12:30 and were expected to stop no later than 1:30, in time for last call. To keep up its food-to-booze sales ratio, it offered $1 dinners just before the first set ("Gnosh Before the Mosh") and 75 cent scrambled-egg breakfasts after the last set ("Hash After the Bash").

The only unpredictable element was the audience, which often included suburban goons play-acting at punk. Moshpit fistfights were not uncommon; bouncers sometimes tried to break them up by spraying Mace at fighters and innocent bystanders alike. At least once, dirtheads called in threats to firebomb the place.

By the end of 1991 the Off Ramp went all-music. It booked four bands a night, seven nights a week, and filled up most of them. The 100 or more bands frequenting the Off Ramp once a month or more included many "generic grunge" bands copying the five-year-old looks and riffs of Green River and the U-Men. It became the mecca for people who moved here hoping to become grunge hits, and for college seniors slavishly copying the grunge look and lifestyle (including, alas, the drugs).

Off Ramp T-shirt slogan, 1992: "If Sober, Please Return to Off Ramp."

Off Ramp no-smoking sign, 1993: "We don't care if you smoke, snort, sniff, or shoot. Just don't do it in here."

One dose too many

Mother Love Bone headlined a Central Tavern show in the first week of March 1990, warming up for a tour to support its first full-length album. Andrew Wood climbed up to a ledge 10 feet above the floor, where he'd set up a keyboard. At the time, Wood had been off heroin for almost four months after a 28-day rehab session.

On March 15, Wood gave an interview to the metal magazine *Rip*, then he and his fiancée Xana La Fuente went to an Aerosmith concert at the Tacoma Dome. The next night, La Fuente came home and found him lying on the bedroom floor, overdosed and oxygen-starved. After three days in intensive care, his condition deteriorated. Life support was turned off, and Fuente held Wood in her arms as he passed away. (La Fuente later portrayed a dominatrix in *West Side Heathen*, a music-video compilation by local filmmakers Tim Muck and Rick Fahr, promoted as "a little S&M followed by a little Jesus Christ"; it included clips by Mudhoney, TAD and Girl Trouble.)

A memorial service to Wood was held on March 24 at the Paramount. Wood's death at age 26 drew attention to heroin as the new drug of choice among the grunge inner circle. The introspection, sluggishness and lack of concern for outer appearance in these bands partly reflected a heroin aesthetic, even among members who didn't use it themselves. It was out of sync with the beer aesthetic of heavy metal, the marijuana aesthetic of the old and neo hippies, the cocaine aesthetics of yuppie society and of hiphop, and the MDA aesthetic of local '80s punk.

Andrew Wood on the drug-rehab experience in his last interview, to Michael Browning of Rip the day before he overdosed: "…It's a total struggle. When you first get out, you're on this pink cloud, and it's pretty easy. After a while things start getting more real, and you have to just stay straight a second at a time."

Douglas Mays, booking agent and ex-Life in General manager: "I was with Andy and Xana at the Aerosmith show. I was kidding him with Dallas Cowboys jokes, becuase I knew it was his favorite football team…. Everyone had been clinging around him. The real essence of Andy was ignored. That's what I think really got the guy. He got the life sucked out of him. He's probably the A&R guy for God now, telling Him to give his friends a big break."

Susan Freeland, former scene member: "I came back to Seattle after several years in Britain and saw my first Nirvana videos. I thought, this is total heroin imagery, the gun in the pool, the image of danger enveloped in calm."

Andy Wood, R.I.P.

LOVE BATTERY

FREE RECORD RELEASE PARTY · SUB POP

NEW LP 'DAYGLO' OUT NOW
-ALSO APPEARING-
MY DIVA and **POND**

RKCNDY FRI JAN 31

Kate Shatzkin describing the heroin experience in a Times *article: "(Police and drug counselors) say most become addicted and use for years, even after cleaning up for a time. The psychological craving for the drug always endures.... 'High' is the popular word but not so accurate, really; nor is 'rush.' After you've been on the stuff a while, you're taking it just to get normal. But this 'normal' is a place where troubles roll off your back like spring rain and sleep comes easy in an itchy cocoon, until the drug wears off and the sick begins again. You learn to function on heroin, much more easily than one can on crack cocaine, for example. But it takes tricks, faithful adherence to routine and trusting no one, especially no one who's straight."*

PolyGram issued the *Apple* CD several months later, to little promotion and little sales. The surviving Mother Love Bone members negotiated their way out of their contract, leaving them in massive debt to the label with little likelihood that the album would ever recoup its advance. PolyGram kept the Stardog Records name, using it for commercial "alternative" bands like Ugly Kid Joe.

Bruce Fairweather and Greg Gilmore formed the short-lived Blind Horse, with singer Chris Tilden. Fairweather then replaced ex-U-Man Jim Tillman on bass in Love Battery, with Ron Rudzitis, Crisis Party vet Kevin Whitworth and Skin Yard vet Jason Finn. (Tillman had replaced Tommy Bonehead; Jonathan Poneman played bass at LB's first shows.) *Rolling Stone* called the group "touching on the classic Seattle formula of fuzzy guitars and troglodytic drums" while adding "mesmeric rhythms, swirling layers of melodic guitars and lyrics inspired by Beat poetry." It made two Sub Pop 45s and the full-lengthers *Between the Eyes* (early copies included a blotter pad), *Dayglo* (produced by Jon Auer) and *Far Gone*; then signed to an A&M affiliate, Atlas (no relation to the new Olympia-based Atlas label), releasing the EP *Nehru Jacket* to prepare the market for the band's major-label full-length debut *Straight Freak Ticket*.

Kevin Whitworth to Option, *9/93: "A lot of people say 'psychedelic' like it's a dirty word. I think the band is going to continue to make the kind of music we've made—music that leaves a lot of head room—but we are not a psychedelic revival act. Love Battery is not a Sha Na Na for acid casualties."*

Robert Sharp in Pandemonium *on* Straight Freak Ticket, *1/95: "The noise is gone, the strident chord changes are replaced by flowing rhythms, and the rampant voices are gone to make room for knowledgeable outbursts of what having a history behind a band can add to their music lyrically."*

Starting in late 1993, Finn moonlighted in a fun-novelty side band, the Presidents of the United States of America (with Chris Ballew on two-string bass and Dave Dederer on three-string guitar), who got to open (along with the Posies) at a local 1994 campaign appearance by Bill Clinton. Finn left Love Battery just before *Straight Freak Ticket* came out to devote full time to the Presidents; he was replaced by Mike Musburger, who'd worked with the Fastbacks, Flop, and the Posies.

Greg Gilmore drummed in assorted bands and one-off projects until he joined Son of Man. One of those engagements was with El Steiner, formed in 1990 by graphic designer Larry Steiner in the Mr. Epp/Thrown Ups heritage of outrageous stage antics, as backed by a changing array of sidemen including Chris and Rick Friel (see below) and up to three simultaneous drummers. At one 1991 show in the all-ages OK Hotel, the five-foot Steiner appeard on stage in nothing but a rug diaper, which accidentally fell off during the first song. Steiner completed the set *au naturel*. At other shows, he's worn a tutu on his head and showered the dance floor with whipped cream. A *Times* reviewer claimed his act "appears to combine Native American dancing, crowd activity at Woodstock and professional wrestling techniques."

No more Central

The Central Tavern closed as a full time new-music outlet at the end of 1990. The space ended with a night-long blowout featuring acoustic singer Kristen Barry, Son of Man, My Sister's Machine, Paisley Sin, and War Babies. Owners Mike and Donna Downing's final band, on Nov. 30, was the Squirrels. The new owners continued with rock shows for a few months, then turned it into yet another white-macho-blues bar.

The Downings then started the Central Clubhouse at a former Chinese restaurant in the low-rent Tacoma suburb of Milton. A new generation of Tacoma rockers emerged there, as well as at the Red Roof Pub, the Victory Club, and the briefly re-opened Prosito; including Running with Scissors (whose singer Denny Porter had played guitar in Baby Knockors, a gloriously bad 1980 Tacoma sleaze-glam-punk outfit), Rhino Humpers, Sedated Souls, My Name and Seaweed. But the Downings found police and fire-marshal harassment even worse in Milton than in Seattle; under intense pressure, they closed at the end of 1993. The final show was a punk rock fest, with the Lemons playing last and trashing the place. The Downings next opened a new Central Tavern in Tacoma's old Prosito space.

Reluctant successes and golden blunders

Soundgarden's major-label debut won a Grammy nomination for Best Hard Rock Album. Alice in Chains' *Facelift* made *Spin*'s 10-best list. Mudhoney was the #1 band in a *Rockpool* poll of college radio programmers. A *Billboard* headline in August 1990 proclaimed that "At Long Last, Seattle Is Suddenly Hot" in a puff piece about the Posies, Alice in Chains, Screaming Trees and Mother Love Bone—while noting that Sub Pop's releases, while influential within the industry, "simply do not chart."

The Posies sold 100,000 copies of their 1990 major-label debut, *Dear 23*, a slick mix of tight harmonies and clever pop lyrics of love and alienation that featured the coming-of-age cautionary fable "Golden Blunders" (later covered by Ringo Starr) and the marriage-as-drowning allegory "Suddenly Mary." (Twenty-three was Jon Auer and Ken Stringfellow's magic number; as inspired by the writings of William Burroughs and Robert Anton Wilson. The initial self-released tape of their debut *Failure* was on their 23 Records label.) *Dear 23*'s cassette version had a "Side 2" and a "Side 3." Carl Smool, Dennis White and Karen Moskowitz collaborated on the cover, a setting of kitsch furnishings from Upchuck's apartment; Stringfellow said it looked "dark and unfocused, like the record."

From "Golden Blunders": "You're gonna watch what you say for a long time, you're gonna suffer the guilt forever/You're gonna get in the way for a long time, you're gonna mess things up you thought you would never."

Dear 23 was one of the first albums released by DGC Records, the new label run by David Geffen, *the* personification of a corporate rock promoter, and managed by Gary Hersch. Geffen had promoted some of Jimi Hendrix's tours; his Asylum and Geffen labels had poisoned the radio for two decades with overproduced tedium by Linda Ronstadt, the Eagles and Nelson. For his new imprint, Geffen trawled for college-radio acts that could be signed cheaply and marketed efficiently to target audiences for profitable sales at sub-platinum levels—and if one of its bands happened to go platinum anyway, so much the better.

DGC still expected its bands to meet standards of marketability. When the Posies submitted self-produced tapes for a follow-up album, soon after finishing their first national tour, the label rejected them as sloppily-recorded and bereft of potential hits. Posies fans had to wait until early 1993 for a new CD, while the band recorded a new set of songs in New York, produced by ex-Dinosaur Jr. member Don Fleming (who also produced the Screaming Trees' *Sweet Oblivion*). The result was

Frosting on the Beater, a decidedly noisier release that surrounded Auer and Stringfellow's harmonies in some of the guitar heroics now expected of a Seattle band. *Frosting* included the MTV alternative-ghetto picks "(I Could) Dream All Day" and "Definite Door." Jon and Ken also played guitars and lead vocals with two of the three survivors of Alex Chilton's legendary band Big Star (preserved on the CD *Columbia*), and joined a cast of alternative all-stars on the save-the-rainforest children's record *Primary Colors.*

From the Posies' "Definite Door": "Say goodbye to your friends and family/Welcome to the menagerie/Funny how they forget to tell you/this is all you will ever be."

The Posies' initial success vindicated the struggles faced by a decade of indie-pop bands who might have made it had record companies bothered with Seattle bands then. The Young Fresh Fellows were still on Frontier, but that company now had a distribution deal through BMG Music (the German company that bought RCA Records).

Geffen bought out the Posies' PopLlama contract; the cash helped Conrad Uno move his Egg Studios from the garage of his old Northgate-area house into the basement of his new U District house, fitted with the original mixing board from

The Posies
Frosting On The Beater
Featuring: Dream All Day •
Flavor Of The Month

**Below:
Blind Horse**

LOSER

every good boy deserves fudge ..

**Screaming Trees'
"Uncle Anesthesia"**

Below: Love Battery

Memphis's legendary Stax studio.

One of the first projects in the new Egg space was Mudhoney's 1991 Sub Pop CD *Every Good Boy Deserves Fudge* (named after the music students' mnemonic, "Every Good Boy Deserves Favor"). Charles Peterson made a cheap video for the song "Good Enough" (Sub Pop's videos seldom cost more than $3000, compared to $60,000 for an average superstar clip). In the clip, Mark Arm shook his fist and mugged at the camera in a powder-blue leisure suit, while Matt Lukin got kissed by a woman wearing a fez, roller skates and an "I'm a Dolphin" T-shirt (played by Turner's girlfriend Caryn Palmier, later a member of the garage-pop Man Tee Mans). The album itself cost $2000 to record and sold 60,000 copies, Sub Pop's biggest seller to date aside from post-1991 Nirvana sales. It reached #37 on the UK pop album chart, and helped save the company.

Arm and his band returned to Egg for their Reprise debut *Piece of Cake* (see next chapter). Their new label was perfectly willing to send them to a high-priced studio, but the band members believed in making their music their own way. They also believed in conserving their advance money, having seen good bands get caught up in the major-label whirlwind only to get financially ruined.

The Screaming Trees moved from four SST releases and a double 45 on Sub Pop to release *Uncle Anesthesia* and the half-million-selling *Sweet Oblivion* on Epic. Mark Lanegan and Gary Lee and Van Conner plus ex-Skin Yard drummer Barrett Martin (replacing the moonlighting Dan Peters, who replaced Mark Pickerel) evolved into a dynamic, textured sound with lots of potential AOR radio hooks, as evidenced in *Sweet Oblivion*'s hit video "Nearly Lost You." Lanegan also released two Sub Pop solo albums of haunting depressive/assertive ballads, both with somber guitar work by Eugene native Mike Johnson (who also played bass in Dinosaur Jr.), *The Winding Sheet* in 1990 (with Fisk and Endino; Kurt Cobain and Chris Novoselic

played on the melancholy Ledbelly song "Where Did You Sleep Last Night," redone on Nirvana's *MTV Unplugged* special) and *Whiskey for the Holy Ghost* in 1994. The Conner brothers released solo CDs on SST's New Alliance label, Van's *Solomon Grundy* and Gary Lee's *Mystery Love* (under the band name The Purple Outside, with yet another Conner, Mark, on drums).

Non-skinny, non-cute

The one big obstacle to the Trees' career was that the Conners were decidedly non-scrawny. They didn't meet industry standards for rock stars.

The majors were showing their influence on the bands, choosing their level of support based on marketing considerations. Sneery, snotty boys *were* considered marketable, so long as they were still cute or studly. Kurt Cobain would prove to combine the best of both worlds; he'd also claim in print to be quasi-bisexual, just like some of the UK new wave idols he missed out on.

TAD was one of the biggest victims of the marketability issue. Tad Doyle's band rocked as hard as any, but his screaming voice and ample physique were considered unfashionable. The "Woodgoblins" video from his Steve Albini-produced album *Salt Lick* (released after the debut LP *God's Balls*), was turned down by MTV; the channel found the girthy Tadster too ugly to appear alongside the longhair pretty boys of its *Headbanger's Ball* show. Also, Sub Pop sold the UK music press an image of Doyle as a psychotic illiterate lumberjack, which attracted early attention but in the long run hindered the band.

TAD's next Sub Pop LP (in the ultimate sign of coolness, most of the local indie labels still put out vinyl), *8 Way Santa*, became an instant collectible. The band used a photo Palmier found at a garage sale as its cover art. The photo depicted a suburban couple, the mustached, longhaired man holding a hand over the woman's bikinied breast. The woman, who'd become a born-again Christian after

the photo was taken, sued to halt distribution of the cover. Copies that got to stores before the recall now sell for up to $100. The album itself was recorded in Madison, Wisconsin by Butch Vig, and featured Doyle singing instead of just shouting while the band honed its crude of attack into a somewhat sharper blunt instrument. TAD next made a CD single, *Jack Pepsi*, which had to be recalled when the soft-drink company didn't appreciate its logo on the cover. While Sub Pop redid the *8-Way Santa* art three times, TAD went on tour to support a record that wasn't in most stores.

TAD's 1992 CD single *Salem* proved the effective end of the Sub Pop Sound; five years after Green River's *Dry as a Bone*, the last of the label's Seattle punk/metal crossover bands left for Mechanic to record the album *Inhaler*. In keeping with the band's bad-luck streak, the album was set to be released when Mechanic lost its affiliation with BMG; TAD sat and watched the Seattle media hype pass it by, until Mechanic hooked up with Warner and got the record out in late 1993. It proved worth the wait; an intricate switch-off of grinding chords and cleverly nihilistic lyrics about such topics as serial killers, contrasted with lighter moments like the power-poppish "Leafy Incline." *Tower Records Pulse!* called it "music for 1,000 dead-end lives, behemoth rock as infectious as it is oppressive and unnerving."

But Mechanic didn't know how to market the band, and dropped it in mid-1994, just as it was about to tour with Soundgarden. TAD next signed with Elektra's East West label, after recording the live-in-the-studio retrospective *Live Alien Broadcasts* for Mechanic's Futurist imprint, releasing the all-new disc *Infrared Riding Hood* in early 1995. Guitarist Gary Thorstensen left after making the live record; Doyle recorded both guitar parts on *Infrared*.

Ex-TAD drummer Steve Wied met up with Mark Spiders, f-Holes vet Otis P. Otis, and H-Hour vets Johnny Clint and Darren Peters as Willard (named for the 1971 killer-rat movie); Roadrunner Records promised its debut *Steel Mill* would "be having bands like Pearl Jam, Soundgarden and Alice in Chains for breakfast—then vomit the undigested chunks all over Nirvana's nice new house!" (Wied resurfaced again in 1994 with Foil; Otis is now in Texass.)

Skin Yard splits

Daniel House quit Skin Yard to devote his full time to C/Z Records. Poor sales by art-rockers Vexed and Amy Denio's Tone Dogs (the latter release with Fred Frith and Matt Cameron) persuaded House to concentrate on what America was coming to expect from Seattle bands: unrelenting noise, churning guitars and screaming vocals.

By then Skin Yard's singer Ben McMillan and drummer Norman Scott had formed a side project, Gruntruck, with Accused guitarist Tom Niemeyer. Scott and Niemeyer left their other bands to concentrate on Gruntruck, which made the 1990 album

Inside Yours for eMpTy. Roadrunner reissued *Inside Yours* and issued the follow-up *Push*. Niemeyer brought in fellow Accused refugee Alex Sibbald as Gruntruck's bassist, replacing Tim Paul. Skin Yard got another bassist, Pat Pedersen, but Jack Endino's production work kept the band from touring much, leaving McMillan to make Gruntruck his primary outlet.

From Gruntruck's "Crucifunkin'": *"Get off your cross and dance."*

***Review of* Push** *in* The Hard Report: *"Gruntruck supplies plenty of that guitar-driven thickness we've come to expect from the* (Northwest), *but without falling into the same traps. They're spurred on by a powerful rhythm section, and the result is a huge magnetic sound that sucks you in and leaves you gasping."*

Skin Yard finally broke up in late 1991, just as major labels were showing interest in the group. Endino has made the solo records *Angle of Attack* and *Endino's Earthworm* but spends most of his time behind the consoles of studios around the world.

Rathouse arrives

Mia Zapata, Joe Spleen (Andy Kessler), Steve Moriarty, Matt Dresdner and Valerie Agnew moved here as a group from Antioch College in Ohio. The first four had been in a band, the Gits (named after a Monty Python skit), since 1986, built on Zapata's passionate vocals and Spleen's chopping guitar. Their proud defiance sounded like what punk might have become had lowlife hardcore not taken it over. They later estimated that over 100 members of Antioch's 1989 class moved here. Seattle had become a place to escape *to* instead of *from*.

The Gits all lived and practiced in an east Capitol Hill house they christened the Rathouse. So did musician/promoter Bob Jenkins, who became Zapata's boyfriend for a time. Like past band houses, it served as a party space, a rehearsal hall, a free inn for touring bands and visiting friends, and a mailstop for entourage members with no permanent addresses. The Gits shared the basement practice space with other bands, including Alcohol Funnycar (with fellow Ohioan Ben London and Crisis Party vet Tommy "Bonehead" Simpson) and Agnew's new band Seven Year Bitch (with Selene Vigil, Stefanie Sargent and Elizabeth Davis, who'd met while they all had day jobs at the Pike Place Market). They organized themselves as a booking co-op and label.

Rathouse Records debuted with a compilation album, *Bobbing for Pavement*. Its bands, who chipped in to pay for the 1,000-copy pressing, included Gas Huffer, East Coast transplants D.C. Beggars, Big Brown House (with Ben London), the Derelicts, Bay of Pigs, My Name, Hammerbox, and the Gits. The latter three bands soon signed with C/Z Records; so did Alcohol Funnycar and Seven Year Bitch.

Banned Tad cover

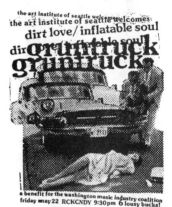

Below: Mark Lanegan

Steve Moriarty: "It was hard to get acclimated into the scene in 1989. We had to forge our own niche. At that time, anything that wasn't on Sub Pop was considered shit. We felt different because we had what we felt was a more expressive, from-the-heart sort of rock. We came out to play music, not to be heavy metal rock stars. We didn't have higher goals than to get people to see our shows.... It took us years of pounding out our own tours and scraping our way to get to the point where we were about to be offered contracts from major labels."

From Mia Zapata's lyric for "Slaughter of Bruce," officially not about Bruce Pavitt: "Some fool came up to me and said/'You'd be a star with that band'/I said, 'That's not why we're doing this/Why can't you fucking get it?' "

Zapata to the Rocket, 12/92: "I do write words to those imbeciles parading around like they know exactly what's up. It's not to be offensive—if it is I don't care, either—it's just, look at yourselves, c'mon, look look, don't think this is it, you gotta be kidding. I don't see how you can take the truth and either swallow and shit it out or whatever you have to do, it is so there. And everybody has such a hard time, you have to ask yourself and remind yourself the next person is going through just as much hell. No one's better or worse. When I go to write words, I don't mean to be depressing. You should always be searching for something that means something to you, even if it means the worst thing brings that honesty."

Elizabeth Davis, Seven Year Bitch, to the L.A. zine Sonic Black Hole, 6/94: "We never waited until we reached a certain point. We just got songs together and started playing live right away. We

put out our first seven-inch after six months. We didn't wait for things to happen. We just took charge. That's the most important thing, to get out there and do it. Don't let people push you around and tell you what to do, even though I'm telling you what to do now. Okay—after this, don't let anyone tell you what to do."

The Gits opened for Nirvana and TAD in a $4 UW HUB concert on Jan. 6, 1990, that ended with Cobain and Novoselic destroying so much gear they got "banned for life" from UW venues. (TAD's performance at the show was used in the MTV-banned "Woodgoblin" video.) The Rathouse people promoted a few all-ages shows at Washington Hall, with Gas Huffer, the Accused and the Boise-founded Treepeople.

Hammerbox formed in early 1990 when singer Carrie Akre, having achieved her childhood dream "to get the hell out of town" (the Tri-Cities), answered a *Rocket* want ad placed by bassist James Atkins and drummer Dave Bosch; guitarist Harris Thurmond completed the group. *Backlash* described them as having "a tight, aggressive edge, precise and coordinated, but hard-hitting like a well-planned assault," led by Akre's range of vocal expressions "from alluring, haunted whispers to unrestrained wails." Their first 45 was on graphic artist Lisa Orth's Big Flaming Ego label; the band then made a self-titled album on C/Z and the poorly-promoted *Numb* on A&M before breaking up. Akre and her drumming brother Eric (formerly in Treepeople) then formed the more singer-songwritery Goodness.

Big Flaming Ego also put out a CD and 45 by Char Easter and Mary Lake's dark-romantic Common Language (the single's inner grooves were engraved "Ethereal..." and "...Or Die;" the band signed to England's Blast First label but broke up after the company released only a compilation CD) and a tape and 45 by the percussion/electronics band Infamous Menagerie (named after a Baudelaire book), formed in the mid-'80s by two ex-Atlanta residents, singer-guitarist Erin Schneider and bassist Lisa Puteska; Orth joined it as co-vocalist after the band moved here. Orth performed dissonant noise-guitar (appearing topless at a few gigs); percussionist Tori Roos added shopping carts and kitchen appliances as found instruments. Orth remembers the band's sound as "still so far ahead of their time that they may not be recognized 'til decades from now. They were excruciatingly melodious; sometimes so noisy and painful that you couldn't tell how intricate and beautiful it was."

Orth set the label aside to concentrate on her next band, 66 Saints, a slightly more melodious ensemble whose changing personnel included John Maroney, Mitch Michieli, Molly K. and Kat Carlisle (she calls it "at one point incredibly chaotic, at another point pure pop with intermeshed guitars and pounding drums like a big rolling machine of noise"). Orth and Moroney had previously been in

SAGE
MY DIVA
ANIMAL
KINGDOM

January ③①

all ages

the Shit Kittens; Orth also had an early band called Barbie's Dream Car that included, at various times, all the original members of Seven Year Bitch. She now calls her old bands "the sound of people learning to play their instruments."

Orth and Caroline Davenport formed the booking- promotion co-op Manna (slogan: "An Alternative to the Alternative"), to promote some of the art-rock and experimental bands whose bookings remained scarce as bar owners discovered the beer-selling power of the guitar-noise bands. Manna's chief acts included My Diva (romantic synth-rhythm by Claudia Groom, Chris Roksam and Dale Lloyd), Sage (the grinding power/political trio of Marc Olsen, Guy Davis and Mike Williamson; not related to Wipers leader Greg Sage), and Maxi Badd (a smart-pop trio led by Tess Lotta and Gretta Harley, C/Z Records' receptionist; renamed Danger Gens). Davenport was to have released a Maxi Badd CD when she got into debt and put Manna aside to take a full-time booking job at RKCNDY. Sage released the CD *Forked* on the local indie Will Records, which in 1994 almost signed a distribution deal with Capitol.

William Abernathy in the Rocket *on Sage, 9/94:* "*...A unique mix of abstract lyrics over droning vocals and Asian harmonies fused with occidental rhythms.*"

Comix co-mix

Lynda Barry had long since left town (finally settling in Chicago), but a new stable of local cartoonists made national waves: Gary Larson (*The Far Side*), Mark Zingarelli (*Real Life, Dining Out With Eddie Longo*), Michael Dougan (*East Texas*), Susan Catherine (*Overheard at America's Lunch Counters*), and Peter Bagge, a veteran of New York's original *Punk* magazine who moved here after marrying the sister-in-law of a Seahawks football player. Dougan published two collections of his haunting-outrageous work, *East Texas: Tales From the Pine Curtain* and *I Can't Tell You Anything*, and made a segment for MTV's *Liquid Television*.

Bagge persuaded his publishers, Fantagraphics Books, to move their entire business operation from the outer suburbs of L.A. to a rundown house on Seattle's Lake City Way. Bagge's series *Hate*

used graphic schticks inspired equally by hippie underground comix and hot rod art to chronicle the lowlife and times of Buddy Bradley, a no-future young slacker who comes to Seattle and gets involved in managing a pathetic punk band (typical lyric: "I scream, you scream, we all scream for heroin!"). Fantagraphics' top title, *Love & Rockets* by L.A.'s Jaime and Gilbert Hernandez, was one of the few works of fiction to successfully depict the dysfunctional-extended-family aspect of the punk scene (they're not responsible for the U.K. synth-pop band that stole their name). Fantagraphics also published *Eightball* by Chicago's Daniel Clowes, featuring the surrealistic serial "Like a Velvet Glove Cast In Iron." Clowes created a lot of art for Sub Pop, including a Supersuckers cover and T-shirt mascot Punky; an unsigned Seattle band took its name from a fictional grocery store in *Eightball*, Value Ape.

Dale Yarger, the former *Rocket* designer who had a role in evolving the Sub Pop logo, became Fantagraphics' senior art director, winning several national design awards for his work. Yarger's assistants included Jim Blanchard and Pat Moriarity, who've drawn and/or designed outrageous record covers and show posters for Skin Yard, Coffin Break, Soul Asylum, Fat Tuesday and other bands. The company published a licensed comic book starring the Accused's mascot Martha Splatterhead.

Worshipping at the Temple

Jeff Ament and Stone Gossard joined with Soundgarden's Chris Cornell and Matt Cameron to record a couple of tribute songs to Andrew Wood. Those sessions grew into the *Temple of the Dog* album, named from a line in Wood's song "Man of Golden Words" and released in early 1991 on A&M; initial sales were modest. The CD was a collection of slow blues-rock dirges and power ballads, some with indulgent guitar solos. They weren't all directly about Wood; some were existing Cornell compositions that didn't fit Soundgarden's established format. The record did highlight the new musical direction Gossard and Ament were taking.

The lead guitarist on those sessions, Mike McCready, had been an old friend of Gossard. He'd played guitar since age nine with neighbor brothers Chris and Rick Friel, first in 1979 as a Kiss cover band called Warrior and then from 1982 to 1988 as

Daniel Clowes's "Punky"

FLANNEL FEST '93!
FEATURING...
FASTBACKS · POND
VELOCITY GIRL · HAZEL

Pete Bagge poster for Sub Pop

Common Language

Lost last Charles Garrish record

Shadow, a group that evolved from the metal circuit (opening for Metal Church and TKO in one Moore Theater show, only to get booed by an audience that thought they were too punk) to the downtown club scene. McCready and Ament gigged together in 1990 in Love Chile and LuvCo (the latter with Chris Friel, singer Shawn Smith, and ex-Fastbacks drummer Richard Stuverud). The Friels then joined Michael Foster for the successive bands Jangle Town and Give (originally called Easy, changed for the usual somebody-had-it-first reason). Give has released one CD, titled *Easy*, on Ivy Records. McCready joined Ament and Gossard's next band, along with new drummer Dave Krusen (a veteran of umpteen local bands, including an Astor Park-era new wave outfit called the Boibs).

Cooking the Jam

Before finding Krusen, Ament and Gossard had sent a demo tape to ex-Red Hot Chili Peppers drummer Jack Irons, asking if he'd like to join them and also if he knew an appropriate singer. Irons was starting a new band (Eleven) and turned down the offer, but sent the guitar-bass demo along to a lyricist-singer he knew in San Diego, ex-Chicagoan Eddie Vedder, who'd been in the local band Bad Radio but was presently working at a gas station. Vedder wrote and dubbed words onto the tape, sent it back to Seattle, and a few days later moved into a practice room in the basement of the third Galleria Potatohead space in Belltown. They wrote and practiced for five days, gigged the next night at the Off Ramp (essentially an on-stage audition for Vedder), then went together the next night

to a SuperSonics-Chicago Bulls basketball game. Vedder joined with Chris Cornell to sing *Temple of the Dog*'s single, "Hunger Strike."

The new band practiced and initially gigged as Mookie Blaylock, named after a New Jersey Nets basketball star. When it became apparent that a living celebrity's name would pose problems for the band's future merchandising deals, they changed it to Pearl Jam. Among the different explanations for the name: Vedder supposedly had a Great-Grand-mother Pearl whose jam recipe contained peyote; Blaylock supposedly called his overhand goals pearl jams. (They didn't comment on rumors that the name might be a semen reference, in the tradition of 10cc and the Lovin' Spoonful.) What is certain is that they took their CD title, *Ten*, from Blaylock's jersey.

Michael Goldstone, who'd been Mother Love Bone's A&R rep at PolyGram, soon signed the new band to his new employer, Sony/Epic. The group quickly recorded 11 tracks at Rick and Raj Parashar's London Bridge Studios in north Seattle, filmed scenes for *singles* as Matt Dillon's band Citizen Dick (Ament supplied band posters and records for Dillon's apartment), went to England to supervise the CD's remix, shot "Alive" and "Even-flow" concert videos with Gossard's Northwest School classmate Josh Taft directing, and embarked on a year and a half of nearly constant touring on three continents, much of it in support of established arena-rock acts. The band stopped in town long enough to play a free outdoor show for 4,000 people at the Mural Ampitheatre. Taft went on to direct videos for other acts including Stone Temple Pilots, a San Diego band trashed by some critics as Pearl Jam imitators.

The group's live shows contained long instrumental stretches, during which Vedder showed off his surfer-dude athleticism by climbing up stage rafters and diving into the moshpit while McCready played '70s pop-metal guitar solos. At pre-gig interviews along the tour, Vedder had to field questions about a "Seattle Scene" he'd barely gotten to see.

More people who should have stuck around

Charles "Upchuck" Gerra, instrumental in the early punk scene through the Fags, Clone, Mental Mannequin, Sleeping Movement and the Wad Squad before trying to make it in New York, had come home in the summer of 1986 and scheduled a fundraising "Fags Reunion and Macaroni and Cheese Bake-Off" to finish a record he'd begun back east. He lost his voice at the show, developed what he called "a common cold that was a little heavier than usual," went to a doctor, and learned he'd caught pneumonia after already acquiring the AIDS virus. The vocal paralysis lasted six months; his general condition got better at times and worse at others. To pay his hospital bills (like most musicians, he was uninsured), a "Chaos Against AIDS" benefit was held in October 1988 with Soundgarden, Skin Yard, and the Refuzors. Upchuck passed away in June 1990, shortly after friends helped him

make it to a Tacoma Dome show by his idol David Bowie, on his nostalgia tour.

Homer Spence, who helped start the scene and remained a spiritual leader to it, died of a heart attack in January 1991. He never saw the ultimate popular triumph of the music he'd fought for, but did see his ex-partners in the Telepaths and Blackouts become cult favorites in Ministry and Toiling Midgets.

Jesse Bernstein died of a self-imposed knife wound in October 1991, leaving behind hundreds of stories and poems, several short films and videos, three short novels (plus the unpublished manuscript for a fourth, *Short Skirt*), several plays (including *Dead Dog*), many unreleased tapes of his jazz-folk songs (including one recorded concert at the Monroe state reformatory), the spoken-word recordings *Words and Music* and *The Sad Bag*, and the posthumously-released CD *Prison*, with background music by Steve Fisk (who had completed one track at the time of Bernstein's death). Bernstein's proudest moment came in August 1988 when he opened in a sold-out Moore for his idol William Burroughs, at a show he'd tried to arrange for years. His former stepson Harry Pierce continued in his tradition of outlandish performances, getting banned from the Bumbershoot festival for stripping during an outdoor reading. Pierce has read and sung several Bernstein works.

From Jesse Bernstein's **Prison**: *"I live on a street that has many, many cars and trucks and factories that bang all night and day.... There is so much noise.... The new age people say we choose the things we live among.... Maybe I need the noise to write poems, make love, and eat. I'm going to hang a sign outside my window that says, 'More Noise Please,' or 'Thank You For Making Noise.'"*

Art music, art, and non-art

Fisk had moved from Ellensburg to Seattle in 1989. He continued to produce records for other people (Some Velvet Sidewalk, Unwound, IMIJ, many Kill Rock Stars releases), and he made some electronic scores for local filmmakers (including Alec Carlin's *Immaculate Perceptions*, featuring Carlo Scandiuzzi, and *The Fertillichrome Cheerleader Massacre*, a "cheesy desert epic" directed by his old Olympia cohort P.S. O'Neill, with one Screaming Trees track). But he had to set aside his favorite works, his solo synth-and-samples records, when the industry cracked down on unlicensed samples.

Fisk's work was concurrent with a new scene of experimental and postmodern music, concurrent with the revitalized rock scene. In some ways, these musicians were closer to the smart, curious spirit of Seattle's earliest punks than some of the metal-crossover acts now marketed as punk. New York art-jazz composer Wayne Horvitz and his singer wife Robin Holcomb moved here to join this community, followed by fellow ex-New Yorker and texural guitarist Bill Frisell. Horvitz formed an art-rock band here, Pigpen, with ex-Three Swimmers member Fred Chalenor (Matt Cameron drummed at one OK Hotel gig). Trimpin, a German-born creator of elaborate string and percussion instruments, has lived and worked here since 1979.

Eric Muhs returned from California to take a UW graduate biology scholarship. He performed solo shows on guitar, tape loops and a growing array of homemade and found instruments. He's made three short films and 25 solo and group tape projects (including backing tracks to Deran Ludd's spoken-word tape *Carnage Motel*), distributed by mail order among the international cassette underground. Muhs has also helped run the annual Festival of Improvised Music, showcasing local experimental composers.

Hammerbox

Jesse Bernstein w/ friend

Then: Mookie Blaylock

Sir Mix-A-Lot

Limousines and hamburgers

MTV instituted a rap show in the spring of 1989, just in time to heavily support the first video by Sir Mix-A-Lot. *Posse on Broadway* introduced America to the black-middle-class joys of motoring from the Central District to Capitol Hill in a "Benz-O" crowded with cronies and "girlies," finally hanging out with friends and foes in the parking lot of Dick's Drive-In. It was tame subject matter compared to the earlier New York rap of biting social commentary and the later Los Angeles rap of glorified gangbanging. But it sold a million copies for Ed Locke's Nastymix Records, with virtually no radio play. It also proved that you didn't have to pretend to not be from Seattle, that you could sing honestly about your life here and people across America could identify with it. Mix-A-Lot recorded it on his home four-track recorder; Locke borrowed money from his Boeing-employee mother for the first pressing. Mix-A-Lot's album *SWASS* also spawned a rap remake of the pop-metal classic "Iron Man," recorded with members of Metal Church. It wasn't the first or last Black Sabbath reference in the local scene.

Mix-A-Lot toured with a male hip-hop dance troupe to support *SWASS*. That tour included a headlining gig in the Coliseum during the Bumbershoot festival. Bumbershoot had booked only one previous rap act in its existence; in typical Seattle booking fashion, most of the African-Americans who got to perform there were R&B oldie acts or mellow world-beaters, both intended for white boomer audiences.

Sir Mix-A-Lot to City Heat *on his unabashed materialism, 5/92: "The one thing I do that everyone tends to look at as 'nothing' is owning these cars and this big house.... There's a new push in rap to downplay the importance of material possessions. That's a crock of shit. It's a capitalistic society. All I'm trying to do is let the kids know you can have the Lamborghini and the house, and not have to sell dope. A lot of rappers are hiding their wealth, and the kids see them in a raggedy truck. Then they see a dope man in a Benz. So who do you think they are going to follow?"*

Mix-A-Lot's second album, *Seminar*, sold 750,000 copies. It featured "My Hooptie," the finest ode to junker cars since Jan and Dean's "Schlock Rod," and "National Anthem," a strong tirade against both drugs and the war on drugs, which he described as a one-two punch against inner city youth. Nastymix went on to release cuts by Tacoma rapper Kid Sensation, High Performance, Criminal Nation, America's Most Wanted, and the thrashin' Accused.

Mix-A-Lot moved to the majors, forming his own Rhyme Cartel company through the Def American label (now American Recordings). His move led to a legal dispute with Nastymix over the rights to his old records, which indirectly helped lead to the label's demise (Locke sold its assets to Atlanta's Ichiban Records).

From his new suburban home-studio compound Mix-A-Lot recorded the three-million-selling single "Baby Got Back," a tribute to big bottoms that was promoted with a giant balloon butt that toured America's record stores. In interviews, Mix-A-Lot answered accusations of sexism by claiming the song was a tribute to black women who didn't try to look white.

Mix-A-Lot to Pandemonium *on "Baby Got Back," 8/94: "I have so many female fans that stand behind me, it's almost incredible. You would think that song would piss 'em off. The song seemed to piss more men off than women. You know, those so-called liberal males were telling me what women wanted to hear. That's far more sexist than any of my songs ever could be."*

His *Mack Daddy* CD also included "One Time's Got No Case" (an anti-police rap based on a real case when he was stopped, harassed and searched for drugs just for being a black male in a nice car).

Mix-A-Lot's 1994 CD, *Chief Boot Knocka* (reported working title: *Chief Poon Knocka*) was promoted with a video produced expressly for Playboy TV, "Put 'Em On the Glass," celebrating the perennial male fantasy of topless car-washing. Mix-A-Lot also collaborated with Mudhoney on a cut for the *Judgment Night* movie soundtrack. In January 1995 he became the titular narrator of *The Watcher*, a TV anthology drama on the new United Paramount Network.

Politics return

Anti-authoritarian ideas had always been big among the early punks, but overt political statements had gone out of favor as punk evolved into just another subculture.

This changed in early 1991, as opposition to the Gulf War produced new strains of youth politics, including the Peace Heathens (who ran a storefront on the Ave, selling used jeans and giving away pacifist tracts) and the Autonoms, an anarchist underground. In May 1992, the loudest protests here against the Rodney King verdict in L.A. were by a handful of white anarchists. In January 1991, over 30,000 Seattlites marched for peace the weekend before the air raids on Iraq began. Alice in Chains played a Peace Movement Concert at the Paramount with the Wilson sisters' acoustic band, the Lovemongers.

The American Left latched on to a comment President Bush made in a minor speech defending the war. His call for a "New World Order," a phrase with precedents in both Nazi propaganda and in conservative anti-United Nations conspiracy theories, was used in rallies and articles to symbolize everything the Left hated about the past 10 years of Republican rule. (Third World socialists in the early '80s had called for a "New World Information Order" subverting the big media companies, the same goal the indie-music movement had.) Al Jourgenson and Paul Barker sampled Bush's speech into

Now: Pearl Jam

SirMixaLot

Charles (Upchuck) Garrish, R.I.P.

Motor Sports Int'l Garage
Stewart & Vale

the Ministry track "N.W.O.," a searing statement of disgust against the war and the dealmakers responsible for it. The track became part of Ministry's album *Psalm 69: The Way to Succeed and the Way to Suck Eggs*. It was unplayable on most radio formats and shunted to the alternative-ghetto slots on MTV, but entered the *Billboard* album chart in June 1992 at #27. It was an early sign that the 1992 election might not be the Bush landslide pundits had predicted at the time of the war.

Empire builders

By the time of the anti-Gulf War movement, Queensryche had released the million-selling concept album *Operation: Mindcrime*, an epic tale of censorship and repression in the Reagan-Bush America. It spawned the single "Don't Believe In Love" and the hit video "Eyes of a Stranger," which alternated black-and-white performance footage with a color chase scene involving gangsters and nuns.

Chuck Eddy *reviewing* Operation: Mindcrime *in* Stairway to Hell: The 500 Best Metal Albums Ever Made*: "Never before had so many pretensions been taken on by so few in so short a time (you can hear U2, Midnight Oil, Iron Maiden, The Wall, Hysteria, Sab's Sabotage, Styx's Kilroy Was Here, death-disco) but most of the time it doesn't sound pretentious at all, just ambitious."*

From there, the group went totally commercial with its multi-platinum *Empire*. That CD featured the straight-ahead anthem "Jet City Woman" and the acoustic ballad "Silent Lucidity" (MTV was big on heavy metal love songs in late 1990-early 1991, apparently for lack of a better fad). Its more serious title track (the name referred to "Empire Builder" railroad tycoon James Hill) focused on the

grimmer realities of Seattle, including crack-dealer shootouts and the Wah Mee gambling-club massacre. "Silent Lucidity" was cited by *Billboard* as the #1 single of 1991 according to radio airplay, and by MTV as the most requested video of the year. Released in September 1990, *Empire* stayed on the *Billboard* charts for over 14 months. It was listed on some lists of the top-selling CDs of 1991. *Empire* was a definitive document of '80s hard rock, perfectly encapsulating a formula that seemed to have been around forever, but would seem like ancient history by early 1992—and especially by October 1994, when Queensryche's fifth full-length album came out. That record, *Promised Land*, took the band still further from sociopolitical anthems and into the realm of personal angst and relationship issues. Following the DIY lead of the punks, most of *Promised Land* was recorded on the band members' home DAT recorders.

Kurt leaves home again

In Seattle, it was OK to seek commercial success as long as you didn't "act like a rock star." In Olympia, you weren't even supposed to think of music as a career. To these folks, playing your own music to your friends was the only real reason to start a band. The Oly people shared this philosophy with the scene in Washington, D.C. In the late '70s, *Op* and the Sub Pop cassettes had given early exposure to D.C. scene pioneers like 1/2 Japanese. By the late '80s Oly people stayed in close contact with the D.C. scene, including the bands on Ian McKaye's Dischord label and Mark Robinson's TeenBeat label. This affinity grew into the Olympia-D.C. band connection: musicians and scenesters flying back and forth between the two Washingtons, corresponding and forming bands together.

One of the D.C. scene's top bands was Scream, with the full-bore drumming of Dave Grohl. Grohl had long admired the Melvins and corresponded with Buzz Osborne. When Osborne heard that Scream had folded, he gave Chris Novoselic's number to Grohl. Nirvana finally had a permanent drummer after three years. Grohl first saw Nirvana (with Dan Peters drumming) in June 1990 to 1,500 people at the Motorsports International Garage, a concrete hangar across from the future RKCNDY used for a handful of all-ages shows before it was demolished.

At this point Nirvana was seriously courting major labels. At one Off Ramp show, the record-company "suits" up from L.A. nearly outnumbered the paid fans. Cobain flew down and dined with execs at posh L.A. nightspots, then returned to Olympia and subsisted on corn dogs and canned chili.

Kurt Cobain *in the last issue of* Backlash, *3/91: "We were talking to Susan Silver and said, 'You know, we got this 30-page giant contract from Sub Pop, what should we do?' And she said, 'I think you should get a lawyer. I'm going down to*

L.A. tomorrow; maybe you should go down, too.' So she flew down to L.A. and we drove down and she introduced us to people and we got a lawyer. That was our big education. We were really ignorant of a lot of things before we got that lawyer and then we got a manager and the whole shebang, and we just sort of passed them up.... Six or seven months after the record (Bleach) *came out, we said, 'Let's start promoting it, OK?' And they said, 'No, you've gotta get something new out.'... Another thing is, we've never known how many records we've sold on Sub Pop."*

Flop-py discs

The stripped-down line-up of Pure Joy made the single "Now I Know" and the 1989 LP *Carnivore* for PopLlama, with the acidic (in both senses) ballad "Division," released on the same day Rusty Willoughby disbanded the group.

Willoughby (who also served time as Fastbacks drummer #9) next formed Flop, with Nate Johnson (Fastbacks drummer #8), Bill Campbell (ex-Chemistry Set), and bassist-backup singer Paul Schurr. The hook-laden poppish band delivered intensely witty lyrics via intensely energetic music (described by Scott McCaughey in the *Rocket* as "pretty much blazing relentless volume, a slow song here and there, Rusty wired but wailing behind a curtain of hair") on a self-titled EP for Jay Haskins's Lucky Records and the 45 "Drugs" (b/w the Sweet cover "Action") on their manager Chris Swenson's Dashboard Hula Girl label. They also appeared on the Swenson-organized *Another Damned Seattle Compilation*, in which songs by the Damned were honored and/or demolished by Love Battery, Skin Yard, the Fastbacks and their side band Motorhoney, the Posies, Mudhoney, the Purdins, Coffin Break, Gruntruck, the Chemistry Set side band Whitey, Hammerbox, the Accused, Gas Huffer, the Young Fresh Fellows, the Derelicts, and Swenson's own bands Big Satan Inc. and Freak.

Flop then recorded their full-length debut *Flop and the Fall of the Mopsqueezer* for Frontier. It featured the perfect 1:49 despair anthem "(Sister) Anne," plus the creatively-titled "Ugly Girl Lover," "Tomato Paste," "Zeus My Master" and "Morton the Venereologist." Epic picked up their next album, *Whenever You're Ready*, with the ennui anthem "Regrets," the Shelley Winters tribute "Night of the Hunter," and an ode to the late, beautiful Seattle Woolworth store. British new wave veteran Martin Rushnet got the producer credit. Frontier was licensed to issue a vinyl picture disc, with a "Man Side" and "Woman Side." Both records featured neo-expressionist covers by Ed Fotheringham, who sang with Flop's backing on the Super-Electro EP *Eddy and the Back Nine*, perhaps the world's first golf-themed punk record. (Fotheringham had a golf-themed car, covered in AstroTurf with a golfer doll as a hood ornament.) Epic dropped Flop while it was preparing its 1995 album; the band returned

LOSER

to Frontier.

Bassist Schurr left Flop in early 1994 to join the Best Kissers in the World and was replaced by Prudence Dredge vet Mick Vee; after one tour, Vee swapped bands with the Posies' second bassist, Dave Fox, only to get replaced in the Posies after one tour by Sky Cries Mary vet Joe Howard. (Posies drummer Mike Musburger left shortly after that, replaced in mid-1994 by Brian Young.)

From Flop's "Regrets": "I haven't got a car/You haven't got an opinion."

Jackson Griffith in Tower Records Pulse! *on* Whenever You're Ready: *"Sounding at times like the 1910 Fruitgum Company on steroids or perhaps the Sub Pop All-Stars doing the Sweet, Flop serves up candy-coated latter-day T-Rextasy for charming young moderns.... Elroy Jetson-gonemetal bugglegum."*

Epic PR for Whenever You're Ready: *"Bridging a soundscape that skirts right by Seventies on-thefringe rock and parks boldly in the "this-space-reserved-for" Nineties lot.... Chock full of well-placed harmonies, notes to hum along to, and lyrics that lend a wicked twist to it all."*

From "Under 10 Handicap" on **Eddy and the Back Nine:** *"My drives always slice, my approaches are poor/I'm lying a six and I'm putting a four/A FUCKIN' FOUR!"*

Former Pure Joy/Gnome drummer Andy Davenhall formed Sister Psychic, an unapologetic power pop band, with bassist Christian Fulghum (son of local inspirational author Robert Fulghum) and drummer Ryan Vego (replaced by Purdins vet Mark Lansdowne). Davenhall had drummed in Fulghum's early-'80s power pop band, the Attachments. Another ex-Attachment, Sandi Miller, formed the ethereal-harmony band Charlotte's Webb.

Sister Psychic recorded its bark-and-growl pop sound on the August 1992 CD *Fuel* for the L.A. indie Restless, featuring the folk-rocky family reminiscence "Birdhouse" (formerly part of Gnome's live set). By the time of the group's poppier, more

Left: Homer Spence, R.I.P.

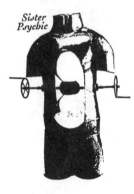
noise better than any band since Television."

Christian Fulghum *to* Hype *on the changed reputation of Seattle, 3/93: "I was in San Francisco a couple weeks ago and this band was on stage and they announced, 'We're moving to Seattle man, it's our last show.'"*

Openings

Skoochies became Oz (now DV8), an 18-and-over dance club (like the Underground, the ex-Hall of Fame in the U District) with occasional live concerts. The town's only true all-ages club was, fortunately, one of the town's best clubs: the OK Hotel. A handful of all-ages gigs took place at the Odd Fellows Hall in the spring of 1990.

The OK didn't remain alone in Pioneer Square for long. Chris Benno and Steve Johnson opened the Colourbox (named for an ethereal-dance band from England) in January 1991, initially with a techno-disco format produced by ex-KCMU DJ Paul Alienkoff and his partner Robin Harnish. The owners smelled bigger money in music performed by live people, and switched to live rock five nights a week under Chris Roberts's management with acoustic and open-mike nights Sunday and Monday. (Alienkoff and Harnish resurfaced in 1995 with Machine Werks, a membership disco in the old Dave's Fifth Avenue space.)

In April 1991 Stephanie Dorgan, a lawyer originally from the Tri-Cities, turned the Athens Cafe, vacant nearly a decade, into the Crocodile Cafe and Live Bait Lounge. It offered full liquor service in a spacious bar and a small, dark, sweaty, sound-proofed music room, plus a full restaurant with conceptual art installations. The opening night starred the Posies, pseudonymously billed as POT (Posies On Tour); original booker Terry Lee Hale also tried to get a Nirvana gig, but they'd stopped playing club gigs in anticipation of their new album. The 189-capacity Croc became the venue of choice for CD release parties and other special events. Mike Melilla, a moonlighting Fire Controlman from the Sand Point Naval Air Station, took over as booker, succeeded in turn by Scott McCaughey.

June 1991 saw the opening of RKCNDY (pronounced "rock candy"). Built into a '60s-era brick garage by local sound man Thomas O'Neil and Stone Gossard's ex-housemate Alex Rosenast, it was sterile and noisy and cavernous; its high ceilings and mezzanine made it seem larger than its 300 capacity. RKCNDY was near the Off Ramp, past the wall of a freeway overpass. Some nights, black-clad couples embracing against this wall were more entertaining than the bands at either club. For a while the two clubs and the nearby Re-bar promoted themselves under the name "Howltown," after Re-bar's address on Howell Street.

One of RKCNDY's first events was a 4th of July show with Mookie Blaylock, the Pearl Jam-to-be. RKCNDY also booked some of the same generic

refined second CD *Surrender, You Freak*, Restless had co-founded the ADA distribution partnership with Warner Bros. (Sub Pop soon joined the venture). The new record included ex-Stumpy Joe guitarist Mark Hoyt, and featured the anti-love anthem "Velvet Dog" and a sweet cover of the Green Pajamas' "Kim the Waitress" (with Jeff Kelly's original lyrics, unlike the better-selling cover by Material Issue). At one 1993 show, Lansdowne broke a drumstick on the side of a snare. A piece of the stick flew into his face and got stuck in the underside of his jaw (no permanent damage). The band broke up in June 1994 (Lansdowne and Hoyt going into a re-formed Purdins), but Davenhall promptly formed a new Sister Psychic with Pat Patterson and John Fleischman.

Andy Davenhall *on Sister Psychic: "We're straight up power pop. We're the Dick's Deluxe, fries and chocolate shake of Seattle Rock. We have more hooks than a tackle box. We're not copping a feel, we're making love."*

J.D. Considine *in* Musician, *1992: "Guitar-crazed and clangorous, Sister Psychic's sound touches on many of the same bases as English shoe gazers like Chapterhouse or My Bloody Valentine. Except that where those bands toyed to hide their pop smarts in a haze of feedback, Sister Psychic uses its grunge to frame the tuneful bits, so* Fuel *balances melodic abandon and guitar*

post-metal rocker bands as the Off Ramp: usually all-male, dressed more or less alike, playing more or less alike. A few of these bands moved here from across the country hoping to discovered; their knowledge of local music came primarily from "Seattle Sound" recordings, without exposure to the wider variety of local live bands.

After almost a decade and a half of people here trying to start and re-start a music scene, the world suddenly believed we had one. Fulfilling the "positive affirmation" rhetoric of local gurus like J.Z. ("Ramtha") Knight, the belief that there was a dynamic Seattle live scene became manifest in physical reality. Not only was the audience pool large enough to support RKCNDY *and* the Off Ramp *and* the OK every night, but new venues kept opening up.

The Weathered Wall (full title: *And the Weathered Wall, the Purity Remains…*), a spacious, elegant, purple-curtained room across from the Westin hotel chain's flagship hostelry on Fifth Avenue, completed the new downtown scene in October 1991. Like the Colourbox, the Weathered Wall opened as a techno-DJ club, but owners Garry McNeill and Nicholas Tran started adding local bands and soon played loud guitar rock heroics most nights. As booked by David Meinert, it settled into a routine of spoken-word cabarets Tuesdays, rock bands Thursdays and Fridays, techno-disco-cabaret shows Saturdays, and fetish-industrial dance nights Sundays. An upstairs lounge opened in 1993 with live jazz, acoustic and cabaret shows.

Some Pioneer Square blues bars, the Swan Cafe and the Owl & Thistle, switched to modern-rock formats at least part of the week. Even a couple of downtown's last working-stiff pubs, Kelly's and Gibson's, began booking bands.

Bands that preferred the community spirit of oldtime punk could perform for free beer and the proceeds of a $1 cover at Phil and John Hendry's Lake Union Pub and (until 1993) at Lenny and Joe Johnson's Storeroom Tavern, workingman's watering holes by South Lake Union between the yuppie lakefront bars and the Howltown triangle. They became home to a new generation of punk revivalists, including the Kent 3 (named for the cigarette, not the south end suburb), the Pullman-founded Sicko (Ean Hernandez, Denny Bartlett, Josh Rubin), Not My Son, Wedgwood Bombers, 4 Hour Ramona (with married vocalists Lisa and Rich Brisbois; named for a dry cleaning sign in Wallingford), Monster Truck Driver, 10:07, Solid Statesmen, Spearhead, North American Bison, Bristle, Fuzzbud, Whipped, Chicken, Whorehouse of Representatives, Piss Drunks (CD title: *Urine Idiot*), James Erdman's Arizona-founded Putters, Russian emigres 17 Pilots On Fire. The Storeroom held Wednesday open mikes where people who now played for big bucks could play for fun.

Ean Hernandez, Sicko co-singer, to the Times *on his band's preference for two-minute songs, 5/94: "There's such a tendancy to overplay. It's really*

pretentious to think people want to listen to the same chorus over and over and over. We like to go up, have fun and want people to get an idea of what we're like. It's more fun if it's like that, rather than a shrine erected to your band for the night."

The new fans for the new spaces

Quite suddenly in the fall of 1991, hundreds of emaciated, leather-clad young people could be seen on the streets nearly every night. There was a seemingly perpetual line for drinks at the Frontier Room. People who'd spent their lives in a Seattle that shut down at 10 p.m. couldn't figure out why they could no longer find a parking place in Belltown on a Friday night.

To an old waver, it looked like a big-budget remake of an old B-movie: a larger cast on larger sets in the same costumes playing the same roles, without the friendly spontenaity of the original. Many scenesters arrived in groups from college towns across the country, including large cliques from Phoenix, Denver, Bennington, and Yellow Springs. Many were locals who, had they come of age a few years before, would have been into big hair and heavy metal. And some were scene veterans who started going out again now that there were new bands and new places.

The new scene was too big for everyone to know everyone else. The extended-family environment of the Central and Squid Row didn't translate to the more spacious RKCNDY and Weathered Wall. The Vogue and Ditto were still small, but their pool of clientele wasn't.

Clubs appeased insurance pressure by discouraging slam dancing; audiences were moving away from moshing anyway, toward attentive listening. The moshpit scenes in Charles Peterson's band photos had already faded by the time mainstream America heard about it.

'80s nostalgia DJ nights began at the Romper Room on lower Queen Anne (the relocated Watertown) and the Belltown Club on First. The new-music scene, which had preached its own obsolescence, now had its own oldies.

The new bands for the new spaces

One by one, the original Sub Pop bands stopped playing club dates just as there were finally enough decent-sized clubs. Instead, the new venues became home to a new explosion of local bands. So many new bands appeared that by the end of 1992 it was just as hard to get bookings in a Seattle with 12 clubs as it had been two years before in a Seattle with three clubs.

Andy Cohen, Joel Phelps and Tim Midgett brought their Montana band Ein Heit here, and added drummer Mike Dahlquist from Olympia's Dump Pump. Their new combo, Silkworm, was driven by equal parts XTC, Husker Du and Neil Young. *Times* reviewer Phil West said they incorporated "a hushed, tense dynamic and a willingness to let

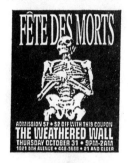

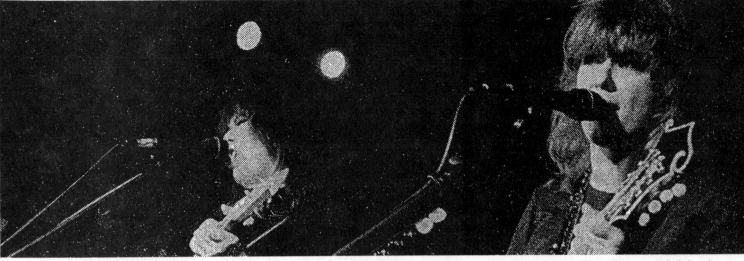

songs breathe, that stays several steps back from their influences.... Vocals are treated more like another instrument than a medium for messages." They released the 1992 CD *L'Ajre* on their own Temporary Freedom label, then recorded *Noise for Heroes* with Steve Albini in Chicago; the latter included a noisy cover of Fleetwood Mac's "The Chain." KNDD DJ Marco Collins put out their next EP, *His Absence Is A Blessing*, on his own Stampede label. It was followed in late 1993 by a power-chord version of "The Little Drummer Boy" on a split C/Z Christmas single with Engine Kid, and in early 1994 by the Albini-engineered C/Z CD *In the West*. Phelps left later that year, after the sessions for the band's follow-up album *Libertine*.

Andy Cohen to the Times *on Silkworm's neo-new wave stage wardrobe of snazzy suits: "It comes down to doing something worthwhile. It's typical in rock music to look like crap, and we like to avoid that syndrome."*

Zipgun was formed by guitarist Neil Rogers of Tacoma's Derelicts, who broke up just as their prophetically-titled Sub Pop EP *I Don't Wanna Live* came out. Rogers, Rob Clarke, Mark Wooten and Dan Cunneen executed what *Urban Spelunker* called "relentless guitars grinding you up with enough hooks to catch a 20-pound steelhead" on the eMpTy album *8-Track Player*. (Clarke had been in the Trids, a Lake Hills-era metal band that performed New York Dolls covers in drag.) Rogers later played guitar in Glazed, fronted by Olympia punk-anthem singer April Glaze.

Gorilla, billed as the world's only punk band with two medical doctors (singer-bassist Dan Merrick and "hardcore organist" Drew McRoberts), recorded singles for Sub Pop, Estrus, the Tacoma-based Aroma and Jimmy Stapleton's Bag of Hammers Records, before releasing the album *Deal With It* through New York's Thrill Jockey label. By that time McRoberts had to leave to devote full time to his practice. (Bag of Hammers has released 18 7" records in two years, including a Refuzors reunion single, plus a CD collection of Gorilla's old singles, *Meconium: The Squid Row Daze*, named after the fecal matter that accompanies childbirth.)

Faith and Disease, fronted by Dara Rosenwasser, revived the gothic stylings of Dead Can Dance and the Cranes without the stereotypes of spider webs and skeletons. They first recorded for the Utah label AIDA House, then released two CDs on Dave Goebel's Ivy label. The second, *Fortune His Sleep*, moved the group away from the 4AD ethereal-pop formula toward hypnotic, non-denominational sacred music.

Tacoma's Seaweed (Wade Neal, Aaron Stauffer, Clint Werner, John Atkins, Bob Bulgrien) held to what the *Times* called "rapid-fire four-on-the-four punk" which served to "whip the kids in the crowd to a pulpy frenzy and throw temper tantrums rather than concerts." They put out singles on Atkins's Leopard Gecko label and K before being grabbed up by Sub Pop, where they released the EP *Despised* and the LPs *Weak* and *Four*; in early 1994 they signed with the Disney-owned Hollywood label. Atkins and Bulgrien were previously in Alphabet Swill, who recorded the fun 45 "Barbie's Dream Townhouse."

Back of a **Seaweed** *T-shirt: "VISUALIZE TACOMA."*

The Pleasure Elite (described in *Hype* as "keyboard-driven techno-pornography") played electronic cabaret ditties of kinky sex with samples of cuckoo clocks, crows, saws, drills, and old TV dialogue, separated by pseudo-erotic poems read by vocalist Rev. V. Blast ("Life is suffering, horror and mortal terror are your friends. Suffer and endure. Pain is enlightenment. Sleep kills. Satisfaction creates rot"). TPE released the 1994 CD *Bad Juju* on Chicago's Red Light label, current home of the Mentors.

Pleasure Elite drummer/percussionist Evan Schiller also performed in Sadhappy, a group that offered no guitars, no vocals. Just ethereal, drifting sax lines by one Skerik onto a solid rhythm foundation laid down by Schiller and bassist Paul Hinklin, previously in the improv/rock Pitbull Babysitter with his brother Rich (who ran Word of Mouth Studios, the former Triangle/Reciprocal space, for two years).

Paul Hinklin was concurrently in the Bellingham-founded Son of Man, fronted by Gig Harbor-native vocalist Tal Goettling and guitarist Brad Kok. It also included ex-Pearl Jam drummer Dave Krusen (who'd gotten his start in Goettling's self-named mid-'80s band); he was replaced by ex-Mother Love Bone drummer Greg Gilmore. The

The Lovemongers

Leopard Gecko

Rocket described its repertoire as "songs about the stupidity of war, the vortex of useless conflicts, the dangers of blind patriotism and the darker side of humanity." In 1993 the group (without Hinklin) moved to Germany. Gilmore moved back soon after; he plays now in Mommy.

The noise-rock genre was also explored by Olympia's Earth (a guitar-distortion instrumental concept led by Dylan Carlson and Dave Harwell with half-hour-long "songs;" Kurt Cobain and Dale Crover played on one of its three Sub Pop CDs) and Burien's Unearth (a quartet described as "concussive psychedelia" that "swirls like a whirling dervish in a mosh pit," as released on New Rage).

Larry Reid: "Earth played its first Seattle show at COCA in 1991. They played just one 'song,' a loud instrumental grating noise thing. Cobain was in the audience; this was while he was still going out in public. He left the room within 10 minutes. Within 20 minutes the only people left were me and another COCA staff member. Even the sound guy had fled. Carlson asked what we were still doing in the room. I told him we worked here. He said, 'You should have told us. We were only going to play until everybody left.'"

Ex-Cat Butt guitarist "Brother James" Birdyshaw formed Sinister Six (described as "hard, bluesy, raw guitar rock with no punches pulled"), along with Doug White and Mark Ferkingstad (both from the Glory Holes) and Erik Hildahl. They recorded 45s for Bag of Hammers, eMpTy, Get Hip, Estrus and In the Red, before issuing the eMpTy CD *Outta Sight.*

An updated throwback to the days of sax-based new wave, Diamond Fist Werny was the first local band to incorporate a bass clarinetist (Axel Mundi). Singer-guitarist Todd Werny contributed what he called "a deep, deep drone" while drummer-sampler Tim Soba mixed up elements of hiphop, Tibetan chanting and assorted kinds of rock and jazz; all fronting Julius Brown's computer-generated video projection images.

Electro-psychedelia was also persued by Jessamine (Rex Ritter, Dawn Smithson, Andy Brown, and revolving drummers). Their songs, lasting as long as 10 minutes, incorporated moody whisper-voices and aggressive guitar-organ jams to create what Tom Kipp in the *Stranger* called "incredible machine lyricism and vocals of almost unutterable sensual beauty and fragility."

More downbeat balladeering was provided by Laundry (Jerret Cortese, Charlie Smyth, Jake McCarter). They plowed out droning tales of realistic and surrealistic despair, punctuated by ex-Chicago punk Cortese's Joy Division-like vocals and beatnik-like bass.

Celibate Twist combined three classically trained musicians slumming on guitars (Craig Corvin, Joe Hauck, Paul Jensen) with former Boy Toast/Arms Akimbo drummer Jeff Mosier to create what they called "hybrids of 20th century composition and '90s noise pop." They made "The Tri-State

Killing Spree Polka" for the Joey Kline-organized LP *Hey Joe: The Seattle Coffee Compilation,* followed by the 45 "Deservedly So" on their own Schwa Sound label.

Bone Cellar (Dave Ellis, Dave Keppel, Dawn Henschen, Matt Marti) played a revived punkabilly, recording two 45s on Portland's Tombstone label. Ellis also played in the power trio Nothing; Henschen also played until early 1995 with Janna Westover and Ashley Nelson in Cat Food, recording the bratty anthem "Bellevue, Washington," about spotting Kurt Cobain and Courtney Love in a mall and not being able to get an autograph, on Brad Gaub's Carving Knife label.

Tyler Willman, Steve Ross, Dan Kempthorne and Bob Martin formed the neo-punk Inspector Luv and the Ride Me Babies in Tacoma, releasing the EP *Another World.* They changed their name to Green Apple Quick Step (from an old slang term for diarrhea), and added bassist Mary Anne Braeden. When they signed to a Warner affiliate and released the 1993 CD *Wonderful Virus,* they became the first local major-label rock act with a non-singing female musician. Warner publicity described GAQS as "fueled by the punk rock of the Heartbreakers and X yet equally adept at conjuring the scope and drama of Blue Cheer and Grand Funk." Former Inspector Luv bassist Eric Munday and drummer Dylan ended up in 3-D S&M, with jazz-trained female singer Dejha and guitarists Shane Forsberg and Dana Turner.

Below: Queensryche

Flop

Freak show

Jim Rose, a former Phoenix pest-control salesman who'd studied some of Europe's last carny shows, showed up at a Capitol Hill belly-dancing club with a one-man show of human oddity. He pounded nails into his nasal passages, lay on a bed of nails, laid face down on broken glass while audience members stood on his head, had darts thrown into his back, and escaped from a strait jacket. Rose recruited for co-stars at his shows and eventually formed the Jim Rose Circus Sideshow. It toured U.S. theaters and European music festivals, and opened for a reading tour by Portland's Katherine Dunn, promoting her carny novel *Geek Love*.

The Torture King (Tim Cridland, who later went solo with his own Incredible Torture Show) ate fire, stuck nails into his face and dragged heavy objects around by wires stuck in his arms. The Enigma (Paul Lawrence) ate bugs and light-bulb shards and showed off his full-body jigsaw-puzzle tattoos. The Tube (Matt Crowley) stuck a tube down his nose and throat, inserted liquids, drained them back out, and offered them to willing attendees. Mr. Lifto (Joe Herman) lifted heavy objects attached by twine to his pierced tongue, nipples and penis; when the group toured with Lollapalooza '92, authorities in Cincinnati and Miami told him not to drop his pants on stage.

Chris Cornell on stage at Lollapalooza '92 in Miami: "Mr. Lifto was going to be thrown in jail if he tried to lift a steam iron with his penis. I think that's bullshit that you can't see the whole show, so I was going to lift an iron with my own penis. Then I thought about how much it would hurt, so I changed my mind."

Singles going steady

In the summer of 1991, Cameron Crowe started filming *singles*, a movie about young relationships with a few characters involved in the Seattle music scene. Members of Pearl Jam appeared as Citizen Dick, a band fronted by Matt Dillon; hence their rewritten Mudhoney song, "Touch Me I'm Dick." Amidst authentically scruffy scenery (the OK Hotel, Re-bar, Crocodile Cafe, Virginia Inn, and an apartment building on Capitol Hill), the film offered sitcom vignettes of light romance among well-scrubbed college graduates Campbell Scott and Kyra Sedgwick. The theme and score were by ex-Replacements singer Paul Westerberg. The soundtrack CD featured a local all-star lineup (Alice in Chains, Screaming Trees, Pearl Jam, the Lovemongers, and an old Hendrix cut) performing tunes you could barely hear for a few seconds in the film. The most telling cut was Mudhoney's "Overblown," in which Mark Arm ranted that everybody now loved his town to the point that he was thinking of leaving. Arm proudly told the *Times* his band got $20,000 for the song, which cost $182 to record.

Beginning of The End

In August 1991, new music returned to local commercial radio for the first time in three years with KNDD-FM ("The End"), on the old KRAB frequency, with old KRAB/KCMU DJ Norman Batley and old KJET DJs Bill Reid and Jim Keller. The new format's first owner, out-of-state station group Noble Broadcasting, was inspired by market research claiming Seattle-Tacoma, America's 13th largest radio market, had become the country's #4 sales market for "alternative" music.

The KNDD playlist alternated current "college radio" hits with power-pop oldies that KJET had played to popular indifference when they came out. Now, the same songs were on a station that, after a couple of disappointing early ratings periods, began to seriously contend for the #1 slot in the 18-34 demographic.

Jesus Christ posers

Soundgarden's second A&M CD, *Badmotorfinger*, took the band further from the underground toward full-tilt anger-rock, not quite as fast or unrelenting as Ministry (labeled by *Variety* as "the ugliest feel-good music ever") but just as bitter, with songs of religion and other dysfunctional relationships ("Jesus Christ Pose," "Holy Water"), corporate greed ("Slaves and Bulldozers"), political collapse ("New Damage") and emotional scars ("Drawing Flies," with ex-KJET DJ Damon Stewart on trumpet).

MTV gave only alternative-ghetto play to the six-minute "Jesus Christ Pose" video, which involved crucifixion scenes with skeletons, robots, women and vegetables on the crosses; A&M later put it out on a home video compilation (with Hammerbox and other A&M acts) sold at the loss-leader price of $2.69. More airplay came from the Led Zep-esque wailers "Outshined" and "Rusty Cage," the latter with Chris Cornell comparing a bad relationship to a horror movie.

Soundgarden held two "Welcome Home" concerts at the Paramount in March 1992, with a surprise introduction by J.P. Patches, who was visibly shaken by the outpouring of cheers by 3,000 grownup Patches Pals. The stage set included *West Side Story*-like alley catwalks for Cornell to climb up and prance around on.

Tom Moon review of Badmotorfinger *in the* Philadelphia Inquirer: *"The guitars splinter into a two- and three-pronged attack: One establishes (and repeats) the riff, another sets up a dramatic ticking-clock pattern, while still another more prominent guitar ad-libs around the vocal lines. It's the typical guitar-god scenario, but because the elements are manipulated so deftly, the result is anything but ordinary."*

The amateur standing of Olympians

In the summer of 1991, Perry Farrell organized the first Lollapalooza festival as a vehicle for his L.A. band Jane's Addiction. It attracted sellout and near-sellout crowds at most of its 17 stops, while corporate-rock dinosaurs toured that summer to pathetic business. The lesson was not lost on the industry, which prepared quickly to get in on the alternative bandwagon. Some people in Olympia wanted to drive that bandwagon off the road be-

LOSER

fore it got bigger.

A lively scene continued to develop around the Olympia entourage. Bands held party gigs in basements and downtown apartments that were often better-attended than their concerts at commercial venues.

In 1989 K honcho Calvin Johnson had launched the Sound Out Northwest package tours (with his brother Streator and bandmate Bret Lunsford), sending Beat Happening, Mudhoney, Anacortes band Pounding Serfs, Girl Trouble, Vancouver's Mecca Normal (singer Jean Smith and guitarist David Lester), Al Larsen's "love rock" combo Some Velvet Sidewalk, Portland's Dead Moon and other bands for all-ages gigs at rental halls in small towns in Washington and Oregon, bypassing Seattle and Portland for Astoria and Aberdeen.

Steve Wtilley in the UW Daily, *11/94: "Some Velvet Sidewalk are lovable punks with an off-kilter pop sensibility that just won't sit still.... Frantic but funny, messy yet magnificent."*

One of Olympia's more active party hosts was an art student from Boston who'd adoped the name Tinuviel. Starting in December 1990, she held monthly basement gatherings with bands and spoken-word artists, called TBS ("Tinuviel's Basement Scene"). Her February 1991 show included four bands: Bikini Kill (Kathleen Hanna, Tobi Vail, Kathi Wilcox, Billy Karren), the Eugene-founded Bratmobile (Allison Wolfe, Erin Smith, Molly Neuman; they later moved to the Maryland suburbs of Washington, D.C.), Vern Lumsey and Justin Trosper's noise-damage Giant Henry (renamed Unwound), and Witchipoo, a band formed by Tinuviel's neighbor Slim Moon. Bikini Kill was named after a line in a parody cabaret song co-written by Lois Maffeo, a KAOS DJ from Arizona. Witchipoo was named for the villain on the kiddie TV show *H.R. Pufnstuf*; the group was planned, Tinuviel said, to be a "great performance thing that always changes." Its line-up that night included Vail's ex-boyfriend Kurt Cobain

Some Velvet Sidewalk

Below:
Courtney Love (the band)

Below: Bikini Kill

(who'd recently lived down the hall from Moon's apartment), Dave Grohl, ex-Melvin Joe Preston, Karren, and future Sub Pop accountant Ian Dickson.

The next month, Moon released *Wordcore Volume One*, a spoken-word 45 with Hanna on the "Girl" side and himself on the "Boy" side. He called his new record label Kill Rock Stars ("after a painting on my wall").

Slim Moon *on the Kill Rock Stars concept, 1993: "Punk has always been defined just as much by what it stands against (bullshit music, bullshit politics, bullshit culture, especially bullshit youth culture) as what it stands for. It's a reaction to things some savvy kids have the good sense to hate, and the creation of a different thing that can be loved. The ideas we have for Kill Rock Stars aren't that new, but they seem to be increasingly rare these days when 'Alternative' is a mainstream genre and 'punk' is a Toyota* (he's really referring to a Subaru slogan by a Portland ad agency, "It's like punk rock, only it's a car").... *Put out stuff by your friends and people you respect; treat them as peers and not as employees or stars; support your local music scene; let the bands and speakers have control of their thing as much as possible— artwork, recording, promotion, advertising, price, etc.; pay the bands fairly and not rip anyone off; put out records which mean something, not just music which sounds nice. Punk is my life. It gets me jumping around and falling in love. Rock Stars and pleasant meaningless music and stupid record labels just looking for a hit make me look for the nearest barf bag."*

With Tinuviel joining as his business partner (she took on more art supervision and band-scouting, he took on more studio responsibility), the label quickly assembled the *Kill Rock Stars* compilation LP. They called some of their favorite bands and within two days had 14 existing tapes; they added one specially-commissioned cut by Unwound. The first 1,000 copies had a silkscreened cover (Tinuviel said, "We didn't think we could sell even that many"). The record was rushed to be available at K's International Pop Underground Convention that August. The 14 mostly-local bands on the record (plus four more on the CD) included Steve Fisk, Seven Year Bitch, Some Velvet Sidewalk, Bikini Kill, Nirvana ("Beeswax," from the band's original demos with Dale Crover), and an Olympia band fronted by Maffeo and named "Courtney Love," after a notorious Portland/ L.A./S.F./Minneapolis/Liverpool singer and party gal. Cobain briefly met the real Courtney Love (Courtney Michelle Menely) after a 1989 Nirvana gig in Portland, and was re-introduced to her when his band went to L.A. to record *Nevermind* in May 1991, three months before the International Pop Underground Convention. Maffeo now records knowing-acoustic-pop tunes for K under the band name Lois. Her partner in "Courtney Love" the band, Pat Maley, started the Olympia-based Yoyo label.

Liner notes *to the* Kill Rock Stars *LP: "All the bands on this record appeared at the International Pop Underground convention or are from OLYMPIA, the Birthplace of Rock."*

Carl Hanni Rocket *review of Unwound's* New Plastic Ideas *album, 7/94: "Three anti-stars from Olympia who forge the sounds of things falling apart and trying to come together... a deep, shifting well of chords, feedback and rolling rhythms that constantly threatens to tear out of control, become fully unwound."*

Keyan Maymand in the Rocket *on Lois, 1/95:* "Lois balances her punk rock roots with softer, traditional acoustic folk influences, but to call Lois folk music would be an error in judgment. The band veers steadily into pop and punk and has only a minor foundation in folk music. Still, it's as safe to mention Lois in the same breath as Joni Mitchell as it is to compare her to Bikini Kill."

Moon and Tinuviel ran the label as a cooperative venture. They split all proceeds 50/50 with the bands, who had total creative control. The KRS partners continued to run the company out of Moon's home (Tinuviel moved to Seattle in 1992 and lived in a loft in the former Lincoln Arts building, then returned home to Boston where she started the Villakula label). By the summer of 1993 they were earning enough from the label to quit their day jobs. By then they had produced nine music 45s, six "Wordcore" spoken-word 45s, three compilation LPs (*Kill Rock Stars, Stars Kill Rock, Rock Stars Kill*), an EP and five albums.

Corporate ogre go away

The six-day IPU Convention gathered over 900 people to the Capitol Theater and three other sites. The convention was intended for people who wanted to strengthen the independent record scene, not to rise above it. Bands were there to play, not to be discovered. Johnson's broadside insisted, "No lackeys to the corporate ogre allowed"—no major labels or bands on them (at the time) could participate. Johnson and Pedersen turned down their pals Nirvana, because they'd gone to the majors (they wound up playing the Reading Festival in England that weekend). Over 50 widely divergent bands did appear, including McKaye's band Fugazi, Mecca Normal, Bratmobile, the Melvins, the Fastbacks, L.A.'s L7 (who were negotiating with a major label but were let in anyway), Jad Fair, England's Thee Headcoats, and Van Conner's side band Solomon Grundy. There was also an all-spoken-word show, a Sub Pop-sponsored barbecue, and a *Planet of the Apes* film marathon. All shows were all-ages; more than half the bands had at least one female member. Johnson and Pedersen had no plans for another IPU Convention, but Yoyo Records mounted its own Yoyo a Go Go convention in Olympia in July 1994.

Johnson said he put on the convention in response to the uncomfortable atmosphere associated with rock concerts, even alternative rock concerts. He also wanted an alternative to institutionalized alternative conventions like the *College Music Journal* show in New York, where bands played for free to houses full of industry people looking for the Next Big Thing. "I wanted to prove that you could put on a show that didn't cost a whole lot of money and still paid the bands, that you could put on a show without all the asshole security, that you could get a lot of people together to have a good time without all the bullshit." A pass to

the entire IPU Convention cost only $35, about as much as it cost to get into the institutionalized atmosphere of Lollapalooza.

Johnson's band, Beat Happening, started releasing its records through Sub Pop after its previous distributor, Rough Trade, folded. Sub Pop, in turn, contracted its retail distribution to Caroline Records, a New York indie that became an autonomously-run division of Virgin—which in turn was soon swallowed by EMI. In 1993 Sub Pop switched allegiances to ADA, half-owned by Time Warner. Other Big Six majors also muscled in on "independent" distribution: Sony owned Relativity Entertainment Distribution (C/Z's distributor); PolyGram owned ILS (Independent Label Sales); and BMG Music started its own "indie" unit. The majors wanted to appropriate the efficiency and street credibility of the indies.

They also wanted to exploit the indies' new sales clout, discovered in early 1991 when *Billboard* switched its Top 200 chart from a corruptible polling system to actual retail sales, tracked by the SoundScan company. SoundScan calculated that indie labels accounted for 15 percent of the record market, three times their previously believed share—even though many smaller stores that carried more indie releases didn't have computers and thus couldn't participate in SoundScan.

Girl germs

Johnson and Pedersen continued to run K in

The Pleasure Elite

Bratmobile

Beat Happening's "Dreamy"

Earth

ries mainly by female writers).

The articles took out-of-context lyrics and quotes from zines to brand the entire movement as separatist man-haters—some zine writers did promote modern stereotypes about Good Women and Bad Men, but others denounced all forms of sexism. The articles also claimed that Bikini Kill ordered men removed from the front of the dance floor at shows—their real policy was to have pushy or violent moshers removed, a policy shared by male bands like Fugazi. (Some other female bands and/or their fans took it upon themselves to enforce "all-girl pits" in front.)

Thanks to the articles, Bikini Kill and Bratmobile may have achieved the biggest ratio of press coverage to sales of any bands in history: aside from their cut on the *Kill Rock Stars* compilation, all Bikini Kill releases were vinyl-only, until the CD *Pussy Whipped* in November 1993. Their first, self-titled EP in 1992 included "Thurston Hearts the Who," the band's jibe at their pals in Nirvana for touring with Thurston Moore of the "mainstream alternative" Sonic Youth (Hanna appeared in Sonic Youth's 1994 video "Bull in the Heather;" she also acted in Jill Reiter's "new wave dyke" movie *In Search of Mango-go*). It made the *Village Voice* annual top-10 list; *Alternative Press* called it "the best punk rock record made." It was rereleased on CD in 1994, packaged with Bikini Kill's half of a joint LP with the English band Huggy Bear.

From Bikini Kill's "White Boy": "*White boy/Don't laugh, don't cry/Just die!/I'm sorry if I've alienated some of you/But your whole fucking culture alienates me!*"

Spin *review* of the Bikini Kill EP, 3/93: "*...Evil sounding guitar, bass and drums aggressively slammed together in a simple catchy punk rock style.... It's Kathleen Hanna's voice that takes this record to a higher level.*"

Hanna had been a spoken-word artist in Portland, then formed the bands Viva Knievel, Amy Carter and Baby Cable before she joined up with Vail. Vail had played for a while in Some Velvet Sidewalk and before that with Karren and Calvin Johnson in Go Team, which released nine K 45s and four cassettes, in monthly sequence, with different musicians on each (Cobain appeared on the seventh single). Vail had been Cobain's girlfriend for a time; he's credited her with helping inspire some of the feminist ideas in his lyrics and record covers. But it was Hanna who scrawled KURT SMELLS LIKE TEEN SPIRIT on his apartment wall, after an all-night graffiti-making session in downtown Olympia. He'd never heard of the deodorant by that name; he claimed never to use such grooming aids.

Bikini Kill and Nirvana both fought against the macho rock-star attitude, one of the main things the original punks were rebelling against, which had infiltrated the alternative scene as mall rats latched onto grunge as low-budget metal. MTV cov-

adherence to the rules of indie rock: spirit is more important than professionalism, 45s are better than CDs, fun is more important than money, corporate-rock-star attitudes suck.

These rules were particularly important on the convention's "girl day." Loosely organized, in part by members of Bikini Kill and Bratmobile, it gathered musicians (some of whom had already met on tour) with editors and readers of a handful of photocopied zines like Tobi Vail's *Jigsaw* and Allison Wolfe's *Girl Germs* (some of whom were already on one another's mailing lists). Some of the attendees had been at an earlier Olympia gathering in 1987, called "'50 Girls From 50 States." They talked about forming bands, making records, recovering from rape and abuse, men they loved and/or hated, and older feminists whose institutional attitudes frustrated them. Performers on "girl day" included Seven Year Bitch, Heavens to Betsy, Kreviss, Bratmobile, Rose Melburg (later in the Sacramento, Calif. band Tiger Trap), and Jean Smith of Mecca Normal.

Many of the Girl Day attendees reconvened the next summer in Washington, D.C. for the International Riot Grrrl Convention (named for a D.C.-based zine co-founded by the members of Bratmobile). There was even a boyfriends' auxiliary at the D.C. meeting, where the outspoken women's softspoken men (many with the same short haircuts as their girlfriends) discussed such issues as collective male guilt. From all accounts, neither the Grrls or their boys discussed what they'd do after the *Washington Post, Newsweek, Sassy, Seventeen* and other media hyped and stereotyped them (in sto-

erage of the first Lollapalooza festival introduced millions to the moshpit phenomenon, which had become far rowdier than the pogo/slamdance from which it had evolved. The mood behind punk dancing evolved from collective tribal rite to aggressive competition. Heavy Dr. Martens boots from England ("Docs") and loose, expendable clothes became the practical uniform for the moshpit.

Five Olympia bands, including Fitz of Depression (self-described as "powercore, great music, high energy"), recorded but didn't release *The Olympia All Male Review*, intended as a tongue-in-cheek response to the Riot Grrrl hype. Their label name was a possible retort to the PC reputation of the Northwest scene—Meat Records.

Believing the Hype

If youth angst was a cultural force (at least to the press), then it would need its own literature. The two authors most closely stereotyped as their generation's New Voices both came from north of the border. Vancouver's William Gibson, a self-professed computer illiterate, speculated about a future world of electronically-created "virtual realities," merged human-computer entities and strange new drugs in his "cyberpunk" adventure novels *Neuromancer* and *Mona Lisa Overdrive*. Fellow Vancouverite Douglas Coupland fooled North America's book critics with *Generation X*, a trendy novella about young wage slaves in California. Thanks to his book, the media saddled young adults with a title Coupland took from Billy Idol's first band, which broke up in 1981 while today's 21-year-olds were still in grade school. Coupland's better second novel, *Shampoo Planet*, was about young wage slaves in eastern Washington's Tri-Cities, home of the massive, messed-up Hanford Atomic Reservation. Seattle artist James L. Acord became obsessed with Hanford and became one of the few civilians with an official license to own small amounts of nuclear material (radium he extracted from old Fiestaware kitchen plates), which he embedded within his sculptures.

Backlash ended in March 1991. Several parties tried to fill its hole. June 1991 saw *Hype*, a free all-music (with lots of bullshitting on the side) tabloid. Because its founders (including Rob Flaggert, Lori LeFavor, J.A. Anderson, Pete Moe, Scott Brown, and Gas Huffer drummer Joe Newton) were more willing than *Backlash*'s backers to lose money, they made big issues full of snide reviews until April 1993.

Hype reviews *of Pearl Jam's Ten by "Adam" and "Pissy the Puppy": "Who ever would've thought that Matt Dillon could sing this good? Is anybody else embarrassed by the idea that a Seattle band needs to import virtuoso-type frontpeople from Cali in an attempt to hit the big time? In all fairness, the new guys are very talented, but the songs, relative to their context, have all the depth of a Domino's pizza in Chicago. Same old FM rock shit."... "Music on the cutting edge of Bad*

Co. revival. I'm embarrassed by the fact that these guys, along with Matt Dillon, will be representing the Seattle scene to the rest of the nation on the big screen. I just don't see anything special about it. Though I will thank Epic 'cause some local fans are easily persuaded to part with their cold, hard cash to get their hands on copies of the promo. Thanks for dinner, Epic."

That September a free weekly tabloid was started by a clique of young adults who came out together from Madison, Wisconsin. *The Stranger* was originally intended to be just a thin package of entertainment listings, cartoons and ads, but it soon became must reading in the coffeehouses and bars with interviews of alternative celebrities, neo-hippie politics, and an explicit sex-advice column. Within three years it was circulating 40,000 free copies a week, overtaking the *Weekly*'s paid circulation of 34,000.

Climbing a Gold Mountain

Another Madisonian, producer Butch Vig, got the nod to produce Nirvana's major label debut. The group had signed with DGC Records and with ex-Led Zeppelin publicist Danny Goldberg's Gold Mountain Entertainment, a high-profile Hollywood management company (both companies represented Sonic Youth). DGC paid the band to set aside seven tracks the band had begun with Vig in Madison for a second Sub Pop album, and to rerecord them with Vig in an L.A. studio. Published reports list DGC as having paid Sub Pop $70,000 and the band $250,000. The latter figure was comparable to PolyGram's advance to Mother Love Bone two years earlier. The MLB advance was treated in the music press as wildly generous; the same press treated Nirvana's advance as a bargain for the label. That money quickly dwindled with deductions for recording and legal expenses, and the band members were slow to see their first checks. Even while they wrote and practiced the album's songs, Cobain subsisted on corn dogs and codeine cough

Below: Green Apple Quick Step

LOSER

Jim Rose

friend) and Kat Bjelland (later of Babes in Toyland; she and her husband later moved here and started the band Crunt). Love's new band Hole (allegedly named from a line in *Medea*) had just recorded the Caroline CD *Pretty on the Inside* after rising through the L.A. rock-hype machine and releasing the Sub Pop 45 "Dicknail." Love once said she turned down a contract offer from Madonna's Maverick label, because she feared Madonna wanted to steal her schtick.

Shortly after the *Nevermind* sessions, DGC sent Nirvana off for seven months of touring and turned the band's tapes over to remixer Andy Wallace, who'd worked with pop-metal bands like Slayer.

Cobain, Novoselic and Grohl held closer to the devil-may-care punk spirit than some of the aging punks. They thrashed around, they mugged it up on stage, they encouraged moshpit shoving up to a point. Yet Nirvana also had publicly expressed reservations about the macho-rock-star image with which Soundgarden, Alice In Chains and Pearl Jam seemed to be compromising. While Nirvana didn't have any calculated plan for commercial success, they knew what they didn't want, and turned down a lucrative offer to tour with Guns n' Roses and Metallica.

Cobain and Novoselic lectured on stage and in print about feminism and the need for men to be reeducated to stop rape: stuff you could hear often from sensitive new age guys and the Riot Grrrl boyfriends, but not from passionate young men who trashed their instruments on stage and got into fights with other guys. Cobain later claimed one of the reasons he left Sub Pop was because he found the label sexist, referring to a CD cover for San Francisco's Dwarves that had two naked women and a bare-chested short man all drenched in animal blood.

Hole opened a few shows with Nirvana on fellow DGC signees Sonic Youth's European tour, as documented in David Markey's concert film *1991, The Year Punk Broke*. Nirvana then went on a six-week US club tour. Love hooked up permanently with Cobain when their paths again crossed in Chicago. She'd gone there to meet up with her long-distance boyfriend, Smashing Pumpkins singer Billy Corgan; had a spat with him, went to see Nirvana's show, and went back to Cobain's hotel room.

A Dallas stop featured a scuffle between Cobain and club bouncer Turner Scott Van Blarcum, a local ex-metal singer with skull tattoos running up the side of his head (his collection of old animal bones became stage props for Ministry's Lollapalooza '92 show). The spat started when a rowdy Cobain flung a guitar into a monitor speaker that belonged to Van Blarcum, who jumped onstage to retaliate. As the *Dallas Morning News* reviewed a home video of the fight, "one can see the soon-to-be-superstar crack Turner over the head with his guitar and a dazed Turner respond with a roundhouse punch that laid out the young punk.

syrup. Somewhere around this time came a bootleg 45, with the title *Nirvana: The Triple Platinum EP*. The name was a joke.

In May, as recording began in the studio where Fleetwood Mac made *Rumours*, Cobain re-met Courtney Love, who'd been corresponding with Grohl since December 1990 about the L.A. rock industry. She told Michael Azerrad that on their first meeting, at a Butthole Surfers show, she expressed her infatuation by punching Kurt in the stomach. He jumped on her and they began wrestling.

Love was the daughter of early Grateful Dead manager Hank Harrison and psychologist Linda Carroll, who made news in 1993 for her involvement with fugitive killer Katherine Ann Power. Love was raised in Eugene, Portland and New Zealand by her mother and a succession of stepfathers. At one point her mom sent her to a reform school to contain her free-spirited nature, unsuccessfully. She spent her young-adult years globetrotting until her trust fund ran out; then she became a self-proclaimed "teenage slut," a stripper, and an early member of Faith No More. She played one of Nancy Spungen's friends in Alex Cox's *Sid and Nancy* and the leading "lady" in Cox's vanity film *Straight to Hell* (she played a pregnant character, brought by the father of her child to an isolated town full of bellicose people who partied too hard and drank too much coffee). In Minneapolis she'd formed the band Sugar Baby Doll with Jennifer Finch (later of L7, and also Grohl's onetime girl-

Turner cemented his legend by pursuing the band out into the parking lot and punching out the window of the cab in which the trio fled." (Scenes from the fight surfaced in the 1994 home video *Live! Tonight! Sold Out!*)

Nirvana's DGC debut, *Nevermind,* was released at the end of September. The band held an autograph party at the Beehive (formerly Peaches) record store in the U District and a record-release party at Re-bar. The release party was Cobain's fi-nal event as a club-level musician, and the last time many of his Seattle friends saw him. He got 86'ed from his own party for starting a food fight. Jeff Gilbert remembered his last sight of Cobain outside that party, smiling, with salad dressing all over his face.

David Geffen later said he'd first hoped *Nevermind* would sell comparably to Sonic Youth's DGC debut, in the 100,000-200,000 range. The initial print run was 50,000 copies in the US, 40,000 in the UK.

Below:
THE Record

CHAPTER TWELVE: IN BLOOM (1992-1994)

"Corporate Magazines Still Suck"

Butch Vig

Peaches In-store

In his 1993 book *From the Velvets to the Voidoids,* English critic Clinton Heylin wrote that the 1970s New York punk bands had "set out to reform rock music, believing in an immutable alliance between pop and rock."

The early Seattle punks had pursued pretty much the same goal, with perhaps a slight digression during the early Sub Pop years. It took a couple of guys who were prepubescents when the Ramones played their hometown to fulfill the task of reuniting pop and rock.

Nirvana's *Nevermind* was a slickly packaged CD whose superficially simple sound masked a wide array of influences, from the Sex Pistols to the Pixies. The band turned the rage of classic punk into a pure, crystalline entity. It turned despair into defiance, depression into urgency. Its ugliness was beautiful.

Its first single and video, "Smells Like Teen Spirit," became an anthem for the ignored, frustrated youth across George Bush's no-future America. Over deceptively simple chords progressing from upbeat radio hooks into full-bore rages, its four-syllable lines painted a lyrical image of disillusion among the misfits and outcasts. Sam Bayer's L.A.-shot video depicted the band in a slam-dancing assembly at a high school in the suburbs of Hell (cheerleaders, played by L.A. strippers, wore black costumes with the anarchist circle-A logo). Kurt Cobain told *Guitar World* that "a film student could've made something just as good for a lot less money." Still, the clip gave listeners not just a new sound but a look and an aesthetic to copy, even if it did so in the familiar milieu of bad boys and dancing girls.

The video for "Come As You Are" brought to film the CD's cover image of an infant underwater, lured out of his innocent state by a dollar bill on a fishhook. Kevin Kerslake (who also directed the live home videos for Soundgarden and Alice in Chains) devised an elaborate studio set with tiered waterfalls and a high chandelier that Cobain swung around upon. The U.K. band Killing Joke unsuccessfully sued, claiming the song's intro copped the riff from their song "Eighties."

The third video, for "Lithium," was a straight forward performance clip in slow motion, corresponding to the lyric's images of a resignation to fate that could be either caused by drugs or merely by being strung out on life.

The next video, "In Bloom" (a previous version was filmed on a much lower budget for a Sub Pop video collection), attacked the jock mentality that had been infiltrating punk audiences even before the record came out, as personalized by a young but ignorant devotee who "likes to sing along and he likes to shoot his gun." Kerslake's video was set on an Ed Sullivan-like variety show from the early '60s (hosted by *People's Court* co-star Doug Llewellyn). Kerslake remembered that live TV cameras used to have four fixed-length lenses affixed to a rotor. He used the lens-switching to transfer from shots of the boys smiling in suits to shots of the boys snarling in white dresses, flailing and busting their instruments. Because the video was released in mid-1992, it qualified for the 1993 MTV Video Music Awards. When they accepted the award for "Best Alternative Video," Cobain dropped his pants (out of camera range).

All four songs mentioned guns, ubiquitous commodities of redneck-town teens whose popularity had spread to city and suburban youth; Cobain had owned shotguns for sport in Olympia, and had gone target shooting with Earth guitarist Dylan Carlson. Other songs took on unwanted pregnancy ("Breed"), everyday moral dilemmas ("Something in the Way"), and the horror of rape ("Polly", based on a Community World Theater patron who was abducted on the streets of Tacoma and escaped by pretending to acquiesce to her assailant).

At least that's what they seemed to discuss. Fans wrote countless zine articles and exchanged messages on computer networks, first trying to figure out what Cobain's lyrics *were,* then trying to figure out what they *meant.* Critics compared his surrealistic verbal imagery to everybody from Artur Rimbaud to James Joyce.

After the first small CD run, subsequent pressings included a bonus track, "Endless Nameless," programmed to play 10 minutes after the last official track; it was mistakenly left off the first run by the mastering engineer. The cut was mostly instrumental but had a few words, apparently about being ready to meet Satan, as if Cobain's words were ever literally "about" one thing.

One million orders came in for *Nevermind* by Christmas. It rose to *Billboard*'s #1 the first week of January.

Cobain was dissatisfied with *Nevermind*'s pol-

**Below:
Nirvana in
the coliseum**

ished-pop sound, according to a *Los Angeles Times* interview: "We really didn't follow through on the mixing. It ended up too commercial and slick." (In other interviews, he said he could've made it rougher if he'd wanted to.) But he didn't take back the money it earned, the three *Village Voice* critics' poll awards, the three MTV Video Music Awards, or the two Grammy nominations. The band made the cover of *Rolling Stone* (Kurt wore a hand-lettered T-shirt reading "Corporate Magazines Still Suck," a variation on SST Records' slogan "Corporate Rock Still Sucks"), *Spin*, and even metal zines *Rip* and *Kerrang!*

Robert Christgau *in the* Village Voice*: "Come on—this is a classic critics' band…. Their multi-platinum takeover constituted the first full-scale public validation of the Amerindie values—the noise, the toons, the 'tude—the radder half of the electorate came up on."*

Nirvana remained on the road through the winter, joining Pearl Jam as opening acts for the Red Hot Chili Peppers. They appeared as solo headliners for a Halloween show at the Paramount; Bikini Kill opened the show in lingirie (including the guy guitarist) with SLUT painted across their bare midriffs. The band appeared on *Saturday Night*

Live on Jan. 11, 1992 with a rendition of "Teen Spirit" that sounded more like the band's punkier live act. The makers of the real Teen Spirit deodorant bought the last national commercial slot before the song. Their second song was the faster, punkier "Territorial Pissing," also performed that month in an MTV studio appearance.

"Teen Spirit" was covered by soft-acoustic singer Tori Amos, sampled by rappers Credit to the Nation in "Call It What You Want," and parodied by Weird Al Yancovic in "Smells Like Nirvana" (Yancovic's video used the set built for the original, and featured some of the same extras). Sara DeBell, a new arrival to Seattle from Massachusetts, made pseudo-Muzak synth arrangements of "Teen Spirit" and other "Seattle Sound" tunes for her novelty CD *Grunge Lite.*

An *Artforum* review by Greil Marcus lauded the "In Bloom" video as a statement against homophobia, even if their drag act was no more threatening than Bugs Bunny's. Cobain *did* make statements against homophobia and sexism in interviews, noting with disgust that the same metal guys who used to fag-bash him in Aberdeen were buying Nirvana CDs. The soap opera *One Life to Live* played "Teen Spirit" during a frat-party scene that culminated in a gang rape. A similar real-life crime had already happened, according to Cobain's liner notes for the *Incesticide* retrospective CD: "Last year, a girl was raped by two wastes of sperm and eggs while they sang the lyrics to our song 'Polly.' I have a hard time carrying on knowing there are bacteria like that in our audience." Cobain closed the statement with a message to hatemongers: "Don't come to our shows and don't buy our records."

Family matters

When Cobain impregnated Courtney Love, the scene had an official Royal Family. When *Vanity Fair* charged that Love shot up smack in New York while carrying her kid (she adamantly denied it), the scene found itself with celebrities big enough to be gossiped about. She married Cobain in February 1992 in a private ceremony in Hawaii, led by a female nondenominational minister, between Nirvana tour segments. Novoselic didn't attend; Dylan Carlson of the band Earth was Cobain's best man.

After 100 shows on four continents in five months, Nirvana had barely started back on the road when Cobain abruptly postponed the band's remaining European dates, officially due to stomach flu. The morning after a July make-up date in Belfast, he collapsed in his hotel. He was rushed to a hospital and treated for what managers called "a weeping ulcer." He retreated to a reclusive existence in Love's Hollywood apartment, fueling rumors about the couple's alleged drug use.

Cobain admitted months later that he (and, to a far lesser extent, Love) had indeed been taking heroin. He'd taken it off and on since 1988, and rediscovered it as a painkiller when his (very real) stomach pains came back on tour. Love quit when

LOSER

she knew she was pregnant, but Cobain continued to use until he developed a $500-a-day habit. He finally undertook a month-long detox, in the same L.A. hospital where Love gave birth, and both were now off the stuff, supposedly for good.

Other rumors claimed that Love wanted to hitch her career wagon to Nirvana's rising star, and even that she was trying to draw Cobain away from Chris Novoselic and Dave Grohl. Still other rumors doubted Nirvana's street credibility: first they put out a pop-rock album on a dreaded *major label* that *sold big*, then the band got dominated by someone from the despised City of Angels.

The Cobains settled in Seattle after the August birth of Frances Bean Cobain, born healthy and with no drug effects. The birth, Cobain's detox, and their battle with California authorities to secure custody of Frances postponed by two weeks Nirvana's Welcome Home show at the only venue in town now big enough for the band, the Coliseum. Its only other official performances in 1992 were a Portland benefit for a campaign against an anti-gay-rights initiative) and on the *MTV Video Music Awards*. Grohl hooked up with a Scream reunion tour.

Cobain and Love insisted they hated the rock-star mentality. They noted that before Nirvana's spring gigs were canceled, the band had declined to open for Guns n' Roses. (Soundgarden had already toured with GN'R, immersing itself into the heart of the corporate-rock universe it had denounced in "Big Dumb Sex.")

GN'R singer Axl Rose denounced Cobain and Love on stage at a Florida show, to a cheering response: "Don't you think Kurt and Courtney ought to be in jail for doing drugs while she was pregnant?"

Backstage at the MTV awards in September, where Nirvana played "Lithium" (in defiance of MTV's threats not to play DGC acts if they didn't play "Teen Spirit") and Grohl shouted "Hi Axl," Love mockingly asked if Rose would like to be her baby's godfather. According to *Entertainment Weekly*, Rose answered to Cobain: "If you don't shut your woman up, I'm going to take you down to the pavement." Rose's date, supermodel Stephanie Seymour, asked Love, "Are you a model?" Love's response: "Yeah, are you a brain surgeon?" Outside later, Duff McKagan and some GN'R roadies surrounded and threatened Novoselic, before bystanders broke up the spat.

Christine Kelly in Sassy, 4/93: "*While watching the inaugural balls, I realized that Hillary Clinton is the Courtney Love of politics. If the people want Kurt (Bill), they have to take Courtney (Hillary) too. People will accuse Courtney (Hillary) of trying to break up the band with her constant meddling and poisoning influence, even though Courtney (Hillary) has her own band (office). Hillary (Courtney) said provocative things to the press about baking cookies (taking heroin). Courtney (Hillary) was on MTV with her hus-*

band. Both chicks have a cute, sassy daughter. There is one major difference: Courtney has too much taste to mix jewel tones like amethyst and royal blue while watching her husband accept an MTV award (get inaugurated)."

Censors, corporations attack

Outgoing Democratic Gov. Booth Gardner invoked Nirvana's success in a speech to the State Legislature in the spring of 1992; weeks later, he signed the Erotic Music Bill, a creation of Republican legislators that would have harassed record stores selling to minors any record deemed "erotic" in court. Musicians (including Chris Novoselic), clubs and record stores formed the Washington Music Industry Coalition to fight the law, which was unanimously declared unconstitutional by the state Supreme Court. Legislators failed to pass a revised law in 1993, which would have made retailers keep up with declarations of officially "erotic" recordings in an obscure state legal journal. Its sponsors introduced another version in the 1994 legislative session; new Gov. Mike Lowry vetoed it. In 1995, Novoselic and members of Soundgarden co-founded the Joint Artists and Music Promotions Political Action Committee (JAMPAC), a full-time lobbying group opposing any future censorship attempts.

Within weeks of *Nevermind*'s release, major-label scouts descended on alternative venues in Seattle (to find the "Next Nirvana") and around the country (to find the "Next Seattle"). At some local club shows in February, industry people on guest lists outnumbered paid attendees.

Pearl Jam's kinder, gentler bleakness

Pearl Jam's *Ten* came out the same month as *Nevermind*, but took a little longer to catch on with the public. Once it did, due to a grueling touring schedule and the stark video for "Jeremy," there was no stopping it.

Ten proved to be among the most carefully crafted mainstream guitar-rock albums ever. Eddie Vedder's painful, triumphant vocal gyrations switched off between enraged shrieks, mournful wails and mumbled profanities. Jeff Ament and Stone Gossard constructed solid riffs that placed Vedder's voice within an assertive but un-pushy

Endfest

Eddie Vedder

context of low-tuned guitar progressions, moody rockers and defiant slow-pop melodies. It was arena rock for sensitive guys, expressing emotions beyond the standard macho-rock poses—hesitancy, uncertainty, desperation. It was especially true of the pain-and-survival power ballads "Alive," based on Vedder's teenage discovery that a late "family friend" had been his real father, and "Jeremy," the searing tale of a child who commits suicide by shooting himself in front of his classmates.

Vedder claimed in interviews that he was surprised so many people could relate to his obtuse tales of young life and death, desire and survival, of bleak human horizons (lacking the catharsis of Nirvana's cynical humor); particularly "Jeremy," which won four MTV awards.

The age-old Seattle drummer shortage resurfaced when Dave Krusen chose to stay home with his new kid rather than live on the road. Matt Chamberlain, formerly with Edie Brickell's New Bohemians, joined the group briefly, then got an offer to join the *Saturday Night Live* band, then came back with fellow ex-Bohemians Brad Houser and John Bush and Sadhappy saxophonist Skerik in Critters Buggin', a combo described by the *Times* as playing "jazzy, funky, and industrial" instrumentals complete with hand drums, sax, didjeridu and clarinet; Gossard signed them in 1994 to his new record label Loosegroove. Chamberlain recommended Dave Abbruzzese, formerly with a couple of Houston bands, to become the permanent Pearl Jam drummer.

By the end of 1992, Pearl Jam members found themselves on *four* of the year's 100 top-selling albums: *Ten*, the reissued Mother Love Bone CD, the reissued *Temple of the Dog*, and the *singles* soundtrack. (*Nevermind*, *Badmotorfinger*, *Dirt*, and *Mack Daddy* also made the list.) The group had appeared on *Saturday Night Live*, the MTV Video Music Awards, its own *MTV Unplugged* special, and the annual Rock n' Roll Hall of Fame show.

Cobain vs. Pearl Jam

Cobain was quoted in *Musician* as calling Pearl Jam a "corporate, alternative, cock-rock crossover"

and in *Rolling Stone* as having "a duty to warn the kids of false music that's claiming to be underground or alternative," charging Pearl Jam with "jumping on the alternative bandwagon." Jeff Ament responded that Cobain seldom spoke to Pearl Jam on their dates together with the Chili Peppers: "To have that sort of pent-up frustration, the guy obviously must have some really deep insecurities about himself. Does he think we're riding his bandwagon? We could turn around and say that Nirvana put out records on money we made for Sub Pop when we were in Green River—if we were that stupid about it."

It wasn't Vedder's fault that *Playgirl* listed him as one of the 10 Sexiest Rockers of 1992 ("A certifiable sex-god-with-a-brain. Here's one hot dude who's really cookin' "). He hadn't posed for the magazine, unlike the Cobains' pose for the cover of *Sassy*.

That fall Cobain and company made up with Vedder, who slow-danced backstage with Love and Cobain at the same MTV Awards show that included the Axl Rose spat. Cobain later said he still expressed distaste for Pearl Jam's commercial sound and lack of "punk ideals." Both bands were multi-platinum commercial successes who deal with the darker side of modern life through pop-song structures; both bands' frontmen had uncomfortable experiences with the industry and the media. The bands' main differences were their musical structures and their initial marketing ambitions. Nirvana was partly influenced by Calvin Johnson's indie ideology and almost stumbled into its fame; the Pearl Jam guys (particularly Ament and Gossard) aspired to the big time, only to find it didn't live up to their fantasies.

Seattle vs. Pearl Jam

Pearl Jam tried to hold a free "Rock the Vote" concert at Gas Works Park (the Lake Union site of a former coal gasification plant) on the Saturday before Memorial Day 1992, at the start of its summer touring schedule, only to get its permits rejected days before the scheduled show. Officials claimed that the crowd would be too big for the place, even though a Memorial Day fireworks show was scheduled with a higher estimated attendance. Officials also objected to the opening act, calling Seaweed a punk band that would attract the wrong element. They may also have opposed a planned between-sets exhibition by local skateboarders, whom "liberal" politicians may have hated more than they hated punk.

During an ACLU seminar with Dave Marsh, previously scheduled to discuss the Erotic Music Bill, Vedder called the city's action blatant censorship. A woman in the audience suggested that politicians didn't want young people to vote. The city was inundated with irate calls, letters and faxes from young fans. It offered to reschedule the show for a Wednesday, but the band insisted on a non-school day. On the day the show was to have occurred, the band members set up the skateboard ramps on a private lot in the suburbs and partied with the skaters and members of Seaweed and Seven Year Bitch.

The non-alternative

Pearl Jam finally had to delay the free concert until the next break in its tours, which included a slot on the second Lollapalooza festival, alongside Soundgarden, Ministry and the Jim Rose Circus Sideshow. Lollapalooza '92 played to 650,000 people at 39 dates, certifying that "alternative" music (or a corporate imitation of it) was the new mainstream. Pearl Jam, signed to the tour before *Ten* broke out, played a 45-minute midday set; at the Los Angeles stop, Jack Irons came out in a Cobain wig to join the band's closing rendition of Neil Young's "Rockin' in the Free World." The Lollapalooza main stage was (except for Ice Cube and U.K. female synth-poppers Lush) all pale penis people playing to lingering hard-rock tastes. Even Ministry, which had never played outdoors in the daytime before, ended its set with a Black Sabbath cover.

Kim Thayil on Lollapalooza to USA Today: *"This is the safest bill I've ever been on. Lollapalooza gives the semi-affluent, leisure-class white youths between 18 and 24 who don't vote an opportunity to relinquish themselves of guilt and practice their civic responsibility. They get style points for that, right?"*

Houston Post *review by* **Claudia Perry**: *"Lollapalooza is really no different from the rest of the music industry in that it's mostly white, mostly male and mostly pugnacious. The squirming pit in front of the stage was the sort of male bonding that, in its most horrific and reckless manifestations, brings on suicide pacts and gang rape. The women who emerged from the pit usually looked dazed and disoriented. The men exchanged high fives and talked about how they had ridden the wave of humanity beneath them."*

KNDD attracted over 20,000 flannel-shirted fans to a multi-act "Endfest" at a suburban fairground with ten bands, including Mudhoney and the Posies. At that event, Jennifer Finch of L7 told MTV that it was hard to tell who was hip or not when the punks looked just like the lumberjacks. Soon after, the station group that started KNDD sold it to MTV's parent company, Viacom.

Free, at last

The free Pearl Jam show finally occurred in September, relocated to Magnuson Park (near the original "Sound Garden" art installation). The 29,000 free tickets were announced on a Saturday morning at 8 a.m. By 8:30, traffic was backed up on Aurora Avenue for a mile each side of the distribution site, the Seattle Center Coliseum. Fans dared traffic by jaywalking across Aurora, leaping over the arterial's barricaded median.

The show itself went much more smoothly; the

LOSER

band provided free bus service from a UW parking lot to the park a mile away. The group footed the entire $100,000 tab for the show. Seaweed played an opening set without incident; but the fire marshals, who controlled the PA, apparently didn't like the pro-marijuana messages of New York rappers Cyprus Hill; their sound was cut off several times during their brief set. Author Robert Anton Wilson got to say all he wanted about the evil New World Order, but few fans seemed interested.

Bill Rieflin, whose career odyssey had stretched from the Telepaths to Ministry, sat in on drums during part of Pearl Jam's set. At another point, Vedder flung his microphone into the air. It accidentally caught on a lighting rafter. He climbed up speakers and a pole until, hanging by his hands

Brad (Shame) in front of Avast! studios

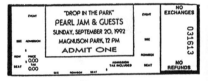

"DROP IN THE PARK"
PEARL JAM & GUESTS
SUNDAY, SEPTEMBER 20, 1992
MAGNUSON PARK, 12 PM
ADMIT ONE

NO EXCHANGES

031613

NO REFUNDS

Below: Pigeonhed

Right: Kevin
Martin of Candlebox

Vedder climbing
the rigging

Jar of Flies

from some guy wires, he retrieved the trapped mike, some 40 feet above the stage. He sang into it as he loosened it and lowered it down. He lost his grip and started to fall; he grabbed the microphone cord and slid down it like a pulley. Then he ran back up on the amps and jumped into the crowd, still singing, using the cord like a bungee rope. On the fifth pass out he executed a perfect flat dive into the audience.

Pearl Jam's subsequent Washington gigs included a handful of surprise gigs warming up for their 1993 second album, and a show with Neil Young at the Gorge Ampitheater in eastern Washington. At that show, Jeff and Stone's old bandmate Mark Arm joined them for a rendition of Mudhoney's "Suck You Dry."

Once Pearl Jam stopped touring for a few months, Gossard recorded for a blue-eyed-soul project, Brad, with former LuvCo singer Shawn Smith and Andy Wood's old Malfunkshun drummer Regan Hagar. The band was to have been called Shame, but some guy named Brad had already signed a band of his own called Shame, so Seattle's Shame changed its name to Brad and used *Shame* as the title of its CD. Hagar and Smith were no strangers to name changes; their main band, the jazz/funk/noise combo Bliss, had to change its name to Satchel. Smith also co-created Pigeonhed, with his vocals fronting Steve Fisk's keyboards, tape loops and samples (including old Kim Thayil guitar tracks).

Gossard was one of the local musicians who gathered for a one-time Seattle all-star picnic, held at the Terminal Sales Building's roof garden in October 1992. Joshua Hardy, a New Hampshire 17-year-old with a terminal brain tumor, was flown here by the Make-A-Wish Foundation to meet a few of his Seattle rock idols. Hardy was feted by members of Soundgarden, the Posies, Seven Year Bitch, Love Battery, TAD, the Fastbacks, Monkeywrench, Truly, the Young Fresh Fellows, Gas Huffer, Steel

Wool and Kill Sybil. He also visited Cobain and Novoselic's homes, the KNDD studios, the Wilson sisters' Bad Animals studio, and Microsoft tycoon Bill Gates.

Alice Mudgarden

Alice in Chains recorded the acoustic-ballad EP *Sap*, with Ann Wilson singing backup on one track and Mark Arm and Chris Cornell on another (billed as "Alice Mudgarden," a name used by Rob Morgan in a Vedder wig at Squirrels shows).

AIC's evolution as rock balladeers continued in 1992 on the million-selling album *Dirt*, featuring the *singles* soundtrack song "Would." Five of *Dirt*'s songs were devoted to the cycle of heroin addiction, from early turn-on to final burnout, an experience singer-lyricist Layne Staley admitted to have lived through. Jerry Cantrell's Vietnam-vet father appeared in the video for "Rooster," a defiant dirge about the horrors of war.

From Alice in Chains' "Junkhead:" "What's my drug of choice? Well, what have you got?"

The group followed *Dirt* with another semi-acoustic EP, *Jar of Flies*, in January 1994. Featuring what the *Post-Intelligencer* called "vibrant, sometimes eerie harmonies" by Staley and Cantrell, it entered the *Billboard* album chart at #1. The disc went far beyond the 1990 stereotype of "acoustic metal ballads," into subtle sonic textures of despair and survival.

The band went on hiatus in the fall of 1994, canceling a tour with Metallica and an appearance at Woodstock '94. Manager Susan Silver's office claimed the hiatus was due to "health problems" within the band, fueling rumors related to Staley's history of drug use. During the layoff Staley recorded backup vocals with the local electronic-rock band Second Coming and make club gigs with Mike McCready, Screaming Trees drummer Barrett Martin and bassist Baker Saunders in the side band

Mad Season (originally named the Gacy Bunch); while Mike Inez appeared on Guns n' Roses member Slash's solo CD. At some Mad Season gigs, Staley was overheard telling fans that Alice in Chains was over; Silver publicly insisted the band was still together and would release another album in 1995.

Soundgarden waited until March 1994 to release its third major-label album, *Superunknown*: 72 minutes of tunes that foresook the metal-crossover shtick for what *Rolling Stone* called "a muscular, melodic accessibility…the most expansive musical terrain the band has ever surveyed." It included "Spoonman" (a stompin' tribute to local street performer Artis the Spoonman), the pseudo-psychedelic ballad "Black Hole Sun," and the grim/defiant "Fell on Black Days," which could be heard as a downbeat epilogue to the band's earlier "Power Trip." It debuted on the *Billboard* album chart at #1, selling over 300,000 copies in its first week of release and over four million by the end of the year. The "Black Hole Sun" video won a 1994 MTV award as Best Hard Rock-Heavy Metal Video. The album received four Grammy nominations.

Soundgarden's rhythm section of Ben Shepherd and Matt Cameron started a side project in 1993 called Hater (no relation to the Haters, a California industrial band) with Andrew Wood's brother Brian, ex-Red Dress drummer Gregg Keplinger, and guitarist John McBain (formerly of New Jersey's Monster Magnet). McBain, Cameron and Shepherd also moonlighted in the garage-pop Wellwater Conspiracy, recording four breezy Super Electro singles (the first, "Sandy," was sung in Japanese); McBain also played with the surviving Wood brothers in Devilhead. Kim Thayil joined DJ Jeff Gilbert in Dark Load, recording the 1994 EP *Loading Zone*. Chris Cornell wrote songs for his old idol Alice Cooper. Cornell's siblings Peter, Katy, and Suzy formed a folk-rock band, Inflatable Soule.

Mudhoney signed to Warner Bros. just before Nirvanamania began (Mark Arm said Warner of-

fered more creative control than Sub Pop) and in mid-1992 released *Piece of Cake*, a Conrad Uno-produced gala of guitars, organs, angst and laffs with separate CD and cassette covers (designed by Art Chantry, with neo-expressionist illustrationss by Ed Fotheringham and lettering by old Andy Warhol associate Nathan Gluck). Nirvana opened for Mudhoney on "secret" pre-tour gigs in Bellingham and at Seattle's Crocodile Cafe. A sold-out Crocodile audience stood in awe and listened carefully to every note Nirvana played, foregoing the participatory moshpit ritual.

The video for "Suck You Dry" showed Mudhoney playing a grunge-nostalgia concert in the year 2002 (filmed by Charles Peterson); Bruce Pavitt, Jonathan Poneman and Fotheringham were the only people in the audience. The album sold 200,000 copies, a figure that would have been considered a smash hit the year before. It was followed by the EP *Five Dollar Bob's Mock Cooter Stew* (with a producer credit for "Kurdt Bloch") and a joint EP on Sub Pop with Austin urban-folk artist Jimmie Dale Gilmore.

Some unapologetic hard-rock bands got signed during the 1992 Seattle-band mania: Sweet Water (Adam Czeisler, Dudley Taft, Rich Albrecht, Cole Peterson, Paul K. Uhlir, some of whom were in thrash-punk band SGM and took the punk-metal crossover all the way), and Brad Sinsel's War Babies.

Adam Czeisler: "Rich and Cole got together again, then they got me to sing for them. We were going to just make a demo and send it to the majors, but people started asking us to play. We got to open for Mookie Blaylock and Alice in Chains at the Off Ramp, and later for Alice in Chains at the Paramount. So when Atlantic came to see us, we were playing to really big houses…. Back when we were in SGM I'd missed my high school graduation party to open for Green River at the

Vogue and thought it was the biggest thing we could ever do, even if it was just 200 or so people."

Bands nobody in Seattle seemed to have heard of started getting signed as "Seattle bands." The chief example was Candlebox, a mainstream style hard-rock band fronted by Kevin Martin (who'd sold shoes in the same store with Susan Silver after he moved from Dallas in 1985). The group (with non-relative Bardi Martin, Peter Klett, and Scott Mercado) formed in the fall of 1991, and concentrated on sending tapes to major labels instead of playing locally. That led to a showcase gig in L.A., which led to a contract with Madonna's Maverick label. Maverick turned their self-titled debut CD into a three-million-copy seller by marketing it initially to hard-rock radio stations in the Midwest and Rocky Mountain states, then letting it spread up to the major markets.

Can't lose for winning

Ten and *Nevermind* each sold four million copies in North America in their first year of release; they've each surpassed 10 million worldwide since. Two years before, merely getting signed to a label bigger than Frontier was a major feat. A scene that had once wanted to smash the record industry's stranglehold was now its darling.

Bruce Pavitt *in the Soundgarden video* Motorvision: *"If you live the myth hard enough, if you believe in the story hard enough, then it becomes true. We used to joke about becoming a multinational conglomerate, and hey, we are. We used to*

joke about Nirvana and Soundgarden and Mudhoney becoming arena rock acts, and hey, they are. Fortunately, in the case of those three groups in particular, I think they've managed to maintain their musical integrity. I think that by starting out on an indie label, I think that gave the artists some leverage that they could use in negotiating a major label deal, and all those groups have maintained control over production, which is the key."

The new superstars bought their own houses (the ultimate sign of wealth within the baby-bust generation's diminished expectations). They gathered staffs, entourages, lawyers, and fan clubs, and made only rare local gigs. As partial proof of their rejecting the rock-star mentality, none of the musicians married fashion models and none moved to L.A. (except the Cobains, temporarily).

Seattle became a state of mind, a different alleged paradise than that promoted by the tourist industry. Despite (or perhaps due to) its cynicism toward the American pop-culture industry, the Seattle myth provided an identifiable, salable voice of youthful alienation. Even the drug scandals added to the bands' street (and mall) credibility.

Hypothetical scene by **Nesbitt Bireley** *in* Tower Records Pulse!, *1993: "Hey, two kids—flannel shirts, backward baseball caps, etc. etc.—in a record store fondling a Mother Love Bone reissue like a religious totem. 'This band is, like rilly important,' sez the larger of the two in the cumbersome tone of the pedant. 'These guys are basically Pearl Jam without Eddie [Vedder] and this guy* *here [points at Andrew Wood] OD'd on heroin so he's not in the band anymore. This is where it all started, man.' The smaller of the two nods his head, taking in the information: One died, so that others might live long and prosper."*

Local indie bands made real money on the road.

Tom Price, *Gas Huffer: "Everywhere we went people looked more like Seattle than anybody in Seattle. We started calling it our Thank You Nirvana Tour."*

Ron Garcia, *Gnome, to the* Rocket, *9/92: "We walked into this club, we looked over behind the bar and there's a RKCNDY flyer with our name on it, and Vogue posters…. It was like a little Seattle club in the middle of Des Moines."*

The time was right. Unit sales of recordings had been in decline for years; only the push toward higher-priced CDs kept profits up. With the teenage population starting to rise again after the baby-bust years, marketers and advertisers wanted to define a New Generation that Pepsi and other products could be the choice of. Thanks to Sub Pop's patient efforts selling an aesthetic of impatience, the industry didn't just get a handful of hit bands, it got a readymade mythology surrounding them.

Looks we never looked like

The national fashion media jumped on the myth of a Grunge Look to be marketed as a prepackaged lifestyle, especially after the release of *singles.* Docs, denim shirts, unwashed long hair beneath wool caps, ripped jeans, ripped long johns under miniskirts (for the layered look), and oversize jackets (for the emaciated look) were originally just some of what a bunch of folks wore because it was cheap and practical and they didn't care about looks. Now, New York designers made "designer grunge" that was ugly and downright ridiculous; and, as MTV's Kurt Loder noted, "which nobody who actually wears the stuff could ever afford to buy." The designer chiefly credited with the fad, Perry Ellis employee Marc Jacobs, had followed the New York underground scene for inspiration for several years (and supplied clothes and models for a Sonic Youth video), but had never been to Seattle. The December 1992 *Vogue* magazine ran a "Grunge & Glory" fashion spread with $500-$1,400 outfits by Ralph Lauren and Calvin Klein as worn by New York waif models, all billed as representing a bold new style that had "broken out of the clubs, garages and thrift shops of Seattle." Poneman's accompanying text had nothing to do with the pictures.

Parade, Details, Spin and the *Boston Globe* ran travel articles that promoted "grunge tourism." The Cyclops Cafe appeared in an AT&T commercial inviting Americans to call up their grungy friends back in Seattle ("a place of all-night talks and part-time jobs"); the ad agency tried to save money by telling the restaurant's owners that they just wanted to shoot stills for a stock-photo bank.

The peak of the silliness came when *New York Times* fashion reporter Rick Martin, believing that "all subcultures speak in code," reprinted a "Glossary of Grunge" from the British fashion magazine *Sky International,* supplied by former Sub Pop sales rep Megan Jasper. Her completely fabricated list of terms included *Lamestain* ("uncool person"), *Wack Slacks* ("old ripped jeans"), *Dish* ("desirable guy"), *Swingin' on the Flippity-Flop* ("hanging out"), and *Tom-Tom Club* ("outsiders"). C/Z Records sold "Lamestain" T-shirts capitalizing on the joke.

To locals used to being jaded and fatalistic, Seattle's "discovery" was either a triumph or a cosmic scam. In the so-called Information Age, the media image of Grunge City USA was quite narrow and misleading. Despite real thriving clubs at last, the Seattle scene often failed to live up to the fantasy. Hype-heavy journalists from the U.S., Canada, Britain, Japan, Germany and Italy were disappointed to learn that (1) only a small portion of Seattle alternative bands were grunge; (2) only a small portion of Seattleites listened to grunge; (3) most local clubs, until recently, weren't too appreciative of grunge bands; (4) except for Nirvana, most of these "working class heroes" were middle- and upper-middle-class college boys; and (5) most of these media-appointed voices of teen angst were in their late 20s and early 30s. When Poneman went to New York to appear on *Sassy* editor Jane Pratt's cable talk show, they asked him to lie about his age (really 31).

With Seattle the music industry's flavor of the month, lots of people tried to cash in. Projects in various stages of completion included an aborted TV series that was to have been taped at the Back-

Lexicon of Grunge: Breaking the Code

WACK SLACKS: Old ripped jeans
FUZZ: Heavy wool sweaters
PLATS: Platform shoes
KICKERS: Heavy boots
SWINGIN' ON THE FLIPPITY-FLOP: Hanging out
BOUND-AND-HAGGED: Staying home on Friday or Saturday night
SCORE: Great
HARSH REALM: Bummer
COB NOBBLER: Loser
DISH: Desirable guy
BLOATED, BIG BAG OF BLOATATION: Drunk
LAMESTAIN: Uncool person
TOM-TOM CLUB: Uncool outsiders
ROCK ON: A happy goodbye

Below: Meddaphysical

stage (it was to have been co-hosted by Norman Batley and Angela Mellini, a Seattle-raised *Playboy* model), a concert film called *Hype* by ex-USC film student Doug Pray (mostly with yet-unsigned local bands), and no fewer than four Nirvana gossip books, all by British and New York-based writers. St. Martin's Press slapped a Nirvana subtitle and cover photo onto *Route 666*, critic Gina Arnold's memoir of her charmed life on the alternative-rock guest list that only had two chapters about Nirvana.

The race is on

The record companies and MTV needed a new fad real bad, preferably a fad that would be "rebellious" but could be successfully executed by young white males. Black rap acts had a considerable white crossover audience; for the first time since the start of rock n' roll, white teenagers were buying large quantities of street-credible black music (not white imitations or "tributes," or white-oriented product like Motown). But the industry still needed white celebrities, and most white rap acts were considered jokes by true fans.

John Leland in Newsweek, 2/93: *"So far, the '90s are shaping up as the decade of anger: angry women, angry African-Americans, angry gays, angry taxpayers. For a $7.8 billion music industry run largely by European white males, punk offers anger without guilt."*

The first-tier grunge bands have all gone on record opposing racism. Chris Novoselic, who is of Croatian ancestry, visited the Bosnian battlefronts for a *Spin* article, and mounted a PR campaign and a benefit concert in San Francisco to protest the Yugoslav civil war. He changed his first name to his father's name, Krist.

The early local scene included only two prominent African-Americans, Vogue DJ/booking agent Randy Carter and Showbox promoter Terry Morgan, who still produces shows in assorted venues and has managed several bands including the Posies.

In the late '80s and '90s, a growing handful of black and mixed-race bands played the local club circuit. They included Action Buddie (Todd Goodson, Dirk Jackson, Dan Harris, Peter Dibuuz, and Cameron Robinson; EP: *World Full of Beat*), Mass Hypnosis (with ex-Prudence Dredge backup singer Ava Chakravarti), Six in the Clip (a six-man multiracial rap team, later revised into Prose and Concepts), the hiphop-thrash crossover unit Meddaphysical (with rapper Mark Henderson and punk guitarist Paul Solger), singer Shelley Doty of the progressive-rock revivalists Jambay, and Love Battery member Kevin Whitworth The major labels skipped most of them over, just as they'd skipped over most of our female-led bands. The outside world saw Seattle rock as a bunch of all-white male bands complaining about white male society. A break from that image might have come with the black rock band IMIJ ("Jimi" backwards); featuring Shannon Funchess's "screaming ambience" vocals with the shredding instrumentation of Lonnie King, Cris Omowale, Cedric Ross and David Carpenter. But Capitol signed and dropped the band without releasing anything. The band finally self-released

The In Gods You Lust EP before breaking up at the end of 1994.

IMIJ *self-description in the* Rocket, *12/90: "Post-apocalyptic sound waves equally attacking and caressing the senses."*

Meddaphysical was one of the first acts on Belltown Records, founded at the start of 1993 by Colourbox booker Archie O'Connor (a 24-year-old ex-skate punk from Ann Arbor, Michigan) and manager-promoter Oscar Mraz. Belltown's other releases included CDs by Gary Heffern, James Palmer's punkabilly Bolos (Walkabouts bassist Michael Wells produced their debut *Hello Danger*), Chris Welch's "psycho-folk-novelty" Ottoman Bigwigs, and Monroe's Fur (plus a 45 by their band with Mark Arm, Blood Loss). Mraz and O'Connor used Belltown to generate interest in bands they were managing and/or promoting, not expecting to make a full-time profit from the records themselves. They got Meddaphysical signed to American Recordings at the end of 1993, but the band was dropped without getting a record out. O'Connor and Mraz downplayed their label in 1994 to concentrate on booking; by the end of the year they ran five stages at three venues (the Weathered Wall, the OK Hotel, and the University Sportsbar).

Seven Year Bitch

Heroin claimed another victim in Stefanie Sargent, the 22-year-old guitarist with Seven Year Bitch. She had been on and off the stuff; on the night of June 28, 1992, she took a lot of booze and a little heroin, then passed out; she was found suffocated on her vomit like Hendrix. (Friends insisted that while there was heroin in her system, her death wasn't an overdose.)

The band pulled through, released a CD (*Sick 'Em*) of its work with Sargent, recruited old friend Roisin Dunne (who'd played with Kurt Bloch in a side band called Wild Betty) to move back from L.A. and join them, and continued to play songs of outrage at a failing society, as sung and snarled by Selene Vigil (songs included "In Lust You Trust" and "Dead Men Don't Rape"). After a second C/Z release, the band signed with Atlantic. The band appeared in two films shot locally in mid-1994, the big-studio drama *Mad Love* (starring Drew Barrymore, who became romantically involved with Hole guitarist Eric Erlandson) and the independent *Odyssey* update *Toast with the Gods*. Singer Selene Vigil also had an acting role in *The Year of My Japanese Cousin*, an independent feature by Fastback Lulu Gargiulo's sister Maria.

Hype *review of* **Seven Year Bitch's** *first single, "Loma": "...A whirlwind of blinding grit and power crunch."*

Elizabeth Davis, *Seven Year Bitch bassist, to* Option: *"I think it's sexy. Maybe guys get hardons when they're watching us. Maybe we should pat their crotches and see. If I was a guy, into dominatrixes and stuff, I'd love it."*

Wilum Pugmire *reviewing Seven Year Bitch in the* Rocket, *11/92: "As I looked around at the large number of women attending the show, I felt a curious peace of mind. Before me, earlier on, had been two delightful dykes, young and in love and grooving to the band. I stopped attending hardcore shows years ago because I had grown weary of the pathetic homophobia I had come to witness. In naive youth I came to punk, thinking that at last I had found a crowd of rebels who would accept me as I am, only to see that they were no different from most others I encountered on the streets.... The older I grow, the more I enjoy being a radical queer. Yet I am still a punk. Punk means more to me now than ever before, for it is the only lifestyle wherein I can be completely myself. As I stood among the sublime women at the Weathered Wall, I felt for the first time in eleven years absolutely safe as a gay man in a punk setting."*

It's different for girls

Female bands had been in the scene since its start. They weren't novelties (at least not more than any other bands). They weren't doe-eyed (like the white-chick blues bands), or bubbly sex objects, or cold anti-sex objects.

Girl Trouble drummer **Bon Von Wheelie** *to the Canadian zine* Cryptic Tymes, *9/93: "Eight years ago when I would set up my drums before a show, the soundman would come over and ask me when the drummer was going to show up. Now the*

Below: Sky Cries Mary

LOSER

soundperson (because that's changing, too) doesn't ask.... It's no longer inconceivable that a girl could lift up her frail feminine little arms and pound the shit out of the skins for an hour."

Soozy Bridges, *manager/promoter: "When I was managing My Sister's Machine there was this L.A. publishing attorney, an English woman who kept telling me that the only way I was going to make it in 'the business' was to get in with 'the boys' club,' to be down there playing golf with the big shots.... A year and a half later she was calling me up saying, 'I think we've got to start paying more attention to the new local managers.'"*

As the scene took a more aggressive, *yang* tone, the more female musicians emerged in it. The female performers were often outspoken radicals, particularly the bands and zines associated with the "Riot Grrrl" scene centered in Olympia and Washington, D.C. Riot Grrrl was estimated by *Newsweek* as consisting of maybe 50 self-published zines and 20 bands scattered across North America and England, connected by common mailing lists. Some were obsessed with getting out their personal stories of past abuse and rape; others were concerned with the larger dysfunctional society. Many felt a need to celebrate their girlhood. They wanted to create a "girl" culture of spontaneous fun and high energy, a rightful counterpart/alternative to the "boy" culture that rock n' roll had always been. Some of the Riot Grrrl zines discussed creating a new "girl music" of impassioned self-expression without mainstream notions of "quality control," something different from both macho hard rock and from the somber acoustic poets of '70s "women's music."

Not all the villains decried in the zines were male; the authors were often frustrated with females who didn't act like they felt females ought to (fashion models, corporate rock singers, women who promoted jealousy and competition among other women). Bikini Kill and England's Huggy Bear, the bands most closely associated with the label, both included male musicians.

The Riot Grrrl hype led to a backlash, with initial supporters distancing themselves from the immaturity and self-righteous posturing the media tacked onto the moniker. As Courtney Love told

Melody Maker, "Girl is not menstruating. Girl is non-orgasmic. Girl is bratty. Girl is non-threatening in her clumsiness and incompetence. Girl is most of all young, it is vanity *in extremis*. I have always called myself a girl but I am going to stop now."

Slim Moon: *"Riot Grrrl is a subculture and a political movement, but it's not a specific genre of music. To call bands 'Riot Grrrl bands' is like talking about 'Democrat bands.'"*

Up in Seattle, meanwhile, a new generation of female and coed bands developed a more melodic but still hard-driving ballad rock: 66 Saints, Juned (Dale Balensiefen, Mike Johnson's wife Leslie Hardy, Claudia Groom, Nalini Cheriel), Violent Green (ex-Some Velvet Sidewalk bassist Jenny Olay, Drew Quinian, and ex-Treepeople drummer Wayne Flower), Job (led by black vocalist Jill Cunningham), Lazy Susan (with Kim Virant), and Sybil Vane (with the alternately lilting and belting vocals of April Devereaux; they signed with Island Records on the basis of a demo tape made before they'd played live).

Aside from Riot Grrrl hype, the media grunge myth treated women as little more than fashionable fans, despite the scene's long heritage of female musicians, promoters, club owners and journalists.

Barbara Dollarhide, *manager/publicist: "If I hear one more male chant: 'yeah, girl bands are cool,' as if it's just another fad, I might just have to stuff my spent tampon straight down his throat. I always assumed that as time progressed, so would people. However, over twenty years after the women's movement began terms such as 'fox-core' are still being invented."* ("Foxcore" was coined as a joke by Thurston Moore of Sonic Youth, but the media turned it into a regular label.)

Dead air revisited

KCMU, the station that nurtured the scene for so long, abandoned its commitment to unfettered music. In 1991-92, manager Chris Knab phased in a watered-down format and an authoritarian management system. The hourly programming "wheel" was revised to give more slots for old-hippie music—blues, folk, and "world beat" (foreign-language acts selected for mild American boomer tastes)—and to eliminate anything too noisy. Knab's ostensible goal was to "mainstream" the station, to attract a broad, upscale audience preferred by corporate underwriters and the national public-broadcasting establishment. Knab was advised by KUOW manager Wayne Roth, who wanted to raise donations and corporate underwriting to a point that would qualify the station for federal grants.

In the fall of 1992, most of the volunteer staffers either quit or were fired for criticizing Knab's policies. As the ex-staffers sued the UW and launched the lobbying group CURSE (Censorship Undermines Radio Station Ethics), the station's ratings and donations collapsed. Knab left the station in late 1993 but Roth dug in, insisting that ratings and revenue growth would vindicate the new policy. Only one local promoter, Backstage owner Ed Beeson, continued to support the station (his club now emphasized a similar "adult acoustic" format). In an ominous repeat of the fall of KRAB eight years before, KCMU floundered as management and CURSE bickered about how to save it. By mid-1994, there was a partial settlement in the lawsuit and some of the ex-DJs returned to the station, which backtracked a bit toward its old freeform format.

Many KCMU listeners switched to KGRG ("Today's Rock"), the Green River Community College station in the working-class suburb of Auburn. It offered no "professionalism," few pledge drives, just great music and no mellow filler.

The RKCNDY raid

Thomas O'Neil, one of RKCNDY's co-owners, was arrested in March 1993 for running a million-dollar pot-growing operation in the basements of four rental houses he owned (including one purchased from *Post-Intelligencer* columnist Susan Paynter). The city moved to seize his share of the club, which remained open; O'Neil's partners claimed the club's books were clean and they shouldn't be punished for anything O'Neil may have done on his own. Cops raided the club but found nothing improper. The club was sold to Matt Baker in early 1994.

O'Neil pled guilty to five of the charges against him, taking a 20-month jail sentence. Also charged were O'Neil's brother Kevin (who was convicted) and a resident of one of their houses, Malfunkshun-Satchel-Brad drummer Regan Hagar (whose charges were dropped).

Still more spaces

At the start of 1994, almost two dozen over-21 clubs and bars played assorted flavors of new music at least once a week in Seattle, Tacoma, Olympia and Bellingham; as well as a half dozen dance clubs, one-shot raves in Seattle and Kent, KNDD DJ nights at suburban bars, regular concerts at the Moore and Seattle Center, and occasional parties at COCA. A dozen bars and cafes served as scene hangouts, with good music in the jukebox or the CD player; most notable was Linda's in the old Capitol Hill restaurant space where Jim Rose gave his first local shows, started with an investment from Bruce Pavitt.

New venues popped up seemingly all over town: the Emerald Diner on Lower Queen Anne; the University Sportsbar and Flowers (a veggie restaurant in an old flower shop with the old neon marquee still up) in the U District; the Tractor Tavern in Ballard; Victor's and Captain Cook's on the waterfront, and the Edge (which folded right after being named the *Weekly*'s favorite club), India Taj and Catwalk in Pioneer Square.

The Belltown Club, which experimented with a number of dance formats in competition with larger and more established clubs, held a gangsta-rap DJ night in April 1992. Some patrons and some hangers-on got into an argument in the parking lot after closing time; somebody fired some shots into the air (no injuries); neighborhood advocates immediately got the place shut down. A few blocks away, a few months before, there had been a fatal shooting outside a meatmarket bar after two men argued over a woman. That bar, with a white upscale clientele, remained open with no harassment.

Tacoma finally got regular venues, bands, and zines after years of attempts; most notably the Red Roof Pub, Victory Club and new Central Tavern.

"Love Song to Barbara Dollarhide"

THE BLOOD OF THE LAMB BAND
THE BARRETTS
FRI. JUNE 25
EMERALD DINER
105 W MERCER

Left: Danger Gens (AKA Maxi Badd)

Tacoma also had a professional music press with *Pandemonium* and the short-lived *Smutch*.

Local bands were showcased on KTZZ's *Northwest Rock* (Frank Harlan's all-local successor to *Bombshelter Videos*) and *The Spud Goodman Show*. New Seattle zines included *Thorozine*, *Patchwerk Press*, *10 Things Jesus Wants You to Know*, *Flavor* (hip-hop), *Pool Dust* (garage punk and skateboarding), and *DystOpinion*.

The Paramount and Moore theaters were bought by a non-profit group launched by Microsoft executive Ida Cole; the Paramount was closed and remodeled into a home for touring musicals.

Former Paramount managers Buddy Williams and Ed Shocker built Under the Rail, a giant Belltown bar in an old warehouse. It opened at the start of 1993 for touring acts once or twice a week, including metal acts that "alternative" acts had shoved out of the big time. It was also the only black-owned live club in town, booking many of the '70s-'80s soul acts that hiphop had shoved out of the big time. It was almost a nostalgia piece for the corporate-music aesthetic, staffed by burly guys from L.A. sporting tuxedos and "all access" patches and boasting that they were going to show this town how to run things.

Sit & Spin, launched by Michael Rose and Lisa Bonney in October 1993, was a concept designed to generate income all day: a cafe-performance space-laundromat on the site of Vic Meyers's old jazz club.

Ex-Crocodile Cafe employees Jerry Everard, Erik Shirley and Craig Graham went on their own at the start of 1994 and built Moe's Mo' Roc'n Cafe, a big bar-restaurant with a 150-capacity music room in a former Salvation Army alcolohic rehab center on Capitol Hill. The bar section had mementos from the Jim Rose Circus Sideshow; all three rooms (bar, band, restaurant) featured conceptual circus-related art by Friese Undine. Moe's quickly rivalled the Crocodile as the top spot to see the top local and touring bands.

When there was no place else to play, bands still played at house parties. On any given weekend night, bands could be heard grinding away for friends and loved ones in a score of basements and living rooms (thrashing, drinking, screaming and running around naked until the cops show up), and at another dozen rehearsal spaces. There also remained an ever-changing line-up of private after-hours clubs and speakeasies.

Inner and other experiences

The ethereal-psychedelic Sky Cries Mary evolved as founder Roderick gathered a new line-up with a lusher sound. The new group included lilting singer Anisa Romero (Roderick's wife), ex-Fags member Ben Ireland on percussion, sample curator DJ Fallout, bassist Joe Howard (later in the Posies), guitarist Marc Olsen (who left for Sage), and former Patti Smith Group guitarist Ivan Kral. Photographer Cam Garrett played guitar at its first gigs.

Roderick and Garrett used a super 8 film camera to make a video for the unsigned group's mood piece "Moon Dream Meadow Allegory" (named after the initials of one of Roderick's favorite chemicals), showing band members at a hot spring wearing only mud. Roderick sent the video and a package of other material to Gordon Raphael, who'd moved to L.A. after his New York misadventure and was working for ex-Gang of Four member Dave Allen's World Domination Records (distributed by Capitol). Raphael helped get the band signed, moved back to Seattle, and joined the band as keyboardist, replacing Penta Swanson's husband Carlo Altomari when that couple moved to Prague. Sky Cries Mary issued the EP *Exit at the Axis* and the album *A Return to the Inner Experience* before Capitol severed its ties with World Domination. The band planned a new CD for independent release in 1994, *This Timeless Turning*, which Raphael described as "even more spacy and out of control." Howard left to become Posies bassist #4; he and Marc Olsen also played in Dave Allen's side band, the Elastic Purejoy (no relation to the former Seattle band Pure Joy). Ben Ireland found time for a couple of side bands, the industrial-noise Bughead (with Raphael and Rich Riggins) and the garage-punk Wasters (with DJ Fallout, Mike Davidson, and Garrett).

Folk angst

The urban folk-rock bands that once played the Central and Squid Row alongside the punks now found themselves scrambling for respect. They found it at Germany's Glitterhouse Records, Sub Pop's first foreign licensee (and its partner in the Sub Pop Europe joint venture), which apparently couldn't get enough Seattle acts. Under the Sub Pop Europe imprint, Glitterhouse exclusively released three CDs by the Walkabouts; Glitterhouse directly signed progressive-folk soloists Terry Lee Hale and Larry Barrett and roots-rock band Kitchen Radio, and was negotiating with the Blood of the Lamb Band and Somebody's Daughter before those groups broke up. These deals helped the artists get professional CDs out and got them choice spots on the European music-festival circuit, but didn't help them get known on their home continent.

Local entrepreneurs Jeff Stuhmer and Tony Hoyt tried to do something about that by starting a label devoted to the lighter side of local pop, called simply Bands We Like. It issued the CD compilation *Shotgun Barbeque*, with Blood of the Lamb, Barrett, the Purdins, the Picketts, Gary Heffern, Fear the Cow, (whose singer, Texas native Derek Horton, later formed the cowboy-parody band Johnny Webelo), Red Eye Special and the Stumpy Joe spinoff Mark & John.

Two older-generation folk combos did achieve domestic deals: the cowgirl-kitsch Ranch Romance on the folk indie Sugar Hill (no relation to the late-'70s rap label Sugarhill), and Charlie Murphy and Jami Sieber's political-folk group Rumors of the Big Wave on a Warner affiliate.

In Utero

With success came the inevitable charges of selling out, and bands' attempts to refute those charges. Members of Nirvana were quoted in mid-1992 as saying they wanted to follow *Nevermind* with a real "punk record."

DGC released *Incesticide* (reported working titles included *Cash Cows*, *Filler* and *Throwaways*) in late 1992. It was a collection with old Sub Pop single tracks ("Sliver," "Dive"), a *Bleach* outtake ("Big Long Now"), BBC Radio performances (including Devo's "Turnaround"), five songs from the band's original demos with Dale Crover, and one track from Steve Fisk's *Blew* session ("Stain"). The group released "Oh, the Guilt" on a Touch and Go split single with the Jesus Lizard. Cobain created an ambient guitar track for William Burroughs's spoken-word record *The Priest They Called Him*, and produced six cuts for the Melvins' major-label debut *Houdini*. Dave Grohl dubbed drum parts for the Beatles bio-film *Backbeat*. Julia Sweeney and Jim Emerson wrote a part for Nirvana in the screenplay for *It's Pat*, but the band was busy and the film role was rewritten for the California band Ween.

Finally, in mid-1993 the band recorded its third real album, *In Utero* (reported working titles included *Verse Chorus Verse* and *I Hate Myself and I Want to Die*) in Chicago, with Steve Albini in the

Below: Mia Zapata, R.I.P.

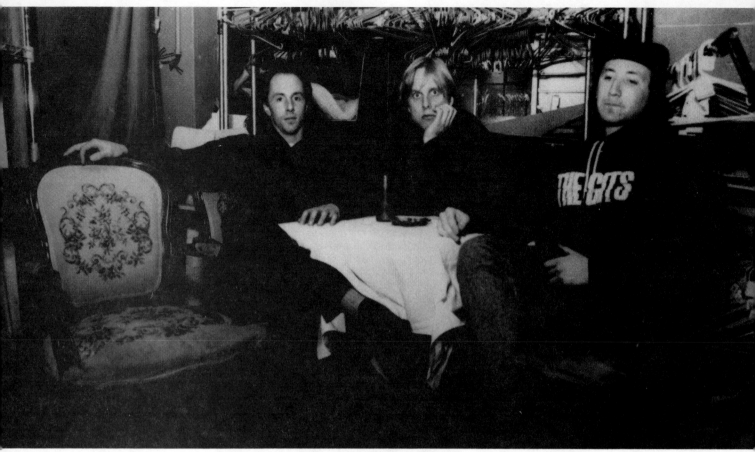

The Gits

booth. According to rumors spread by the *Chicago Tribune*, DGC didn't want to release Albini's hard-driving document of pure noise, with song titles such as "Rape Me," "Heart-Shaped Box" (named after Courtney Love's collection of valentine candy boxes), "Pennyroyal Tea" (after a homeopathic abortion aid) and "Frances Farmer Will Have Her Revenge on Seattle." (Another provocateively-titled song, "Moist Vagina," was saved for a CD-single backing track, where it was listed only as "MV.") The band and DGC released a statement claiming there was no dispute; two songs were being remixed, with the band's approval. Albini wouldn't comment on the Nirvana issue directly, but told *Newsweek* that bands should learn what to expect from the industry:

"The labels have been hiring hip, young people to lull the bands into being comfortable with the big, faceless record company. That way, the band doesn't think, 'Hey, Geffen—this is the company that sued Neil Young! This is the company that gave us Nelson!'"

The result of all the hoopla was a disc harsher than *Nevermind* and even harsher in some ways than *Bleach*, yet slower and steadier, more a sustained growl than a series of roars. With no further need to dress his anger in pop-rock hooks, Cobain's music more fully matched the rage and despair of his words. He delivered immoderate statements at moderate tempos. Despite his assertion to *Spin* that he hoped *In Utero* would "inspire women to pick up guitars and start bands," it was a very mascunine work that appropriated feminist righteousness in much the same way other liberal artists ap-propriated black and gay cultures. The record's power came from enveloping of those themes within robust masculine passion.

It premiered on the *Billboard* album chart at #1 in its first week of release, and sold 1.5 million copies by the end of the year. It topped the *Rolling Stone* critics' poll as Best Album and Best Band (Pearl Jam won as Artist of the Year, Best Male Singer and Best Album Cover; Alice in Chains won as Best Metal Band).

K mart and Wal-Mart refused to carry *In Utero*, the latter chain claiming "lack of customer demand" but more likely disliking the Cobain-designed cover: on the front, a clear plastic female figure revealing organs and muscles; on the back, fetuses in a bed of flowers, surrounded by neo-pagan symbols. (DGC issued a censored cover six months later, with "Rape Me" billed as "Waif Me"). More surrealist imagery showed up in Dutch director Anton Corbijn's "Heart Shaped Box" video: A heavy woman in a muscles-and-organs body suit and wings reaching for plastic fetuses on a tree, a little girl in a white-witch costume that turns black in a lake of ink, an emaciated guy with a Victorian Santa beard climbing onto a cross. Corbijn achieved a look of oversaturated color by filming in black and white and having the whole thing computer-colorized.

Kurt Cobain to Rolling Stone, *1/94:* "*For a few years in Seattle it was the Summer of Love, and it was so great. To be able to just jump out on top of the crowd with my guitar and be held up and pushed to the back of the room, and then brought* back with no harm done to me—it was a celebration of something that no one could put their finger on. But once it got into the mainstream, it was over. I'm just tired of being embarrassed by it. I'm beyond that."

Along with the album came the now-usual assortment of outtakes, CD single backing tracks and compilation tracks, including "Verse Chorus Verse" on the AIDS benefit *No Alternative* and "I Hate Myself and I Want to Die" on the MTV *Beavis and Butt-head Experience* CD.

*Children's entertainer **Fred Rogers** to USA Today on "I Hate Myself and I Want to Die": "Is that supposed to be funny or is it a cry for help?"*

Hole numbers

Love re-formed her band Hole after moving here; she brought guitarist Eric Erlandson up with her and added bassist Kristen Pfaff (from Minneapolis's Janitor Joe) and ex-Kill Sybil drummer Patty Schemel. Hole signed with DGC Records after a voracious bidding war; the label then took its time on releasing anything by the group, finally scheduling the CD *Live Through This* for April 1994. It proved a vindication of Love's talent and determination: a disc of melodic angry pop, slick yet consistently edgy, highlighted by the beauty-queen exposé "Miss World" and the Riot Grrrl backlash rant "Rock Star."

In June 1993 Cobain was arrested on "investigation of domestic violence" at his home on Lake Washington, after neighbors made complaints about his loud practicing in his garage. According to the police record, Love told officers they'd been frustrated when their new juicer wouldn't work properly, and also had argued about Kurt's new gun collection. She threw a glass of juice at him, they pushed each other around, then he pushed her to the floor and allegedly choked her. He was released on bail without charges being filed. Love told the *Post-Intelligencer* that they'd not maliciously fought, just playfully roughhoused: "My husband's a feminist. He's nonviolent. We get along great…I'm this normal girl. We live on the lake. We're just like two kids. We both have these punk-rock bands. We drive a Volvo and a Dart." She added that she'd had no intention of filing domestic-violence charges, but that the cops still insisted on bringing him in with them.

Hole performed a scheduled gig at the Off Ramp the same day that the arrest was made public. The group cooked, but Love stumbled some of her lines, and about halfway into the set stopped playing guitar. She was able to joke about her media image: "This next song's about domestic violence—not!"

Not revealed at the time was another incident back in May. Love had called 911 to report that Cobain had apparently overdosed on heroin. He was sent to Harborview Medical Center, where he came to and was released.

LOSER

The backlash; the backlash against the backlash

With the local Endfest II (co-starring Hammerbox) and Grungefest I (starring Mudhoney), and the touring Lollapalooza '93 (co-starring Alice in Chains) set for the summer, some local wags predicted that 1993 would be the Summer of Hate. Other wags said (hoped?) that it would all collapse any day now, that North Carolina or Oregon or Nova Scotia would become the "Next Seattle" and we could go back to our familiar defeatist attitudes, out of the national spotlight. What happened instead was an influx of young tourists from Europe, Japan and the U.S., pounding the downtown streets in their new Doc Martens and searching upscale-oriented guidebooks in vain to find clubs the guidebook writers hadn't heard of.

Duff McKagan started asserting his Seattle roots in interviews promoting his first solo album. He moved back here and even drummed for the encore of a Fastbacks show at the Crocodile, sporting the prettiest hair and only silk scarf in the building. Early 1995 rumors spoke of McKagan teaming up with Bruce Fairweather to form a new 10 Minute Warning.

Tess Lotta, Maxi Badd/Danger Gens bassist, to the Vancouver zine Geezuz: "When I first got here (from L.A.), this city's scene was very supportive. Everyone came to each other's shows—that's all you ever saw at shows, other musicians. You'd loan each other equipment. What's happened now is that everyone's thinking has gone through a metamorphosis from 'we are musicians creating music' to 'we are musicians,' from 'we' as a community to 'I.' And people here now equate their success with money, getting on a label, who's seeing them, what rag they're in.... This town has been fuckin' brainwashed by magazines and media so they think they're unsuccessful unless they're getting 'mawneee' or they're on a 'laaaay-bulll' or getting airplay, and people are buying in-

**Below:
Layne Staley of
Alice In Chains**

Built to Spill

Red Rocket

to it. *Not everyone; there are still pockets of really cool people with old community ideals and haven't been brainwashed by what this big machine has done to Seattle—and it's done it.... Everyone's trompin' over each other 'cause they've bought into this idea of success instead of just playing.... I can't wait 'til the hype dies down—back to the bare bones—when we're left with just the real thing."*

Some music lovers hoped grunge would die and soon, so a greater diversity of the city's bands could get the attention they deserved. The chart failure of major-label debuts by Sky Cries Mary and Hammerbox underscored the need felt by many locals to overthrow the "Seattle Sound" stereotype. Saying what now was referred to as "the G-Word" in Seattle instantly identified the speaker as an ill-informed wannabe from the outside. Like Dr. Seuss's Sneetches rushing to the Star-Off Machine, locals *en masse* mended their jeans and cut their hair to disassociate themselves from the hype.

From the summer of 1992 on, virtually *every* press review or profile of any local band used the terms "not grunge," "an alternative to grunge," or "not a typical Seattle band." The new Red Rocket label promoted the techno-rave band Roulade with the slogan "95% Grunge-Free Seattle Dance Music." Industrial bands formed a booking collective, the Northwest Elektro-Industrial Coalition (NEC), to persuade the now-successful clubs to book them; its flyers expressed a sense of romantic martyrdom for bands who didn't conform to yesterday's alternative. Sir Mix-A-Lot used "No Grunge" in the subti-

tle for a compilation of rappers on his Rhyme Cartel label, *Seattle: The Dark Side.*

Eddie Vedder *to* Guitar World, *6/92: "We're all really sick of the whole Seattle Scene thing, and I don't think it's something anybody asked for. It's nothing Soundgarden asked for and it's certainly not something that we asked for. It's rare and cool and something to be proud of. Too bad they put it on* Entertainment Tonight *and embarrassed us all."*

Steven Blush *in* Paper, *5/93: "From Marc Jacobs's laughable 'something grungy, something new' vibe, to Christian Francis Roth's 'It's the idea of looking like you don't really care' pitch, to even J. Crew's mail order weekend grunge uniform, what these pretenders don't get is that the most* uncool *thing in rock right now is Pearl Jam. Now that the mall rats have been invited in, there's a huge grunge backlash brewing; and for those caught in the crossfire, it'll be harsher than a stage-diving combat boot to the head."*

Mark Lanegan *to* Option: *"I've been ridiculed by people for wearing a flannel shirt. But, fuck it, I'm not going to stop wearing something I've worn for 27 years 'cause someone's going to say we're part of some fashion thing…"*

Jack Endino *to the* Times, *4/92: "We were all very happy. Everyone was doing their thing. We were all surviving. The original sense of the Seattle scene as an innocent thing, people just making* a sound they wanted to make, ended around 1989. Bands got so big it changed things. Sub Pop spent more than they needed to. A bunch of bands jumped ship. And as recently as a year ago, Sub Pop was doing very badly. I was touring with Skin Yard, trying to get established, and actually we didn't do too bad. Then the Nirvana thing happened and basically changed everything."

Portland indie Elemental Records put out a compilation CD of white-funk (Jumbalassy, Idaho's Black Happy) and dance bands (including the Tiny Hat Orchestra, an 11-piece ska-revival act from Bellingham with a full horn section and mournful-clownish singer Rudy Yuly) under the name *Northwest Ungrunge*. Dance bars like the Fenix Underground (co-owned by *Northern Exposure* costar John Corbett) promoted fratboy funk and reggae as the latest thing in mindless safe entertainment (including Mo'Lasses, co-founded by Malfunkshun vet Regan Hagar, and Portland's Crazy 8's and Sweaty Nipples). The Fenix became the hub of a dance-bar circuit whose spokes included the Swan Cafe in Pioneer Square and Lox Stock & Bagel in the U District, booking a variety of black dance music performed by mostly-white bands: reggae, ska and Afropop as well as homeboy-wannabes.

Larry Rosen in Pandemonium *on the white-funk fad:* "I went to a party in Bellevue and ran into a couple of guys I used to know back when everyone wore volleyball shirts and pretended they lived in California. These guys walked into the party with stocking caps, enormous shorts and forty-once bottles of St. Ides in paper bags.... Look around every day and you will see packs of rich white boys all dressed like Dr. Dre. Try to talk to them. They even sound like Dr. Dre. They may even break into an impromptu rap."

Sub Pop USA

Jonathan Poneman and Bruce Pavitt won the annual Joel Webber Award for excellence in music and business at the 1992 New Music Seminar in New York, while Sub Pop retreated from the bidding wars for Seattle bands. Poneman claimed in *Billboard* that the city's good bands were all taken; he could have added that they'd been taken either by the majors or by upstart indies with less overhead. Sub Pop broke with EMI-Caroline in the fall of 1993; the label wanted to move to a more effective distributor, and signed with Time Warner's 50-percent-owned ADA. In mid-1994 the label resumed distributing other local labels' releases (K, Super Electro, Up, Flydaddy). At the end of 1994, Time Warner bought a 49 percent stake in Sub Pop for a reputed $20 million.

With TAD and Love Battery splitting for major-affiliated labels, the label repositioned itself back toward Pavitt's first love, independent music from all over. The label's 1993-94 roster included Portland's Sprinkler, Pond, Spinanes and Hazel, Vancouver's Zumpano, Dallas's Reverend Horton Heat, Cincinnati's Afghan Whigs, Washington, D.C.'s Velocity Girl, Amherst, Massachusetts's Sebadoh, Detroit's Big Chief, Rhode Island's Six Finger Satellite and Combustible Edison, Japan's Supersnazz, and England's Thee Headcoats, as well as the local Fastbacks, Earth, Supersuckers, and Sunny Day Real Estate plus one-offs by Mark Lanegan and ambient-rockers Jessamine. The label released a one-shot 45 by neo-punkers Sick and Wrong (whose two female singers wore strap-on dildos and sometimes little else) that led to the band's appearance in a grunge-hype documentary on Britain's Channel 4 Television.

The Dwarves tried to pump their hype with a

Below: Sunny Day Real Estate

The Halobenders

THE GITS

ENTER: THE CONQUERING CHICKEN

7 YEAR BITCH

¡Viva Zapata!

DaNgeR GeNs
life BeTWeen CigARettes

faked announcement that their guitarist, known as "Hewhocannotbenamed," had died in a bar fight shortly before the release of the band's second CD. Sub Pop learned of the fraud and dropped the band. The label would accept a cover with naked women in blood, but actual death was beyond its boundary of taste. The band broke up; Danny Bland returned to Seattle to manage his old pals the Supersuckers.

Viva Zapata!

Less than two weeks after the Dwarves incident, Gits singer-lyricist Mia Zapata left a group of friends at the Comet Tavern; they'd gathered to mark the one-year anniversary of Stefanie Sargent's death. She left the bar for a friend's apartment a block away, then left there at 2 a.m. Zapata, 27, was found at 3:20 a.m., strangled, in an alley two miles away. No suspects were known, even a year later.

On stage, Zapata had given a powerful straight-ahead re-creation of the early punk spirit: no lowlife wallowing, no image hype, just healthy defiance. Off stage, Zapata could be extremely shy, sometimes slipping away to the band's van right after shows. She was a poet, a painter (often depicting her distant ancestor, Mexican revolutionary Emiliano Zapata) and an advocate for women's rights. She'd scheduled to finish vocals on the Gits' second CD, *Enter: The Conquering Chicken*, and had booked gigs in New York and Europe.

Pete Sheehy in the Stranger, 1/94: "Perhaps the most insightful and poetic lyricist in all of punk rock, Mia wrote songs about the pain and frustra-

tion of trying to live a life true to oneself without being selfish."

*From the **Gits** song "Second Skin": "I need a second skin/Something to hold me tough/Can't do it on my own/Sometimes I just need a little more help/I've got that change to give every drop that's left in me."*

The day after her death was made public, over 300 friends of the band gathered for a wake at the Weathered Wall. The hastily-printed poster for the wake was headlined "Viva Zapata!" Over 600 attended a benefit concert at RKCNDY the next week; Love Battery, Maxi Badd, D.C. Beggars and Sage played to support a reward fund for information on the case. The other Gits announced they wouldn't continue without her, beyond finishing the record; they later changed their minds and (with Joe Spleen on vocals and Julian Gibson from D.C. Beggars added on guitar) performed gigs under the names Spear and Magic Helmet (from a Gits song inspired by a Bugs Bunny cartoon) and the Dancing French Liberals of '48. Gary Heffern and Carrie Akre made a tribute single, "The Beauty of the Little Things in Life." Seven Year Bitch named its second album *Viva Zapata!* in her honor. Danger Gens devoted most of its first full-length album, *Life Between Cigarettes*, to songs about the killing and about violence in general. Joan Jett included a song and video dedicated to Zapata, "Go Home," on her 1994 album *Pure and Simple* (which also included several songs co-written by Kathleen Hanna of Bikini Kill; Jett produced BK's

45 "This Is New Radio.") Jett toured with the Dancing French Liberals in 1995 as Evil Stig ("Gits Live" backwards).

The house of House

Zapata's band, like Sargent's, was signed to C/Z Records. The dual tragedies marred a year of breakthrough growth for the label. Daniel House and his promo honcho Tim Cook scored a succession of underground successes by Alcohol Funnycar; Loren Evans and David Bond's Gnome (described by bassist Ron Garcia as "beach blanket bubble-grunge for the '90s...like warm, fuzzy slippers on a cold marble floor"); Tacoma punk/poppers My Name; hardcore vets Greg Anderson and Brian Kraft's Engine Kid; the Iowa-born retro-metal Voodoo Gearshift; Sara DeBell's *Grunge Lite*; Porn Orchard (not from Port Orchard, Wash. but Athens, Ga.); Calgary's Huevos Rancheros; and Idaho-formed popsters Dirt Fishermen (with the harmonies of Gina Gregerson and K.T. Shanafelt; typical lyric: "Cops Like Girls Who Plant Red Flowers").

C/Z promo copy for Voodoo Gearshift: "...V.G.'s sound could best be described as a large weight falling into a 100 gallon bucket of that goo you find in lava lamps, but not before it crashes through at least a couple of window panes balanced precariously on top of the bucket—heavy, melodic and loud."

Brian Willis in the UW Daily on Engine Kid: "What starts out slowly, ends with a clash of sounds that is revved up and up until you think they are going to blow a fuse. One minute accelerating, the next applying the brakes, they hold you firmly in their clutches. They reach highs and lows within each song."

Gina Gregerson, Dirt Fishermen guitarist: "We would love to be accused of being 'punk as fuck,' but I think the best label we can hope to be stuck with is 'pop as fuck.'"

Sara DeBell on the meaning of Grunge Lite: "Why did I do this? Because every authentic artistic and hormonal expression I've ever seen in my life has been, often improbably, bled dry and turned into an advertisement for unnecessary crap. So I join with Seattle artists in celebrating 'fuck you' in the face of abject hopelessness. This IS nevermind. It IS touch me I'm sick. It IS my denial. It's just a sick idea, and if you have to ask why, don't ask."

By mid-1992, House and his small staff were putting out an average of an album a month, plus scattered singles and EPs. But he faced cash-flow problems resulting from the distribution problems that had helped kill Rough Trade and other indies. In February 1994, just as Silkworm's *In the West* was coming out, House laid off Cook and three other staffers. Cook formed the El Recordo label, issuing Silkworm's next album *Libertine*. Sony made offers to take over C/Z's distribution or even buy the company. House turned down Sony's overtures, but over the course of the year most of C/Z's bands moved to other labels or broke up. By early 1995 House had laid off most of the rest of his staff and moved the company into his basement.

When Hammerbox left for A&M, C/Z got a sublicense to put out a vinyl edition of the band's CD *Numb*. Hammerbox singer Carrie Akre's brother Eric drummed for the Boise punk band Christ on a Crutch and then became the third successive drum-

Below: Team Dresch

mer in Treepeople, a melodic pop-punk group that evolved in 1988 from the Boise punk band State of Confusion; that group's ever-changing lineups included Scott Schmaljohn, Doug Martsch, Pat Brown, John Polle, Tony Reed and Eric Carnell. With Steve Fisk producing, Treepeople made the self-released EP *Time Whore* and the album *Guilt, Regret, Embarrasment* (released by Arizona's Toxic Shock). A *Stranger* review described the Treepeople sound as "transcending punk's one-dimensional posturing" thanks to "Martsch's plaintive, sometimes strident songwriting" and his "guitar swirling with Schmaljohn." The group moved to C/Z for the albums *Something Vicious for Tomorrow*, *Just Kidding* and *Actual Reenactment*, the latter recorded after Pat Brown and Doug Martsch went back to Boise. There, Martsch began the "snide rock" Built to Spill, recording the noise-ballad masterpiece *Ultimate Alternative Wavers* for C/Z and the follow-up *There's Nothing Wrong With Love* for ex-*Rocket* writer Chris Takino's Up label; he also recorded with Calvin Johnson as the Halo Benders. During production of the last Treepeople record, Schmaljohn and Polle followed Martsch back to Boise and formed Stuntman.

Former Christ on a Crutch bassist Nate Mendel started the wall-of-sound band Sunny Day Real Estate (with Jeremy Enigk, Dan Hoerner, and William Goldsmith), making two 45s on their label One Day I Stopped Breathing before signing with Sub Pop. The *Rocket* called SDRE "the best new band of 1994 and one of the most iconoclastic." When their Sub Pop debut *Diary* came out they refused to give interviews or to tour in California (they backed off from the latter demand). They appeared on the syndicated *Jon Stewart Show* and started public petitions to persuade MTV to play their video "Seven." The band's future became cloudy at the start of 1995, after singer Enigk "found religion" and began to question his commitment to the commercial music business. Mendel and Goldsmith reportedly made plans in 1995 to perform with Dave Grohl and Pat Smear as the Foo Fighters (named after a 1940s term for UFOs), supporting Grohl's solo recording project of the same name. (Krist Novoselic formed his own new band at the same time, Sweet 75.)

Adam Tepedelen in the *Rocket* on *Sunny Day Real Estate's* *Diary*: "...A nearly hour-long epiphany of bittersweet, two-guitar thick, passionate rock.... The songs are long (only one is less than four minutes and most are closer to five) and filled with quiet twists and expressive turns. They weave a complex forest of contrasting musical energy that is as enthralling as it is intimidating."

Eric Akre also drummed for Tammy Watson and Dale Balensiefen's fun-punk Kill Sybil (originally just Sybil, before a disco queen of the same name showed up). He replaced Patty Schemel, who joined the re-formed Hole. (Schemel had previously been in the Doll Squad, who'd appeared with Cri-

sis Party and Jim Rose in a cheap shot-on-video movie spoof, *The Rock n' Roll Mobster Girls*.) Kill Sybil recorded a self-titled album for eMpTy in 1993, then broke up. Watson then formed the Executioners with Ian Dickson and Robin Peringer; Balensiefen and Leslie Hardy ended up in pop-balladeers Juned, with Claudia Groom from My Diva and Nalini Cheriel from Eugene's Adickdid.

Another Adickdid member, Kaia Wilson, joined guitarist Donna Dresch (who'd briefly played guitar for Van Conner in Screaming Trees) in a Portland all-lesbian punk band, Team Dresch (also with Jody Bleyle, concurrently in the hard-acoustic-pop trio Hazel). Its first album was co-released by Dresch's Chainsaw label and Bleyle's label Candy-Ass, the latter named after an insult Courtney Love once made against K's Candice Pedersen. Team Dresch became part of the "homocore" sub-scene of gay/lesbian punks, whose other regional members included the male Olympia band Mukilteo Fairies (a pun on the Mukilteo ferry dock near Everett).

Treepeople profile in Alternative Press: "...One can tell Treepeople are very smart. Behind those beards, thick glasses and stocking caps, they don't have to fake angst. They're from Boise and their lives really do suck."

Review in Urban Spelunker: "...In live performance, Kill Sybil has two gears: frightfully sloppy and delightfully sloppy."

Tammy Watson: "I've gotten fan letters from 14- and 15-year-old girls and boys who said that without punk records they'd have no friends, but now they have their own thing. I tell them, 'right on!'... We were at a picnic with some people from the Fastbacks, Mudhoney and some of the other local bands. When we tried to choose sides for a volleyball game, everybody said they'd been the people who were picked last for sports in their schools: the four-eyed computer nerds or the butch gals. It's a whole network of misfits who've made something for themselves."

An even greater number, and variety, of local acts were released on a crop of indie labels including eMpTy (Sicko, Arizona transplants Earl's Family Bombers and the Putters, Spokane's Fumes, Portland's Crackerbash), Sounds of Seattle (slop thrashers Dumt), 3:23 (compilations curated by Art Institute of Seattle students, advised by Tom Dyer), New Rage (Stymie), Carving Knife (Monster Truck Driver), Meat (Tsunami, the Fuckers, Treehouse, Big Satan Inc.), Insight (the *Seattle Women in Rock* and *Seattle Music Scene* compilations), Terry Morgan's Sirius (Peace Love and Guitars), Up (Built to Spill spinoff band Butterfly Train), IFA (neo-thrashers Zeke and Texass), Rob Middleton's Y label (Softy, Chet, Spike, Job, Flake), Crunch Melody (Danger Gens), Wallace Hargrave's Estate (Rent-A-Wally, the Wasters, the *Designer Drug* compilation), Ivy (Diamond Fist Werny, Faith and Disease),

the Issaquah-based Regal Select (the *Puget Power* compilation EPs), Tacoma's Wrecking Ball (Deflowers) and Collective Fruit (the *South End All-Stars* compilation), Estrus (Fall-Outs, Superchargers, Spokane's Makers), and Kill Rock Stars (girl-punk duo Heavens to Betsy, boy-noise bands Unwound and KARP, the latter described in the zine *10 Things* as "hilarious and fun noise"). One Kill Rock Stars act, Boston-raised acoustic soloist Mary Lou Lord, broke with the label's indie-rock ideology and signed a publishing contract (but not a recording contract) with BMG Music.

Back to the garage

Seattle's recording studios (including Egg, Avast, Word of Mouth, Bad Animals, Hanzsek, Laundry Room, House of Leisure, London Bridge, and the Music Source) were booked with bands that had made the majors and bands that wanted to. The latter included dozens of unimaginative combos that tried to copy the successful Seattle bands.

Johnny Rubato: "I had a studio on Queen Anne Hill for about a year. It was making money, but it wasn't any fun. We kept getting these bands that just wanted to be grunge. In the old days the scene was pure because people wanted to make music they liked. Now there are all these bands coming up here just trying to get a contract."

But not all the new Northwest bands slavishly pursued big bucks. A new generation of garage bands started showing up throughout the state. These bands explored everything from power surf instrumentals to parodies of '60s country music to new wave nostalgia.

Dave Crider of Bellingham's Estrus Records gathered some 30 new underground bands for each of his annual Garageshock Festivals, starting in May 1992. The bands came from Washington small towns, from across the country, and from Japan (where old Northwest bands like the Ventures were reissued on CD box sets). Unlike the International Pop Underground convention, Garageshock had no overt political-economic agenda and permitted major label reps to attend (few did). Fun, self-expression, and beer were the convention's priorities.

One of the top bands at both Garageshocks was Gravel, a neo-acid-pop combo from Anacortes with ex-Pounding Serfs Bryan Elliot and Dale Robinson plus guitarist Rich Papritz and drummer Bob Vaux. Singer-lyricist Elliot added a moody, mournful side to the band's aggressive sound. Bassist Robinson, the first wheelchair-based musician in a local rock band, rocked on stage with the best of them.

Bob Vaux to Pandemonium *on the power of negative music, 12/93: "Expressing darkness can be an empowering feeling. Instead of letting it drag you down, you can deal with what's bothering you. It's a release. That's just the way Bryan is—there's always something chasing him around."*

Matt Cameron to Spin, *9/92: "I still have a lot of hope for younger musicians around here. They seem somewhat pissed off by what's going on right now (politically), and hopefully that'll add to the desire not to follow any formula and go for a big record contract. Just try to make that music or that art or whatever—totally stand up to what's going on right now."*

Chris Crass, Rockinghams: "It was very hard to come back and start over from the ground up after being in the Muffs, who were one of the top L.A.

Mudhoney at the I.O.O.F. CURSE benefit

club bands. I'm now playing with all these bad bands, with all these bad names. It's like all the bands here that had it in them got picked up by the labels already."

Scott McCaughey: *"There are still a lot of people making great music here, in a wide variety of forms. It's still growing."*

Douglas Mays: *"People say there are too many clubs now, that they can't all attract enough business. I say they could all be doing much better if they became more professional. Each club should have its own identity—I don't mean one narrowly-defined kind of music, but a personality or head space. The club bookers should work as live A&R reps, putting the right bands in the right shows and promoting them right. They should breed bands, work to build their popularity. They need to book bands that complement each other; if you have four bands that are too different, you bring in fewer people than you would if you had just one of those bands.... Seattle now has more different kinds of good bands, and more studios per capita, than maybe any other city in America. We've always had more people going to shows—I used to study Billboard's tour reports in the early '80s, and a lot of bands made more money in Seattle than at any other stop. We still need a pressing plant, but we have just about all the other elements to become an industry city. We should be placing tourist ads in national magazines inviting people to visit the capital of rock music."*

Kurt Danielson *to Seconds, 9/94: "The whole Seattle 'scene' in the first place is a fabrication constructed by the media. So people move to Seattle expecting to find this so-called scene and now there's a half dozen clubs where there used to be one or two. There's all these bands moving in*

from out of town who hope to get signed. The thing is, there never really was a scene there in the first place. What there was was Sub Pop Records and a few bands rediscovering the music they grew up with, heavy rock. After years of punk rock, rediscovering the old stuff. There were a few bands like Soundgarden, the Melvins, Malfunkshun, Green River and before them it was the U-Men. These bands were the first ones to put records out and it was like, 'Maybe we can actually get a record out.' That was the first big goal and then once Sub Pop came out they gave Mudhoney, TAD, Nirvana and Soundgarden the chance to put records out. Then, all this press hype was created to promote all the bands. In retrospect, there was no scene, just a half dozen bands that played for each other."

Sir Mix-A-Lot *in the same issue of Seconds: "I always compare Seattle music—not just the rap scene, but the music scene in general—to mildew in a basement. It's been left alone for so many years that it just grew and grew and grew. Now it's blowin' up. For so long, you'd go to New York or L.A., and no one took the Seattle scene seriously. Especially in New York, they still don't take it seriously—they're in their own world. In that way it's good because you have some creativity goin' on there; some people don't want to sound like everyone else. The down side is, especially in the hip hop scene, a lot of people are so into the other sounds they're hearing—Compton and all that shit, the different vibes—that they try to imitate it. Some local rappers don't want to have their own sound. That's why people ain't believing 'em."*

Seattle vs. teenagers

The City of Redmond, home of Microsoft's sprawling office park, sponsored biweekly all-ages shows at a YMCA gym. But in Seattle, the Teen Dance Ordinance remained a major obstacle to a healthy scene. It gave police, who seemed to have a religious conviction against youth culture, a tool to shut down all-ages concerts at the Greenwood Masonic Temple and assorted rave dances at warehouse spaces around town.

One rave promoter, Chris Rosemond, managed to cover all the assorted legal hurdles and mount regularly scheduled, legal shows; he had to give up one part of the rave aesthetic, the undisclosed warehouse location, and establish a semi-permanent site in a West Seattle rehearsal building. Rosemond held a sold-out, all-night, 18-and-over party there the night before the Fourth of July with Sky Cries Mary, Six in the Clip, and tribal-circus-rock band ¡TchKung! (who included a fire-eater and up to six percussionists at a time, performing angry political rants) as well as the usual crew of DJs; overflow crowds danced on the building's front lawn, while those who could get inside danced amidst six-foot mask props left over from an Alice in Chains video for the *Last Action Hero* soundtrack.

At the Odd Fellows Hall, where our saga began back in 1976, promoters Caroline Davenport and David Meinert launched Friday and Saturday all-ages concerts, at first unadvertised. They were

ter, the Enterprise Rent-A-Car garage on Westlake Avenue, Rm. 608 on Capitol Hill (a tiny storefront performance-art space), and at the Velvet Elvis Arts Lounge (another of the old Pioneer Square Theater's spaces, where *Angry Housewives* had debuted a decade before). Some Velvet Elvis shows were promoted by Meg Watjen, others by Curtis Pitts, a Sub Pop office drone who got his grinning mug on a compilation album, *Curtis W. Pitts: Sub Pop Employee of the Month*, that showcased the label's new cross-country roster.

The Washington Music Industry Coalition, which forged public opposition to the Erotic Music Bill, scheduled meetings with city brass to try to negotiate an alternative to the Teen Dance Ordinance. The last full time all-ages space, the OK Hotel Cafe, finally went 21-and-over by adding a bar in the fall of 1994.

University Way became home to as many as 500 teenage runaways and homeless young adults. A new squatting scene emerged in 1992-93, despite publicized evictions of teens from UW-owned vacant houses and police harassment against panhandling by street teens.

Robert Bennett was working with Jean Baptise and other promoters on turning the 1962-built King Theater, a cavernous 900-seat movie house in Belltown, into an all-ages concert venue at the time of

wildly popular (600 shoved and stage-dived to a sizzling Mudhoney set at a CURSE benefit on Feb. 10). Despite Davenport and Meinert's attempts to cooperate with the police and fire departments, plainclothes cops appeared at most shows and tried every trick to find a reason to close the space. Threatened with prosecution under the Teen Dance Ordinance, the promoters reluctantly took an 18-and-over policy. Even then, the fire department shut down all public events at the ancient building. A month later, the theatre groups using the building were allowed back, but the ballroom remained closed. New promoters mounted a handful of 18-and-over shows in the building over the summer.

Shows took place for a couple of months at the Pioneer Square Theater, the former Palace Theater where *Angry Housewives* closed. Other promoters mounted all-ages shows at a couple of school buildings, the Langston Hughes Cultural Arts Cen-

his escort-service indictment. A company called Grass Roots Promotions assumed charge of booking shows at the place. The first King show, in August 1993, starred TAD, Voodoo Gearshift and Kill Sybil in a benefit for a private investigation into Mia Zapata's murder. The afternoon of the show, KNDD reported that Nirvana would also perform (their first official local gig in a year), guaranteeing a sellout. The band performed blistering previews of songs from *In Utero* and closed with a Led Zeppelin cover, "No Quarter." The show served as a warm-up for the *In Utero* tour and an *MTV Unplugged* special, both of which featured guitarist Pat Smear (of L.A.'s hardcore-pioneer Germs) and cellist Lori Goldston (of Seattle's Black Cat Orchestra).

Tammy Watson: *"The guys in Nirvana were so excited; they couldn't wait to play. I was really disappointed with their Coliseum show; they*

The Eastlake scene

Below: Eddie Vedder

were herded around by security and it was a lot like any big arena rock show. But this time, when they played it just came out purely for the thrill, the release and abandon of it. I regained my faith in them that night."

Test of *Time*

Pearl Jam's second CD was released with far less of a promotional push than the first: just a handful of rock-mag interviews (including a *Rolling Stone* puff piece by Cameron Crowe), a syndicated radio interview show, a listening party-slide show at a Seattle movie theater, a few warm-up tour dates opening for Neil Young in the summer, a national tour in the winter. The band declined to participate in a *Time* cover story, "All the Rage," which called the group "angry young rockers" who "give voice to the passions and fears of a generation." Christopher John Farley's story attempted to lump "alternative" bands together as one big genre of rehashed hippie moves.

Time on Eddie Vedder: *"They haven't built that Rock n' Roll Hall of Fame in Cleveland, Ohio, yet, but when they do, they'd better save a room for Vedder.... He's got all the rock-idol moves down. Does he have a painful, shadowy past? Check. Does he have an air of danger and sensuality reminiscent of Jim Morrison? You bet. Does he refuse to adopt the trappings of a rock star, thus demonstrating that he's such a genuine article he doesn't need stardom? Absolutely. Is he happy to be on the cover of* Time*? No way."*

Eddie Vedder to the radio show Rockline *on* Time: *"I think this is a bunch of crap. To look at it is very strange. It looks like one of those things you get at Magic Mountain for $10 or whatever where they impose your image on the cover of a famous magazine.... This is my parents' magazine, if I had parents...We're on the cover as entertainment. Am I paranoid by thinking that we're just a decoy? Do you know we're declaring war on Haiti?"*

The album was to have been titled *Five Against One*, continuing the band's basketball theme. It was changed to *Vs.* at the last minute; the limited vinyl edition and the first run of CDs were untitled. The cover art featured cute sheep, just like the inside of *Grunge Lite*'s CD booklet.

If Nirvana went to a softer voice of irritation on its follow-up, PJ went in a harder direction. The first few songs continued in the mellow-blues-rock revival vein of much of *Ten*, but with even bleaker stories and more energetic riffs. By "W.M.A." (White Male American), a searing attack against three white Detroit cops who beat a black man to death with their flashlights, the CD entered a full-bore sonic attack. It also included "Glorified G.," an attack on American gun culture; "Go," a violent boyfriend's plea for a second chance; "(Don't Call Me) Daughter," featuring the male singer lashing out against patriarchal society; and "Rats," an animal-rights anthem attacking the concept of house pets.

Despite the wishes of many in the local scene that the furor over Seattle bands would die down, *Vs.* sold 950,000 copies in North America in its first week and another 2.8 million over the next three months. It was the fastest-selling record in SoundScan's three-year history. Sony reportedly had to delay other new releases so it could devote its manufacturing capacity to *Vs.*

The band faced some hassles on the road, including a near-riot at a Colorado show. They announced in *Billboard* in early 1994 that they were trying to keep ticket and merchandise prices down, wouldn't play venues that took more than 30 percent of T-shirt sales, played several small-hall shows primarily for fan club members, and were working to reduce ticket-agency charges to no more than 10 percent of ticket prices, and to keep advertising off the tickets. These moves got the band in trouble with Ticketmaster, the nation's biggest ticket-handling service, which had just been bought by Microsoft co-founder Paul Allen (who was also promoting the proposed Jimi Hendrix Museum and Experience Music Project). The band's magagement filed a complaint with the U.S.

Antitrust Division. The complaint charged that Ticketmaster pressured local promoters to boycott Pearl Jam tours if the band didn't allow full service charges. Ament and Gossard brought their charges to a Congressional committee hearing investigating the Ticketmaster monopoly; the band received letters of support by acts ranging from Garth Brooks to the Grateful Dead.

Vedder to Spin, *12/94: "Everyone is so fucking cynical that you can't even do something good without someone thinking that you've got another play on it. No one seems to know how to deal with honesty anymore. They see someone being honest and they think there's got to be a hidden agenda there. And it's really fucking it up for some of us who are coming clean. I'm just totally vulnerable. I'm way too fucking soft for this whole business, this whole trip. I don't have any shell. There's a contradiction there, because that's probably why I can write songs that mean something to someone and express some of these things that other people can't necessarily express."*

When the group put out no videos at the release of *Vs.*, MTV had nothing to show from 1993's top-selling rock record except a live performance of "Animal" from that September's *Video Music Awards* show. The channel signed Pearl Jam to perform with its ol' critics Nirvana in a New Year's special, taped in mid-December in a Seattle waterfront warehouse, but Vedder called in sick the day of the show. The show was a complete industry affair, the sort of overstaged big schmooze-fest that Vedder and Kurt Cobain both insisted they hated. An L.A. art director devised an ugly set in what he claimed were "grunge" colors, which Nirvana thoroughly trashed at the end of its set.

Pearl Jam sold out three December shows at the Seattle Center Arena in one hour; Nirvana "bested" them by selling out two Arena shows in 15 minutes. Those shows, on Jan. 7 and 8, turned out to be Nirvana's final U.S. performances.

Kurt finds his numbness

With his habit apparently behind him and his stomach problems apparently in control, Cobain agreed to another European tour. Shortly into it, he complained of health problems. Nirvana played for the last time on March 1 in Munich; Cobain lost his voice halfway through the show and was told by a doctor to take several weeks' rest. Cobain postponed the tour's last dates, and retreated to a Rome hotel.

On the morning of March 4, 1994, Courtney Love found him passed out in a deep coma after taking a non-narcotic prescription sedative and drinking champagne (in *Come As You Are*, he'd told Michael Azerrad that he knew to never mix downers with alcohol). He was rushed to a hospital, where he regained consciousness after five hours and promptly asked for a strawberry milkshake. While the incident was officially ruled an accident, sources later said he'd taken 50 individual-

Kurt Cobain's troubled last days

Drugs, guns and threats; and then he disappeared

Cobain's music full of anger, confusion

Salmon fishing off coast hit hard

Many additives too toxic for food are in cigarettes, radio reports says

Jesse Jackson caught in ... 'tle of Palestinian-Isr'

Left: Times cover w/ sleazy photo

Seattle Post-Intelligencer

Cobain's suicide note ended with 'I love you'

ly-packaged pills and left a suicide note.

Cobain retreated to a luxury home in the Madrona area, overlooking Lake Washington, that he and Love bought in January from the daughter of *Seattle Weekly* co-owner Bagley Wright. During what his PR people called a period of "recuperation," Cobain canceled negotiations for Nirvana to headline the Lollapalooza '94 tour, plans that had confounded some of the punk purists. The band had been courted to co-headline the Woodstock '94 festival (Alice in Chains, Pearl Jam and Soundgarden were also reportedly sought for the show).

Back in Seattle, Cobain got back on heroin. On March 18, Love called police to report a suicidal threat; they confiscated a gun and unnamed drugs. He told officers he'd simply retreated to his bedroom to escape a combative situation with Love; the gun was there by coincidence.

On March 22, Cobain and Love allegedly quarreled viciously in the back of a taxi heading to a used-car lot where the couple had bought a Lexus on Jan. 2 but returned it a few days later; Love said she'd wanted to keep the luxury car, according to an employee of the lot, but Cobain was more comfortable with a more downscale car. They bought a Dodge Dart that day for $2,500; the owner of the lot later told the *Times* that he saw an "unstable" looking Love drop several pills.

On March 25 Love orchestrated an "intervention" for Cobain, a technique in which an addict is confronted by friends and experts. She'd planned to group-confront him a week before; but someone tipped him off to the scheme and the surprise confrontation was canceled. This time, Love brought

Below: At the memorial

10 friends and record-company people, including Novoselic, Grohl, Gold Mountain founder Danny Goldberg (who'd become president of Atlantic Records and now runs the Warner Bros. label) and Nirvana's current manager John Silva, to meet Cobain at the couple's home; they pleaded with him for over four hours. Goldberg later said Cobain had been "extremely reluctant" and "denied that he was doing anything self-destructive." But at the end of the session, he apparently agreed to go to a treatment program in California that day. Love flew to California alone that day, to promote the Hole CD *Live Through This* and also to treat a dependence on prescription tranquilizers. She took outpatient psychiatric therapy from a $500-a-day Beverly Hills hotel suite.

Cobain failed to get on a plane on March 25. Instead, he took a cab back into Seattle from the airport and hung out with a friend who supported herself as a heroin dealer.

A March 27 statement credited to Cobain, posted to a Nirvana mailing list on the Internet computer network, said the band would lay off of touring ("We're all taking a break from the music and touring for a bit. I'm still a little freaked over the Rome thing and need some time to rest and get over it, you'd think they could make a good milkshake, but

no") and that Nirvana would soon start work on "a calmer, moodier album" ("If you're expecting the same verse-chorus-verse, well, I suppose you have but two choices: don't buy the new album when it's released in early '95, or get used to the fact that the band is changing. Longevity folks"). An Internet user in Victoria, B.C. later claimed to have fabricated the statement.

On the morning of March 30, Cobain took Dylan Carlson to a gun shop and gave him $300 to buy a shotgun for him. Cobain dropped the gun off at his house before he drove to the airport to go to the Exodus Treatment Center outside L.A.. Love talked to Cobain by phone several times while he was there. The last call came around 6 p.m. on Good Friday, April 1, an hour before he walked away from the treatment program by claiming he was stepping out to get cigarettes; he told her, "Just remember, no matter what happens, I love you." He'd also taken a call from his mother in Aberdeen; she pleaded with him not to join what she called "that stupid club" of dead rock stars.

Cobain briefly reappeared at his house on Saturday, after a cab took him to buy shotgun shells. He was seen at the house by Michael DeWitt, Frances Cobain's nanny, who later said Kurt "looked bad" and was "acting weird." DeWitt called Carlson, who told him to confiscate the shotgun if he knew where it was. Cobain's whereabouts after that became unknown, though he'd apparently been sighted around town and at the couple's country home in east King County.

On April 4, O'Connor phoned a missing-person report to the Seattle Police. Love had already hired detectives (including L.A. private eye Tom Grant) to stake out their house and the Capitol Hill apartment of Cobain's alleged drug connection; the Dart was parked outside the house, with two flat tires, but he wasn't spotted. She'd canceled their joint credit card, but attempted charges on it from unknown locales continued to be made. Carlson, Mark Lanegan and other friends scoured Cobain's regular haunts and the Madrona house; they didn't bother to look in the garage building next door.

On April 6, Love called 911 from her Beverly Hills hotel room; she later said it was for an allergic reaction to medication. Police arrested her on suspicion of narcotics possession; she was taken to a hospital and from there to jail, from which she was bailed out later that day. All charges against her were later dropped.

On April 7, *USA Today* and the *Los Angeles Times* published rumors that Nirvana was breaking up, that Cobain wanted only to make music with R.E.M. singer Michael Stipe (who'd moved to Seattle following bandmate Peter Buck, who in turn had fathered twins borne by Crocodile Cafe owner Stephanie Dorgan).

At 8:40 a.m. on Friday, April 8, an electrician came to the Cobain home to install a new security system. He saw a body through the second-story window of a greenhouse room above a garage next to the house, behind a door that had been blocked

from the inside—a room that Carlson, DeWitt, and the private eyes hadn't bothered to explore. Cobain had shot himself in the face that Tuesday afternoon, medical examiners determined, after taking a large dose of heroin and valium and writing a long suicide note in red ink. The note, which was stuck into a plant container with a pen, ended with: "Please keep going Courtney, for Frances, for her life which will be so much happier without me. I LOVE YOU. I LOVE YOU." The shotgun rested on his chest; a cigar box full of heroin supplies lay next to the body.

The electrician reported the body to his dispatcher, who called KXRX before he called 911. Within minutes of the first radio reports, fans started gathering at a small city park adjacent to the house. At least one local youth killed himself in response to Cobain's death; suicide hotlines and radio stations across the country were flooded for a week with calls from distraught people who'd identified with Cobain.

The black circle

That night, Pearl Jam and Mudhoney performed their scheduled tour stop at Fairfax, Virginia. Pearl Jam's set was performed on a stage lit with candles. Vedder told the audience, "Sometimes, whether you want it or not, people elevate you. It's really easy to fall. I don't think any of us would be here if it weren't for Kurt Cobain."

Sub Pop had scheduled its sixth anniversary party for that Saturday at the Crocodile. Despite press reports that the party would become a wake, the 300 invited guests (including many out-of-town media people) kept their spirits up and mostly avoided talk of the tragedy. That same night, 300 people attended a candlelight vigil in Aberdeen.

The next day, members of Pearl Jam visited the White House and reportedly discussed the tragedy with President Bill Clinton. Eddie Vedder closed a *Saturday Night Live* appearance the following week by quietly opening his vest to reveal a black "K." drawn on his T-shirt over his heart. The band postponed its remaining dates, and eventually canceled them during its dispute with Ticketmaster.

Pearl Jam drummer Dave Abbruzzese either quit or was fired following sessions for the band's third album, *Vitalogy* (the name came from a 1927 personal-health guidebook Vedder had found), released in November 1994. It furthered the band's evolution away from the stadium-rock revivalism of *Ten* toward a more textured but still high-energy sound, exemplified on the anthems "Not For You" and "Whipping" and the angry ballad "Tremor Christ." Vedder accompanied himself on accordion in the novelty tune "Bugs;" the disc closed with a melodyless tape-loop track, "Stupid Mop." In keeping with the pro-vinyl sentiment of its first single, "Spin the Black Circle," *Vitalogy* was released on LP three weeks before it came out on CD; the vinyl version debuted at #55 on the *Billboard* album chart. The CD sold 877,000 copies in its first week, again with no video or tour support.

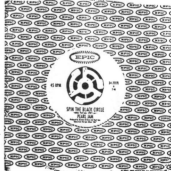

Courtney Love (the person)

At the end of the year the band announced its new drummer—Jack Irons, who'd given that original Gossard-Ament demo tape to Vedder four years before. To avoid Ticketmaster, the band planned to perform in outdoor venues or in theaters that didn't have exclusive ticketing contracts. The band (with a guest appearance by Neil Young) filled two Moore Theater shows in February 1995 by mailing free tickets to fan club members; Pearl Jam was billed on the marquee as "Piss Bottle Men."

Andrew Mueller in Melody Maker: *"Their most intense album.... The PJ of* Vitalogy *are staggeringly shell shocked across a irreparably desecrated rock landscape, struggling to find some kind of resolve in the void. Eddie Vedder is out there alone now, and has the humanity to sound more than a little frightened by the prospect."*

Corporate media still suck

A media feeding frenzy began before Cobain's body got to the medical examiner. MTV went all-Nirvana the day his body was found, and ran a four-hour retrospective a month later. TV commentators Andy Rooney, Rush Limbaugh and John McLaughlin took the death as an excuse to berate the entire younger generation as pathetic losers. The Monday

Right: Kristen Pfaff, R.I.P.

**Jonathan Poneman
Joins Rotary Club**

**Even Jim Rose makes
the Wall Street Journal**

after his death, Cobain's face appeared on the cover of *Newsweek*. Dave Thompson, a British rock writer who'd lived in Seattle since 1990 and married *Rocket* writer Jo-Ann Greene, supplied St. Martin's Press with a paperback bio, *Never Fade Away: The Kurt Cobain Story*; it reached stores five weeks after the death. A week later, it was optioned by a Hollywood agency for a feature film, over the objections of Love and Kurt's family. Amy Jo Merrick, a sculptor and conceptual artist who'd moved into the former Rathouse space on Capitol Hill, put up a temporary memorial in the house called *Never Fucking Mind: Sculptures for Kurt*, opening in October 1994 on the six-month anniversary of his death.

A private memorial was held at the Unity Church of Seattle on Sunday, April 10. That evening, nearly 10,000 fans attended a free candlelight memorial at the Seattle Center Flag Plaza. Three local DJs, a Unity minister and a suicide prevention counselor gave brief statements. Love supplied an audiotaped statement; she read parts of Cobain's suicide note ("All the warnings from Punk Rock 101 courses over the years since my first introduction to the, shall we say, 'ethics' involved with independents and the embracement of your community have proven to be very true. I haven't felt the excitement of listening to as well as creating music, along with really writing something, for too many years now.... When we are backstage and the lights go out and the manic roar of the crowd begins, it doesn't affect me.... The worst crime I can think of would be to pull people off by faking it and pretending as if I were having 100 percent fun.... I'm too much of an erratic, moody person, and I don't have the passion anymore"). She interspersed the reading with her own comments about how stupid he was to think death was the only answer ("No, Kurt, the worst crime I can think of is for you to just continue being a rock star when you fucking hated it. Just fucking stop"). She denounced drug intervention tactics ("They just don't work") and wished she had "let him have his numbness. We should have let him have the thing that made him feel better."

Novoselic supplied a less emotional message: "We remember Kurt for what he was: caring, generous, and sweet. Let's keep his music with us; we'll always have it, forever. Kurt had an ethic toward his fans that was rooted in the punk rock way of thinking: no band is special, no player royalty. If you've got a guitar and a lot of soul, just bang something out and mean it. You're the superstar, plugged into tones and rhythms that are uniquely and universally human; music. Heck, use your guitar as a drum; just catch a groove and let it flow out of your heart. That's the level that Kurt spoke to us on, in our hearts. And that's where he and the music will always be, forever."

Love showed up in person later in the evening, while many attendees were still on the grounds. She gave some of Cobain's T-shirts to some young fans who sat around a shrine of Cobain momentos, while others climbed on and around the nearby International Fountain in what a *Times* headline called a "fountain of teen spirit."

Love donated Cobain's guns to be destroyed by a stop-the-violence group, and shared her inner turmoils with the world via a series of highly emotional public messages on the America Online computer service. Love's father, Hank Harrison, announced a Kurt Cobain Foundation for Suicide Prevention; Love, still estranged from Harrison, declined to participate.

From an open letter by **Hank Harrison** *to President Clinton, 4/19/94: "Millions of Kurt's fans (and Courtney's) are seriously depressed now and will remain so for many years if they do not receive help. Kurt's violent death has a much greater impact on youth than did the drug overdoses of Elvis or Jim Morrison or Jimi Hendrix—the pain is deeper, the nerves are closer to the surface."*

Tom Grant, the private investigator hired by Love after Cobain's disappearance, went on talk radio shows in December claiming Cobain had really been murdered by unidentified persons who "had an interest in increasing the value of his recordings." Grant's charges echoed similar allegations by Richard Lee, a local public-access TV commentator. Grant's and Lee's allegations were emphatically denied by Cobain's family and Seattle police. Among the "evidence" cited by Grant and Lee was a claim that Cobain's suicide note was really just an announcement that he was quitting the music business so he could turn his life around.

One who had tried to turn her life around in time was Hole bassist Kristen Pfaff, who'd undergone drug rehab over the winter. After Cobain's death canceled Hole's tour plans, she planned to move back to Minneapolis. She was found dead in the bathtub of her Capitol Hill apartment on June 16, the day she was to have moved out, an apparent heroin overdose.

Love recruited Melissa Auf Der Maur from Montreal to become the third Hole bassist, touring with Nine Inch Nails in September 1994 to promote the official re-launch of *Live Through This*, which sold a half million copies by Christmas. At some tour stops Love stage-dived into the audience, re-emerging with her clothes torn to shreds. Media stories of Love's outrageous behavior and celebrity hobnobbing partly inspired Mudhoney to record a musical hate letter to the Hole entourage, "Into Your Shtick."

At the tour's start, Hole performed at a KNDD-sponsored benefit for Artists for a Hate-Free America, an Oregon group formed to fight anti-gay campaigns and hate crimes. In her first Seattle appearance since her widowhood, Love brought out the two-year-old Frances Bean Cobain (outfitted with ear-protecting headphones) and blew the roof off the Arena. She closed with a screaming-sad rendition of Ledbelly's "Where Did You Sleep Last Night?", the song Nirvana made famous on its *MTV Unplugged* special. Fans close to the stage saw tears in Love's eyes. Just before she left the stage she cautioned, "Now don't you guys tell anybody I got sentimental and did that song."

Conclusion: What if this *is* normal from now on?

By the time of Cobain's final struggles, the music industry had switched its focus back to commercial soft rock, in the form of R&B harmony groups and "adult acoustic alternative" balladeers.

Some Seattlites predicted (or even hoped) that the end of Nirvana would finally end the Seattle-rock media mania. Even before, many locals had expressed wishes that the media would leave Seattle alone so things could return to "normal." Yet between September 1993 and March 1994, *In Utero*, *Vs.*, *Jar of Flies*, and *Superunknown* all debuted at *Billboard*'s #1. The area's 20 other major-label acts and indie bands like Seaweed, Sunny Day Real Estate and Bikini Kill gained converts at home and abroad.

This current rock, whatever you call it, has gestated for almost 20 years. Before long, people conceived on the Vogue fire escape will be old enough

to go there. The best Seattle bands rock hard without being pretentious or slaves to fashion. They speak directly to people in a way no groomed-for-stardom act can. Even the biggest acts in the scene speak toward a post-Hollywood era, when art and entertainment are wrested from centralized corporations to become direct expressions of people's hearts. After 25 years of leftist artists distancing themselves from the working class, the new punk identified with the downscale youth of the generation after the Blank Generation. It's instantly accessible, and (as the knockoff bands still moving here prove) easy to learn. The trappings of grunge may have never existed as publicized, but the DIY ethic behind it can only grow.

But with the Teen Dance Ordinance still preventing larger all-ages concerts and the city now enforcing a new, tougher ban on street posters, Seattle still has a ways to go toward supporting live original music. And the Seattle Commons Committee, a group of suburban go-getters led by Microsoft/Ticketmaster mogul Paul Allen, wants to replace nearly 100 blocks northeast of downtown with a square-mile "urban village" of luxury condos. Its plan calls for the demolition of the Off Ramp, RKCNDY, Lake Union Pub, and at least half a dozen band practice spaces.

If the destructive plans of the Commons can be revised, and if the city can allow more all-ages shows and cheap ways to promote them, this could truly become a place where people gather to create new art forms for the post-mass media age, works that directly communicate to people's souls, that help people express their anger, their joy, their aggression, their sex, their love, their fear, and their togetherness.

That's as good a definition of nirvana as I can imagine.

Above:
There's hope yet

UNPLUGGED
IN NEW YORK

Some Product

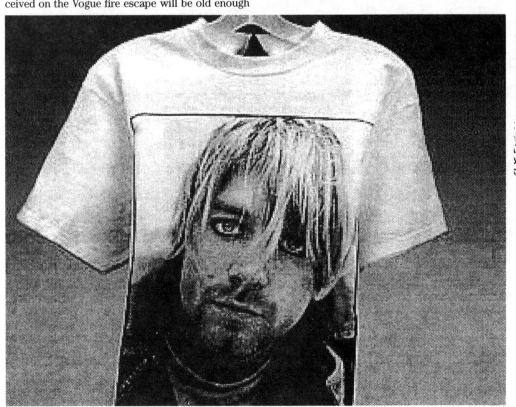

Kurt Cobain R.I.P.

PART THREE

CHAPTER THIRTEEN: APPENDICES

SEATTLE MUSIC SPACES OVER THE YEARS
(in approximate chronological order)

RENTAL HALLS
IOOF *1976-79, 1985-86, 1993*
FREEWAY HALL *1976-82*
IOGT *1976-81*
OLYMPIC HOTEL *1977*
WASHINGTON HALL *1977-85, 1989-91*
CARPENTERS HALL *1977-79, 1990-91*
NORWAY CENTER/MOUNTAINEERS *1977-81, 1985*
UW ETHNIC CULTURAL THEATRE *1978-84*
POLISH HALL *1978-90 sporadically*
LANGSTON HUGHES CENTER *1979-80, 1993*
UW KANE HALL *1979-81*
MASONIC TEMPLE *1979-80*
UNITED COMMERCIAL TRAVELERS *1981-1986 sporadically*
WILSONIAN HOTEL BALLROOM *1981-83*
ST. JOSEPH'S CHURCH *1982-83, 1992-93*
THE CLUB/FREMONT PALACE *1983, 1988-92*
SERBIAN HALL *1983*
BELLEVUE VFW HALL *1983-89*
MUSIC HALL *1983-84*
UNION STATION *1984*
SEATTLE BOXING CLUB *1988*
BEST WAREHOUSE *1992*
N.A.F. STUDIOS *1993-94*
SAILORS UNION OF THE PACIFIC *1995*
...and a score of one-time-only rave sites.

ALL-AGES SPACES
PARAMOUNT *1969-present*
NEPTUNE THEATRE *1976*
THE BIRD #1 *1978*
THE BIRD #2 *1978*
UW HUB AUDITORIUM *1978-present*
FUNHOLE *1978, 1981*
PUPPET THEATER *1978*
HARVARD EXIT *1979*
EDMONDS THEATRE *1979*
PIKE PLACE CINEMA *1979*
GOLDEN CROWN *1979*
EAGLES NEST *1979, 1982-83*
SHOWBOX *1979-83, 1987-88*
MR. BILL'S *1980-81*
GORILLA ROOM *1980*
DANCELAND USA *1980-81*
PARADISE LOFT/KIT KAT KLUB *1981-83*
ENEMY STUDIO/66 BELL/LINCOLN ARTS *1981-87*
EAGLES AUDITORIUM *1967-70, 1981-83*
STRAND HOTEL *1982*
PIKE PLACE CINEMA *1983*
MOORE *1983-present*
METROPOLIS *1983-84*
MUNRO'S DANCE PALACE *1984*

MEATLOCKER *1984*
TOP OF THE COURT *1984*
LE CLUB HIT *1984-86*
SPIDER'S WEB/BARRICADES *1984, 1993*
GORILLA GARDENS #1/ROCK THEATER *1984-85*
GORILLA GARDENS #2 *1985*
1411 GALLERY *1985*
UNIVERSITY COFFEE #1 *1986-88*
LUNA *1987-88*
THE ALAMO *1988*
OK HOTEL *1988, 1990-94*
LAKE CITY CONCERT THEATRE *1990*
MOTORSPORTS INTERNATIONAL GARAGE *1990*
BALIARD HIGH SCHOOL *1991*
GREENWOOD MASONIC TEMPLE *1992*
THE PENNY UNIVERSITY *1992-93*
NIGHTLIFE/REDMOND YMCA/OLD FIREHOUSE *1992-present*
PIONEER SQUARE THEATRE *1993*
INGRAHAM HIGH SCHOOL *1993*
ROCKHAUS (Old Lincoln H.S.) *1993-present*
ENTERPRISE RENT-A-CAR *1993*
EASTLAKE CAFE *1993-present*
RENDEZVOUS UPSTAIRS *1993*
KING THEATRE *1993-95*
VELVET ELVIS ART LOUNGE *1993-present*
GROUND ZERO (Bellevue) *1994*
CAFE PARADISO *1994-present*
PIONEER SQUARE JUICE & JAVA *1994-present*
CAFE CAPELLA *1994-present*
SALOTTO COFFEEHOUSE *1994-present*
CAFE ALLEGRO *1994*
LUX COFFEEHOUSE *1994-present*
CLUB 449 *1995*

ALL-AGES (or 18-and-over) DISCOS
THE MONESTARY *1979-85*
SKOOTCHIE'S/OZ *1984-present*
CLUB BROADWAY *1983-86*
STALLIONS/CLUB MECCA *1985-86*
RETRO *1987*
UNDERGROUND *1987-present*
42nd STREET ANNEX *1988-92*
KING THEATER *1993-95*

INTIMATE BARS
DOUBLE HEADER *1977*
BAHAMAS UNDERGROUND *1979-80*
GOLDIE'S ON BROADWAY *1979*
NEW MELODY/OLD TOWN/TRACTOR *1979-present*
GORILLA ROOM *1980-81*
WREX *1980-82*
PANCHO'S *1980-81*
EASTLAKE ZOO *1980-present, intermittently*
DEZ'S 400 *1981-82*
BABY O'S *1981-83*

SHIRE *1981-82*
STAMPEDE *1982*
TWO BELLS *1982-present*
DRAGON PALACE *1982-83*
EMBERS (West Seattle) *1982-83*
AD LIB (Kent) *1983-84*
MEEKER'S LANDING (Kent) *1983*
HOLLYWOOD UNDERGROUND *1983-85*
G-NOTE *1983-84*
MEDIEVAL CELLAR *1983*
RIO CAFE *1983*
BACK COURT *1983-84*
TALK OF THE TOWN *1984*
MICHAEL J'S *1984*
FIVE-O *1984-86*
NEW CENTURY/BOOM BOOM ROOM/UNIVERSITY SPORTSBAR
  1985-95, intermittently
SOHO RESTAURANT & CLOTHING *1985-86*
OXFORD *1985-89*
DITTO *1985-87, 1989-present*
ATTIC *1986-87*
JILLY'S EAST *1986-87*
TRADE WINDS *1986-87*
FAR SIDE/MAD DOGS *1986-93*
SQUID ROW/BEATNIX *1987-90, 1994-present*
SCOUNDREL'S LAIR *1987-88*
FIVE POINT *1987-88*
LILLIAN'S *1987-88*
CANTERBURY ALE & EATS *1987-88*
UNIVERSITY BISTRO *1987-89*
ALAMO *1988*
RENDEZVOUS *1988-present*
LOX STOCK & BAGEL *1990-present*
SWAN CAFE *1990-94*
EMERALD DINER *1991-94*
STORE ROOM *1991-93*
EDGE *1991-92*
DETOUR (Renton) *1991-92*
KELLY'S *1992-93*
GIBSON'S *1992-present*
PINK RESTAURANT *1992*
LAKE UNION PUB *1992-present*
SIT & SPIN *1993-present*
PANKO'S *1993*
LAKE CITY TAVERN *1993*
BOGART'S *1993*
OWL & THISTLE *1993*
CAPTAIN COOK'S PUB *1993-present*
VICTOR'S *1994*
INDIA TAJ/RED SEA *1994-present*
LAVA LOUNGE *1995-present*

SHOWCASE BARS (capacity 150+)
PARKER'S/AQUARIUS *1932-93*
BUFFALO *1968-80*
RAINBOW *1973-86*
ASTOR PARK *1978-83*
GOLDEN CROWN *1979-86*
ATHENS CAFE *1981-83*
99 CLUB (Sea-Tac) *1981-83*
BACKSTAGE *1983-present*
CENTRAL TAVERN *1983-90*
BALLARD FIREHOUSE *1984-present*
OFF RAMP *1990-present*
COLOURBOX *1991-present*
CROCODILE CAFE *1991-present*
RKCNDY *1991-present*
WEATHERED WALL *1992-present*
UNDER THE RAIL *1993-present*
FENIX UNDERGROUND/ABOVE GROUND *1993-present*

MOE *1994-present*
OK HOTEL *1994-present*
ROCKSPORT (West Seattle) *1995-present*
METROPOLIS *1995-present*

PERFORMANCE ART SPACES WITH MUSIC
WASHINGTON HALL/ON THE BOARDS *1974-present*
and/or *1974-82*
SEATTLE CONCERT THEATRE *1979-82*
PARADISE LOFT/KIT KAT KLUB *1981-83*
NEW CITY THEATER *1982-present*
CENTER ON CONTEMPORARY ART #1 *1982-83*
FOCAL POINT MEDIA CENTER *1982-86*
911 MEDIA ARTS *1984-present*
FREMONT PALACE *1984-92*
CENTER ON CONTEMPORARY ART #2 *1985*
FREE MARS *1985-86*
CENTER ON CONTEMPORARY ART #3 *1986*
CENTER ON CONTEMPORARY ART #4 *1988-94*
PILGRIM CENTER *1988-present*
FRYE WAREHOUSE *1989*
RM. 608 *1992-94*
CLUB PAGODA *1993-present*
CENTER ON CONTEMPORARY ART #5 *1995-present*

ART GALLERIES WITH BANDS
ROSCO LOUIE #1 *1978-79*
ROSCO LOUIE #2 *1979-82*
OUR OWN DAMN GALLERY *1981*
GROUND ZERO *1982-84*
GRAVEN IMAGE *1983-84*
GALLERIA POTATOHEAD #1 *1983-85*
HERE TODAY *1984*
WE "B" ART *1983-85*
AFLN *1988-91*
GALLERIA POTATOHEAD #2 *1987-90*
GALLERIA POTATOHEAD #3 *1990-92*
ART/NOT TERMINAL #1 *1990-92*
WONDERFUL WORLD OF ART *1991-94*
OFFBEAT CAFE *1993*
THE POUND *1993-present*

DISCO BARS
WATERTOWN *1976-89*
TUGS BELLTOWN *1979-89*
VOGUE *1983-present*
TALK OF THE TOWN *1984*
BOREN ST. DISCO/CITY BEAT *1985-86*
PIER 70 *1985, 1993-present*
DJ'S NIGHTLIFE/1501 AKA THE CLUB *1989-90*
RE-BAR *1990-present*
BELLTOWN CLUB *1990-91*
CLUB PHANTOM *1990-91*
ROMPER ROOM *1990-present*
CELEBRITY'S *1991*
FLOWERS *1992-present*
ORESTES/THE BLOB/14 ROY *1993-present*
CATWALK *1994-present*
VICTOR'S *1994-present*
2218 *1994-present*
MACHINE WERKS *1995-present*

SEATTLE CENTER *1962-present*
COLISEUM
EXHIBITION HALL
MURAL AMPITHEATRE
OPERA HOUSE
ARENA
FLAG PLAZA AND PAVILION
CENTER HOUSE

NORTH COURT ROOMS
MEMORIAL STADIUM
PACIFIC SCIENCE CENTER
NILE TEMPLE/PACIFIC ARTS CENTER

OUTDOOR SHOWS
GAS WORKS PARK
CITY HALL PARK
U DISTRICT STREET FAIR
FREMONT FAIR
PIKE PLACE STREET FAIR

RECORD STORES
DISCOUNT RECORDS *1969-80*
MUSIC STREET/MUSICLAND U DISTRICT *1970-91*
CAMPUS MUSIC *1970-79*
2ND TIME AROUND *1969-present*
ROXY MUSIC *1971-84*
GOB SHOPPE *1971-present*
YESTERDAY & TODAY *1972-89*
TOWER MERCER ST. *1973-present*
BOP STREET *1974-present*
CELLOPHANE SQUARE #1 *1975-95*
CELLOPHANE SQUARE #2 *1994-present*
TIME TRAVELERS/ACME/CORPORATE *1975-95*
PEACHES U-DISTRICT/BEEHIVE *1977-92*
RUBATO BELLEVUE *1978-present*
BUDGET TAPES & RECORDS U-DISTRICT *1979-81*
MT. OLYMPUS IMPORTS #1-2 *1979-81*
PENNY LANE/EASY STREET WEST SEATTLE *1979-present*
TOWER U DISTRICT *1980-present*
EASY STREET BELLEVUE *1980-87*
RUBATO BROADWAY *1983-84*
RECORD GALLERY/BOMBSHELTER *1983-84*
FALLOUT *1984-present*
ORPHEUM *1986-present*
MT. OLYMPUS #3/EXOTIQUE #1 *1986-present*
URBAN RENEWAL *1986-87*
PEACHES BALLARD/BACKSTAGE MUSIC *1988-present*
EXOTIQUE #2 *1989-90*
SOUND AFFECTS #1 *1989-90*
SOUND AFFECTS #2 *1990-present*
WALL OF SOUND *1990-present*
EASY STREET KIRKLAND *1991-present*
BEDAZZLED DISCS *1991-present*
SUB POP MEGA MART *1993 – present*

UNADVERTISED AND AFTER-HOURS CLUBS
(incomplete)
LOVE CANAL *1978-79*
BLANCHARD STUDIOS *1980-82*
FASHION MEDIA *1980-81*
GREY DOOR *1983-84*
INCUBATOR #1 *1985-87*
THE CHURCH *1986-87*
INCUBATOR #2/KALBERER HOTEL SUPPLY *1987-89*
THE SPEAKEASY ON HOWELL ST. *1988-90*
OCCUPIED SEATTLE *1989-90*
PARTY HALL ON MADISON *1989-91*
RED FARM FILMS *1990-91*
STUDIO 1210/THE POUND *1990-present*
7TH AVENUE STUDIOS *1990-present*
SUNNY ACRES *1990-92*
K9 RANCH *1990-91*
PIN DOWN GIRL *1992*
AVAST! *1992*
HOUSE OF LEISURE *1992-1993*
THE BRIDGE *1993*
THE HOUSE *1993*
SQUISH *1993*

ATOMIC THEATRE *1993*
THE RUINS *1993*
THE CLUB WITH NO NAME *1993*
JALAPENO HOUSE *1993-94*
BLUE ROOM *1994*
THE BASEMENT *1994*
GOAT HAUS *1994-95*
UNIVERSAL JOINT *1995*

HANGOUT BARS (no live bands)
FIVE POINT CAFE *1929-present*
MECCA CAFE *1930-present*
BLUE MOON *1934-present*
COMET TAVERN *1945-present*
FRONTIER ROOM *1950-present*
ERNIE STEELE'S *1950-93*
NITELITE *1950-present*
DELUXE BAR & GRILL *1962-present*
JADE PAGODA *1964-present*
UNIQUE GRILL #1 *1979-83*
VIRGINIA INN *1981-present*
PIONEER SQUARE SALOON *1991-present*
LINDA'S TAVERN *1994-present*

HANGOUT CAFES (no live bands)
DOG HOUSE *1934-94*
HASTY TASTY *1934-80*
JOKER NITE & DAY *1951-93*
DICK'S DRIVE-INS *1954-present*
LAST EXIT ON BROOKLYN *1967-93*
MORNINGTOWN PIZZA/BLACK CAT CAFE *1967-present*
COLLEGE INN CAFE-PUB *1969-present*
CAFE ALLEGRO *1975-present*
456 CAFE *1975-79*
RUBATO RECORD ESPRESSO *1983-84*
CAFE SEPTIEME #1 *1985-89*
FREE MARS/CAFE MARS/CYCLOPS *1985-present*
UNIVERSITY COFFEE #2 *1988-present*
ESPRESSO ROMA BROADWAY *1988-present*
GLOBE CAFE *1988-present*
ROCKET PIZZA *1988-present*
CAFE SEPTIEME #2/THE BATTERY *1989-present*
ESPRESSO ROMA U DISTRICT *1990-present*
ROCKET PIZZA *1990-present*
HOT LIPS PIZZA *1991-present*
UNIQUE CAFE *1991-present*
WORLD PIZZA *1993-present*
HURRICANE CAFE *1994-present*
THE PUPPY CLUB *1994-present*
CAFE SEPTIEME BROADWAY *1994-present*

TACOMA
TACOMA DOME (arena) *1982-present*
BEDROCK LOUNGE/PROSITO/CENTRAL TAVERN
    1985-present, intermittently
CLUB TACOMA (all ages) *1985-93*
CRESCENT BALLROOM/LEGENDS (all ages) *1986-90*
COMMUNITY WORLD THEATRE (all ages) *1987-88*
RED ROOF PUB *1991-94*
CENTRAL CLUBHOUSE (Milton) *1991-93*
VICTORY CLUB *1991-present*
BUZZ CITY (all ages) *1991-92*
BROOKLAKE HALL (Federal Way, all ages) *1991-93*
TEMPLE THEATER *1992-present*
HEIDELBERG BREWERY (all ages) *1993-94*
SLAVONIAN HALL *1994*
24TH ST. TAVERN *1994-present*
PROPELLER CLUB (all ages) *1994-present*
RIALTO THEATER (all ages) *1994*
JAVA JUMP (Fife, all ages) *1994-present*

MOUNTAINEERS CLUB (all ages) *1995*

OLYMPIA
EVERGREEN BALLROOM *1958-66, 1986-87*
GNU DELI *1980-83*
TROPICANA (all ages) *1984-85*
G.E.S.C.C.O. (all ages) *1985-87*
CAPITOL THEATRE (all ages) *1986-present intermittently*
PACIFIC SURF CLUB *1986-89*
REKO-MUSE (gallery with bands) *1988-90*
NORTH SHORE SURF CLUB *1990-92*
CHAMBERS PRAIRIE GRANGE HALL *1990-present, intermittently*
CHARLIE'S BAR AND GRILL *1991-present*
UNCOLA (all ages) *1992*
THEKLA *1993-present*
SLOWRIDE PUB *1994-95*
MIDNIGHT SUN *1994-present*
STUDIO 3.2.1 *1994-95*
CHUNDER BLOW *1994-95*
GIGGLING GOOSE *1995*
McCOY's TAVERN *1995*
...and many basement/party spaces.

BELLINGHAM
WWU VU (all ages)
MATRIX/MASONIC LODGE (all ages) *1982-83*
3B's *1991-present*
UP & UP *1992-present*
SPEEDY O'TUBS *1992-93*
BEACHHOUSE
SHOW OFF GALLERY (all ages)
KID'S PLACE
CLUB USA (all ages)
ECHO HOUSE (all ages)

BREMERTON
NATACHA'S (all ages) *1963-82, intermittently*
EASTSIDE TAVERN
KITSAP CO. FAIRGROUNDS *1991-present, intermittently*
SCHOONER (Kingston) *1992*
PRESIDENT'S HALL (all ages) *1993*
ROXY THEATER (all ages) *1993*
CAFE ZZOO (all ages) *1994-present*

EVERETT
THE TRESSEL *1993-94*
EVERETT THEATER (all ages) *1994*
JIMMY Z's *1994-95*

SHOWBOX SHOWS

• *FIRST PUNK BAND AT SHOWBOX* •
12/31/78   chinas comidas, jr. cadillac, sundance rhythm band
• *MODERN PRODUCTIONS LEASES THE BUILDING* •
9/8/79   magazine, blackouts, dr albert
9/29/79   Rocket benefit: dishrags, look, macs band, enemy
10/6/79   pointed sticks, wipers, female hands
10/27/79   halloween party: blackouts, urge, red dress
11/17/79   dk's, pink section, young scientist
11/24/79   iggy pop, bags, blackouts
12/11/79   motels, live wire (albatross)
12/21/79   sports, blackouts, macs band (albatross)
1/8/80   ultravox, macs band, exquisite corpse
2/1/80   police, specials
2/7/80   muddy waters
2/23/80   fingerprintz, pink section, minimal man, debbies
2/29/80   xtc, blackouts, beakers
3/13/80   jam, the beat (albatross)

3/15/80   999, dickies
3/28/80   pearl harbor & the explosions (albatross)
4/4/80   rachel sweet (albatross)
4/13/80   mi-sex, reactive wear fashion show
4/17/80   ramones
4/18/80   ramones
4/19/80   selecter
4/24/80   troggs reunion, blackouts (left bank concert cie.)
4/25/80   cretones (albatross)
5/8/80   blackouts record release party
5/9/80   macs band, fred, debbies, beakers
5/10/80   missing link, psycho pop
5/13/80   king bees, magnetics
5/17/80   a.k.a.
5/18/80   cramps, debbies (st. helens eruption day)
5/25/80   gang of 4, beakers, customer service
5/30/80   doa
6/7/80   sonny terry & brownie mcghee
6/8/80   sam rivers, dave holland
6/13/80   sonny fortune
6/14/80   squeeze, humans
6/27/80   young scientist
7/15/80   dead kennedys
7/18/80   mental mannequin
7/19/80   mental mannequin
7/23/80   psychedelic furs
8/9/80   tuxedomoon, dna, minimal man
8/12/80   devo (2 shows)
8/13/80   black flag, solger
9/24/80   mo-dettes, mental mannequin, kitchy koo fashion show
10/4/80   delta 5, blackouts, beakers
10/10/80   psychedelic furs, blackouts
11/7/80   iggy pop
• *STEVE PRITCHARD TAKES OVER* •
12/14/80   food bank benefit: johnny & the distractions,
            dynamic logs, palmolives
12/22/80   beatles film screening
12/31/80   new years party
1/9/81   jim carroll band
1/15/81   captain beefheart, beakers (on the boards, 21 & over)
1/19/81   tom robinson's sector 27
1/29/81   specials
1/30/81   doug & the slugs, freddie & the screamers
2/6/81   romantics
2/13/81   johnny & the distractions
2/14/81   cowboys, impacts
2/15/81   rail
2/20/81   alley brat
2/21/81   alley brat
3/7/81   joan jett, pudz
3/8/81   toots & the maytalls
3/13/81   heats
3/15/81   rescue the rock of the '80s benefit: cowboys, connec
            tions, enemy, features, numatics,
            michael o'beill band, pudz, rockefellers,
            sex therapy, skeezix, student nurse, shivers, spectators,
            visible targets, x-15
3/21/81   taj mahal, sonny terry & brownie mcghee
3/27/81   new deal rhythm band
4/17/81   international punk explosion: uk decay, social unrest,
            rpa, refuzors, subhumans, fartz
4/18/81   freddie & the screamers, heats
4/19/81   rescue the rock of the '80s benefit:
            clash *rude boy* film screening, enemy, visible targets,
            student nurse, byrons, sex therapy
5/13/81   stranglers, idiot culture
5/16/81   enemy, no cheese please, impacts
5/30/81   rescue the rock of the '80s spring collection
• *SPACE MUFFIN TAKES OVER* •
6/6/81   b-sides

6/7/81	kzok jimi hendrix memorial benefit: jr. cadillac, dynamic logs, hi-fi, kidd afrika, ronnie lee, skyboys, annie rose	PALACE OF LIGHTS *1982-88*
6/17/81	equators	DOG TAPES/BOX DOG *1983-present*
6/23/81	vapors, impacts	GREEN MONKEY *1983-91*
6/24/81	john cale, x-15	GROUND ZERO *1983-84*
6/25/81	plasmatics	FARM PRODUCT *1983-85*
7/10/81	gang of 4, 3 swimmers, little bears from bangkok	SUSHI *1983*
7/12/81	dead kennedys, doa, husker du	TELEMUSIC *1983*
7/23/81	psychedelic furs, veil of tears	K.D.T. *1983-89*
7/25/81	999, plimsouls, pudz	POPLLAMA *1983-present*
7/28/81	split enz	DR. STIMSON *1984*

• *CONCERTS WEST TAKES OVER* •

9/23/81	go-gos	BOMBSHELTER *1984*
9/24/81	myth (queensryche predecessors), queen annes	K *1985-present*
9/25/81	leon redbone, baby gramps	EXPLODING *1985*
9/29/81	echo and the bunnymen, enemy	DeDbeet *1985-93*
11/14/81	x, napalm beach	NASTYMIX *1985-92*
11/27/81	iggy pop	ALCHEMY *1985-87*
11/30/81	king crimson	COMA *1985-86*
12/6/81	steve hackett of genesis	C/Z *1986-present*

• *BIG Z PRODUCTIONS TAKES OVER* •

		FIN DE SIECLE *1986*
4/10/82	xtc, jools holland	GEMINI *1986-87*
4/20/82	professionals (steve cook & paul jones of sex pistols)	EVER RAT/EVER RAP/EVER DREAD/EVER RUS *1987-present*
5/9/82	kcmu benefit: vizible targets, 3 swimmers, napalm beach	PENULTIMATE *1987-90*
5/15/82	brando bogart, no cheese please	eMpTy *1987-present*
6/4/82	waitresses, moving parts	ESTRUS *1987-present*
6/20/82	dave edmunds, dynette set	NO BIG BUSINESS *1987*
8/20/82	burning spear	MIRAMAR *1988-present*
9/4/82	fear, fartz, silly killers	SUN AND STEEL *1988-89*
9/11/82	exploited, fartz, rejectors, poison idea	ENGISN *1988-90*
9/26/82	kcmu benefit: 54/50, life in general	LEOPARD GECKO *1988-91*
10/21/82	x, life in general	SPOOT MUSIC *1988-91*
11/9/82	nina hagen, race age, rally go, mr. epp	AROMA *1989-92*
11/12/82	public image ltd., napalm beach	APRAXIA MUSIC RESEARCH LTD. *1989-present*
11/19/82	visible targets, 3 swimmers, beat pagodas	NEW RAGE *1989-present*
12/10/82	sights, gun club	RHYME CARTEL *1989-present*
12/17/82	lounge lizards	THE CRUDDY RECORD DEALERSHIP *1989-present*
2/12/83	tsol, memory	FATBALD *1989*
4/22/83	dead kennedys, 10 minute warning	MEAT *1989-93*

• *ONE-OFF SHOWS* •

		HORTON/REFLEX *1989-90*
7/4/87	big black, u-men (coca)	CHESTNUT *1990*
4/1/88	psychic tv video screening (coca)	BIG FLAMING EGO/WHITE TRASH *1990-present*
2/1/90	mudhoney, gas huffer, coffin break, common language, dickless, adrian's childhood (nw aids foundation)	CARVING KNIFE *1990-present*
		RATHOUSE *1990-present*

WHITE AND LAZY *1990*

STEVE PRIEST FAN CLUB *1990-91*

LUCKY *1990-present*

REGAL SELECT *1990-present*

SOME LOCAL RECORD LABELS (modern era)

(incomplete; not counting self-released tapes)

DASHBOARD HULA GIRL *1990-92*

KILL ROCK STARS *1991-present*

BLATANT *1991*

PERISCOPE *1991-93*

FIRST AMERICAN/GREAT NORTHWEST *1976-83*

WILL *1992-present*

EDGE CITY *1977*

BAG OF HAMMERS *1992-present*

MONSTER WAX/EXQUISITE CORPSE *1977-79*

SUPER-ELECTRO *1992-present*

LITTLE ORANGE BABIES *1977*

TOP DRAWER *1992-present*

PRECEDENT *1977-80, 1983-85, 1993-present*

DEKEMA *1992-present*

KING TUT *1978-82*

3:23 *1992-present*

SCRATCHED *1978*

ESTATE *1992-present*

MODERN *1979-81*

INSIGHT *1992-present*

NO THREES *1979-88 intermittently*

WRECKING BALL *1992-present*

DOG STAR *1979*

CHUCKIE BOY *1992-present*

SUB POP *1979-83, 1986-present*

SPOO *1992*

MR. BROWN *1980-81*

FOR ART'S SAKE *1992*

SAFETY FIRST *1980*

TEMPORARY FREEDOM *1992-93*

ENGRAM *1980-84*

JAEGERMONKEY *1992-present*

GLASS MOUTH *1980*

BELLTOWN *1993-present*

ALBATROSS *1981-84*

PLUTO *1993-present*

TEENIE WOMPUM/DU-TEL *1981*

ONE DAY I STOPPED BREATHING *1993*

FARTZ WRECKORDS *1981-82*

VAGRANT *1993-present*

206 *1982*

STAMPEDE *1993-present*

SUBCORE *1982-87*

GREEN DRAGON *1993-present*

IGLOO *1993-present*
IVY *1993-present*
BANDS WE LIKE *1993-present*
CHROMOTOSE *1993-present*
SIRIUS *1993-present*
BROUN SOUND *1993-present*
UP *1993-present*
CHER DOLL *1993-present*
RED ROCKET *1993-present*
NEGATIVE FEEDBACK *1993-present*
HARRIET *1993-present*
MOPE *1993-present*
FLAMING COW'S HEAD *1993-present*
GRITTY KITTY *1993-present*
YOYO *1993-present*
MOTHER *1993*
SYLVIA *1993-present*
WATERHOUSE *1993-present*
EXCURSION *1993-present*
CHAINSAW *1993-present*
KNW YR WN *1993-present*
TEAM FRIENDLY *1994*
BEDAZZLED COMPACT DISCS *1994-present*
LOOSE GROOVE *1994-present*
BLOTTER *1994-present*
CM *1994-present*
NOTEWORTHY *1994-present*
FLYDADDY *1994-present*
FRUMUNDA *1994-present*
MAKE-OUT *1994-present*
NEGATIVE FEEDBACK *1994-present*
UP *1994-present*
Y *1994-present*
UNMITIGATED GALL *1994*
RAT CITY *1994-present*
ENDGAME *1994-present*
OPTIONAL ART *1994-present*
LAUNDRY ROOM *1994-present*
CONCEPTION *1994-present*
RAISED *1994-present*
ATLAS *1994-present*
ENDGAME *1994-present*
EL RECORDO *1994-present*
HORN HUT *1994*
CRUNCH MELODY/NEW ROSE
1994-present
COLLECTIVE FRUIT *1994-present*
JETT CITY *1994*
IFA *1994-present*
(YOUR NAME HERE) *1994-present*
TOOTH & NAIL *1994-present*
IT IS *1994-present*
ULTRASOUND *1994-present*
OUTCAST *1995-present*
CHARLATAN *1995-present*

FASTBACKS DRUMMERS
(#1-10 with comments by Kurt Bloch from the Rocket, *6/91)*

1. Kurt Bloch. Original drummer. Played on original demo tape.
2. Duff McKagan. In another band. Played on "It's Your Birthday" 45.
3. Richard Stuverud. In many bands (including TKO and War Babies). Played on *...Play Five of Their Favorites.*
4. Danny Zakos. In Boomslang.
5. Tad Hutchison. Played one show. Now in the Young Fresh Fellows. Fastest-ever, says Kim.
6. Tom Hendrikson. Seen recently at QFC.
7. Richard Stuverud. Back in again. Played on *Every Day Is Saturday* and *...And His Orchestra.* Back out again. (Recently in Lazy Susan.)
8. Nate Johnson. At Mariners game (in Flop, 1990-1994). Played on

Bike Toy Clock Gift, Very Very Powerful Motor and *The Answer Is You.*
9. Rusty Willoughby. Not kicked out yet (in Flop).
10. Nils Bernstein. In training for '92 (didn't perform in any shows).
—
11. Mike Musburger, on loan from the Posies.
12. Rusty Willoughby again; played on *Zucker.*
13. John Moen, formerly of Portland's Dharma Bums.
14. Mike Musburger again, now an ex-Posie.
Drums on *Answer the phone, dummy.* played by Willoughby, Johnson, Musburger, Moen, Jason Finn, and Dan Peters.
Bill Rieflin was asked to drum for the group sometime in the late '80s but declined.

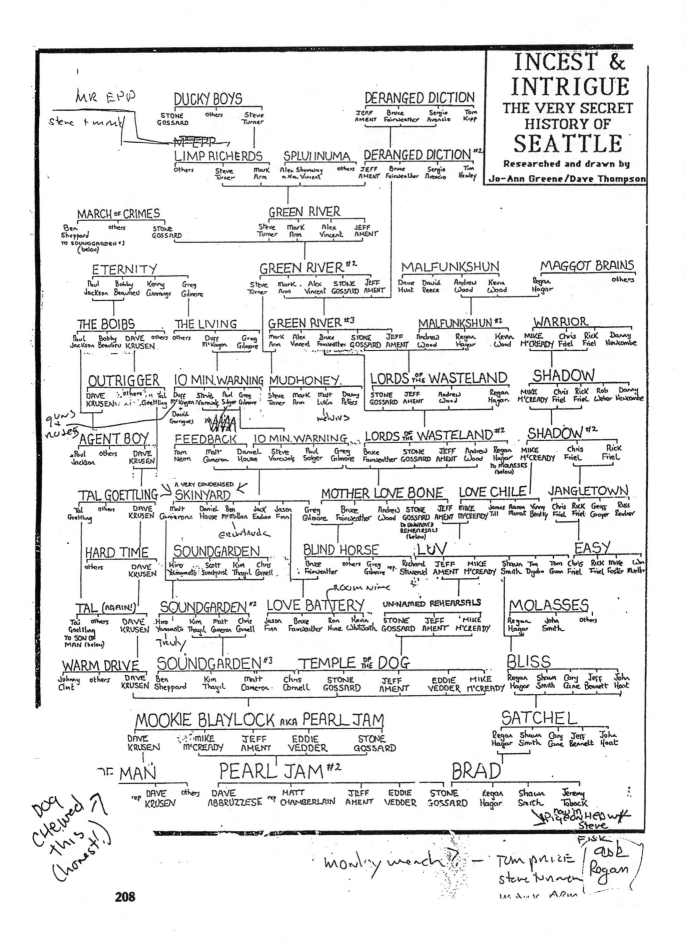

INCEST &
INTRIGUE
THE VERY SECRET
HISTORY OF
SEATTLE
Researched and drawn by
Jo-Ann Greene/Dave Thompson

208

CHAPTER FOURTEEN: DISCOGRAPHY

ESSENTIAL (IN-PRINT) DISCOGRAPHY
A list of over 500 key albums and a few singles, tapes and videos, in approximate order of recording (not necessarily of release), by people who've worked in Western Washington; either in print or still in stock through some channels. Some will undoubtedly become unavailable before you read this. This list doesn't include promos, bootlegs, most singles by bands who've also made albums, most foreign releases, out-of-state bands on local labels, or pre-punk stars who grew up here but didn't record here (J. Hendrix, Q. Jones).

THE EARLY ROCK YEARS
DON AND THE GOODTIMES
Don and the Goodtimes (Jerden)
FLEETWOODS
The Best of the Fleetwoods (Rhino compilation)
Come Softly To Me: The Very Best of the Fleetwoods (EMI compilation)
KINGSMEN
The Kingsmen In Person Featuring Louie Louie (Sundazed)
The Best of the Kingsmen (Rhino compilation)
Shindig Presents: Frat Party (Rhino Video)
Live and Unreleased (Jerden compilation)
PAUL REVERE AND THE RAIDERS
Greatest Hits (Columbia compilation)
SONICS
Here Are The Ultimate Sonics (Etiquette compilation)
Maintaining My Cool (Jerden)
VENTURES
Greatest Hits (Curb compilation)
Walk Don't Run: The Best of the Ventures (EMI compilation)
WAILERS
Tall Cool One/Golden Classics (Capitol Collectables compilation)
The Boys From Tacoma (Etiquette compilation)
COMPILATIONS
Cruisin' 1966 (Increase; hosted by Pat O'Day)
Cruisin' 1968 (Increase; with Merillee Rush)
The Del-Fi and Donna Story (Ace import; with Ron Holden)
Louie Louie by the Best of the Northwest (Jerden)
Marry Christmas from the Wailers, Sonics and Galaxies (Etiquette)
The History of Northwest Rock Vol. 1 (Jerden)
Rock n' Roll Guitar Greats (K-Tel; with Ventures, Frantics)

THE MODERN ERA
ACCUSED
More Fun Than An Open Casket Funeral (Combat)
Martha Splatterhead (Combat)
The Return of Martha Splatterhead (Combat)
Martha Splatterhead's Maddest Stories Ever Told (Combat)
Hymns for the Deranged (eMpTy)
Grinning Like An Undertaker (Nastymix/Ichiban)
Straight Razor (Nastymix/Ichiban)
Splatter Rock (Nastymix/Ichiban)
ALCOHOL FUNNYCAR
Burn (C/Z EP)
Time to Make the Donuts (C/Z)
Shapes (Columbia)
ALICE IN CHAINS
Facelift (Columbia)
Live Facelift (SMV Video)
Sap (Columbia EP)
Dirt (Columbia)
Jar of Flies (Columbia EP)
Layne Staley with other people:
Mad Season: Above (Columbia)
AND CHRIST WEPT
Destroy Existence (NEC)
ATOMIC 61
Heartworm (Box Dog EP)
Tinnitus in Extremis (Cavity Search)
BAM BAM
Pollywog (self-released tape)
PAUL BARKER/BILL RIEFLIN (also see Blackouts)
with Lead Into Gold:
The Age of Reason (WaxTrax)
with Ministry:
The Land of Rape and Honey (Sire)
The Mind Is A Terrible Thing To Taste (Sire)
In Case You Didn't Feel Like Showing Up (Sire EP/Warner Video)
Psalm 69 (Sire)
Pig's Food (Sire; Barker only)
with Pigface (Rieflin only)
Notes from the Underground (Invisible)

with Revolting Cocks:
Linger Ficken' Good (Sire)
LARRY BARRETT
Flowers (Glitterhouse import)
LYNDA BARRY
The Lynda Barry Experience (Gang of Seven/BMG)
JIM BASNIGHT
The Moberlys (Precedent)
Pop Top (Precedent)
BEAT HAPPENING (also see Halo Benders, Dub Narcotic Sound System)
1983-85 (K compilation)
Jamboree (K/Rough Trade/Sub Pop)
Black Candy (K/Rough Trade/Sub Pop)
Beat Happening/Screaming Trees (K)
Dreamy (K/Sub Pop)
You Turn Me On (K/Sub Pop)
BELUGA
Nuke the Gay Whales (CM)
JESSE BERNSTEIN
Words and Music (Original Cast tape)
The Sad Bag (Trigger tape)
Prison (Sub Pop)
BEST KISSERS IN THE WORLD
Best Kissers in the World (Sub Pop EP)
Puddin' (MCA EP)
Been There (MCA)
BIKINI KILL (also see Fumpies)
Bikini Kill/Yeah Yeah Yeah Yeah (Kill Rock Stars)
"This Is New Radio" (Kill Rock Stars 45)
Pussy Whipped (Kill Rock Stars)
Peel Sessions (Strange Fruit EP)
Kathleen Hanna with other people:
Viva Knievel (Ultrasound EP)
Wordcore Vol. 1 (Kill Rock Stars split 45, with Slim Moon)
Fakes: Real Fiction (Chainsaw)
BITTER END
Harsh Realities (Metal Blade)
BLACK CAT ORCHESTRA
...Plays for Dante's Inferno (self-released)
BLACKHUMOUR
Peace in Our Time (We Never Sleep)
BLACKOUTS (also see Paul Barker/Bill Rieflin)
Blackouts compilation (C/Z, due late 1995)
BLANKET
"Ocean" (Cher Doll 45)
BLOOD CIRCUS
Primal Rock Therapy (Sub Pop)
BLOOD LOSS (also see Green River, Mudhoney, Monroe's Fur)
In-A-Gadda-Da-Change (Sympathy for the

Record Industry)

Ten Solid Rocking Inches of Rock-Solid Rock
     (Sympathy for the Record Industry EP)

Live My Way (Reprise/In The Red)

BLOOD OF THE LAMB BAND

Let It Bleat (self-released tape)

Cowtown to Exstasy (self-released tape)

Earl Brooks with other people:

Crop Circles: Born With a Bad Heart (self-released)

BLOWHOLE

Uncoastin' (Apraxia EP)

BOLOS

Hello Danger (Belltown)

This Is You (Belltown)

BONE CELLAR

Now That It's All Over (Your Name Here)

BRATMOBILE

Pottymouth (Kill Rock Stars)

The Real Janelle (Kill Rock Stars EP)

Peel Sessions (Strange Fruit EP)

BUILT TO SPILL (also see Treepeople, Halo Benders)

Ultimate Alternative Wavers (C/Z)

There's Nothing Wrong With Love (Up)

Built to Spill/Caustic Resin (Up split CD)

CANDLEBOX

Candlebox (Maverick/Warner Bros.)

CAPPING DAY

Post No Bills (PopLlama)

CAT BUTT

Journey to the Center of Cat Butt (Sub Pop EP)

CAT FOOD

50 Beautiful Girls and 3 Ugly Ones (Carving Knife)

CAUSTIC RESIN

Fly Me to the Moon (Up)

Built to Spill/Caustic Resin (Up split CD)

CELIBATE TWIST

"Amok" (Schwa Sound 45)

CENTRAL DISTRICT POSSE

Life in the Central (Come Up)

CHET

Chet (Y)

CHRIST ON A CRUTCH

Crime Pays When Pigs Die (New Red Archives)

CHURN

Titus (Laundry Room)

COFFIN BREAK

Rupture/Psychosis (C/Z)

No Sleep 'Til the Stardust Motel (C/Z compilation)

Thirteen (Epitaph)

Crawl (Epitaph)

COMMON LANGUAGE

Scar (Big Flaming Ego)

COVEN

Death Walks Behind You (Ever Rat/Medusa)

Blessed Is the Black (Ever Rat/Medusa)

Boneless Christian (Ever Rat/Red Light)

CRABS

Jackpot (K)

ROBERT CRAY

Who's Been Talking (Charly)

Too Many Cooks (Tomato)

Strong Persuader (Mercury)

Don't Be Afraid of the Dark (Mercury)

Midnight Stroll (Mercury)

I Was Warned (Mercury)

Robert Cray Collection (PolyGram Video)

Shame + A Sin (Mercury)

Some Rainy Morning (Mercury)

CRIMINAL NATION

Trouble in the Hood (Nastymix)

CRITTERS BUGGIN

Guest (Loosegroove/Epic)

CROWS

Crows (Amphetamine Reptile)

CRUNT

Crunt (Trance Syndicate)

DANCING FRENCH LIBERALS OF '48 (also see Gits)

Scream Clown Scream (Broken EP)

Powerline (Broken)

DANGER GENS

Evil Bed Set (Crunch Melody EP)

Life Between Cigarettes (Crunch Melody)

DEAD PRESIDENTS

South Tacoma Way (K)

SARA DEBELL

Grunge Lite (C/Z)

DEFLOWERS

Shiny New Pony (Platypus)

STUART DEMPSTER

On the Boards (self-released tape)

AMY DENIO

No Bones (Spoot Music tape)

No Elevators (Spoot Music tape)

Never Too Old to Pop a Hole (Spoot Music)

Birthling Chair Blues (Knitting Factory Works)

Tongues (FOT)

with the Billy Tipton Memorial Saxophone Quartet :

Saxhouse (Knitting Factory Works)

Make It Funky God (Horn Hut)

with Blubber:

Grows Down (Invisible Music tape)

with Couch of Sound:

Rabagubus (Spoot Music tape)

with Curlew:

A Beautiful Western Saddle (Cuneiform)

with the (EC) Nudes

Vanishing Point (ReR/Cuneiform)

with Entropics:

Spagga (PopLlama)

with Tone Dogs:

Ankety Low Day (C/Z)

The Early Middle Years (Soleil Moon)

DERELICTS

Love Machine (Penultimate)

Going Out Of Style (eMpTy compilation)

DEVILHEAD (also see Fire Ants)

Your Ice Cream's Dirty (Loosegroove/Epic)

DIAMOND FIST WERNY

Diamond Fist Werny (Rudy/Ivy)

DIRT FISHERMEN

Glenn's Car (Silence)

Vena Cava (C/Z)

DUB NARCOTIC SOUND SYSTEM (also see Beat Happening, Halo Benders)

Rhythm Record Vol. 1 (K)

Industrial Breakdown (K)

DUMT

in...Humor Core Galore (Ever Rat)

P.K. DWYER

How Can I Go Wrong (self-released)

EARL'S FAMILY BOMBERS

Earl's Family Bombers (eMpTy EP)

Earl's Family Bombers (Kept in the Dark)

EARTH

Bureaucratic Desire for Revenge (Sub Pop EP)

Earth 2 (Sub Pop)

Earth Phase 3: Thrones and Dominions (Sub Pop)

JACK ENDINO (also see Skin Yard)

Angle of Attack (Bobok)

Endino's Earthworm (Cruz)

ENGINE KID

Bear Catching Fish (C/Z)

Astronaut (C/Z EP)

Iceburn/Engine Kid (Revelation split CD)

Angel Wings (Revelation)

EXECUTIONERS (also see Kill Sybil)

1493 Steps to My House (Last Minute/eMpTy EP)

FAITH AND DISEASE

Beauty and Bitterness (Ivy)

Fortune His Sleep (Ivy)

FALL-OUTS

Here I Come and Other Hits (Estrus compilation)

Fall-Outs (Super-Electro)

Sleep (Super-Electro)

FASTBACKS

...And His Orchestra (PopLlama; CD includes EPs

     ...Play Five of Their Favorites and *Every Day Is Saturday*)

Bike Toy Clock Gift (Lucky)

Very, Very Powerful Motor (PopLlama)

The Answer Is You (Sub Pop double 45)

The Question Is No (Sub Pop compilation)

Zucker (Sub Pop)

Gone to the Moon (Sub Pop Europe EP)

Answer the Phone Dummy (Sub Pop)

FIRE ANTS (also see Devilhead)

Stripped (Dekema EP)

STEVE FISK

Over & Thru the Night (K compilation)

448 Deathless Days (SST)

S.J. Berrnstein: Prison (Sub Pop)

Pigeonhed (Sub Pop)

with Pell Mell:

Flow (SST)

The Bumper Crop (SST)

Interstate (DGC)

FITZ OF DEPRESSION

Fitz of Depression (Negative Feedback)

Let's Give It A Twist (K)

Pigs Are People Too (Negative Feedback EP)

FLAKE

Box (Y)

FLOOD

Satan Touched My Hat (self-released)

FLOP (also see Pure Joy)

Losing End (Lucky EP)

Flop & the Fall of the Mopsqueezer (Frontier)

Whenever You're Ready (Frontier/Epic)

Eddy and the Back Nine (Super-Electro EP)

World of Today (Frontier)

FORCED ENTRY

As Above So Below (Combat)
Uncertain Future (Combat)
ED FOTHERINGHAM
Thrown Ups: Melancholy Girlie Box (Amphetamine Reptile 45 box set)
Icky Joey: Pooh (C/Z)
Love and Respect: Record (Penultimate)
Sad and Lonely(s) (Super-Electro EP)
Eddy and the Back Nine (Super-Electro EP)
4 HOUR RAMONA
4 Hour Ramona (self-released)
BILL FRISELL (since moving to Seattle; also see Wayne Horvitz)
Before We Were Born (Elektra)
Is That You? (Elektra)
Where in the World? (Elektra)
Have A Little Faith (Elektra)
This Land (Elektra)
FRUMPIES (also see Bikini Kill)
Babies and Bunnies (Kill Rock Stars 45)
Tommy Slich (Lookout)
FUMES
Knock Out the Axis (eMpTy)
GAMELAN PACIFICA
Trance Gong (self-released)
GARDENIAS
We're Sorry, But We're the Gardenias (self-released tape)
GAS HUFFER
Janitors of Tomorrow (eMpTy)
Integrity Technology and Service (eMpTy)
The Shrill Beeps of Shrimp (eMpTy EP)
One Inch Masters (Epitaph)
The Del Lagunas: Time Tunnel (Estrus 45)
GIRL TROUBLE
Hit It or Quit It (K/Sub Pop/Estrus)
Thrillsphere (PopLlama)
Stomp and Shout and Work It On Out (Dionysus EP)
New American Shame (eMpTy)
GITS (also see Dancing French Liberals of '48)
Frenching the Bully (C/Z)
Enter: The Conquering Chicken (C/Z)
Joan Jett and the Gits: Evil Stig (Reprise)
GIVE
Easy (Ivy)
GNOME
Six Hi Surprise Tower (C/Z)
Fiberglass (C/Z)
GODHEADSILO
Elephantitus of the Night (Kill Rock Stars)
PAMELA GOLDEN
Happens All the Time (Park Avenue)
GOODNESS
Goodness (Y)
GORILLA
Meconium: The Squid Row Daze (Bag of Hammers compilation)
Deal With It (Thrill Jockey)
GRAVEL
No Stone Unturned (Estrus)
Break a Bone (Estrus)
GREEN APPLE QUICK STEP
Wonderful Virus (Medicine/Warner Bros.)
Reloaded (Medicine/Warner Bros.)
GREEN PAJAMAS
Ghosts of Love (Green Monkey/Bomp)
"Song for Christina " (Endgame 45)

GREEN RIVER
Come On Down (Homestead)
Dry As A Bone/Rehab Doll (Sub Pop)
JEFF GREINKE
Timbral Planes (Linden)
Changing Skies (Multimood)
Aerial #2 (Non Sequitor)
Lost Terrain (Silent)
Crossing Ngoli (Ear-National; with Rob Angus)
Places of Motility (Dossier import)
In Another Place (Linden)
Big Weather (Linden)
with Land:
Land (Extreme)
GRUNTRUCK (also see Skin Yard)
Inside Yours (eMpTy/Roadrunner)
Push (Roadrunner)
TERRY LEE HALE
Oh What A World (Normal import)
Frontier Model (Glitterhouse import)
Tornado Alley (Glitterhouse import)
HALL AFLAME
Guaranteed Forever (IRS)
HALO BENDERS (also see Beat Happening, Built to Spill, Dub Narcotic Sound System)
Canned Oxygen (Atlas EP)
God Don't Make No Junk (K)
HAMMERBOX
Hammerbox (C/Z)
Numb (A&M)
HAPS
Back to the House (PipTone)
HEART
Dreamboat Annie (Mushroom/Capitol)
Little Queen (Capitol)
Magazine (Capitol)
Dog and Butterfly (Portrait)
Bebe Le Strange (Epic)
Greatest Hits Live (Epic)
Private Audition (Epic)
Passion Works (Epic)
Heart (Capitol)
Bad Animals (Capitol)
Brigade (Capitol)
Lovemongers: The Battle of Evermore (Capitol EP)
Desire Walks On (Capitol)
20 Years of Rock n' Roll (Compton CD-ROM)
The Road Home (Capitol)
HEAVENS TO BETSY
Calculated (Kill Rock Stars)
GARY HEFFERN
Bald Tires in the Rain (Nocturnal)
Askew (Belltown)
Painful Days (Glitterhouse import)
HELL UPSIDE DOWN
The Bovine Years (Y)
ROBIN HOLCOMB
Robin Holcomb (Elektra)
Rockabye (Elektra)
HOLE
Pretty on the Inside (Caroline)
Asking For It (Caroline compilation)
Live Through This (DGC)
HOLIDAYS
Every Day's A Holiday (Chuckie Boy)
Holidays (Chuckie Boy)
WAYNE HORVITZ

This New Generation (Elektra)
Todos Santos (Sound Aspects; Robin Holcomb cover album)
The President: Miracle Mile (Elektra)
Bring Yr Camera (Elektra)
with Naked City, including Bill Frisell:
Naked City (Elektra)
The Torture Garden (Toy's Factory/Shimmydisc)
Heretic: Jeux Des Dames Cruelles (Avant soundtrack)
Leng Tch'e (Toy's Factory)
Grand Guignol (Avant)
with Pigpen:
HalfRack (Tim/Kerr EP)
Pigpen (Cavity Search EP)
Miss Ann (Tim/Kerr)
V As In Victim (Disk Union/Sphere)
PENELOPE HOUSTON
Avengers (CD Presents compilation)
The Whole World (Heyday)
HUSH HARBOR
I'm Not Impressed (Up EP)
IMIJ
The In Gods You Lust EP (Babylon Burnin' EP)
INFAMOUS MENAGERIE
"Toast" (Big Flaming Ego/K 45)
INFLATABLE SOULE
So Sad (Silver Management)
JAMBAY
Run If You Can (self-released)
Live in the Northwest (self-released)
JESSAMINE
Jessamine (Kranky)
MIKE JOHNSON
Where Am I? (Up)
JUNED
Juned (Up)
KALBERER HOTEL SUPPLY
Kalberer Hotel Supply (self-released tape)
CHET KANE
Tears for Columbia (self-released)
KARP
KARP (Kill Rock Stars EP)
Mustaches Wild (K EP)
Bastard Swords (K)
KENT 3
Coin of the Realm (eMpTy EP)
Screaming Youth Fantastic (Bag of Hammers)
KICKING GIANT
Alien I.D. (K)
KID SENSATION
Seatown Funk (Ichiban)
KILL SYBIL (also see Executioners)
Kill Sybil (eMpTy)
KILL SWITCH...KLICK
Beat It to Fit, Paint It to Match (Cleopatra)
Oddities and Versions (Cleopatra)
KITCHEN RADIO
Virgin Smile (Glitterhouse import)
JOEY KLINE (also see Squirrels)
Prudence Dredge: Big Ellen (Green Monkey)
Pomp and Circus Pants (PopLlama)
Hat Ashbury (Bands We Like)
LAZY SUSAN
Twang (self-released)
Sink (Ivy)

PETE LEINONEN
Ashfall (Original Cast EP)
Words & Music (Original Cast tape, with Jesse Bernstein)
Lemminkainen's Adventures (Original Cast tape)
LEMONS
Marvel (Macola/Pacific Inland)
Sturdy (Macola/Pacific Island)
Sturdy (Mercury)
LIAR'S CLUB
Evolution #9 (self-released)
Drop Dead (Collective Fruit)
LIFE LIKE FEEL
Life Like Feel (Phisst)
LOIS
Butterfly Kiss (K)
Strumpet (K)
Shy Town (K EP)
Bet the Sky (K)
MAN TEE MANS
Man Tee Mans (Bag of Hammers EP)
MAVIS PIGOTT
Late Bloom (Flydaddy EP)
MARY LOU LORD
Mary Lou Lord (Kill Rock Stars EP)
LAURA LOVE
Venus Envy: I'll Be A Homo for Christmas (Ladyslipper)
Z Therapy (Octoroon Biography)
Pangea (Octoroon Biography)
Helvetica Bold (Octoroon Biography)
The Laura Love Collection (Putumayo World Music compilation)
Jo Miller and Laura Love Sing Bluegrass and Oldtime Music (Rockin' Octoroon)
LOVE BATTERY
Between the Eyes (Sub Pop)
Dayglo (Sub Pop)
Far Gone (Sub Pop)
Nehru Jacket (Atlas/A&M EP)
Straight Freak Ticket (Atlas/A&M)
LYNC
These Are Not Fall Colors (K)
MAKERS
Hip Notic (Sympathy for the Record Industry EP)
Howl (Estrus)
The Devil's Nine Questions (Estrus)
All-Night Riot!! (Estrus)
MALCHICKS
Bad Acid Comedy (Other Rivers)
MALFUNKSHUN
Return to Olympus (Loosegroove/Epic compilation)
MAN TEE MANS
Man Tee Mans (Bag of Hammers EP)
DUFF McKAGAN
Believe In Me (Geffen)
with Guns n' Roses:
Appetite for Destruction (Geffen)
GN'R Lies (Geffen compilation)
Use Your Illusions I/II (Geffen)
The Spaghetti Incident? (Geffen)
MEDDAPHYSICAL
Flow (Belltown)
MEDICINE HAT
Medicine Hat (Collective Fruit)
MELVINS
10 Songs (C/Z)

Gluey Porch Treatments (Alchemy/Boner)
Ozma (Boner)
Bullhead (Boner)
Eggnog (Boner EP)
Salad of a Thousand Delights (Box Dog video)
King Buzzo, Dale Crover, Joe Preston (Boner solo EPs)
Lysol (retitled *Melvins*) (Boner)
Houdini (Atlantic)
Snivlem: Prick (Amphetamine Reptile)
Stoner Witch (Atlantic)
MENTORS
Up the Dose/You Axed For It (Combat)
The Wretched World of the Mentors (self-released video)
Sex, Drugs, and Rock & Roll (Ever Rat/Red Light)
El Duce solo:
Slave To Thy Master (Ever Rat/Red Light)
METAL CHURCH
Metal Church (Elektra)
The Dark (Elektra)
Blessing in Disguise (Elektra)
The Human Factor (Epic)
Hanging in the Balance (Blackheart)
MODEL ROCKETS
Hilux (Lucky)
MO'LASSES
Straight From the Players (Belltown)
MOMMY
Mommy (Ivy)
MONO MEN
Stop Draggin' Me Down (Estrus)
Wrecker (Estrus)
Shut Up! (vinyl title: *Shut the Fuck Up!*) (Estrus EP)
Lost in Europe (Lucky EP)
Back to Mono (1+2 import)
Bent Pages (Semaphore import)
Sin & Tonic (vinyl title: *Skin & Tonic*) (Estrus)
Live at Tom's Strip & Bowl (Estrus)
MONROE'S FUR
Sadistfactory (Belltown)
MONSTER TRUCK DRIVER
Monster Truck Driver (Carving Knife EP)
MORAL CRUX
Moral Crux/Load of Dead Tracks (DeDbeet compilation)
The Side Effects of Thinking (CM)
...And Nothing But the Truth (Vandal Children)
I Was A Teenage Teenager (Monitor)
MOTHER LOVE BONE (also see Pearl Jam)
Mother Love Bone (Stardog/Mercury)
The Love Bone Earth Affair (PolyGram Video)
MUDHONEY
Superfuzz Bigmuff plus Early Singles (Sub Pop)
Mudhoney (Sub Pop)
Every Good Boy Deserves Fudge (Sub Pop)
Let It Slide (Sub Pop EP)
Piece of Cake (Reprise)
Five Dollar Bob's Mock Cooter Stew (Reprise EP)
Mudhoney and Jimmie Dale Gilmore (Sub Pop EP)
My Brother the Cow (Reprise)

Mark Arm with other people (also see Green River, Blood Loss):
Mr. Epp: Of Course I'm Happy, Why? (Box Dog/Super-Electro compilation)
Mr. Epp: Live As All Get Out (Box Dog tape)
Thrown Ups: Melancholy Girlie Box (Amphetamine Reptile 45 box set)
The Freewheelin' Mark Arm (Sub Pop 45)
The Monkeywrench (Sub Pop)
Junkyard Dogs: Good Livin' Platter (Sympathy for the Record Industry EP)
ERIC MUHS
Presto Vim: The Salad Days (Invisible Music tape; with Audio Leter and Student Nurse)
Notochord (Invisible Music; with Myles Boisen)
Carnage Motel (Invisible Music tape; with Deran Ludd)
MUKILTEO FAIRIES
Special Rites (Kill Rock Stars EP)
MY DIVA
My Diva (Manna EP)
MY NAME
Megacrush (C/Z)
Wet Hills and Big Wheels (C/Z)
MY SISTER'S MACHINE
Diva (Caroline)
Wallflower (Chameleon)
NIGHT KINGS
Increasing Our High (Super-Electro)
NIRVANA
Bleach (Sub Pop)
Hoarmoning (DGC Japan compilation)
Incesticide (DGC compilation)
Nevermind (DGC)
1991: The Year Punk Broke (Geffen Video)
Live! Tonight! Sold Out! (Geffen Video)
In Utero (DGC)
The Nevermind and In Utero Singles (DGC Japan box set)
MTV Unplugged in New York (DGC)
Kurt Cobain with other people:
Mark Lanegan: The Winding Sheet (Sub Pop)
Earth: Bureaucratic Desire for Revenge (Sub Pop EP)
Melvins: Houdini (Atlantic)
Wm. Burroughs: The Priest They Called Him (Tim/Kerr CD single)
Dave Grohl solo:
Foo Fighters (Roswell/Capitol)
Dave Grohl and Krist Novoselic with other people:
Stinky Puffs (Elemental of New Jersey EP)
NORTH AMERICAN BISON
Expect the Worst (self-released)
PANIC
Epidemic (Metal Blade)
Fact (Metal Blade)
PEACH
Siesta (Caroline)
Dead Soldier's Coat (Caroline EP)
Peach II (Caroline)
PEARL JAM (also see Green River, Mother Love Bone, Soundgarden/Pearl Jam side projects)
Ten (Epic)

Vs. (Epic)
Dissident (Sony Europe three-EP series)
The Singles Collection (Sony Europe box set)
Vitalogy (Epic)
Neil Young: Mirror Ball (Reprise)
RICHARD PETERSON
Love on the Golf Course (PopLlama)
PICKETTS
Paper Doll (PopLlama)
Pick It (Cruddy/PopLlama EP)
The Wicked Picketts (Rounder)
PISS DRUNKS
Urine Idiot (Ransom Note)
PLEASURE ELITE
Bad Juju (Red Light)
Brutal Tutu (Quivering Submissive Flesh)
POOR OLD LU
Sin (Alarma/Zoe)
POPDEFECT
Live With This (self-released)
Playing for Time (self-released EP)
Live With This: Adrift in America (Reality Train video)
Punch Drunk (Flipside)
Don't Be Hateful (Flipside EP)
POP SICKLE
Under the Influence (C/Z EP)
Here Today… (Collective Fruit 45)
PORTRAIT OF POVERTY
Term in Hell (Mother)
POSIES (also see Squirrels)
Failure (PopLlama)
Dear 23 (DGC)
Frosting on the Beater (DGC)
Big Star: Columbia (Zoo/BMG)
Minus Five: Old Liquidator (East Side Digital)
What Color Is A Red Light? (DGC; due early 1996)
PRESIDENTS OF THE UNITED STATES OF AMERICA
Presidents of the United States of America (PopLlama/Columbia)
PROSE AND CONCEPTS
Procreations (Loosegroove/Epic)
PURDINS
Greatest Hits (Bands We Like compilation)
PURE JOY (also see Flop)
Unsung (Flydaddy)
Carnivore (PopLlama)
PUTTERS
Fear of Women (eMpTy)
QUEENSRYCHE
Queensryche (206/EMI EP)
The Warning (EMI)
Rage to Order (EMI)
Operation: Mindcrime (EMI)
Video Mindcrime (EMI Video)
Operation: Livecrime (EMI Video)
Empire (EMI)
Building Empires (EMI Video)
The Promised Land (EMI)
QUEER THE PITCH
Little Freddy (Mother)
RANCH ROMANCE
Flip City (Sugar Hill)
Western Dream (Sugar Hill)
Blue Blazes (Sugar Hill)

RED DRESS
The Collection (PopLlama compilation)
REFUZORS
"I Think I Lost My Faith" (Bag of Hammers 45)
RORSCHACH TEST
The Eleventh (DC)
JIM ROSE CIRCUS SIDESHOW
Jim Rose Circus Sideshow (American Recordings Video)
ROULADE
Late Night Rain (Red Rocket EP)
RUMORS OF THE BIG WAVE
Burning Times (Earth Beat/Warner Bros.)
RUNNING WITH SCISSORS
The Turkey Album (Procession/Instant)
Single Bullet Theory (Procession/Instant)
Ordinary Leper (Instant)
SADHAPPY
Depth Charge (Periscope)
Live: Before We Were Dead (Periscope)
The Good, The Bad… and the Scary (Bedazzled)
SAGE
Forked (Will)
7th Standard Rd. (Will)
SANCTUARY
Refuge Denied (Epic)
Mirror Black (Epic)
SCREAMING TREES
Other Worlds (Velvetone/SST)
Even If And Especially When (SST)
Invisible Lantern (SST)
Buzz Factory (SST)
Anthology (SST compilation)
Beat Happening/Screaming Trees (K)
Change Has Come (Sub Pop EP)
Uncle Anesthesia (Epic)
Sweet Oblivion (Epic)
Mark Lanegan solo:
The Winding Sheet (Sub Pop)
Whiskey for the Holy Ghost (Sub Pop)
Gary Lee Conner solo:
The Purple Outside: Mystery Lane (New Alliance)
Van Conner solo:
Solomon Grundy (New Alliance)
SEAWEED
Seaweed (Leopard Gecko EP)
Despised (Sub Pop EP)
Weak (Sub Pop)
Four (Sub Pop)
Spanaway (Hollywood)
SECOND COMING
L.O.V.Evil (Red Rocket)
SEVEN YEAR BITCH
Sick 'Em (C/Z)
Viva Zapata (C/Z)
WALLY SHOUP
Project W (Aparaxia tape)
Alto Sax (self-released tape)
TRAVIS SHREDD
Headbanger's Square Dance (Siruis)
SIBYL VANE
Sibyl Vane (Island)
SICK AND WRONG
Sick and Wrong (Sub Pop EP)
"Pickup (Some Beer)" (Rat City 45)
SICKO
You Can Feel the Love In This Room

(eMpTy)
Laugh While You Can Monkey Boy (eMpTy)
SILKWORM
…his absence is a blessing (Stampede EP)
In the West (C/Z)
Libertine (El Recordo)
JIMMY SILVA
Heidi (East Side Digital)
Near the End of the Harvest (East Side Digital)
SINISTER SIX
Outta Sight (eMpTy)
Nobody Rides For Free (Bag of Hammers)
SIR MIX-A-LOT
SWASS (Nastymix/Def American)
Seminar (Rhyme Cartel/Def American)
Mack Daddy (Rhyme Cartel/Def American)
Maconomics (Def American Video)
Chief Boot Knocka' (American Recordings)
SISTER PSYCHIC
Fuel (Restless)
Surrender, You Freak! (Restless)
66 SAINTS
Dreamdate (Big Flaming Ego)
SKIN YARD (also see Gruntruck, Jack Endino)
Skin Yard (C/Z/Cruz)
Hallowed Ground (Toxic Shock)
1000 Smiling Knuckles (Cruz)
Fist Sized Chunks (Cruz)
Undertow (Cruz EP)
Inside the Eye (Cruz)
SKY CRIES MARY
Until the Grinders Cease/Don't Eat the Dirt (New Rose/World Domination compilation with Auer and Stringfellow; to be reissued mid-1995)
Exit to the Axis (World Domination/Capitol EP)
A Return to the Inner Experience (World Domination/Capitol)
This Timeless Turning (World Domination)
SLEEP CAPSULE
Mousepuss (Spanish)
SHAWN SMITH
Brad: Shame (Epic)
Pigeonhed (Sub Pop)
Satchel: EDC (Epic)
SLEEP CAPSULE
Mousepuss (Spanish)
SOLGER
Solger (Bag of Hammers reissue EP)
SOME VELVET SIDEWALK
I Scream (K EP)
Appetite for Extinction (K)
Shipwreck (K)
Avalanche (K)
Whirlpool (K)
SOULFOOD
Velour (Zoe)
SOUNDGARDEN
Screaming Life/Fopp (Sub Pop)
Ultramega OK (SST)
Flower (SST EP)
Louder Than Love (A&M)
Louder Than Live (A&M Video)
Badmotorfinger (A&M)
Motorvision (A&M Video)
Superunknown (A&M)

Soundgarden/Pearl Jam side projects:
Temple of the Dog (A&M)
Brad: Shame (Epic)
Hater (A&M)
Wellwater Conspiracy (Super-Electro 45 series)
Mad Season: Above (Columbia)
SPIKE
Whelmed (Y)
SQUIRRELS
What Gives? (PopLlama)
Harsh Toke of Reality (PopLlama)
Don't Fear the Snowman/Son of Snowman (PopLlama Xmas tape)
SQUIRT
See You In Heck (Red Rocket)
STATICS
Statics (Super-Electro EP)
Rat City (Rip Off)
STEEL WOOL
Simple Men Who Like Working With Their Hands (eMpTy)
Lucky Boy (eMpTy)
STUMPY JOE
One-Way Rocket Ride to Kicksville! (PopLlama)
Poor, Poor Stumpy Joe (Bands We Like tape)
STYMIE
Other (New Rage EP)
SUNNY DAY REAL ESTATE
Diary (Sub Pop)
SUPERSUCKERS
The Songs All Sound the Same (eMpTy compilation)
The Smoke of Hell (Sub Pop)
La Mano Cornuda (Sub Pop)
Supersuckers and Rev. Horton Heat (Sub Pop EP)
Junkyard Dogs: Good Livin' Platter (Sympathy for the Record Industry EP)
On the Couch (Sub Pop Europe EP)
Sacrilicious (Sub Pop)
SWALLOW
Swallow (Sub Pop/Tupelo)
SWEET WATER
Sweet Water (Atlantic)
Superfriends (EastWest)
SYMON-ASHER
Three Color Sunday (Miramar)
TAD
God's Balls/Salt Lick (Sub Pop)
8-Way Santa (Sub Pop)
Salem (Sub Pop CD single)
Inhaler (Giant/Mechanic)
Live Alien Broadcasts (Futurist)
Infrared Riding Hood (East West/Elektra)
¡TCH'KUNG!
¡Tch'Kung! (Belltown)
TEAM DRESCH
Personal Best (Candy-Ass/Chainsaw)
TEEN ANGELS
Teen Angels (Sub Pop 45)
TEN-O-SEVEN
Chainsaw Orchestra (Excursion)
You're Cool (Excursion)
TEXASS
Chanel #5 (IFA EP)
Texass (IFA)

TINA CHOPP
Nebbish (self-released)
TINY HAT ORCHESTRA
Noon at Nine (self-released)
Funhaus (Scrapyard)
TRANSIENT LOVE
I Learned (self-released)
TREEPEOPLE (also see Built to Spill, Halo Benders)
Guilt, Regret, Embarrassment (Toxic Shock)
Something Vicious for Tomorrow/Time Whore (C/Z)
Just Kidding (C/Z)
Actual Reenactment (C/Z)
TRULY
Married in the Playground (Sub Pop EP)
Leslie's Coughing Up Blood (Sub Pop EP)
Fast Stories… From Kid Coma (Capitol)
U-MEN
U-Men collection (Sub Pop/Amphetamine Reptile compilation; due late 1995)
Step on a Bug: The Red Toad Speaks (Black Label/Tupelo)
UNDERTOW
At Both Ends (Excursion)
UNEARTH
Everything Was Beautiful and Nothing Hurt (New Rage/C/Z)
UNWOUND
Pure Pain Sugar (Honey Bear/PNMV)
Fake Train (KIll Rock Stars)
New Plastic Ideas (Kill Rock Stars)
The Future of What (Kill Rock Stars)
VEXED
The Good Fight (C/Z EP)
Cathexis (C/Z)
VIOLENT GREEN
Eros (Up)
VOODOO GEARSHIFT
Glue Goat (C/Z)
It's About Time (Your Name Here)
WALKABOUTS
See Beautiful Rattlesnake Gardens (PopLlama)
Cataract (Sub Pop)
Rag and Bone (Sub Pop EP)
Where the Deep Water Goes (Sub Pop EP)
Jack Candy (Sub Pop EP)
Dead Man Rise (Sub Pop EP)
Scavenger (Sub Pop)
Chris and Carla: Shelter for an Evening (Sub Pop Europe)
New West Motel (Sub Pop Europe/Creative Man)
Satisfied Mind (Sub Pop Europe/Creative Man)
Setting the Woods On Fire (Sub Pop Europe/Creative Man)
To Hell and Back: The Walkabouts Live in Europe 1994 (K7/Music Video Inc. video)
Chris & Carla: Life Full of Holes (Glitterhouse import)
WAR BABIES
War Babies (Columbia)
WASTERS
"The Thrill" (Estate 45)
JOHNNY WEBELO
Extended Play (Bands We Like EP)

MARK WHEATON
Plays America's Favorite Award-Winning Tunes (Catasonic)
WILLARD
Steel Mill (Roadrunner)
WITCHYPOO
Mixed Metaphor (Kill Rock Stars EP)
YAB YUM
It's Delicious (Rosasham)
YOUNG FRESH FELLOWS (also see Squirrels)
Fabulous Sounds of the Pacific Northwest/Topsy Turvy (PopLlama/East Side Digital)
GAG Fah (PopLlama)
The Men Who Loved Music/Refreshments (PopLlama/Frontier)
Totally Lost (PopLlama/Frontier)
This One's For the Ladies (Frontier)
Electric Bird Digest (Frontier)
It's Low Beat Time (Frontier)
Temptation on Saturday (PopLlama EP)
Take It Like a Matador: Live in Spain (Impossible import)
Scott McCaughey solo:
My Chartreuse Opinion (PopLlama/East Side Digital)
The Boatrampmen: Rampage (Cruddy EP)
Minus Five: Old Liquidator (East Side Digital; with Peter Buck, Auer/Stringfellow)
ZEKE
West Seattle Acid Academy (Wrecking Ball EP)
Super Sound Racing (IFA)
ZIPGUN
8-Track Player (eMpTy)
Baltimore (eMpTy)

COMPILATIONS
C/Z
Deep Six
(with Soundgarden, U-Men, Malfunkshun, Melvins, Skin Yard, Green River; reissued by A&M)
Teriyaki Asthma Vol. I-V
(with Nirvana, Coffin Break, Daddy Hate Box, Dickless, Gas Huffer, Icky Joey, My Name, Vexed, others)
Hard to Believe: The KISS Tribute Album
(with Melvins, Nirvana, Skin Yard, others)
Something's Gone Wrong Again: The Buzzcocks Tribute Album
(with the Accused, Coffin Break, Lunachicks, others)
A Far Cry: Women in Independent Music
(with Juned, DeDuo, Crypt Kicker 5, Danger Gens, Dirt Fishermen, others)
Three on the Tree
(EP with Wreck, Vexed, Engine Kid)
ESTRUS
Here Ain't the Sonics (co-release with PopLlama)
(with Mono Men, Gravel, Young Fresh Fellows, others)
Estrus Lunch Bucket, Estrus Gear Box, On the Rocks, Tales from Estrus, Estrus Cocktail Companion
(7" box sets with Mono Men, Fastbacks, Makers, Gravel, Gas Huffer, Fall-Outs, Girl Trouble, others)

INSIGHT

Seattle Music Scene Vol. 1
(with Fosso, Spoonbender, Sadhappy, Pleasure Elite, Grin, Medicine Hat, others)

Seattle Music Scene Vol. 2
(with Sadhappy, Pleasure Elite, Diamond Fist Werny,
Running With Scissors, Willard, Life Like Feel, others)

Seattle Women In Rock: A Diverse Collection
(with Sky Cries Mary, Seven Year Bitch, Lazy Susan, others)

K

International Pop Underground
(with Beat Happening, Melvins, Seaweed, Some Velvet Sidewalk, the band "Courtney Love," Unwound, Bratmobile, Girl Trouble, Fastbacks, others)

International Hip Swing
(with Beat Happening, Some Velvet Sidewalk, Girl Trouble, Seaweed, Gravel, Mecca Normal, others)

KILL ROCK STARS

Kill Rock Stars
(with Bratmobile, Some Velvet Sidewalk, the band "Courtney Love," Nation of Ulysses, Unwound, Mecca Normal, Nirvana, Bikini Kill, Steve Fisk, Witchypoo, Melvins, Infamous Menagerie, Fitz of Depression, Seven Year Bitch)

Stars Kill Rock
(with Mary Lou Lord, KARP, Adickdid, Frumpies, Nikki McClure, others)

Rock Stars Kill
(with Team Dresch, Mukilteo Fairies, Kathleen Hanna, Severed Lethargy, others)

SUB POP

Sub Pop 200
(with Beat Happening, Cat Butt, Girl Trouble, Green River, Mudhoney, Nirvana, Screaming Trees, Soundgarden, TAD, Thrown Ups, others)

The Grunge Years
(with Beat Heppening, Dickless, Love Battery, Nirvana, Screaming Trees, TAD, others)

Fuck Me I'm Rich (Austrailian import)
(with Mudhoney, Blood Circus, Soundgarden, Swallow, TAD)

Afternoon Delight: Love Songs from Sup Pop
(with Beat Happening, S.J. Bernstein, Green River, others)

Say Hello to the Far East (Sub Pop/Sony import)
(with Fastbacks, Supersuckers, Seaweed, Beat Happening)

1989-1993: The John Peel Sub Pop Sessions
(with Mudhoney, TAD, Seaweed, others)

3:23
The End Unleashed
(with Mudhoney, Flop, Sister Psychic, Mudhoney, Fastbacks, Truly, Inflatable Soule, Posies, Purdins, Gnome, Diamond Fist Werny, Treepeople, Best Kissers in the World, Sky Cries Mary, Supersuckers)

Warm and Fuzzy Feelings
(with Pleasure Elite, Sadhappy, Blackhappy, Maxi Badd, Inflatable Soule, Blood Loss, Sage, Mommy, My Name, Lemons, Grin)

YOYO

Throw
(with Kicking Giant, Bratmobile, Some Velvet Sidewalk, Bikini Kill, Lumihoops with Lois Maffeo, Crayon, Go Team, McTells, others)

Julep
(with Heavens to Betsy, Bratmobile, KARP, Kicking Giant, others)

Periscope
(with Mukilteo Fairies, Fitz of Depression, Copass Grinderz, Neutral Milk Hotel, Cub, Team Dresch, others)

OTHER LOCAL COMPILATIONS

Dope Guns & Fucking in the Streets Vol. 1-3 (Amphetamine Reptile)
(with U-Men, Mudhoney, Thrown-Ups, TAD, others)

Dope Guns & Fucking in the Streets Vol. 4-7 (Amphetamine Reptile)
(with Crows, Gas Huffer, Melvins, Lubricated Goat, others)

Another DAMNED Seattle Compilation (Dashboard Hula Girl)
(with Young Fresh Fellows, Flop, Posies, Fastbacks, Purdins, Coffin Break, Skin Yard, Gas Huffer, Gruntruck, Hammerbox, Motorhoney, Derelicts, Big Satan Inc., Whitey, Love Battery)

Bobbing for Pavement (Rathouse/Broken)
(with the Gits, Gas Huffer, Hammerbox, My Name, Derelicts, Big Brown House, D.C. Beggars, Bay of Pigs)

Singles soundtrack (Epic)
(with Pearl Jam, Mudhoney, Heart, Lovemongers, Alice in Chains, Screaming Trees, others)

Northwest Ungrunge (Elemental)
(with Sadhappy, Mommy, Jolly Mon, others)

Seattle: The Dark Side (Rhyme Cartel/American Recordings)
(with Sir Mix-A-Lot, Kid Sensation, E-Dawg, Jay-Skee, others)

Puget Power Vol. 1-4 (Regal Select EPs)
(with Gas Huffer, Derelicts, Statics, Night Kings, Mudhoney, others)

Shotgun Barbeque (Bands We Like)
(with Larry Barrett, Blood of the Lamb Band, Bolos, others)

Hodge Podge Barrage from Japan (1+2 import)
(with Young Fresh Fellows, Fastbacks, Mono Men, Girl Trouble, Stumpy Joe)

The Way Things Really Ought to Be (The Labels United double 45)
(with Chicken, Sourpuss, Whipped, Meatminder, others)

eMpTy Sampler (eMpTy)
(with Gas Huffer, Kill Sybil, Girl Trouble, Sicko, the Putters, Meices, Sinister Six, others)

South End All Stars (Collective Fruit)
(with Rhino Humpers, Spontaneous Funk Whorehouse, Unspun, Running With Scissors, Redneck Girlfriend, Portrait of Poverty, the Lemons, Smelter, and 10 other Tacoma bands)

Here's To the Losers: The Store Room Compilation (Store Room)
(with Cat Food, Monster Truck Driver, Piss Drunk, Patchouli Sewer, Sore Jackson, Sick

and Wrong, Well Hung Over, Zulu Chainsaw, 17 others)

Designer Drug Vol. 1 (Estate)
(with Wasters, Rent-A-Wally, Foil, Mustard, Weird Feeling #3, Dead Man Walking, Skin-n-Bones, Michael Rook)

Northwest Postgrunge (Elemental)
(with Artis the Spoonman, Built to Spill, Dirt Fishermen, Hitting Birth, IMIJ, Rorschach Test, Running With Scissors, Tiny Hat Orchestra, more)

East of Eden (BopTone)
(comp. of Eastern Washington bands)

World of the Zombies (PopLlama)
(with Flop, Fastbacks, Young Fresh Fellows, Posies, Model Rockets, others)

Tribute to Poison 13 (Bag of Hammers)
(with Sinister Six, Gas Huffer, Sugar Shack, Big Foot Chester)

13 Soda Punx (Top Drawer)
(with Fastbacks, Kim Warnick/Bum, Young Fresh Fellows, Sicko, Model Rockets, Primate 5, others)

Universal Choking Sign (Excursion)
(with Undertow, Ten-O-Seven, Jayhawker, Has Been, Greg Bennick, Brand New Unit, Bicker, Sparkmarker, others)

We Are All Guilty (Outcast)
(with the Dunderheads, Portrait of Poverty, Berzerkers, Zeke, Chicken, Whorehouse of Representatives, Pregasm, Whipped)

Stacked Up! (Up)
(with Violent Green, Juned, Mike Johnson, Halo Benders, Hush Harbor, Butterfly Train, Built to Spill, Caustic Resin)

Ace • High • Straight (Lucky)
(with Supersuckers, Best Kissers in the World, Mono Men, Model Rockets, Fastbacks, Scott McCaughey/Supersnazz, others)

Your Hair Is Too Long And So Is Your Set: Live at the Colourbox (Red Rocket)
(with with 3DS&M, Dancing French Liberals of '48, Kitchen Radio, Lloyd's Rocket, Rorschach Test, Flood, Ondine, Supersonic Soul Pimps, others)

COMPILATIONS WITH A FEW SEATTLE ACTS ON THEM

Say Anything soundtrack (WTG/Sony)
(with Nancy Wilson)

Alternative N.R.G. (Hollywood)
(Greenpeace benefit with Soundgarden, Pearl Jam)

Born to Choose (Rykodisc)
(with Soundgarden)

Judgment Night soundtrack (Epic)
(with Mudhoney/Sir Mix-A-Lot)

Last Action Hero soundtrack (Columbia)
(with Alice in Chains, Queensryche)

Bonograph: Sonny Gets His Share (Bogus)
(with the Young Fresh Fellows)

Blah Blah Blah! Buy Buy Buy! (Geffen)
(Geffen sampler with Nirvana, Posies)

14 Songs for Greg Sage and the Wipers (Tim/Kerr)
(with Nirvana, Hole, others)

Sweet Relief: A Benefit for Victoria Williams (Chaos/Columbia)
(with Pearl Jam)

In Defense of Animals (Restless)

(PETA benefit with Pearl Jam, Sister
Psychic)
Stone Free: A Tribute to Jimi Hendrix
(Reprise)
(with Ament/McCready/Cameron/Cornell)
No Alternative (Arista)
(AIDS benefit with Nirvana, Soundgarden)
The Beavis and Butt-Head Experience
(Geffen)
(with Nirvana, Sir Mix-A-Lot)
20 More Explosive Fantastic Rockin' Mega-
Smash Hit Explosions!
(Pravda of Chicago)
('70s covers compilation with the Posies,
Fastbacks, Squirrels)
Reality Bites soundtrack (RCA)
(with the Posies)
Primary Colors (Kid Rhino)
(children's environmental musical with
Auer & Stringfellow)
P.C.U. soundtrack (Fox)
(with Mudhoney)
Rarities Vol. 1 (DGC)
(with Nirvana, Hole, Posies)
S.F.W. soundtrack (A&M)
(with Soundgarden, Chris Cornell solo,
Hole)
You Got Lucky: A Tribute to Tom Petty
(Backyard)
(with Engine Kid, Silkworm)
Clerks soundtrack (Chaos/Sony)
(with Alice in Chains, Seaweed)
Decade of Disaster: The Toxic Shock Years
(Westworld)
(with Skin Yard, Jack Endino, Treepeople)
Punk-O-Rama (Epitaph)
(with Gas Huffer)
Outpunk Dance Party (Outpunk/Revolver)
(with Mukilteo Fairies)
There's A Dyke in the Pit (Outpunk/Revolver
EP)
(with Seven Year Bitch, Bikini Kill)
This Is Fort Apache (Fort Apache/MCA)
(with the Walkabouts)
Happy Birthday Baby Jesus: The Second
Coming
(Sympathy for the Record Industry)
(with the Supersuckers, Mono Men)
Dangerhouse Vol. 1 (Frontier)
(with Avengers)
Caged/Uncaged (Kenwood import)
(with Amy Denio)
Killed By Death #2 (Redrum import)
(with Vains)
Give Me Back (Ebullition)
(with Bikini Kill)
Punk USA (Lookout)
(with Moral Crux)
Yellow Pills Vol. 2 (Big Deal/Caroline)
(with the Posies, Jim Basnight)
Tank Girl soundtrack (Elektra)
(with Hole)
The Basketball Diaries soundtrack (Island)
(with Pearl Jam, Soundgarden, Posies,
Green Apple Quick Step)
Batman Forever soundtrack (Atlantic)
(with Sunny Day Real Estate)
A Saucerful of Pink: A Tribute to Pink Floyd
(Cleopatra)
(with Sky Cries Mary)

Red Hot and Bothered (Elektra)
(with Built to Spill, Lois, Team Dresch)

HOME VIDEOS (also see individual band list-
ings)
Birthright (Birthright Film Production)
Both Parts Live
(with the Accused, Forced Entry, Panic,
Coffin Break, Skin Yard, and the industrial-
noise version of Sky Cries Mary)
Comic Book Confidential (Voyager/Stream-
line)
(documentary with Lynda Barry, Charles
Burns)
Frances (HBO)
Funny Ladies
(documentary with Lynda Barry)
Hard 'n' Heavy Vol. 9
(with Soundgarden, Queensryche, Forced
Entry, Bitter End, Panic, Mother Love Bone,
Andrew Wood interview)
Hoop Skirt/Loop Yarn (Box Dog)
(with Mr. Epp, Mudhoney, Steel Pole Bath-
tub, Melvins,
Fred's Crash Shop)
It Happened At the World's Fair (MGM/UA)
Joy of Six (Ensign)
(with the Posies and five other Bellingham
bands)
J.P. Patches Vol. 1-4 (City Dump Productions)
Molted: Hunt & Gather (A&M)
(with Soundgarden, Hammerbox)
Northwest Rock Music Video Compilation #1
(No-Budget)
(with Applied Science, Variant Cause,
Young Fresh Fellows,
f-Holes, U-Men, Blackouts, Steve Fisk,
Acoustinauts, Boom Boom GI, Prudence
Dredge)
Northwest Rock Music Video Compilation #2
(No-Budget)
(with Sir Mix-A-Lot, Posies, Purdins, and
scenes from
Little Boy Goes to Hell)
Rock n' Roll Mobster Girls
(amateur thriller spoof with Doll Squad,
Crisis Party, Girl Trouble, Cat Butt, Jim
Rose)
Seattle Chronicle (Tartu Productions)
The Seattle Slam (Underground Productions)
(with Slam Suzanne, Dumt, Date Rape, Bit-
ter End, others)
Shredder Orpheus (AIP Video)
singles (Warner)
The Stan Boreson Show Vol. 1-2 (Stan Bore-
son Video)
Straight to Hell (CBS/Fox)
Streetwise (Starmaker)
Sub Pop Video Network Vol. 1 (Atavistic)
(with Nirvana, Mudhoney, TAD, Mark Lane-
gan, Seaweed, Beat Happening, Walkabouts,
others)
Sub Pop Video Network Vol. 2 (Atavistic)
(with Fastbacks, Supersuckers, Love Battery, Earth, Beat Happening, S.J. Bernstein,
Seaweed, Mudhoney, others)
Sub Pop Video Network Vol. 3 (Atavistic)
(with Fastbacks, Supersuckers, Sunny Day
Real Estate, Mark Lanegan, others)

Trouble in Mind (Charter)
We've Come For Your Daughters: C/Z Video
Compilation (Atavistic)
(with Coffin Break, Hammerbox, Icky Joey,
Tone Dogs, Treepeople, Vexed, others)

CHAPTER FIFTEEN: BIBLIOGRAPHY

Alden, Grant, with Jeff Gilbert and Nils Bernstein: "Grunge Makes Good." *Spin*, September 1992. New York: Camouflage Associates.

Arnold, Gina: *Route 666, On the Road to Nirvana*. New York: St. Martin's Press, 1993.

Azerrad, Michael: *Come As You Are: The Story of Nirvana*. New York: Bantam Doubleday Dell, 1993.

Bernstein, S.J.: *More Noise Please*. Seattle: Left Bank Publishing, 1995.

Blecha, Peter: *Northwest Music Archive, 1958-1970*. Unpublished manuscript, 1994.

Book, John: "Seattle Heavy." *Goldmine*, Vol. 18, No. 17, Aug. 16, 1992. Iola, WI: Krause Publications.

Brewster, David, and David M. Buerge, eds.: *Washingtonians*. Seattle: Sasquatch Books, 1989.

Chantry, Art, ed.: *Instant Litter: Concert Posters from Seattle Punk Culture*. Seattle: Real Comet Press, 1985.

Danen, Fredric: *Hit Men*. New York: Vintage Books, 1990.

DeBarros, Paul: *Jackson Street After Hours*. Seattle: Sasquatch Books, 1993.

Dorpat, Paul, writer/director: *Seattle Chronicle*. Seattle: Tartu Productions videocassette, 1992.

Duncan, Don: *Meet Me at the Center*. Seattle: Seattle Center Foundation, 1992.

Eddy, Chuck: *Stairway to Hell: The 500 Best Heavy Metal Albums in the Universe*. New York: Harmony Books, 1991.

Gaar, Gillian G.: "The Dark Side of Innocence: Nirvana and the Rise of the Seattle Sound." *Goldmine*, Vol. 19, No. 25, Dec. 10, 1993.

George-Warren, Holly, ed.: *Cobain by the Editors of Rolling Stone*. Boston: Little, Brown & Co., 1994.

Gilbert, Jeff: *Grunge: Inside Seattle's Music*. New York: Western Publishing Co./Angel Entertainment Inc., 1993.

Greene, Jo-Ann: "Intrigue and Incest: Pearl Jam and the History of Seattle." *Goldmine*, Vol. 19, No. 17, Aug. 20, 1993.

Guitar World Presents Nirvana and the Seattle Sound. New York: Harris Publications, 1993.

Hale, Mark: *HeadBangers: The Worldwide Megabook of Heavy Metal Bands*. Ann Arbor, MI: Popular Culture Inc., 1989-93.

Heylin, Clinton: *From the Velvets to the Voidoids: A Pre-Punk History for a Post-Punk World*. New York: Penguin Books USA, 1993.

Johnstone, Milo: *The Magic Decade: A Street Level Glance at Seattle During the Mutinous Sixties*. Seattle: Johnstone & Durham, 1994.

Kelly, "Doc Rock": *Liberty Records*. New York: McFarland & Co. Inc., 1994.

Lanza, Joseph: *Elevator Music*. New York: St. Martin's Press, 1994.

Mark, Mary Ellen: *Streetwise*. New York: Aperture, 1985.

Marsh, Dave: *Louie Louie*. New York: Hyperion, 1993.

Morgan, Murray: *Skid Road: An Informal Portrait of Seattle*. New York: Viking, 1951-60.

Morrell, Frank: *Nirvana and the Sound of Seattle*. London: Omnibus Press, 1993.

Morrell, Frank: *Pearl Jam: The Illustrated Biography*. London: Omnibus Press, 1993.

Newell, Gordon: *Totem Tales of Old Seattle*. Seattle: Superior Publishing Co., 1956.

Robbins, Ira, ed.: *The Trouser Press Record Guide*. New York: Collier Books, 1983-91.

Sale, Roger: *Seattle Past to Present*. Seattle: University of Washington Press, 1976.

Shamash, Diane, and Steven Huss, eds.: *A Field Guide to Seattle's Public Art*. Seattle: Seattle Arts Commission, 1991.

Thompson, Dave: *Industrial Revolution*. Los Angeles: Cleopatra, 1993.

Thompson, Dave: *Never Fade Away: The Kurt Cobain Story*. New York: St. Martin's Press, 1994.

Watson, Emmett: *Digressions of a Native Son*. Seattle: Pacific Institute, 1982.

Woog, Adam: *Sexless Oysters and Self-Tipping Hats*. Seattle: Sasquatch Books, 1992.

This index covers principal bands, individuals, companies, and concepts in the text. It does not list individual recordings, except compilations, or songs.

Hoerner, Dan: 190
Hoke, Eldon ("El Duce"): 33, 39
Holcomb, Robin: 151
Holden, Ron: 12
Hole: 166, 179, 185, 190, 195, 198-199
Holidays, the: 60
Hollingsworth, Harold: 75
Hollywood Records: 141, 158
Hollywood Reporter, The: 61
Holm, Toni: 47
Holmes, Jeff: 118: 143
Holy War Cadet Productions: 87
Homestead Records: 91, 104
Hood, Paul: 33, 36, 74, 100
Hoquiam: 82, 139
Horn, Tony: 91
Horrible Truth, the: 103
Horton, Derek: 183
Horvitz, Wayne: 151
House of Leisure: 191
House, Daniel: 73, 88, 96, 103, 109, 114, 129, 141, 147, 189
Houston Post: 173
Houston, Penelope: 33
Howard, Joe: 182
Howe, Mike: 82
Howltown: 156
Hoyt, Mark: 136, 156
Hoyt, Tony: 183
Hubbard, Hanmi: 96
Hubbard, Neil: 31, 32, 33, 39, 56, 71
Hudson Brothers: 19
Huevos Rancheros: 189
Huggy Bear: 164: 180
Hugo: 87, 95, 107
Humble, Mary: 86
Hunt, Kathleen: 91
Hunter, Chick: 108
Huntley, Chet: 4
Husbands, Roger: 35, 37, 39, 41, 53, 55, 57
Husker Du: 97, 157
Huskinson, Brad: 78
Husted, James: 57, 71
Hutchison, Tad: 79
Hype: 156, 165, 178, 179

I Love You to Death: 128
Ichiban Records: 152
Icky Joey: 140
Icons: 80
Idaho: 189
Identity Crisis: 88
Idiot Culture: 74
Idol Worship: 97
Idol, Billy: 165
IFA Records: 190
Iffland, Chuck: 117
ILS (Independent Label Sales): 163
IMIJ: 151, 178-179
Immoral Roberts: 97
Improvisation, the: 120
In Search of Mango-go: 164
In the Red: 159
Incubator: 101
India Taj: 181
Industrial Workers of the World: 3
Inez, Mike: 122
Infamous Menagerie: 148
Inflatable Soule: 175
Insight Records: 190
Inspector Luv and the Ride Me Babies: 159
Interbay neighborhood: 88, 93
International Donut House: 59
International Pop Underground: 162, 191
Interstate 5: 18, 20
IOGT Hall: 42
Ireland, Barbara ("Barbie"): 40, 59, 116
Ireland, Ben: 40, 59, 74, 124, 182
Ireland, Dan: 25

Irish Potato Famine: 80
Irons, Jack: 150, 173, 196
Ironwood Studios: 103
IRS Records: 54, 83
Irwin, John: 72
Isaac, Jay: 72
Island Records: 135, 180
Isley Brothers: 17
Itchy Brother: 84
Ivan, Hank: 99, 100
Ivy Records: 150, 158, 190
Iyall, Deborah: 78

J. Crew: 186
Jack Straw Memorial Foundation: 13, 76
Jackson, George Michael: 37
Jackson, Henry: 6
Jacobs, Karrie: 47
Jacobs, Marc: 177, 186
Jam, the: 49
Jambay: 178
Jane's Addiction: 126, 161
Jangle Town: 150
Janitors of Love: 42
Japan: viii, 62, 106, 126, 132, 177, 185, 191
Jasper, Megan: 177
Java Jive: 128
Je Ka Jo: 15
Jefferson Airplane: 103
Jenkins, Bob: 68, 891, 101, 117, 147
Jenniker, Bob: 80
Jennings, Kim: 35
Jensen, Paul: 159
Jerden Records: 12, 14
Jessamine: 159, 187
Jesse Bernstein Band: 91
Jesters of Chaos: 113
Jesus Lizard: 183
Jesus People: 25
Jett, Joan: 83, 188
Jewett, Doug: 97
Jigsaw: 164
Jim Rose Circus Sideshow: 102, 173, 182
Jimi Hendrix Museum/Experience Music Project: 77, 194
Jitters: 36
Job: 180, 190
Jody Foster's Army: 93
Joe Despair and the Future: 17, 61
Joel Phelps: 157
Joel, Billy: vii
John and Stu's Place: 104
John, Elton: 135
Johnny and the Distractions: 54, 133
Johnny Webelo: 183
Johnny's Handlebar: 53
Johnson, Calvin: vii, 48, 66, 67, 89, 90, 102, 106, 125, 161, 162, 164, 172, 190
Johnson, Eric: 118
Johnson, Lenny and Joe: 157
Johnson, Mike: 146, 180
Johnson, Nate: 155
Johnson, Steve: 156
Joint Artists and Music Promotions Political Action Committee (JAMPAC): 171
Jones Fantastic Museum: 64
Jones, Jim: 119
Jones, Pontiac: 35
Jones, Quincy: 4
Jones, Tamara: 35
Joplin, Janis: 26
Jourgenson, Al: 72, 100, 153
Jr. Cadillac: 26, 34, 78
Judgment Night: 153
Jumbalassy: 187
Juned: 180, 190

K: 47, 62, 67, 90, 104, 106, 128, 130, 158, 162, 163, 164, 187, 190

K., Molly: 148
K mart: 184
Kahn, Doug: 50
Kalberer Hotel Supply: 101
Kalmar, Veronika: 113, 136
KAOS: 47, 50, 66, 67, 89, 161
KARP: 191
Kaukola, Gina: 107
Kaye, Danny: 9
Kaye-Smith Enterprises: 18, 27
KAYO: 9
KCMU: vii, 48, 53, 64, 76, 79, 82, 84, 100, 102, 103, 106, 119, 121, 122, 156, 160, 180
KCTS-TV: 27, 108
KDT Records: 102
Keister, John: 42, 46, 47, 61, 68, 78, 81, 141
Keister, Paul: 78
Keliehor, Jon: 15
Keller, David: 43, 101
Keller, Jim: 43, 100, 101, 160
Kelly, Christine: 171
Kelly, Dani: 125
Kelly, Jeff: 106
Kelly's: 157
Kempthorne, Dan: 159
Kent 3: 157
Keplinger, Gregg: 175
Keppel, Dave: 159
Kerr, Tim: 140
Kerrang!: 82, 170
Kerslake, Kevin: 169
Kertzer, Jon: 76
KGRG: 181
KHIT: 107
Kid Sensation: 152
Kill Rock Stars: 151, 162, 191
Kill Sybil: 99, 174: 185, 190, 193
Killing Joke: 169
Kincaid, Dave: 78
King County: 1
King Crimson: 135
King Krab: 101
King Theater: 192
King, Lisa: 100, 114
KING-TV: 7, 13, 20, 78, 108, 115, 141
Kingdome: 2, 64
Kingsmen: 11, 104
Kinks: 13
Kinnear, Ken: 42
Kinney, Sean: 85, 122
Kipp, Tom: 159
KIRO-TV: 7, 98, 99
Kiss: 60, 62, 75, 76, 109, 129, 135, 138, 149
KISW: 27
Kit Kat Klub: 86
Kitchen Radio: 183
Kitchy Koo: 58
KJET: 77, 79, 100, 106, 115, 121, 129, 160, 161
KJR: 9, 18, 27
Klein, Calvin: 177
Kline, Joey: 79, 105, 107, 159
Knab, Chris: 76, 121, 122, 180
KNDD: 158, 160, 173, 174, 181, 193, 198
KNHC: 76, 107
Knight, J.Z. ("Ramtha"): 157
Knobs, the: 35
Koch, Lisa: 116
Koda-Kahn: 82
Kok, Brad: 158
KOL: 10, 12
KOMO-TV: 61
Kondrak, Bob: 40, 41, 42
Koo Dat Tah: 102
Kool, Harry: 46
Koonce, Johnny: 54
KRAB: 12, 17, 33, 55, 56, 64, 66, 67, 76, 101, 107, 160, 181
Krafft, Charles: 19
Kral, Ivan: 182

Kramer, Stella: 39, 41, 46, 47
Krogstad, Karl: 117
KROQ: 74
Krusen, Dave: 150, 158, 172
KSTW: 118
KTZZ: 108, 118, 182
KUGS: 90
Kulczyk, David: 80
KUOW: 66, 121, 180
KXRX: 115, 196
KYYX: 77, 78, 95, 107, 115
KZAM: 50, 57, 60, 61, 64, 76, 78, 117
KZOK: 27, 42, 77, 121

L.A. Weekly: 61
L7: 163, 166, 173
La Conner: 7, 19, 24
La Fuente, Xana: 143
Ladd, Ted: 84
Lake, Mary: 148
Lake Hills Roller Rink: 81, 158
Lake Union: 3
Lake Union Pub: 157, 199
Lake Washington: 24
Lamar Harrington Band: 20, 28
Lame Fest: 139
Lame Festival: 140
Land of Look Behind, The: 101
Lande, Alan: 57
Landes, Bertha: 2
Lanegan, Mark: 101, 146, 186, 187
Langill, Norm: 28
Langston Hughes Cultural Arts Center: 88, 192
Lansdowne, Mark: 155
Lapses In Grammar (Afforded To Avoid Sexism): 80
Larry and the Mondellos: 67
Larsen, Al: 161
Larson, Gary: 149
Larusson, Jodi: 68
Last Action Hero: 192
Lateef's: 106
Laton, Michael: 86
Laundry: 159
Laundry Room: 191
Laurelhurst: 62, 68
Lavine, Michael: 125
Lazy Susan: 180
Le Club Hit: 97
Learned, Bryan: 115
Led Zeppelin: 13, 17, 28, 46, 75, 81, 82, 85, 165, 193
Ledbelly: 146, 198
Lee, Bruce: 19, 85
Lee, Gypsy Rose: vii, 2, 4, 49
Lee, Laura: 9
Lee, Richard: 198
Legends Ballroom: 84
Leimer, K. (Kerrie): 101
Leinonen, Henry: 10
Leinonen, Pete: 10, 20, 21, 54, 59, 91, 124
Leinonen, Walter: 10, 124
Leland, John: 178
Lemons: 131, 145
Lennon, John: 61, 116, 133
Leopard Gecko Records: 158
Lerner, Michael: 20
Lethal Dose: 98
Levy, Herb: 101
Lewd, the: 28, 34, 35, 39, 44, 45, 83
Lewis, Dave: 11, 12, 133
Lewis, Heather: 89
Lewis, Rick: 97
Liberty Records: 9
Life: 59
Life, the: 132
Life in General: 71, 77, 87, 108, 143
Lightfoot, Jim: 45, 49, 55, 56